Sport in the Global Society

General Editor: J.A. Mangan

SPORT IN THE GLOBAL SOCIETY

General Editor: J.A. Mangan

ISSN 1368-9789

The interest in sports studies around the world is growing and will continue to do so. This unique series combines aspects of the expanding study of *sport in the global society*, providing comprehensiveness and comparison under one editorial umbrella. It is particularly timely, with studies in the political, cultural, social, economic, geographical and aesthetic elements of sport proliferating in institutions of higher education.

Eric Hobsbawm once called sport one of the most significant practices of the late nineteenth century. Its significance is even more marked in the late twentieth century and will continue to grow in importance into the next millennium as the world develops into a 'global village' sharing the English language, technology and sport.

Other Titles in the Series

Footbinding, Feminism and Freedom
The Liberation of Women's Bodies in Modern China
Fan Hong

The Games Ethic and Imperialism
Aspects of the Diffusion of an Ideal
J.A. Mangan

The Nordic World
Sport in Society
edited by Henrik Meinander and J.A. Mangan

The Race Game
Sport and Politics in South Africa
Douglas Booth

Rugby's Great Split
Class, Culture and the Origins of Rugby League Football
Tony Collins

Sporting Nationalisms
Identity, Ethnicity, Immigration and Assimilation
edited by Mike Cronin and David Mayall

Cricket and England
A Cultural and Social History of the Inter-war Years
Jack Williams

The First Black Footballer
Arthur Wharton 1865–1930: An Absence of Memory
Phil Vasili

SCORING FOR BRITAIN

International Football and International Politics, 1900–1939

PETER J. BECK
Kingston University

FRANK CASS
LONDON PORTLAND, OR

First published in 1999 in Great Britain by
FRANK CASS PUBLISHERS
Newbury House, 900 Eastern Avenue
London, IG2 7HH

and in the United States of America by
FRANK CASS PUBLISHERS
c/o ISBS, 5804 N.E. Hassalo Street
Portland, Oregon 97213-3644

Website: http://www.frankcass.com

British Library Cataloguing in Publication Data

Beck, Peter
    Scoring for Britain: international football and
    international politics, 1900–1939. – (Sport in the global
    society; no. 9)
    1. Soccer – Political aspects – Great Britain – History
    2. Great Britain – Foreign relations – 20th century
    I. Title
    796.3'34'0941

            ISBN 0-7146-4899-X (cloth)
            ISBN 0-7146-4454-4 (paper)
            ISSN 1368-9789

    Library of Congress Cataloging-in-Publication Data

Beck, Peter (Peter J.)
    Scoring for Britain: international football and international
politics, 1900–1939 / Peter J. Beck.
                    p.   cm. – (Sport in the global society, ISSN 1368-
9789; vol. 9)
    Includes bibliographical references (p.   ) and index.
    ISBN 0-7146-4899-X (cloth). – ISBN 0-7146-4454-4 (pbk.)
    1. Soccer – Political aspects – Great Britain – History – 20th century.
    2. Soccer – Social aspects – Great Britain – History – 20th century.
    3. Nationalism and sports – Great Britain.
    I. Title.   II. Series: Cass series – sport in the global society; 9.
    GV944.G7B43   1999
    796.334'66'0941 – dc21   98-47283
                                                                    CIP

Printed in Great Britain by
Bookcraft (Bath) Ltd, Midsomer Norton, Somerset

Contents

	List of Tables and Figures	vi
	Acknowledgements	vii
	Abbreviations	ix
	Series Editor's Foreword	xi
1.	Introduction: Eleven Footballers Do a 'Good Job' for Britain in Germany, May 1938	1
2.	Presenting Britain as a Great Nation on the World's Screen through International Football	17
3.	Conquering the World through Football: 1900–18	50
4.	Responding to 'New Developments' in International Sport after 1919	79
5.	'Football by Order of the Foreign Office'? The 1920s	101
6.	' "To Intervene in International Football, or Not to Intervene?", That is the Question': The Early 1930s	130
7.	'The Greatest ever Triumph of the "Keep Politics Out of Sport" Brigade'? England versus Germany, 1935	173
8.	Footballing Examples of British Propaganda as it Should, and Should Not, Be: The Mid to Late 1930s	213
9.	Britain's 'Football Ambassadors' Perform Work of 'National Importance': The Late 1930s	238
10.	Conclusion: 'Good Kicking is Good Politics'	272
	Bibliography	286
	Index	300

Tables and Figures

Table 2.1   The British Football Associations   25

Table 2.2   British football and the World Cup, 1930–50   26

Table 2.3   British football versus foreign teams, 1908–39   32

Table 3.1   FIFA membership   51

Table 3.2   England's amateur internationals before 1914   53

Table 3.3   England versus Germany, 1900–54   4

Table 5.1   British representative team tours to the dominions, 1910–39   107

Table 6.1   *Pesti Naplo*'s European football rankings, 1933   131

Table 6.2   Foreign spectators in Britain, early 1930s   161

Table 8.1   1936 Olympic Games' unofficial points table   215

Table 8.2   Foreign Office survey of official attitudes regarding sport in other European countries   224

Table 10.1   British football becomes less isolationist, 1900–39   280

Figure 3.1   British football and FIFA membership   51

Figure 10.1   England's record versus foreign teams, 1908–39   275

Figure 10.2   Percentage of internationals versus British teams   281

Acknowledgements

This research project commenced in the late 1970s, as suggested by the interviews conducted in 1980 with Sir Stanley Rous and Frank Broome as well as the initial outcomes published in the early 1980s. In the event, other publication commitments led to the project's delay, and then suspension for over a decade. What particularly encouraged me to take up the study again during 1992–93 was the growing interest shown in sport by historians, and particularly the broader foreign policy context provided by Martin Polley's PhD thesis.

Of course, things change over time. Not only does each age view the past differently, but also previously closed archival sources become available for research. Despite possessing a lengthy manuscript written in the early 1980s, I decided in effect to start again, that is, to re-read previously used archives as well as to scrap most of my draft chapters. In addition, the project, having focused originally on 1920–54, was changed in the light of research to concentrate on the period 1900–39, although I plan to cover the period 1939–54 in another monograph, entitled provisionally *Good Kicking is Good Politics*. As ever, research was conducted simultaneously on several fronts, as indicated by my work in press on Anthony Eden, historians and appeasement or the 1938 Munich Crisis. Although such publications have further delayed completion, this monograph has benefited from numerous insights yielded by private papers consulted for my work on Anglo-German relations, but rarely figuring on the research schedule of sports historians. Also, whereas previously I included a whole chapter justifying the historical study of sport, today such a rationale seems superfluous, even if my experience of service on the history panels for the 1992 and 1996 Research Assessment Exercises as well as for the Humanities Research Board, among other bodies, leads me to believe that the history of sport has yet to be fully accepted by all academic historians. Admittedly, there are still too many weakly researched studies – for example, a reliance on newspapers is not always accompanied by a preparedness to consult relevant archival sources – and too much recycling of the same material, but already a large number of sports history monographs, chapters and articles merit comparison with those found in any other field of history.

Archival and library research was conducted with the help of the History Research Fund of Kingston University. A special word of thanks is due to Lyn Porteous, the history librarian, and inter-loans staff at Kingston University library; David Barber (FA); Rose Marie Breitenstein; Frank Broome; William Campbell (IFA); Christopher Cobb; David Collins (FAW); Christiane Eisenberg; Richard Holt; Jan Hoskins (FAW); the late Sir Stanley Rous; Marius Schneider (FIFA); Philip Taylor; Alan Tomlinson; the Imperial War Museum; and staff at the archives and libraries listed in my bibliography. The advice and support of Professor Mangan, the series editor, and of Jonathan Manley at Frank Cass is gratefully acknowledged. My wife, Barbara, and son, Jonathan, offered their usual support and understanding, while my other son, Richard, provided invaluable IT advice and prepared certain diagrams.

I am grateful to the following for permission to quote from copyright materials: Baron Aberdare (Lord Aberdare); Hon. Francis Noel-Baker (Lord Noel-Baker); Master and Fellows of Trinity College, Cambridge (Lord Butler); Mark Farrrer, Farrer & Co. (Sir Alexander Cadogan); Christine Penney, Special Collections Librarian, University of Birmingham (Neville Chamberlain); Curtis Brown Ltd. London, on behalf of the Estate of Sir Winston Churchill (Sir Winston Churchill); J. Davies, Archivist, Carmarthenshire Archives Service (Viscount Cilcennin); Michael Simmonds, Director, Conservative Political Centre (Conservative Party); William Bell (Geoffrey Dawson); Alex di Carcaci, executor of the estate of Edward Millington Drake (Eugen Millington Drake); FIFA; the Football Association; Football Association of Wales; Professor D.M. Smith, Director, Borthwick Institute of Historical Research, University of York (Lord Halifax); Irish Football Association; Dr John Charmley (Lord Lloyd); Master and Fellows of Churchill College, Cambridge (Sir Eric Phipps); Scottish Football Association Museum Trust; and Christie Viscountess Simon (Lord Simon).

Every effort has been made to trace the owners of copyright material, but in some cases they proved untraceable. If any copyright has been inadvertently infringed, the author is willing to acknowledge copyright in any relevant future publication.

Abbreviations used in the text

AAA   Amateur Athletic Association
BAOR   British Army on the Rhine
BBC   British Broadcasting Corporation
BOA   British Olympic Association
BWSA   British Workers' Sports Association
BWSF   British Workers' Sports Federation
DFB   *Deutscher Fussball Bund*
FA   Football Association
FAI   Football Association of Ireland
FAW   Football Association of Wales
FIFA   *Fédération Internationale de Football Association*
IAAF   International Amateur Athletics Federation
IARHC   Inter-Allied Rhineland High Commission
IFA   Irish Football Association
IFAB   International Football Association Board
IOC   International Olympic Committee
MOI   Ministry of Information
NUR   National Union of Railwaymen
OFB   *Oesterreichischer Fussball-Bund*
RFU   Rugby Football Union
SFA   Scottish Football Association
TUC   Trades Union Congress

Abbreviations used for archival sources can be checked in the bibliography.

Series Editor's Foreword

In March 1969 Chinese and Russian troops clashed on Damansky Island on the Ussuri River on the Chinese–Russian border. Then there were later clashes. Rumours filtered through to China from Eastern Europe that the Russians were contemplating a nuclear strike against Chinese nuclear weapon sites. A famous diplomatic friendship was fractured. More to the point, China was threatened by 'Big Brother'!

The outcome of this confrontation between socialist comrades and political allies was a reassessment by the Chinese of relations with the United States of America. Mao thought long and hard about the form this was to take and the manner by which it would be communicated.

The first attempt by the Chinese to indicate a change of diplomatic heart was the invitation by Mao to Edgar Snow, the distinguished American author of *Red Star Over China*, published in 1938, to stand beside him in Tiananmen Square for the celebrations commemorating the twenty-first anniversary of the creation of the Peoples' Republic of China.

Ironically, the gesture was unappreciated by the American government. The Western mind, not for the first nor the last time, failed to read the Eastern mind – and vice versa. Mao tried again. Following an invitation to the Chinese by the Japanese hosts to attend the Thirty-First World Table Tennis Championships, Mao gave orders that not only were his players to attend but they were to act with cordiality towards the Americans! The outcome was a request by the encouraged and surprised American Table Tennis Association to visit China. Mao graciously, and no doubt contentedly, agreed.

In April 1971 the Americans were greeted in the Peoples' Hall, Beijing, by Premier Zhou Enlai with these words: 'You have opened a new chapter in the relations of the American and Chinese people ... You are welcome.'

The famous 'Era of Ping Pong Diplomacy' had come to pass. In July of the same year Henry Kissinger visited China on behalf of President Nixon to pave the way for a visit by Nixon himself – the rest, as they say, is history. The whole affair was a 'heart-warming' story of sport as an instrument of diplomacy – with a happy ending!

On occasion sport can be diplomacy by other means.

As Isaac Goldberg once cuttingly remarked: 'Diplomacy is to do and say the nastiest things in the nicest way'. A propos of this, Peter Beck notes, in this fascinating story of soccer and politics in the first 39 years of the twentieth century, the notorious match between England and Germany in Berlin in May 1938 is viewed more often than not as a historic Anglo-Saxon humiliation. England won the European small game but lost a European Great Game. The English players' presence in Berlin, and more to the point their infamous Nazi salute, still represents for many an abject gesture of appeasement that mocked the inmates of the concentration camps, the trampled territories and their brutalised peoples. Yet with hindsight a more benign view may be taken of the match. It was a boost to British morale and a triumph of democracy over totalitarianism – at a pressing time in pressing circumstances.

With its wealth of detail, meticulous research, and thoughtful commentary, *Scoring for Britain* is an important contribution to the history of sport, and to the series Sport in the Global Society.

It is with the most complete pleasure that I comment that one of the virtues of Peter Beck is his ability to link his long-term studies of the history of appeasement to more recent studies in the history of sport. He reads widely – and it shows – to the advantage of his readers. While, as he asserts rightly, many monographs, chapters and articles in historical studies of sport 'merit comparison with those found in any other field of history', he implies correctly that too many historians of sport remain parochial in their perspectives, narrow in their imaginative vision, restricted in their cultural horizons. Consequently from an informed perspective, he remarks:

> ... my experience of service on the history panels for the 1992 and 1996 Research Assessment Exercises as well as for the Humanities Research Board, among other bodies, leads me to believe that the history of sport has yet to be fully accepted by all academic historians. Admittedly, there are still too many weakly-researched studies – for example, a reliance on newspapers is not always accompanied by a preparedness to consult relevant archival sources – and too much recycling of the same material. (p.vii)

He points the way forward to the post-Millennium – and in doing so, does us all a service.

As we approach the next century of opportunity, we might usefully recall the remark of John Stuart Mill in *Auguste Comte and Positivism*: 'as often as a study is cultivated by narrow minds, they will draw from it narrow conclusions'.

J.A. Mangan,
International Centre for Sport, Society, Socialisation,
University of Strathclyde
January 1999

Introduction: Eleven Footballers Do a 'Good Job' for Britain in Germany, May 1938

Looking back with the benefit of hindsight, the Chamberlain government's pursuit of détente with Hitler's Germany is easily dismissed as a study in failure, most notably during 1938, when both Austria (March) and the Czech Sudetenland (September–October) fell under German control.[1] Within one year, the two governments were at war. Against this background, the infamous photograph, showing England's footballers giving the Nazi salute before their game played against Germany at Berlin on 14 May 1938, has often been depicted as evidence of yet another Munich-style national humiliation, given the manner in which Chamberlainite appeasement provided a supportive policy framework for the match. From this perspective, the Football Association (FA), which not only arranged a fixture played in Berlin two months after the German takeover of Austria (i.e. the *Anschluss*) but also congratulated Chamberlain for the Munich Agreement resolving the Sudeten crisis, might easily be added to Cato's cast list of 'Guilty Men'.[2] By contrast, contemporary assessments often proved more positive, especially as the notorious salute, given in part in the light of official advice, was adjudged to have helped to maximise the fixture's perceived contribution to national interests.

'ENGLAND CONQUERS GERMAN ELEVEN, 6-3'

Watched by a capacity crowd of *circa* 110,000 at Berlin's Olympic stadium, England triumphed 6-3 in a match seemingly impressing a wide range of people in both Germany and the wider world with the qualities characterising not only British football but also Britain itself. Although Cliff Bastin gave England the lead within 15 minutes, Germany soon got back on level terms through Josef Pesser, its most dangerous forward. But goals by Jack Robinson, playing his first international, and Frank Broome restored England's lead, which was further extended following a typical example of individualism by Stanley Matthews. Then, a poor clearance by

Vic Woodley, England's goalkeeper, allowed Josef Gauchel to reduce the deficit to 2-4 before half time. During the second half, further goals were added by Pesser and Robinson for both teams before Len Goulden, driving the ball hard into the roof of the net from outside the penalty area, struck England's final goal to 'gasps of admiration' from the crowd.[3] Reportedly, his shot, together with Matthews' 'individual brilliance', proved 'the talk of the town'. On the following afternoon, the 3-2 victory of Aston Villa, 1937–38 Second Division champions, over a 'German XI' before another large crowd in Berlin rounded off, it was reported, 'a good weekend's work for the prestige of British sport'.

In many respects, England's victory offered a rare, but welcome, British success *vis-à-vis* Germany, as acknowledged by the *Daily Express*: '1938's snappiest blow for our prestige was struck by the England eleven who trounced Germany by 6-3 here yesterday. It has been rocketed sky high. You should be here properly to appreciate the magnificence of the achievement.'[4] Nor, despite the determined efforts of successive governments to stress the separation of politics and sport in Britain, did the game, sandwiched between Hitler's state visit to Rome (3–9 May) and the Czech 'May Crisis' (19–20 May 1938), remain a mere football match. Inevitably, the British government's prime role in seeking to manage, hopefully to resolve, the German problem as part of a comprehensive European pacification as well as to uphold the interests of the liberal democracies in the ongoing European 'civil war', ensured that any Anglo-German sporting contest became 'embroiled in politics'.[5]

THE FA PRESENTS THE FOREIGN OFFICE WITH ANOTHER *FAIT ACCOMPLI*

Between the wars, 'football became an integral part of totalitarian rule'.[6] The political control exerted over German sport meant that the invitation despatched to the FA by the *Deutscher Fussball Bund* (DFB) in June 1937 would have required the approval of the relevant political authorities, most notably Captain Hans von Tschammer und Osten, the *Reichssports Führer*. Perhaps the latter was already thinking along the lines suggested by Nevile Henderson, the British ambassador in Berlin (1937–39), who warned one journalist in May 1938: 'Be cautious in advocating contests between British and German individuals or teams. The Nazis are looking for easy opponents and victories to boost their regime. It is their way of claiming a super race.'[7]

By contrast, the four British football associations, operating as nongovernmental bodies, possessed a considerable degree of autonomy, most notably regarding their choice of international opponents. Naturally, fixtures had to be in conformity with the overall framework of British foreign policy; for example, it would be impossible to play a national team representing a country lacking diplomatic relations with Britain. Notwithstanding this proviso, there occurred frequent complaints within official circles about the FA's failure to engage in meaningful consultations about the political suitability of opponents, let alone provide advance notification of forthcoming club and national fixtures against foreign teams. From this point of view, the 1938 German game proved no exception, for the FA, having accepted the German invitation, proceeded to agree terms with the DFB.[8] There is no evidence of British government involvement in these negotiations. Normally, the FA insisted on sharing profits from foreign internationals, but German exchange controls meant that the fixture was treated as part of a special two-match home and away package allowing both associations to retain net receipts from their respective home games.[9] The return fixture was scheduled for 1939–40! Significantly, in June 1937, that is, at roughly the same time as it took up the DFB's invitation, the FA arranged a mid-season international against Czechoslovakia – as we know now, this country was high on Hitler's shopping list – to be played at Tottenham's ground on 1 December 1937 (England won 5-4).[10]

Although the FA and DFB finalised arrangements by November 1937, the Foreign Office only learned of the forthcoming fixture on 4 May 1938 from Harley Usill (general editor of the *Year Book of Education*), who also apprised officials of the 'great importance' attached to the game for reasons of national prestige by the German government and people.[11] Once again, the British government, presented with a fixture as a *fait accompli*, faced a major dilemma, most notably, was it in the national interest either to stop the match or to allow it to go ahead? Much depended on assessments of the national interest, and, in this vein, the seemingly more active and urgent search for détente with Germany, ushered in by Chamberlain's accession to the premiership in May 1937, might be deemed as providing an appropriate policy framework for the FA's response. At the same time, there existed an awareness of the impact of any interference on traditional images concerning the separation of politics and sport in Britain.

In the event, the British government, realising that the game's imminence severely limited its options, decided that any matter affecting Anglo-German relations was too important to be left entirely to the FA, even if it took care to ensure that any official action occurred behind the scenes. Basically, a reluctance to do anything liable to threaten the prospects of appeasement, alongside a belief that sporting exchanges benefited Anglo-German relations, fostered a strong disinclination to stop the game, especially as any last-minute ban would be viewed in Germany as the consequence of a government decision, no matter how things were presented in public. Instead, non-intervention emerged as the product of a deliberate policy decision, given not only the perceived disadvantages of cancellation but also the fixture's perceived potential advantages for Anglo-German relations. To some extent, this line had been foreshadowed earlier in the year, when no official objections were raised to a proposed Easter visit to Wuppertal by a Brighton police football team as part of a regular interchange scheme, even if the Home Office instructed players to travel in civilian clothes in order to avoid providing any pretext for visiting German teams and spectators to wear uniforms and/or Nazi insignia within Britain.[12]

Despite being merely the first stage of a three-match close season tour also involving Switzerland and France, the German game was interpreted by the British government, the FA and the media as by far the 'most important' fixture.[13] Notwithstanding Germany's impressive recent record, this assessment largely reflected non-sporting factors, since Switzerland posed an equally strong footballing challenge. Reportedly, England's visit occasioned 'great excitement' throughout Germany, where extensive media coverage was accompanied by a massive demand for tickets.[14] Despite the British government's assumed apolitical stance and *The Times*' somewhat fanciful claim that 'the German public thrust politics into the background', the result was bound to be interpreted in Germany and elsewhere through political spectacles.[15] Indeed, hopes that the national side, boosted by a fortnight's special training, would prove at least the equal, if not the superior, of England were boosted by Germany's recent run of 14 games without defeat – this proved a far better recent record than that of England – as well as by the fact that Germany's takeover rendered Austrian players eligible for selection. The *Anschluss*, highlighting Hitler's growing threat to international order, exerted also a major impact upon the world of football, since the resulting incorporation of the *Oesterreichischer Fussball-Bund* (OFB) into the DFB terminated Austrian membership of FIFA (*Fédération Internationale de Football Association*), while promising to strengthen the German national team, given Austria's status as a leading footballing power boasting a recent 2-1 victory over England (May 1936).[16] Those inclined to maximise the impact of sport might even present this as one motivation for the *Anschluss*, an event which prevented Austria from completing its games in the fourth edition of the International Cup and taking its place in the 1938 World Cup finals! Surprisingly, only one Austrian, Pesser, was selected for the England match – reportedly, he proved Germany's most dangerous forward and scored two goals – even if Austrians, including three players who had faced England in 1936, dominated the 'German XI' chosen to play Aston Villa one day later.

UPHOLDING 'OUR PRESTIGE' THROUGH FOOTBALL

Upon learning of the forthcoming game, Sir Stephen Gaselee, the Librarian and Keeper of Records, and Sir Robert Vansittart, the Chief Diplomatic Adviser, drew attention to the implications of such a 'tremendous occasion' for national images projected in both Germany and the wider world;[17] thus, it seemed essential – to quote the clumsy wording of one departmental minute – to ensure that England's performance was 'as efficacious as possible': 'for our prestige, it is really important that we should either win or put up a very good fight'.[17] Despite the media's long-standing uncritical acceptance of British footballing supremacy, the game's continued growth across the channel by Britain's former 'pupils' meant that – to quote the *Daily Express* – 'no game can be looked upon as a walk over'.[18] The Foreign Office, acknowledging the usual difficulty of persuading British clubs to release players for internationals, noted reports about the extensive preparations undertaken by Germany for the England game. Although the game had yet to go professional, Germany, like several other countries, adopted a far more professional approach towards internationals than the FA: 'The British team, though it will be selected from our best professionals, has at present the disadvantage that it does not seem likely that it can be got together for practice matches and instructions until shortly before it leaves for Germany'.[19] In addition, sportsmanship's integral role in British values identified for propaganda purposes, in conjunction with an official desire to minimise the risk of political complications arising from incidents on or off the field, led officials to expect high standards of behaviour from the England team.

As a result, the Foreign Office, having exchanged views informally with Stanley Rous, the FA's Secretary (1934–61), despatched a 'semi-official' letter from Vansittart reminding the FA about the match's broader political significance: 'it is really important for *our prestige* that the *British team* should put up a really first class performance. I hope that every possible effort will be made to ensure this.'[20] This request-*cum*-instruction also illustrated the frequent departmental tendency to equate 'England' with 'Britain', while devoting minimal, if any, attention to foreign internationals played by the other home countries. In response, the FA, though failing to spell out ways of implementing its promise, reassured the Foreign Office that 'every member of the Team will do his utmost to uphold the prestige of his country'.[21] The government's position had been made extremely clear – a 'first class performance' was interpreted to mean a good result achieved in a sporting manner – but the FA was left to draw its own conclusions and act accordingly. Rous, far from resenting government interference, positively welcomed Vansittart's despatch for use in his campaign to persuade the FA to adopt a more progressive approach concerning the introduction of special training for internationals or the use of air travel for lengthy foreign journeys.[22] But, the FA proved a very conservative institution, and Rous' efforts exerted minimal impact, at least in the short term, as evidenced in May 1938 by the failure to introduce any special pre-tour training and the fact that the England party, comprising 15 players plus accompanying officials led by C. Wreford Brown, travelled to Berlin via the Hook of Holland on a lengthy and tiring rail-sea journey. As Stanley Matthews observed, England underwent the usual preparations, that is, an eight-and-a-half-month season of league and cup games plus a two-day journey across Europe![23]

In Berlin, players, having been welcomed by the German authorities, the British embassy and the German-English Society, were soon made aware of not only widespread German interest in the game but also the latter's political dimension and relevance to British prestige.[24] According to Frank Broome, 'Sir [sic] Stanley told us that this was one we mustn't lose. He said it was as important politically as it was sporting.'[25] Stanley Matthews also acknowledged the way in which Germany viewed the match as 'a test of the New Order': 'There was not any doubt in any of our minds that the Nazis wanted to win this match more than anything else in the world. Equally certain was the fact that we realised there was more at stake than just a football game. This day as never before we would be playing for England.'[26]

THE NAZI SALUTE

As mentioned earlier, subsequent accounts have often concentrated on a notorious pre-match incident, that is, photographs of England players, lined up before the game during the playing of the German national anthem, giving the straight-armed Nazi salute. FA officials, guided by Henderson's advice about his use of the Nazi salute when greeting Hitler, decided unanimously the previous evening that it would be diplomatically prudent to make such a gesture.[27] Subsequently Rous justified this controversial decision in terms of responding to official pressure to ensure the match's success, particularly given his personal recall of Hitler's alleged irritation about the failure of British team members to turn their eyes while passing him at the opening parade for the 1936 Berlin Olympics. For the FA, the players' action, occasioning a thunderous response from the crowd, 'did much to ensure a friendly reception by the huge crowd present' as well as to create the 'right atmosphere' for the game.[28]

Writing in his memoirs, Rous claimed that players, who first learned of this 'bombshell' in the dressing room immediately prior to the game, 'had no objections, and no doubt saw it as a bit of fun rather than of political significance'.[29] Ivan Sharpe, a journalist, agreed: 'there was no appeasement about it'.[30] Bastin, who scored England's first goal, echoed such sentiments: 'Personally, I did not feel very strongly about the incident'.[31] But other players' memoirs suggest strong resentment about a proposal sprung on them at the last minute and implemented only under protest in obedience to the alleged interests of the team as well as the threat that 'if we didn't give the salute we wouldn't be selected for any future England games'.[32] Eddie Hapgood, the England captain, claimed to be sickened by the episode, while Stanley Matthews said that the 'order' 'caused everyone to stop what he was doing and look up with some alarm'.[33]

> What would all our friends back home think? … I wonder how many of the boys were tossing up with the idea of rebelling against this FA order which seemed so weak – the idea of crawling to Hitler and his thugs did not appeal to Englishmen … Even to this day, I still feel shame whenever I sit by the fire and glance through my scrap-book and gaze on that infamous picture of an England football team lining up like a bunch of Nazi robots, giving the dreaded salute.

Naturally, the historian would prefer to know what players really thought at the time, given the filtering effect of having lived through a long war against Germany. Moreover, players, or rather their respective ghost writers, would treat the incident as a way of attracting attention and sales: 'such excuses are the lifeblood of sport's self-image of neutrality, and as a result certain important political issues are marginalised into humorous farce'.[34] Nevertheless, contemporary press reports, though tending to be generally uncritical, offer some corroboration for players' disclaimers; for example, Henry Rose, writing for the *Daily Express*, recorded Hapgood's opinion that merely standing to attention would have been sufficient.[35] The following day's match played between Aston Villa and a 'German XI' offers conflicting evidence. The British team, which included one player (i.e. Broome) who had represented England the previous day, agreed to give the Nazi salute after the game, but then refused to implement this promise because of the way in which its offside tactics were booed by the crowd.[36] From this perspective, *The Times'* above-mentioned positive comments about Aston Villa's match must be treated with caution, especially as an unnamed FA official was quoted as saying that the resulting controversy undermined the 'good work' done by the England game.[37]

FIXING THE LABEL 'PRESTIGE' TO BRITISH FOOTBALL?

Even so, the Germany-England international continued to occupy centre stage. Henderson, who joined the German leadership to watch the game from the Führer's box, expressed great satisfaction that a clean and entertaining encounter free of incident resulted in a decisive England win. Hitler, having just returned from Rome, was absent, but prominent spectators included Rudolf Hess, the deputy Führer, as well as Joseph Goebbels (Minister for Propaganda), Joachim von Ribbentrop (Foreign Minister) and Von Tschammer und Osten. For British representatives in Germany, the game, in conjunction with the overall impression of bonhomie cultivated at the post-match dinner, presided over by the *Reichssports Führer*, brought significant propaganda benefits.[38] The British consul-general in Berlin, reporting to London, felt that this 'thoroughly enjoyable' game helped to reverse the deleterious impact of recent club visits upon Britain's footballing reputation: 'It is now recognised that the excellence of English football is still something to be admired and coveted … The game undoubtedly revived in Germany British sporting prestige.'[39] According to *The Times*' Berlin correspondent, England players, 'always a fraction of a second faster in tackling and shooting', were 'so much superior at all points of the game that the game will be remembered here less as a match than as a splendid exhibition of football'.[40] Indeed, the British press, glossing over Italy's status as 1934 World Cup victors as well as the forthcoming World Cup finals in France, employed the occasion to proclaim that 'once again, England had been proclaimed the leading football nation in the world' (*Daily Mail*), while taking delight in quoting *Fussball Woche*'s view that, despite non-entry to the World Cup, England were the 'world champions of football after all'.[41] The *New York Times*' headline, 'England conquers German Eleven, 6.3', suggested the match's global impact.[42]

More importantly, the German authorities and people, though hoping for a home victory, appeared to accept defeat in a magnanimous manner. British representatives in Germany, impressed by the welcome given to the England team, believed that 'the immediate contacts made between sports leaders of both countries gives prospect of cordial relations in the future insofar as sporting fixtures are concerned'.[43] Of course, Anglo-German relations depended on far more substantial considerations; indeed, the following weekend's Czech war scare crisis – this coincided with England's next tour game in Zurich – suggested the continued German threat to the territorial *status quo*. Nevertheless, sport offered one instrument capable of both reflecting and influencing the course of international relations. From this perspective, a football international, proving a highly visible bilateral contact, reinforced the British government's efforts at national projection in a country, whose controlled nature meant that any propaganda therein had to be – to quote a 1938 Cabinet paper – 'unobtrusive and unprovocative' to avoid arousing German sensitivities and worsening relations.[44] Reportedly, Henderson, 'a tall distinguished-looking gentleman', visited the England dressing room after the game to congratulate the team: 'Well played. You have done a good job for England this afternoon.'[45] In this manner, 'quiet' and 'restrained' cultural propaganda was viewed as possessing greater utility than more overt propaganda, especially if, as in this case, the event presented Britain in an extremely favourable light.[46]

By 1937–38, the Foreign Office concluded that the British Council, having been created a few years earlier to project positive British images in the wider world, had more than 'justified its existence' by encouraging other countries to direct their political, economic and cultural orientation towards Britain.[47] Indeed, international conditions rendered its work a 'vital necessity': 'Good cultural propaganda cannot remedy the damage done by a bad foreign policy, but it is no exaggeration to say that even the best of diplomatic policies may fail, if it neglects the task of interpretation and persuasion which modern conditions impose'. A continued programme of national projection – in Britain, this term was preferred to 'propaganda' – was required to counteract negative images of Britain, and particularly to establish that – to quote Anthony Eden (Foreign Secretary, 1935–38) – 'we are not the effete and degenerate people we are misrepresented as being by our totalitarian rivals'.[48] Similarly, Lord Lloyd, the British Council's chairman (1937–41), referred frequently to the ongoing 'fierce war of ideas' when identifying its role in countering the 'serious and perhaps irreparable damage' inflicted by foreign propaganda on Britain's image as a great nation.[49] Nevertheless, despite Germany's status as the prime focus for British policy-makers during the late 1930s, for reasons mentioned above, the British Council was assigned a virtual non-role therein.[50] However, sport meant that there was not a complete void respecting British propaganda in Germany, where athletics, motor cycling and tennis, among other sports, joined football in providing not only a meaningful point of contact throughout the period immediately preceding the outbreak of the Second World War but also an effective instrument for projecting British values and qualities to a captive, seemingly receptive, audience within and outside Germany.

Despite its prominence in official, media and public thinking in Britain, the Berlin match was merely the opening fixture of a three-match tour during the course of which wins over Germany (6-3) and France (4-2) were offset by a defeat (1-2) by Switzerland, whose strength was reaffirmed soon afterwards by its 4-2 victory over Germany in the early stages of the 1938 World Cup finals. Even so, the German match continued to be viewed by the government, media and people as the most important tour game. This point was reaffirmed in June 1938, when the FA, concluding that the team had fulfilled the government's highest expectations, decided to award a special gift to each player as 'special appreciation that, in the match against Germany, every member of the England team, even though determined to win, realised that his play must be consistent with the best British sporting traditions'.[51] Naturally, the British government was pleased with the win, England's sporting performance, and the absence of incident on and off the field. As a result, the Foreign Office, seeking to dispel the usual impression given by its contacts with Rous – 'usually we send him nothing but complaints' – informed the FA about the government's pleasure at the 'success' of the German visit, as verified by favourable reports from British overseas representatives.[52]

WAS 'GOOD KICKING' REALLY 'GOOD POLITICS'?

The Second World War (1939–45), in which Britain and Germany proved major protagonists, foiled plans for the return match scheduled for London during 1939–40. As a result, the two countries did not play each other again until December 1954, when the game's changing fortunes were highlighted by the fact that West Germany arrived at Wembley as recently crowned World Cup champions. A few months earlier, Theodor Heuss, the Federal Republic of Germany's President, presented players with a silver laurel, the nation's highest sports award, for overcoming Hungary 3-2 in the 1954 World Cup final: 'We can all rejoice about the German victory but nobody should believe that good kicking was good politics'.[53]

Despite such disclaimers, during preceding decades several governments deliberately politicised international football because of their clear belief that 'good kicking was good politics'; thus, 'in the gathering gloom of the late 1930s the label "prestige" was firmly fixed to football'.[54] International fixtures came to be viewed and presented as far more than mere sporting encounters, especially as the game's universal appeal made such matches a prime target for propaganda. In May 1938, the scale of foreign interest in British football was shown by not only large-scale media coverage but also capacity attendances for England's appearances in Berlin and Paris; thus, the 110,000 crowd in Berlin exceeded crowd figures for Germany's recent home games against Switzerland (30,000) and France

10

(65,000). Similarly, the final tour match, played at a recently enlarged Colombes stadium in Paris, attracted 65,000 people, hitherto the largest attendance in French footballing history.[55]

Frequently, internationals played against England or Scotland were interpreted in overseas countries as a useful way of testing the rapidly emerging strength of their national sides. As Rous observed about England, 'we were the side every country wanted to play and beat'.[56] At the same time, the British media, though assuming national primacy in a sport originated and developed by Britons, was forced to acknowledge that foreigners were proving themselves to be quite good at the game. For example, previewing the 1938 Germany-England game for the *Daily Express*, Henry Rose noted the changing balance of power in the world of football: 'Years ago this would have been looked upon as a joy ride. The Continentals were easy meat ... Time has marched on, the arts and crafts of the game have been mastered with Continental thoroughness. Under British tuition mark you, so that now no game can be looked upon as a walk over.'[57] Within this context, in May 1938 England's victories over France and Germany, in conjunction with Scotland's 3-1 tour win over Holland, reinforced the impression of British primacy, even if England's defeat by Switzerland gave substance to Rose's comments about the march of time.[58] Meanwhile, within days of the return of England and Scotland from abroad, the fact that their four opponents travelled to France for the 1938 World Cup finals highlighted the refusal of British teams to see any reason to prove themselves therein. Italy emerged triumphant yet again, and hence, in many respects, as discussed in the penultimate chapter, a more meaningful test of footballing primacy came one year later, when England travelled to Rome to play the reigning World Cup holders. Yet again, an international fixture became a highly visible event, whose footballing significance – the fixture was presented as the 'masters of the game' versus the world champions – was reinforced by the contemporary focus upon Anglo-Italian relations at a time of growing international tension.

PUTTING SPORT INTO HISTORY

'Though sport, like it or not, is everywhere, its historians have been nowhere – until recently.'[59] Today, sport has emerged as a more accepted area of historical study, but most historians, albeit often turning first to the sports pages of their daily newspaper, continue to gloss over Britain's sporting dimension regardless of its intrinsic interest, relevance to a wide range of political, social, economic, cultural and other concerns, and the high quality of many sports history monographs and journals, like the *International Journal of the History of Sport* or *The Sports Historian*.[60] In particular, there exists an enduring tendency to treat sports history as not meriting comparison with studies of, say, Lloyd George or Neville Chamberlain and British politics.

But, there are exceptions, perhaps inspired by Barbara Tuchman's claim that '*homo ludens*, man at play, is surely as significant a figure as man at war or at work. In human activity the invention of the ball may be said to rank with the invention of the wheel.'[61] Nor should one overlook the contribution of James Walvin, whose *The People's Game* (1975) helped to establish football as a valid field for historical study.[62] More recently, Peter Clarke's *Hope and Glory: Britain 1900–1990*, the final volume in the Penguin 'History of England', acknowledged sport's role, while taking up an often quoted assertion uttered by Liverpool's Bill Shankly (1913–81):

> For some people, the joke goes, sport is not a matter of life and death: it is more serious than that. When it is referred to as a religion, the comment may be suggestive as well as ironic. The ability of sport to capture the popular imagination, to infuse a sense of common commitment in the outcome of an epic contest, to provide a strong narrative line – even when busy people can only eavesdrop on the story on the back page of a newspaper or snatch at the latest Test score – this is not just a trivial matter. In twentieth-century Britain organised mass sport may have filled some of the psychic space which was being evacuated by organised mass Christianity.[63]

Similarly, Eric Hobsbawm, echoing a theme articulated during the early 1900s by J. Astley Cooper, among others, has presented footballers as 'primary expressions of their imagined communities' engaged in some kind of 'national struggle' in which political considerations imparted an extra edge to the usual element of sporting competition.[64] Footballers might see themselves as engaged in a purely sporting activity, but in practice they have often been perceived by governments, the media and public opinion as representatives embodying and projecting national values and qualities in some kind of gladiatorial contest.

> What has made sport so uniquely effective a medium for inculcating national feelings, at all events for males, is the ease with which even the least political or public individuals can identify with the nation ... The imagined community of millions seems more real as a team of eleven named people. The individual, even the one who cheers, becomes a symbol of his nation himself.[65]

Hobsbawm himself recalled listening with several Austrians to a radio commentary of the Austria-England match played at Vienna in 1930: 'I was England, as they were Austria … In this manner did twelve-year-old children extend the concept of team-loyalty to the nation.'[66] One of the more vivid examples of this instrumental use of football occurred in September 1981, when Norway, having traditionally proved weak opposition, overcame England 2-1 in a historic victory eulogised in extravagant terms by Bjorge Lillelien, the match commentator: 'We have beaten England, Lord Nelson, Lord Beaverbrook, Sir Winston Churchill, Sir Anthony Eden, Clement Attlee, Henry Cooper, Lady Diana. We have beaten them all. Maggie Thatcher, can you hear me? Maggie Thatcher, your boys took a hell of a beating. Norway have beaten England at football.'[67] Lillelien's complex mix was revealing in a range of ways, but establishes the manner in which the overseas mind has often linked the performance of England's football team to Britain's place in the world.

Today, British politicians, the media and opinion polls suggest that football still represents 'the most significant source of national pride in the modern world'.[68] Early in 1995, Tony Blair (then Leader of the Opposition, Prime Minister 1997–), addressing the Football Writers' Association on the occasion of Sir Stanley Matthews' 80th birthday, conceded that 'I know from my own children the pleasures they get in identification with their heroes, and the pride we all get in identification with our club or our national side'.[69] A few months later, John Major (Prime Minister, 1990–97), supporting his government's *Raising the Game* policy initiative, identified the centrality of sport in the contemporary world, including the manner in which national teams engaged the wider British community. He also raised several questions for historians.

> Some people say that sport is a peripheral and minor concern. I profoundly disagree. It enriches the lives of the thousands of millions of people around the world who know and enjoy it. Sport is a central part of Britain's National Heritage. We invented the majority of the world's great sports … It could be argued that nineteenth century Britain was the cradle of a leisure revolution every bit as significant as the agricultural and industrial revolutions we launched in the century before.
>
> Sport is a binding force between generations and across borders. But, by a miraculous paradox, it is at the same time one of the defining characteristics of nationhood and of local pride. We should cherish it for both those reasons.[70]

NOTES

1. John W. Young, *Britain and the World in the Twentieth Century* (Arnold, London, 1997), pp.122–5; R.A.C. Parker, *Chamberlain and Appeasement: British policy and the coming of the Second World War* (Macmillan, London, 1993), pp.132–81.
2. Football Association, London (hereafter FA), W. Pickford, FA, to N. Chamberlain, 4 Oct. 1938, encl. Consultative Committee, 19 Oct. 1938, minute 18, 1938–9; Cato, *Guilty Men* (Gollancz, London, 1940), p.6.
3. *The Times*, 16 May 1938.
4. *Daily Express*, 16 May 1938.
5. Sir Stanley Rous, *Football Worlds: a lifetime in sport* (Faber, London, 1978), p.64; Peter J. Beck, 'England v Germany, 1938', *History Today*, 32 (June 1982), 29–34.
6. Bill Murray, *Football: a history of the world game* (Scolar, Aldershot, 1994), p.96, pp.134–5.
7. Quoted, Ivan Sharpe, *Forty Years in Football* (Hutchinson, London, 1952), p.73. Note that Henderson's Christian name was spelt 'Nevile', not 'Neville'.
8. FA, International Selection Committee (hereafter ISC), 26 June 1937, minute 6, 11 Nov. 1937, minute 8, 1937–38.
9. FA, Joint Meeting of ISC and Finance and General Purposes Committee, 13 Dec. 1937, 1937–38; ISC, 10 Jan. 1938, minute 8, 24 Jan. 1938, minute 6, 29 April 1938, minute 3, 1937–38.
10. FA, ISC, 26 June 1937, minute 7, 1937–38. Czechoslovakia played Scotland in Glasgow one week later (Scotland won 5-0).
11. Public Record Office, Kew (hereafter PRO), minute, S. Gaselee, 4 May 1938, FO395/568/P1718.
12. PRO, J. Burrell, Home Office, to Gaselee, 14 Jan. 1938, FO395/568/P275; R. Kenney to Burrell, 29 Jan. 1938, Burrell to Kenney, 5 Feb. 1938, FO395/568/P444.
13. FA, Report on Continental Tour 1938, encl. ISC, 24 June 1938, minute 2, 1935–46.
14. PRO, Monthly Report from G. Lyall, consul-general in Berlin (hereafter Consular Report), n.d. (May 1938), encl. Henderson to Foreign Office, 9 June 1938, FO395/568/P2054. Gate receipts were £23,000.
15. *The Times*, 14 May 1938.
16. FIFA Archives, Zurich (hereafter FIFA), R. Ebersteller to I. Schricker, 28 March 1938, encl. FIFA Circular 1938/7, 29 March 1938, Austria 1935–57; Michael John, 'Österreich', in C. Eisenberg (ed.), *Fussball, soccer, calcio: ein englischer Sport auf seinem Weg um die Welt* (DTV, Munich, 1997), p.75. The FA denied press reports that it pressed for the exclusion of Austrians from the German team: *Daily Express*, 10 May 1938.
17. PRO, minute, Gaselee, 4 May 1938, R. Vansittart to S. Rous, 6 May 1938, FO395/568/P1718.
18. *Daily Express*, 10 May 1938.
19. PRO, minute, Gaselee, 4 May 1938, FO395/568/P1718.
20. PRO, Vansittart to Rous, 6 May 1938, FO395/568/P1718.
21. PRO, Rous to Vansittart, 10 May 1938, FO395/568/P1718.
22. Author's interview with Sir Stanley Rous, 28 March 1980; PRO, H. Usill to Gaselee, 13 May 1938, FO395/568/P1718.
23. Stanley Matthews, *Feet First* (Ewen & Dale, London, 1948), p.85.
24. PRO, Consular Report, May 1938, encl. FO395/568/P2054; *Daily Express*, 13 May 1938. Apparently Jimmy Hogan, the Aston Villa manager, translated German press reports for the benefit of players: author's interviews with Frank Broome, 6, 10 May 1980.

25. Charles Nevin, 'Adolf's lads: my part in their downfall', *Daily Telegraph*, 14 May 1988. Rous was not knighted until the late 1940s.
26. Matthews, p.85.
27. Author's interview with Rous, 28 March 1980; *Daily Express*, 13, 14 May 1938; Richard D. Mandell, *The Nazi Olympics* (Macmillan, New York, 1971), p.149.
28. FA, Report on Continental Tour, 1938, encl. ISC, 24 June 1938, minute 2, 1935–46; *Daily Express*, 14 May 1938; *The Times*, 16 May 1938.
29. Author's interview with Rous, 28 March 1980; Rous, *Football Worlds*, pp.64–5; John Cottrell, *A Century of Great Soccer Drama* (Hart-Davis, London, 1970), pp.94–5.
30. Sharpe, *Forty Years*, p.74.
31. Cliff Bastin (with B. Glanville), *Cliff Bastin Remembers. An Autobiography* (Ettrick Press, London, 1950), pp.113–14.
32. Stan Cullis, quoted, Rogan Taylor and Andrew Ward, *Kicking and Screaming: an oral history of football in England* (Robson Books, London, 1995), p.52. Cullis was not selected anyway for the German game, but played in the French fixture.
33. Eddie Hapgood, *Football Ambassador* (Sporting Handbooks, London, 1945), pp.26–8; Matthews, pp.86–7; Matthews (7 June 1981), quoted Stephen G. Jones, 'State intervention in sport and leisure in Britain between the wars', *Journal of Contemporary History*, 22 (1987), 170.
34. Martin Polley, 'The Foreign Office and International Sport, 1918–1948' (unpublished PhD thesis, St David's University College, University of Wales, 1991), p.xxvii.
35. *Daily Express*, 16 May 1938.
36. Ibid. See Eric Houghton, quoted Taylor and Ward, pp.52–3.
37. PRO, Henderson to Foreign Office, 9 June 1938, FO395/568/P2054; *The Times*, 16 May 1938; *Daily Express*, 16 May 1938.
38. *The Times*, 16 May 1938.
39. PRO, Consular Report, May 1938, FO395/568/P2054.
40. *The Times*, 16 May 1938.
41. *Daily Express*, 16 May 1938; *Daily Mail*, 16 May 1938.
42. *New York Times*, 15 May 1938.
43. PRO, Consular Report, May 1938, FO395/568/P2054.
44. PRO, Lord Halifax, 'British propaganda in Germany', 8 Dec. 1938, Cab24/281, CP384.
45. Matthews, p.83; author's interview with Rous, 28 March 1980.
46. PRO, Sir Eric Phipps, British ambassador in Berlin, to A. Eden, 7 Feb. 1936, BW32/1; R. Leeper to Lord Lloyd, 21 Nov. 1938, BW32/2.
47. PRO, Eden to Sir John Simon, Chancellor of Exchequer, 23 Dec. 1937, T161/907/S35581/03/38/1.
48. Ibid.
49. PRO, Lloyd to Eden, 22 Dec. 1937, T161/907/S35581/03/38/1.
50. PRO, R. Leeper to Hale, Treasury, 18 Jan. 1938, T161/907/S35581/03/38/1.
51. FA, ISC, 24 June 1938, 1937–38. Aston Villa's five-match German tour saw mixed results; for example, the next game at Dusseldorf was lost 1-2, while the third match at Stuttgart was won 2-1.
52. PRO, C. Warner to Rous, 25 June 1938, FO395/568/P2054; FA, ISC, 24 June 1938, 1937–38.
53. *The Times*, 17, 19 July 1954. The official publication has a slightly different translation: 'Not "a German Football Wonder" ', *The Bulletin* (Bonn), 25 Nov. 1954, 6; *Deutschland Weltmeister im Fussball, 1954* (Wilhelm Limpert, Frankfurt am Main, 1954), p.71.

54. Percy M. Young, *A History of British Football* (Stanley Paul, London, 1968), p.184.
55. *The Times*, 27 May 1938; *Daily Express*, 27 May 1938.
56. Rous, *Football Worlds*, p.62.
57. *Daily Express*, 12, 23 May 1938.
58. Bastin, complaining that England was 'kicked off the field' in Zurich, presented the Swiss match as one of the dirtiest games he had played in, even including the 1934 'Battle of Highbury': Bastin, pp.145–6.
59. Gareth Williams, *1905 and All That* (Gomer, Llandysul, 1991), p.1.
60. Roy Hattersley, formerly deputy leader of the Labour party, stated that he read the sports pages before any other section of his daily paper: 'Who Goes Home?', *BBC Radio Four*, 9 Jan. 1995; Richard Holt, 'Sport and History: the state of the subject in Britain', *Twentieth Century British History*, 7 (1996), 251; Pierre Arnaud, 'Sport – a means of national representation', Pierre Arnaud and James Riordan (eds), *Sport and International Politics: the impact of fascism and communism on sport* (E. & F.N. Spon, London, 1998), p.3.
61. Barbara Tuchman, *Practicing History: selected essays* (Ballantine, New York, 1982), p.234.
62. James Walvin, *The People's Game: a social history of British football* (Allen Lane, London, 1975; rev. edn Mainstream, Edinburgh, 1994).
63. Peter Clarke, *Hope and Glory: Britain 1900–1990* (Allen Lane, Penguin Press, London, 1996), p.53.
64. Eric Hobsbawm, *Nations and Nationalism since 1780: programme, myth, reality* (Cambridge University Press, Cambridge, 1990), p.143; Barrie Houlihan, *Sport and International Politics* (Harvester Wheatsheaf, Hemel Hempstead, 1994), p.170; Neil Tranter, *Sport, Economy and Society in Britain, 1750–1914* (Cambridge University Press, Cambridge, 1998), pp.55–6; J. Astley Cooper (1908), quoted, Polley, *Foreign Office and International Sport*, p.xi; Arnd Krüger, 'On the origins of the notion that sport serves as a means of national representation', *History of European Ideas*, 16 (1993), 863–7; Arnaud, *Sport – a means of national representation*, p.6. In particular, Arnaud raises questions about whether national teams represent specific governments, states or the nation.
65. Hobsbawm, p.143.
66. Ibid. Hobsbawm gives the wrong date (1929) for the match, which was played in 1930.
67. Quoted (9 Sept. 1981), *Sunday Times*, 8 Oct. 1995.
68. *The Independent*, 18 June 1995; *Sunday Times*, 21 Sept. 1997; *Daily Telegraph*, 22 Nov. 1997.
69. Tony Blair, 'Stan's my man', *New Statesman and Society* (20 Jan. 1995), 19.
70. Foreword by John Major, July 1995, in *Sport: raising the game* (Dept. of National Heritage, London, 1995), p.ii.

2

Presenting Britain as a Great Nation on the World's Screen through International Football

In September 1997 Chris Smith, the Secretary of State for Culture, Media and Sport in Tony Blair's recently elected Labour government, conceded the perennial problem of defining 'culture' as a governmental responsibility, even if his department's work, like that of its predecessor (i.e. Department of National Heritage), highlights the treatment of British sport as an integral part of national culture.[1] Today, it remains difficult also to establish the actual foreign policy contribution of cultural propaganda, including specific cases where it has made a real difference, especially as compared to 'hard power', like economic and military strength.[2] Even so, cultural propaganda, though depicted by contrast as 'soft power', has been perceived as an effective and powerful form of British diplomacy, as reaffirmed in the mid-1980s by the Thatcher government: 'Our cultural diplomacy helps to make Britain and British standards better known and understood, so we may pursue British interests more effectively'.[3]

PRESSING BRITISH CULTURE INTO 'POLITICAL SERVICE'

Some 50 years earlier, Richard Butler, speaking in May 1938 as Parliamentary Under-Secretary of State at the Foreign Office (1938–40), acknowledged the continued growth of propaganda in an increasingly tense world:

> Propaganda, as practised by the totalitarian states, is not only part of the new technique of government, but is used as a potent instrument … to make known the achievements of the regime both at home and abroad. Mass production of news and opinion accompanies the mass production of armaments. This is a new and important phenomenon in modern life and it would be foolish to underestimate it.[4]

In 1936, the British Council, created during 1934–35 to 'make known the achievements' of Britain in the wider world, received a lengthy

17

memorandum about cultural propaganda in the Mediterranean region from C.G. Hardie, Director of the British School at Rome. For him, the fundamental problem was that 'we are too apt to trust to the weight of our already established position to carry us on progressively, and to think that because we and the Americans still learn no other language, everyone else will end by learning English'.[5] His views, reflecting those of a Briton working overseas, typified complaints about British inertia, most notably the repeated failure to capitalise on national strengths at a time when other countries approached propaganda in a more businesslike manner: 'the Germans perhaps most thoroughly of all understand what they want and provide means sufficient to that end'.

Hardie advocated a strong push overseas harnessing Britain's cultural potential to the full: 'English language and culture are important in themselves, but to the foreigner their importance is immensely increased by their extension and the political and economic weight of Britain, the British Empire and the United States'. British diplomats might think twice about the American link, given the ambivalent nature of Anglo-American relations in the 1930s, even if they would have echoed Hardie's view that the propaganda attractions of cultural activities derived from their seemingly innocuous appearance, including the fact that 'their primary and ostensible purpose is not political … Political propaganda tends to defeat its object unless it is indirect.' At the same time, patience was required: 'It is a mistake to demand an immediate and visible return in these matters. To a long-sighted view, the bread we cast on the troubled waters of international relationships will be seen not to be wasted, but return a hundredfold though in unsuspected forms.'

Similar thoughts were articulated within the British Council, where Kenneth Johnstone drafted a lengthy 23-page memorandum on the Mediterranean region. Johnstone, whose comments possessed a broader relevance for the Council's activities in Europe and Latin America, echoed Hardie's concerns: 'national culture, like every other asset of the nation, has been pressed into political service, and cultural propaganda, exceeding its legitimate and useful function of interpreting one people to another, has become a weapon of aggression'.[6] Britain, having been drawn reluctantly into this 'struggle', proved far less active than, say, Germany or Italy, whose governments undertook a range of ostentatious and expensive projects designed to publicise the qualities and values of their respective regimes as well as to act as 'the *servant* of a restless and ambitious foreign policy'. Despite statistical uncertainties, Johnstone estimated that Germany and Italy each spent at least the equivalent of one million pounds *per annum*.[7] France, described as the 'original home of cultural propaganda', appeared equally active, thereby prompting frequent British complaints that French governments always seemed to find enough money for everything, excepting the repayment of war debts!

Of course, Britain, though less busy and more parsimonious than most other countries, was no stranger to propaganda.[8] The writings of Philip Taylor, among others, have provided a relatively full picture of British propaganda during, between, and after the two world wars. Between 1914 and 1918, propaganda, centred on the Ministry of Information (MOI), represented a major part of the total war strategy, but soon after the end of the First World War 'the propagandists were closed down'.[9] Subsequently, cultural diplomacy fell largely within the ambit of the Foreign Office, wherein the News Department, supported by both the Library and Political Departments, assumed responsibility for 'stating public policy clearly and accurately to the public throughout the world' and keeping 'a watchful eye' on the propaganda conducted by other countries.[10] Informed appraisals of practice elsewhere, alongside the advice of British diplomats overseas, reinforced the need for caution, including the risks of blatant propaganda on the German or Italian model, given the fact that – to quote Sir Malcolm Robertson (Chairman, British Council, 1941–45) – 'most countries welcome what we call cultural propaganda, but don't like political propaganda'.[11] The Foreign Office frequently criticised the over-politicised character of French propaganda, which was dominated by images drawn from the First World War and '99 times out of 100 overshoots the mark and does more harm than good'.[12] By contrast, more restrained cultural propaganda, exploiting economic (e.g. growth of media), social (e.g. increased leisure) and technological advances (e.g. broadcasting, film), was adjudged capable of greater penetration, even by-passing the obstacles deriving from censorship and other restrictive measures prevalent in other countries.[13]

In June 1934 Rex Leeper, counsellor in the News Department, codified the state of official thinking on the subject: 'Cultural propaganda has been recognised of late years as an effective and necessary instrument of national policy. It has been pursued vigorously by most Governments in one form or another, either directly or indirectly, and the efforts made to promote it have been steadily increasing.'[14] Confronted by a wide-ranging, escalating, well-funded, and state-directed propaganda challenge from overseas, British policy-makers realised that a 'policy of abstention' based on the role of a 'disarmed bystander' was no longer a profitable course: 'In the last resort, like can only be met with like, and propaganda with propaganda'.[15] In many respects, Britain became, as Johnstone admitted, 'an unwilling participant in the cultural struggle' conducted on the global stage.[16] The post-war world could not be taken for granted: 'Modern conditions require something more than a mere negative complacency. Sound policy cannot usefully speak without an opportunity to be heard.'[17] British interests and values had to be protected and promoted overseas, foreign policy explained, and misrepresentations corrected, and even sceptics came round to the view, as stated by Sir Arthur Willert (former Press Officer in the Foreign Office), that an allegedly unBritish activity like propaganda represented a 'fact of modern political and diplomatic life'.[18]

> It is obviously difficult for a school of statesmanship so long inculcated with the idea of the inevitable and automatic supremacy of Great Britain in world affairs to realise how things have changed in that respect and how thoroughly the present precariousness of our position, both political and economic, justifies the growing demand for an adequate system of national advertisement.[19]

During the early 1930s, anxieties articulated in official circles about the growth and impact of foreign propaganda, in conjunction with its seeming lack of policy priority in Britain, prompted Sir Stephen Tallents, head of the Empire Marketing Board, to write *The Projection of England* (1932).[20] Soon afterwards, the extra edge imparted to German propaganda by Hitler's advent to power (1933), alongside the politico-ideological rivalries underlying the European Civil War, merely accentuated the force of his demands for a more effective approach.[21]

THE BRITISH COUNCIL IN THE EUROPEAN CIVIL WAR

In July 1934, British missions overseas were instructed henceforth to monitor and report back regularly about the relative impact overseas of British cultural activities as well as the nature of propaganda conducted by other countries.[22] In effect, as Vansittart noted, the initial political and economic responsibilities of British diplomats overseas were now extended in 'a cultural direction'.[23] These moves prepared the way for the British Council, known initially as the Cultural Relations Committee and instructed to maintain close contact with the Foreign Office, while linking up, as appropriate, with other government departments. In many respects, this format reflected Leeper's stress on the advantages of distancing the government from such activities: 'the propaganda promoted by the Foreign Office should, so far as possible, be conducted through private organisations which should be encouraged to stand on their own feet and not be entirely dependent on official assistance'.[24]

The British Council's activities focused largely on 'high culture', that is, English language teaching and libraries, drama, art exhibitions, films, music, educational scholarships, and cultural exchanges undertaken by prominent musicians and writers, among others. The target audience comprised influential opinion-makers, not the general public, in foreign countries; indeed, in 1937 one British Council official, referring to the masses, noted that the 'unintelligent ... do not matter to us anyway'.[25] Even so, there remained a niche for less elitist activities, like sport, directed at specific local audiences: 'the fact that some particular activity is not mentioned does not exclude other suggestions from being put forward either in London or by Missions abroad'.[26]

Although its contribution should not be exaggerated, the British Council provided an invaluable prop to diplomacy and military preparedness, particularly at a time when the British government was engaged – to quote Lord Lloyd, the Council's chairman (1937–41) – 'in the fierce war of ideas to which we are inevitably, if defensively, committed'.[27] In June 1937, Lord Eustace Percy (1936–37), Lloyd's predecessor, apprised Anthony Eden, the Foreign Secretary (1935–38), about its changing role: 'The Council is no longer expected merely to rescue British prestige from neglect; it has to defend that prestige from deliberate attack'.[28] Certainly, the Council helped 'to prevent England being lost sight of or relegated to the position of a second-rate power' as well as to 'correct the impression which has gained currency abroad that this country is decadent' (Lloyd).[29] Eden proved a ready listener for such promptings: 'It is perfectly true that good cultural propaganda cannot remedy the damage done by a bad foreign policy, but it is no exaggeration to say that even the best of diplomatic policies may fail, if it neglects the task of interpretation and persuasion which modern conditions impose'.[30] Neville Chamberlain, the Prime Minister (1937–40), was less enthusiastic, but accepted the Council's 'urgent national importance', even if limited funding, in conjunction with Leeper's view that 'success depends on quality and not quantity', compelled a 'concentration of effort'.[31]

Cultural propaganda's policy impacts, albeit invisible and incapable of measurement, were real in the sense that other states were encouraged to direct their political orientation towards Britain in preference to any other state. Nor should the commercial case be overlooked during a decade characterised by generally depressed economic conditions, as stressed by Samuel Hoare, Eden's predecessor at the Foreign Office:

> The commercial arguments in favour of intensifying the work of British
> cultural propaganda are no less strong than the political arguments. In

all, the danger of German cultural and commercial penetration, which may be expected to increase as the power and wealth of Germany revive, makes it particularly desirable for British cultural propaganda to secure as firm a hold as possible in the minds and interests of the population, and particularly on the younger generation before the counter attraction becomes too strong.[32]

The old maxim of trade following the flag appeared to be giving way to an alternative sequence involving trade following culture.[33]

SPORT AS CULTURAL PROPAGANDA

Cultural propaganda was defined normally to emphasise the promotion and dissemination of ideals, beliefs and achievements in a general rather than a specifically politico-economic format. Negative aims, reflecting a desire to contain and counter the impact of hostile propaganda, went hand-in-hand with more positive considerations related to a belief in the intrinsic value of propagating British cultural values in the wider world as an alternative philosophy and way of life to doctrines propagated by other states. Despite conceding the value of alternative 'supplementary methods' of national projection, historians have concentrated upon artistic, dramatic, film, literary, and musical manifestations of British culture.[34] By contrast, the contribution of more popular forms of culture, most notably sport, have been overlooked in a manner tending both to reflect and reinforce impressions about the autonomy of sport in Britain.

However, international sport was equally capable of fulfilling a cultural propaganda role in terms of not only promoting a favourable image of Britain as a great nation characterised by an ability to win well in a fair and sporting manner but also countering the detrimental effects of foreign propaganda. Writing in 1928, Philip Noel-Baker, currently teaching international relations at London University (1924–29), felt that sport had every right to be treated like more elitist forms of art: 'To lots of people running means more than any game or any sport. It is on a plane with the great forms of art ... It has a dramatic power that nothing else has .... And what makes it most important is that it is so simple that its appeal is universal.'[35] Several games, sporting events and values featured in Tallents' *The Projection of England* (1932), which influenced the thinking underpinning the British Council:

If we want to know what material England should project, it is wise to ask ourselves what are the English characteristics in which the outside world is most interested. It is an entertaining pursuit – this breaking up of

22

the fame of England into its primary colours. At one end of the spectrum are to be found, I suppose, such national institutions and virtues, as: the monarchy ... parliamentary institutions ... Shakespeare, and Dickens.[36]

Nor was sport neglected in his list of points worthy of projection: 'In sport – a reputation for fair play. At the other end of the spectrum might be found such events as the Derby and the Grand National ... the Boat Race, Henley, Wimbledon, the Test Matches, and the Cup Final.' Between these two extremes, Tallents, typifying the official tendency to conflate 'England' and 'Britain', identified a 'medley of institutions and excellencies', including 'Oxford and St Andrews' and 'football and foxhunting'. 'Of some such elements as these is the standing raw material of England's esteem in the world composed. There should be added to them all those achievements which by a sudden stroke place England from time to time on the world's screen and win her there a favourable reflection.'

Any sport, like football, capable of contributing to national projection on the 'world's screen', became also an *essentially political activity* supporting policy-makers, regardless of the position taken by British governments. In reality, Britain was not unaffected by what was happening in the wider world, where international sport in general and football matches between teams representing the major powers in particular were often viewed through political spectacles. During the 1920s and even more so during the 1930s, it proved difficult for any country, even Britain, to remain immune from such external pressures; thus, British governments, regardless of their *laissez-faire* pronouncements, were unable to prevent any football match played by England against Germany or Italy from being interpreted, at least overseas, in a political mindset defined by, say, the struggle between liberal democracy and fascism. Governments, media and opinion increasingly regarded sporting prowess as a gauge of national power, values, prestige, influence and vitality.[37] In this vein, a letter, written to the FA by its Spanish counterpart to confirm a forthcoming fixture, proved rather revealing, particularly given Spain's historic victory over England the previous year: 'we would have a great honour in *fighting* in England a return match of that played in Madrid in May 1929'.[38] Of course, this was a mistranslation, but what happened on the field was often endowed with an extra-sporting significance. Indeed, to use cricketing terminology, football internationals were depicted in effect as 'test matches' for national power and prestige, even if such a descriptor was employed only for matches played by representative teams touring the dominions (see Table 5.1, Chapter 5), where it offered a way of exploiting the more significant cricketing connection.[39]

A WORLD GAME 'MADE IN BRITAIN'

In 1948, the Duke of Gloucester, formally welcoming representatives to the FIFA Congress, held at London to coincide with the Olympics Games, pressed football's British dimension, including 'the remarkable fact that the game which began among a handful of boys on the playing fields of English schools had not only spread throughout the world, but [was] being played everywhere according to the same rules'.[40] Indeed, only the previous year, FIFA members fielded a representative side against Great Britain to express thanks for the 'gift of football'.[41] Football's propaganda potential was enhanced by Britain's central role in the origin and development of a sport which acquired the strongest claim to be the world game in terms of participants and spectators, in spite of being the undisputed major sport in only Britain, continental Europe and Latin America. Association football was, as Frederick Wall, the FA Secretary (1895–1934), reminded the Home Office during the early 1920s, 'the largest National Sport in the country'.[42] Moreover, the game, benefiting from the growth of the media in reporting and focusing public attention on matches, flourished as both a leisure activity and spectator sport, often attracting a level of enthusiasm comparable to something akin to religion.

British football was controlled by four national associations, which were founded between 1863 and 1880 (Table 2.1), that is, prior to any foreign governing body (i.e. Denmark 1889). Basically, each British association, acting in accordance with its own agenda and regulations, constituted an autonomous non-governmental organisation exercising considerable authority over the game within their respective countries, including the selection of representative sides, the arrangement of international fixtures, and the approval of club visits overseas, among other functions. Moreover, acting through the International Football Association Board (IFAB), they exerted a dominant role in making and amending the laws of the game as played throughout the world. In 1935, the FA was described by one British minister as a 'quite independent body', and, during the inter-war period, the non-governmental nature of football's governing bodies, like those responsible for other sports (e.g. Amateur Athletic Association), was frequently presented as a distinctive British trait in a world characterised by ever-closer politico-sporting links.[43] Certainly, British governments, media and opinion continued to accept, and even to emphasise, this feature for a nation, where, to quote *The Times* (1929), 'the game's the thing': 'Football to Englishmen is a recreation, an amusement, a help to physical fitness. There is certainly no case for official interference by the British Government; and, of course, there never has been any.'[44]

TABLE 2.1
THE BRITISH FOOTBALL ASSOCIATIONS

Name	Date of founding	Area of control	FIFA membership
Football Association	1863	England	1906–20 1924–28 1946–
Football Association of Wales	1876	Wales	1910–20 1924–28 1946–
Irish Football Association	1880	Northern Ireland*	1911–20 1924–28 1946–
Scottish Football Association	1873	Scotland	1910–20 1924–28 1946–
Note also:			
Football Association of Ireland	1921	Republic of Ireland	1923–

* The Irish Football Association's claims to control the game in, and select players from the whole of Ireland, proved a major source of contention with the Football Association of Ireland during and after the 1920s.

Despite implying their predilection for more elitist sports, in January 1929 both *The Times* and *The Scotsman* reminded readers – undoubtedly, these included members of the Foreign Office – that 'the full extent of its (i.e. association football) importance is still not generally realized': 'How greatly the vogue of football has grown abroad during the present century, and especially since the War, may be observed by all who have travelled on the Continent of Europe in spring or summer during the last quarter of a century ... Association football has indeed come into its own on the Continent.'[45] The thousand-plus football clubs in Portugal, like the hundred clubs found in Prague alone, were quoted to establish the game's spread throughout Europe as well as the rapid growth of international matches between national and club teams often watched by large crowds. By contrast, sports, like cricket and rugby football, more familiar to their

25

typical readers had made limited progress elsewhere, with the exception of the British empire; for instance, rugby had made minimal impact in continental Europe, excepting France and Italy.

However, the game's hold, even within Europe, proved somewhat variable. For example, the *Daily Express* recorded football's primacy in Madrid café society, where 'footballers are quite as popular as bullfighters … Many Spaniards confess that they really prefer football to bullfighting.'[46] By contrast, Ernest Rennie, writing from Helsingfors during the early 1920s, reminded the Foreign Office that, though sport represented a 'special feature' of Finnish national life, athletics and winter sports attracted far more attention than football.[47] Winter sports represented, he reported, the 'most engrossing topic' of conversation for the younger generation, while the country's strong performance at the 1920 Olympic Games explained why athletics was followed with an enthusiasm reminiscent of that shown for football elsewhere. Similarly, across the Atlantic the game's popularity in, say, Argentina, Brazil and Uruguay was not replicated in all Latin American countries. Nor were North America, Asia, Australasia, and Africa major areas of footballing activity prior to the Second World War.[48]

TABLE 2.2
BRITISH FOOTBALL AND THE WORLD CUP, 1930–50

Year	1930	1934	1938	1950
Entrants	13	29	36	33
British entry	No	No	No	Yes

Source: 'A short history of the World Cup competition', *FIFA Official Bulletin*, 22 (May 1958), 25.

Inevitably, football's advent as the national game in an ever-increasing number of countries was reinforced by the growth of cross-border contacts, as domestic league and cup competitions were supplemented by international fixtures and tournaments.[49] The long-standing home international championship in Britain, described by FIFA as 'the most senior of all international competitions', dated back to the early 1880s. It was followed by the Olympic football tournament (1908), the South American championship (1916), the Scandinavian championship (1924), the International Cup in central Europe (1927), the Baltic Cup (1928), the

Balkan Cup (1929), and, most notably, the World Cup (1930). Even so, the initial World Cup tournaments, albeit imparting a more meaningful global dimension to the 'world game' and attracting large total attendances (1930: 434,500; 1934: 395,000; 1938 483,000), were devalued by the deliberate non-participation of leading footballing countries (Table 2.2).[50] British teams refused to enter until 1950, while the absence of most European countries from the inaugural tournament held at Montevideo in 1930 was followed by limited Latin American participation in the 1934 and 1938 World Cup finals played in Europe. The football tournaments of successive Olympiads – only the 1932 Los Angeles Olympics lacked a football competition – were recognised by FIFA as 'the amateur championship of the world of association football' and assumed a more global appearance through the participation of China (1936), Egypt (1920–36), Japan (1936), and the USA (1924–36).[51] From this perspective, the cancellation of the 1940 Tokyo Games deprived the game of an opportunity to enhance its position in Asia.

The global impact of British football, though deriving largely from the game's world-wide popularity, was helped also by close season overseas tours undertaken by British national and club teams, which were often interpreted as epitomising the nation's footballing qualities and values. Regular mid-season internationals played at home against foreign teams did not commence until the 1930s. Less visible, but frequently exerting a more enduring influence, British footballing coaches were employed throughout Europe and Latin America, occasionally under the auspices of the British Council. British football adopted a somewhat ambivalent approach towards international fixtures, as highlighted in the 1930s by repeated refusals of FIFA's invitations to enter the World Cup. For Britain, the key 'international' tournament remained the home international championship (1884–1984), even if for both England and Scotland their annual fixture proved the 'big match'. Whereas the Irish Sea failed to prevent close and regular footballing 'cross-Channel' links between the Irish Football Association (IFA) and the other home countries, the English Channel, like the Atlantic Ocean, proved more of a physical and psychological divide for British football. England developed its continental fixture list to a far greater extent than other home countries, but never played a non-European team at full international level until after the Second World War. During the 1930s, Scotland, moving out of its previous self-imposed isolation, played more continental teams home and away, particularly as compared to Wales, whose full national side crossed the Channel only twice prior to the Second World War. By contrast, Northern Ireland, though regularly crossing the Irish Sea for home championship matches, never played a full international in continental Europe at all during this period.[52] Prior to 1939, British teams venturing further afield, such as to Australia, Canada, South Africa, South America or the USA, tended to be either touring teams representing one of the football associations or, more usually, a club side engaged on a close season tour.

The relatively cautious attitude assumed by British football towards international, and particularly inter-continental, fixtures, derived from a range of factors, including a deep-seated isolationism, a belief in national footballing superiority, and the high priority attached to the domestic game. Nor were logistical considerations, particularly concerning transport and player availability for lengthy overseas visits, irrelevant to the consideration of tours to more distant parts. International travel remained a tiring, time-consuming and often difficult process, even if the 1930s saw the gradual advent of the aeroplane, as highlighted in 1935 when the German team flew to London to play England. But aircraft did not become the norm for intra- and inter-continental travel until the post-1945 period, when 'physical distance no longer prevents regular meetings of nations, clubs and players'.[53] Meanwhile, for most British teams, motor coaches, ships and trains remained the principal means of transport within and between continents; indeed, the FA's continued refusal to use air travel for lengthy journeys prompted press criticism during the late 1930s about the adverse impacts exerted upon the performance of players by reliance on traditional forms of travel.[54]

BRITAIN'S MAJOR EXPORT

In March 1934, Sir John Simon, addressing the 'Lords and Commons Cricket Dinner', pointed to cricket's perceived place in external images of Britain:

> The observant and judicious foreigner, if asked to select the two institutions of our country which are most characteristic of the English spirit, would unhesitatingly reply – 'Cricket' and 'the House of Commons' ... Cricket furnishes a storehouse of the most delightful memories which will remain with us as long as life lasts ... The Frenchman thinks of his early love affairs; the American gloats over his most successful speculation; the Hindu contemplates his previous existence; and the happy Englishman dreams of cricket.[55]

Simon moved on to identify also the merit attached by foreigners to British values, like 'to play cricket', that is, 'to be modest in victory, to fight your hardest when things are going badly, to play for your side and not for yourself, to accept the decision and to obey the rules'. Although Simon's status as Foreign Secretary (1931–35) imparted significance to these remarks, they were merely personal views illuminating both contemporary tendencies to conflate 'English' with 'British' and elitist prejudices respecting association football. For many foreigners, football, rather than cricket, proved 'most characteristic' of the 'English spirit'. Moreover, the FA was equally conscious of the need to establish the way in which the game epitomised British sporting values, as evidenced in 1939, when the Earl of Athlone, the FA's President (1939–55), exhorted players to 'make your sportsmanship an everyday affair. Tenacity and determination, the will to win, but the power to lose, and the ability to act as a member of a team, even whilst developing individuality and initiative.'[56]

More recently, Alan Tomlinson, pointing to popular culture's propaganda potential, claimed that 'the game of football was exported to the world by all-confident Britons. Football became one of Britain's most successful cultural exports, more resoundingly successful than Shakespeare, and more smoothly adaptable than, say, a Gilbert and Sullivan opera.'[57] Britain's undoubted role as an originator, leader and teacher for many games meant that sport, figuring prominently in both self-images and other countries' perceptions, represented both a cause and an effect of the extension of British influence, values and prestige in the wider world. Such cultural imperialism, though often underrated by ministers and officials and ignored by most histories, was recognised during the 1920s, such as by James Douglas, editor of the *Sunday Express*, who expressed great pride in 'our position as the greatest exporters of sport in the world. We teach other nations to play our national games, and they prove such apt pupils.'[58] A few years later, the Archbishop of York made a similar point:

> It is difficult, perhaps, for an Englishman, so I have been told, to realise the enormous prestige of Great Britain in the world of sport, a prestige which is unaffected either by our victories or by our defeats in particular sporting events, but which depends on the fact that we invented most of the games which we have taught the world to play, and that we are still regarded as the final court of appeal in everything which concerns the spirit in which games should be played … We in our country claim a great deal for sport. Expressions such as 'playing the game' have found their way into our language.[59]

Nor was the point lost on those active in the world of football, who often depicted themselves as 'missionaries of sport' (Wall) responsible for 'spreading the gospel of football to foreign parts'.[60] Of course, spreading the word to fortunate foreigners was a double-edged sword, since other spheres of activity, like industrialisation, in which Britain took an early lead had already demonstrated that any benefits accruing from being originators, leaders and teachers were liable to be counter-balanced by the fact that some 'pupils' proved fast learners. Looking back to the late 1930s, George Graham, the Scottish Football Association (SFA)'s Secretary, acknowledged the changing balance of footballing power: 'Time was when our clubs went on "holiday" tours to European countries and enjoyed themselves, but the foreigners have proved apt pupils in the science of the game, and now Jack is as good as his master. No team from this country can afford to go to any capital of Europe and treat the match in the holiday spirit – those days have gone for ever.'[61] Even worse, 'Jack' was soon to prove that he was much better than his British 'master'! Unsurprisingly, Britain's enduring image as 'masters of the game' meant that visits by British club and national sides were seen elsewhere as a good way to advance the game, particularly as good performances against visiting British teams, even club sides from lower leagues, came to be regarded as a kind of rite of passage, that is, an excellent way to establish one's credentials in the world's major sport.[62]

According to *The Times* (1929), 'Europeans' – the newspaper seemed to exclude Britons from this descriptor – took their major game so seriously that internationals were viewed through political spectacles as a reflection of not only a country's footballing abilities but also the strength and dynamism of its politico-social system.[63] Association football was increasingly treated as far more than a sport, as recorded in 1928 by the British consul in Turin, who identified what he saw as the 'different mental angle' of continental countries towards the game.[64] Wall agreed: 'People in Continental countries take Association Football very seriously, and even go so far, I suppose, as to rate another country's national quality by the prowess of its representatives at international sports gatherings'.[65] He elaborated the point in his memoirs:

> Abroad, international sport has a political aspect. Football in England is not carried on for the purposes of playing a foreign country and gaining a victory. Football in dear old England is merely a sporting entertainment ... England regards international matches as a game, but continental countries look upon these matches as a test of strength, spirit and skill. Victory increases national prestige, and defeat is a sign of decadence. To them, success is vital.[66]

Obviously, national sides proved the central focus, but British clubs engaged on foreign tours were equally capable of depiction as representing their county of origin. Of course, even seemingly apolitical assertions, like those articulated by Wall about the alleged distinctiveness of a British game unburdened by political values, were underpinned by notions of 'Englishness' or 'Britishness' based on superior liberal democratic values.[67] In this vein, one is tempted to recall the claims made by J.E.C. Weldon, headmaster of Harrow (1881–95), to the effect that 'Englishmen are not superior to Frenchmen or Germans in brains or industry, or the science or apparatus of war' but rather in the qualities 'which games impart'; indeed, traits, like team spirit and energy, 'which merit success in cricket or football, are the very qualities which win the day in peace or war'.[68]

Whether or not the outcome of football internationals actually reflected national power, values and ideologies is less important than the fact that many people, even those denying any inter-connection, perceived or implied a meaningful linkage.[69] By implication, as *The Times* noted in 1929, there existed a Darwinian belief that, if any nation's teams were continually beaten, 'the race which produced them must be decadent'.[70] Subsequently, the advent of Hitler's Germany, highlighting sport's central role in national propaganda machines, reinforced the hold of such perceptions, while prompting warnings to 'beware of too much nationalism in our football'.[71] Within this context, Britain, a leading force in both the international political and sporting spheres during the pre-1914 and inter-war periods, might be interpreted as having little to gain and much to lose from international football (Table 2.3). Victories over foreign teams, albeit reinforcing images of national footballing prowess, lost some impact because of expectations of British success, as acknowledged by one player: 'I have found that when England lose abroad, they are damned categorically; when they win, it is taken for granted'.[72] Indeed, this feature enabled other countries to excuse defeats to British sides with minimal loss of prestige, while allowing other governments to exploit any successes to the full in terms of establishing simultaneously their dynamic impact on all spheres of life and the decline, even decadence, of Britain as the hegemonial power. In this manner, international sport, attracting considerable domestic and external visibility, exerted a levelling effect, especially as lesser powers, like Austria, Portugal or Uruguay, gained the opportunity to acquire kudos by challenging, perhaps even defeating, a team representing a major power. Subsequently, this prompted the jibe that 'Uruguay cannot afford a nuclear force ... or a fleet of supersonic aircraft, but she has won the World Cup twice. "Uruguay has no history, only a football team".'[73]

British embassies and missions, like foreign diplomatic representatives based in London, ensured that government ministers and officials in Britain were fully apprised of the growing political significance attached to sport

TABLE 2.3
BRITISH FOOTBALL VERSUS FOREIGN TEAMS, 1908–39

	England		Northern Ireland	Scotland		Wales	Home International Tournament Winners
1907–8	Austria	(a) 6-1					Scotland/England
	Austria	(a) 11-1					
	Hungary	(a) 7-0					
	Bohemia	(a) 4-0					
1908–9	Hungary	(a) 4-2					England
	Hungary	(a) 8-2					
	Austria	(a) 8-1					
1909–10							Scotland
1910–11							England
1911–12							England/Scotland
1912–13							England
1913–14							Ireland
			First World War (1914–18)				
1918–19							Not held
1919–20							Wales
1920–21	Belgium	(a) 2-0					Scotland
1921–22							Scotland
1922–23	Belgium	(h) 6-1					Scotland
	France	(a) 4-1					
	Sweden	(a) 4-2					
	Sweden	(a) 3-1					
1923–24	Belgium	(a) 2-2					Wales
	France	(a) 3-1					
1924–25	Belgium	(h) 4-0					Scotland
	France	(a) 3-2					
1925–26	Belgium	(a) 5-3					Scotland
1926–27	Belgium	(a) 9-1					Scotland/England
	Luxemb'g	(a) 5-2					
	France	(a) 6-0					
1927–28	France	(a) 5-1					Wales
	Belgium	(a) 3-1					
1928–29	France	(a) 4-1		Norway	(a) 7-3		Scotland
	Belgium	(a) 5-1		Oslo XI	(a) 4-0*		
	Spain	(a) 3-4		Germany	(a) 1-1		
				Holland	(a) 2-0		
1929–30	Germany	(a) 3-3		France	(a) 2-0		England
	Austria	(a) 0-0					
1930				*World Cup – No British Entry*			
1930–31	France	(a) 2-5		Austria	(a) 0-5		Scotland/England
	Belgium	(a) 4-1		Italy	(a) 0-3		
				Switzl'd	(a) 3-2		
1931–32	Spain	(h) 7-1		France	(a) 3-1		England
1932–33	Austria	(h) 4-3				France (a) 1-1	Wales
	Italy	(a) 1-1					
	Switzl'd	(a) 4-0					
1933–34	France	(h) 4-1		Austria	(h) 2-2		Wales
	Hungary	(a) 1-2					
	Czech.	(a) 1-2					
1934				*World Cup – No British Entry*			
1934–35	Italy	(h) 3-2					England/Scotland
	Holland	(a) 1-0					
1935–36	Germany	(h) 3-0					Scotland
	Austria	(a) 1-2					
	Belgium	(a) 2-3					
1936–37	Hungary	(h) 6-2		Germany	(h) 2-0		Wales
	Norway	(a) 6-0		Austria	(a) 1-1		
	Sweden	(a) 4-0		Czech.	(a) 3-1		
	Finland	(a) 8-0					
1937–38	Czech.	(h) 5-4		Czech.	(h) 5-0		England
	Germany	(a) 6-3		Holland	(a) 3-1		
	Switzl'd	(a) 1-2					
	France	(a) 4-2					
1938				*World Cup – No British Entry*			
1938–39	FIFA/Rest			Hungary	(h) 3-1	France (a) 1-2	England/Scotland/
	Europe	(h) 3-0*					Wales
	Norway	(h) 4-0					
	Italy	(a) 2-2					
	Yugo.	(a) 1-2					
	Romania	(a) 2-0					
				Second World War (1939–45)			

* Inserted to link with the text, but not a recognised full international.
Note: The British team's score is given first for both home and away matches.

in the wider world on the part of not only governments and the media but also the masses, given the widespread popular interest taken in association football. For people resident in continental Europe and beyond, British sport was not only held in high regard but also treated as newsworthy, since the intrinsic interest exhibited in, say, information about individual players and teams was reinforced by the relevance of the results to football pools and betting in the Netherlands and Sweden, among other countries.[74] Dutch press reports, even extending to cover the England-Australia cricket tests, suggest that the level of overseas interest in British sport *per se* should not be underestimated; indeed, in July 1921 H.A. van Karnebeek, the Dutch Foreign Minister, specifically asked Sir Ronald Graham, the British Minister, for news about recent cricket, polo and tennis events in Britain.[75] It was, of course, the close season for football, the country's major sport. Graham, having reminded the Foreign Office about van Karnebeek's cricketing past, identified sport's propaganda potential: 'This country has by no means escaped the world-wide wave of sporting enthusiasm, which is but a natural reaction from the terrible events of past years ... I regard the very considerable sporting element in the Dutch public as a very favourable field for British propaganda, which should on no account be neglected. I have endeavoured to make full use of it and shall continue to do so.'[76]

FOOTBALL AS CULTURAL PROPAGANDA

In September 1946, one British diplomat, reviewing a proposed football tour to Turkey, minuted that 'experience has shown that sporting fixtures tend to be political rather than cultural in their implications'.[77] Whether or not association football, or any other sport, warranted definition as 'cultural propaganda' was considered from time to time in official exchanges, principally between the British Council and Foreign Office. For instance, in December 1937 Rowland Kenney responded positively to a proposal for the British Council to send a football coach to Greece: 'I suppose to include football under the general heading of "culture" is to make the term somewhat elastic, but we have given some assistance to football teams in the past, and we very much hope that the Council will consider helping in this particular instance'.[78] In turn, the British Council, attaching 'considerable importance' to this project, made a presentation about its work to encourage the FA to play its part in helping to 'make the life, thought, and achievements of British people more widely known abroad'.[79] Certainly, visits by British teams came to offer an extra dimension to cultural propaganda in a way articulated clearly by the British legation at Berne soon after the Second World War: 'Such visits make a stirring appeal to the Swiss heart, the effect of which far outweighs the effect of propaganda directed at the Swiss head'.[80]

In practice, there were, and still are, as Peter McIntosh has written, 'very few governments in the world which do not accept the political importance of success in international sport'.[81] Britain proved no exception. Despite carefully cultivated non-interference images, British governments, finding themselves unable to remain on the sidelines, adopted a more intervention-ist strategy towards international sport, such as to fine-tune the process through the occasional exertion of pressure in support of good results and behaviour. Within official circles, success, defined roughly speaking as a good performance, as measured through results, remained the primary goal, as acknowledged in the late 1920s by Arthur Yencken, 'it is still true that success is by far the best form of propaganda'.[82] Victories on the football field, particularly in matches versus teams representing a major footballing or political power, came to be valued officially in terms of enhancing Britain's reputation as masters of the world game, reaffirming its status as a liberal democracy occupying a leading role among the great powers, and confronting images of decline. Wins remained the key requirement, but what was described by *The Scotsman* as a 'worthy display', defined to involve fair play and good conduct, was also valued: 'Whether they win or lose is a secondary consideration, the important matter is that they should be such as to give a worthy display'.[83] Certainly, fair play, viewed and presented as a distinctive and commendable feature of British sport, had already won widespread praise, most notably as a form of moral training worthy of emulation.[84] Reportedly, in 1931, even Mussolini told a British journalist that 'you have taught people the meaning of those words "fair play" … the entire world recognises in Great Britain the old country of fair play'.[85] A few years later, I.K.C., a Polish newspaper commenting critically on Chelsea's visit, reaffirmed this point in picturesque terms: 'The word gentleman is indissolubly bound up with England and the English. We had the opportunity to see eleven gentlemen, not in top hats, it is true, but in football clothes, which comes to the same thing in England, for the word gentleman was born in playing fields and it can well be replaced in England by the word sportsman.'[86]

Generally speaking, association football was regarded as essentially a working-class sport. Indeed, the British football associations, albeit wishing to avoid 'social cleavage in the matter of football' by offering 'boys of every social type' the opportunity to play the game, rejoiced 'that our game is that of the masses'.[87] In effect, football displaced religion for the working man, who watched and played the game, did the pools, and voted Labour: 'the football grounds of England were the Labour party at prayer'.[88] Even so, as the *Manchester Guardian* argued in the early 1930s, this did not mean that the game lacked cultural merit: 'To the working man football is a serious occupation, an art; his attitudes to his heroes, to the Arsenal, is that of the German to Furtwängler and the Berlin Philharmonic Orchestra. And how much more sincere is the devotion of the English working man than that of the English devotees of higher things.'[89] Nor did repeated references to its working-class character, including its tag as a man's game 'quite unsuitable for females', prevent football from assuming a national character.[90] Negative images, consequent upon a reputation for spectator hooliganism and disorder, were displaced with the help of the media by 'the notion of the football crowd as an embodiment of the stable, disciplined and ordered nature of English (and, indeed, British) society': 'from 1919, football came to be seen not as something antagonistic to the national project, but rather at its very heart'.[91]

Obviously, it took time to shake preconceived official notions dismissing football as a lowbrow activity possessing limited appeal to opinion-formers in other countries, especially as compared to, say, cricket or its rugby variant, but as the inter-war period progressed the game's apparent ability to reach an alternative mass audience came to represent a bonus point as compared to more elitist forms of culture. Propaganda presupposes an audience, and football guaranteed large, captive, and potentially responsive crowds for visiting British teams. For example, England players, 'literally overwhelmed' by the vast crowds in, say, Bucharest or Milan greeting their overseas tours during the late 1930s, attracted the kind of 'hero worship' accorded to film stars.[92] British teams were usually watched by large crowds, as highlighted by the fact that the 65,000 attendance at the France-England international played at Paris in May 1938 was never exceeded for any game, even including the France-Italy quarter final (58,455), in the subsequent World Cup tournament. Certainly, British teams playing abroad attracted larger audiences than either visiting politicians or more elitist cultural activities, for the large crowd at the ground was supplemented by readers of newspaper match previews and reports, listeners to the radio commentary, and cinema-goers watching the newsreel. The visibility acquired overseas by British football, even in countries seeking to keep out British propaganda, was verified in December 1935 when William Dodd, the American ambassador in Berlin, informed the State Department about the recent England-Germany match played in London: 'The game – which Germany lost 3:0 – was given much space in the German press'.[93]

In 1944, Dugdale claimed that football internationals, involving visits by 'similar' types of people, were widely welcomed by the masses in continental Europe: 'we wish to encourage visits by similar classes of people; and if booksy boys go over, why not footballers? This match wd appeal to people who are not affected by more cultural propaganda.'[94] Following Lord Balfour's comments about the cinema, football possessed the useful ability 'to reach the intelligence of the least intelligent'.[95] Moreover, despite its working-class image, international football offered meaningful points of contact at all social levels, given the game's elitist origins and widespread appeal across the social stratum in overseas countries, where leading public figures often occupied prominent positions in foreign national football associations. As Lord Decies, who served on the British Olympic Association (BOA) Council, observed in the early 1930s, association football proved 'a thoroughly democratic game – and yet one that is enjoyed by princes'![96]

Of course, it is unwise to view foreign audiences in British terms, as suggested in October 1936, when Geoffrey Dawson, editor of *The Times*, was apprised by one of his New Jersey contacts of the low American propaganda potential of leading British politicians, like Stanley Baldwin (Prime Minister, 1935–37) or Neville Chamberlain (Chancellor of the Exchequer, 1931–37), 'about whom he [i.e. the average American] knows little'.[97] As Christopher Brasher, an athletics gold medallist at the 1956 Melbourne Olympics, observed, 'in peace the masses turn to the sports pages for their heroism', and for the masses, at least in Europe and Latin America, British footballers meant much more than, say, a visit by a famous British politician, actor or musician.[98] Looking back in 1954, Philip Noel-Baker recalled a conversation conducted during the late 1930s with a Yugoslav friend, Vlada Dedyer:

> In our talk, I asked him if people in Jugoslavia were interested in world affairs. 'It depends what you mean', he answered; 'Ask any schoolboy in Belgrade: "Who is Bastin?", and he will reply at once: "Outside left for the Arsenal, the greatest forward in the world". But ask him: "Who is Winston Churchill?", and he will say: "I am sorry, I do not know that player".'[99]

In this manner, sporting heroes, possessing 'major instrumental power' as symbols for their respective national communities, came to exert significant propaganda impacts across borders.[100]

36

INTERNATIONAL SPORT AS THE 'PEACEMAKER' OR 'WAR MINUS THE SHOOTING'?

According to Alan Tomlinson, 'large scale international sports were trapped, from their beginnings, in a major tension. They represented an attractive cosmopolitanism and a meeting-ground between cultures. But equally they were always a forum for the assertion of particular national strengths.'[101] There was, and remains, strong disagreement regarding the precise nature of links, if any, between international sport, international relations, and the policies of individual states. Inevitably, this long-running controversy, centred on the question of whether international sport serves either to promote or to hinder the construction of a peaceful and stable international political framework, proves omnipresent throughout this study.

Normally, Pierre de Coubertin's ideas, despite displaying contradictory elements, are taken as championing sport's cooperative potential through bringing together nations in friendly competition: 'Let us export our oarsmen, our runners, our fencers into other lands. That is the true Free Trade of the future; and the day it is introduced into Europe the cause of peace will have received a new strong ally.'[102] In many ways, these pacifist and international-ist themes were taken up also by the workers' sports movement, which arranged its own version of the Olympics and was active within and outside Britain.[103] Within Britain, Philip Noel-Baker (1889–1982), whose lifetime work in the cause of disarmament and international organisation was recognised by the 1959 Nobel Peace Prize, proved one of the more articulate advocates of this 'comradeship through sport' view; indeed, Guttmann described him as 'the foremost British symbol of the idealist-athlete'.[104] Noel-Baker, whose opinions about sport's 'broader political importance' gained greater credibility through his status as one-time Olympic athlete (competitor in 1912 and 1920 Olympics; silver medallist in 1920; captain of track team in 1920 and 1924 Olympics; deputy high commissioner at 1928 Olympics; commandant of British team at 1952 Olympics), university professor, and politician, claimed that international sport helped to 'promote not ill will, but friendship, not international friction, but mutual respect and admiration'.[105] Participation in the 1912 Olympics transformed his thinking: 'We went to Stockholm as British athletes. We came home Olympians, disciples of the leader, Coubertin, with a new vision which I never lost.'[106] In particular, 'we saw national differences merged into the greater unity of a common fellowship among sporting men and women of many lands'.[107] Commenting on the 1928 Amsterdam Olympics, he asked: 'Who can doubt that such a movement as this for the promotion of International Sport, under the best possible conditions, is a movement that may do much for the promotion of

37

that good understanding among the nations upon which peace depends?'.[108] For Noel-Baker, who was both a Quaker and a pacifist, 'sport as part of culture, inseparable from democracy, would bring out the best in the individual and enlist cooperative talents harmoniously. Faith in the sportsman as peacemaker was to sustain him until the end of his long life' (Whittaker).[109]

In this vein, British footballers, like those touring Germany or Italy in the late 1930s, were often presented as 'ambassadors in soccer kit' (G. Allison) building bridges between Britain and other countries.[110] For instance, Jimmy Hogan, drawing on his experience of British and continental football, argued that 'I am firmly of the opinion then that international matches with our foreign cousins are a surer way to peace and friendship than anything which our statesmen and politicians have ever tried to accomplish'.[111] Similarly, Sir Stanley Rous (FA Secretary 1934–61), treating international football as a highly specialised form of communication, believed that football gave the world 'a much needed international language. Through FIFA, it maintains links that cut through national frontiers and other barriers.'[112] 'Off-side', like other footballing terms, was familiar, he argued, to people in all corners of the world, whether living in 'London, Rome, Moscow, Washington, Delhi, Peking, or Buenos Aires'.

Against this background, Lord Decies, a former international show jumper and one-time BOA vice-president, even claimed that 'Sport can kill war'.[113] But there was another view, which was partly encouraged by the way in which Hitler's accession to power gave substance to the ideas of Carl Diem, who had told the Wuensdorf Army School in 1931 that 'war is the noblest and most genuine sport, the sport *par excellence*'.[114] For Brian Glanville, who watched many of England's internationals in the 1930s, 'international sport is no pacifier of nations, and the specious efforts of certain governments to use it for propaganda have made it still more of a divider'.[115] In this vein, the 1936 Berlin Olympics provided the context for Winston Churchill's claim that 'sport, when it enters the international field in Olympic Games and other contests between countries, may breed ill-will rather than draw the nations closer together'.[116] Subsequent chapters establish that such thinking proved commonplace in British governmental circles, most notably on the part of those working within the Foreign Office; but perhaps this view was expressed most vividly in 1945 by George Orwell in the light of a recent British tour by a Soviet football team: 'Serious sport has nothing to do with fair play. It is bound up with hatred, jealousy, boastfulness, disregard of all rules and sadistic pleasure in witnessing violence: in other words, it is war minus the shooting.'[117] For Orwell, de Coubertin and Noel-Baker, among others, would seem 'unusually starry-eyed idealists'.[118]

FOOTBALL AS THE 'MARK OF A LEADER'

In 1990 Richard Turner claimed that 'politicians of all shades have shown absolutely no interest in football, unless there are votes to be won in condemning football hooliganism or turning up at the Cup Final for a press photo-call'.[119] Even so, it is one thing for politicians to be either interested or disinterested in football. It is entirely another matter for them to allow such personal interests to influence the formulation and conduct of government policy. However, excepting Margaret Thatcher (Prime Minister, 1979–90), who reportedly 'found it difficult to understand why anyone would want to go to a football match at all', during recent decades British politicians have appeared increasingly willing, even anxious, to associate themselves personally with the game.[120] Indeed, one of Thatcher's predecessors, Harold Wilson (Prime Minister, 1964–70, 1974–76), who supported Huddersfield and presided over England's World Cup victory in 1966, irritated some ministerial colleagues, most notably, Richard Crossman, by identifying an interest in football as 'the mark of a leader'.[121] In retirement, he presented Stanley Matthews as a 'national symbol' projecting fair play and other British values to the wider world.[122]

Similarly, Thatcher's successor, John Major, though wondering 'how a Prime Minister can be expected to find time to be a football fan', made no secret of his sporting interests, most notably, his passion for cricket and personal support for Chelsea football club: 'Even on the busiest of Government engagements, I make sure someone is on hand to pass me the results as soon as they are available'.[123] Football offered a welcome diversion from the burdens of office, even if 'there is a close similarity between football and politics. Abrupt swings of fortune are common in both, although there are, thank goodness, fewer teams to beat in politics.'[124] Tony Blair has also taken pains to establish his footballing credentials, including support for Newcastle United, even if he employed a eulogy of Stanley Matthews to express reservations about certain aspects (e.g. commercialism) of the modern game.[125] Whether or not this trend represents another manifestation of the gentrification of association football *à la* Nick Hornby's best-seller *Fever Pitch* (1992) remains questionable, but, today, football, presented as crossing class, race, and religion in Britain to become a true national game, provides a much-needed sense of passion and community.[126]

By contrast, it is far more difficult to provide a similar listing for politicians active in public life between 1900–39. In part, this situation might reflect the relatively unexplored nature of the sporting interests of individual ministers, politicians and officials, since sport seldom figures, even in passing, in their memoirs and biographies, except perhaps during their school and university days. Nor is the situation helped by the fact that normally the raw materials used by biographers, that is, the private papers of ministers and officials, treat sport as a marginal activity covered, if at all, in only a cursory manner, perhaps because of long-standing impressions regarding the separation of politics and sport in Britain. Significant exceptions, albeit concerned more with sports other than football, are those of Philip Noel-Baker (later Lord Noel-Baker) and Samuel Hoare (later Viscount Templewood). The former's ministerial career did not commence until the early 1940s, but an extensive archival collection establishes Noel-Baker's prominent contribution to exchanges about the place of sport in international relations.[127] Unsurprisingly, Noel-Baker's biographer, though concentrating on the political dimension, devotes more space than usual to sport.[128] Viscount Templewood's private papers prove more limited in terms of their sports coverage, but their historical value is reinforced by his lengthy periods in office (Secretary of State for Air: 1922–24, 1924–29, 1940; Secretary of State for India: 1931–35; Foreign Secretary 1935; First Lord of Admiralty: 1936–37; Home Secretary: 1937–39; Lord Privy Seal 1939–40; ambassador to Spain: 1940–44). Like Noel-Baker, Templewood moved on from being an active sportsman (e.g. Oxford tennis blue, golf, skating, cricket) to work for various sporting bodies and clubs.[129] Thus, his work for, say, the Lawn Tennis (president, 1932–58) and National Skating Associations (president, 1945–57) was paralleled by Noel-Baker's involvement with both the Amateur Athletic Association (AAA) and Achilles Athletic Club.[130]

Fishwick mentions one overt political link, that is, a 1931 general election poster, which depicted a footballer in England colours and carried the following slogan: 'Playing the game for England. You can play for England now by voting for the National Government candidate.'[131] He refers also to the interest shown in the game by Lloyd George, Ramsay MacDonald and Stanley Baldwin – reportedly, in 1929 the latter even gave a talk thereupon – but during the period covered by this book, relatively few ministers, politicians and officials displayed any obvious personal enthusiasm for association football; indeed, at times, there existed a marked reluctance to accept invitations to attend prominent football internationals on behalf of the government.[132] To some extent, this feature might be taken as reaffirming the game's character as a working-class game, particularly as compared to the more elitist images characteristic of, say, cricket, golf or rugby. For example, the cricketing interests of Sir John Simon, who proved influential in the official exchanges concerning the 1935 England-Germany football fixture, were mentioned earlier, but he was also keen on golf, as highlighted during 1936–37 when he was elected captain of St Andrews Royal and Ancient Golf Club.[133] In March 1935 he commented on the death of a former minister, Sir Arthur Steel-Maitland, who apparently dropped dead on the eighth tee at Rye after hitting a shot close to the pin: 'A good end'![134] Another enthusiast was Vansittart's successor, Alexander Cadogan, whose disclaimers – 'I played in my time a great deal of indifferent golf' – obscured the fact that his handicap went as low as eight at one stage.[135]

Nor, unlike today, did association football appear to inspire a ready supply of suitable phrases, metaphors and clichés for ministers and officials, who relied heavily on other games, most notably, cricket. Paradoxically, one reported exception was Clement Attlee (post-1935 leader of the Labour Party), whose passion for cricket failed to prevent an occasional footballing metaphor, such as one describing himself as the government's 'centre half'.[136] Clearly, the cult of sport inculcated by public schools – Robert Graves' memoirs highlighted its primacy, even over academic work, at Charterhouse – made games, and particularly cricket, a natural metaphor for people prominent in public life, even for those, like Neville Chamberlain, relatively indifferent to what went on at either Highbury, Lords or Wimbledon.[137] In a very real sense, the language of cricket (e.g. 'straight bat', 'to play cricket') became an extended metaphor for acceptable codes of behaviour and values, while serving also as a useful descriptor; for instance, in November 1936, the British ambassador in China, lapsed into cricketing jargon when describing China's attitude towards Britain: 'we are on a very good wicket, watered and rolled for us by our Japanese friends'.[138] For Lord Halifax (Lord President of the Council, 1937–38; Foreign Secretary, 1938–40), hunting yielded a ready stream of phrases, as confirmed by Richard Butler: 'the best insight into Halifax's character is that he is an M.F.H. [Master of Fox Hounds]. Many of his metaphors come from the chase. He advises one not to jump into a field until one can see a way of jumping out.'[139] Even so, Lord Halifax's blow-by-blow account of the events culminating in Anthony Eden's resignation from the Foreign Office in February 1938 hinted at his interest in boxing.[140] Clearly, football's day had yet to come as a major source of metaphorical inspiration for British political life.

CONCLUSION: A FRAMEWORK FOR RESEARCH

Kenneth Clarke, who occupied ministerial office under both Thatcher and Major, has implied continued acceptance of the separate worlds of football and politics: 'When I go to a football match, I like to lose myself in it. I forget about politics and everything else besides.'[141] In many respects, these sentiments harmonised with Richard Holt's summary of British history: 'Sport in Britain, central as it has been to elite and to mass male culture, has not historically been a matter for governments. The very essence of British sport, so long associated with the idea of amateurism, embodied the principle of voluntarism and minimal state interference.'[142]

This study seeks to illuminate the international politics of British football between 1900 and 1939, with special reference to the extent to which footballing realities conformed to public images regarding the alleged uniqueness of the British situation based on the autonomy of sport. Naturally, at this stage, it is easier to pose questions than to furnish clear-cut answers, particularly respecting a topic frequently surrounded by myth and rhetoric rather than critical informed analysis.[143] Indeed, during this period, British governments, the media and football associations went out of their way to deny any meaningful politico-sporting linkages. Nor is the situation helped by potential tensions between any fixture's overt and covert purposes. For example, how far did a football international's alleged objectives to make foreign contacts and create goodwill obscure the underlying aim to demonstrate national superiority and values through victory, especially at a time when it seemed natural for Britons to accept not only that 'our great game has been made, controlled and advanced by Britishers' (FAW) but also their status as masters of the game.[144] Similarly, given Murray's assertion that the idea of fair play has won more respect for Britain than all the gun boats, was this much vaunted sense of fair play little more than British self-interest in terms of reflecting a belief in the assumed superiority of liberal democratic values?[145] There are, of course, several other questions.

The focus will be placed upon Britain, even if, unlike other countries, the United Kingdom fielded four national football sides (i.e. England, Northern Ireland, Scotland and Wales), which have been depicted increasingly as not only strong popular expressions of national feeling but also for three of the home countries symbols of resistance to English political, economic, and cultural hegemony.[146] In practice, this challenge to the concept of the unitary state failed to prevent a common foreign tendency to conflate 'England' and 'Britain' in both footballing and political terms.[147] Tallents' *The Projection of England*, listing 'St Andrews' among national institutions, showed that the practice was not confined to foreigners.[148] Similarly, in May 1938, Lyall, the British consul-general in Berlin, commenting on the Germany-England football international, claimed that 'the excellence of *English* football … undoubtedly revived in

Germany *British* sporting prestige'.[149] Of course, this tendency to equate England and Britain overlooked the highly competitive nature of the home international championship, including the fact that England was far from being always the strongest British side (see Table 2.3). Wales had a good spell during the early 1930s, while throughout the inter-war period Scotland, building on pre-1914 achievements, had an impressive record against England (1920–39: Scotland won 11, lost 6, drew 3). Nevertheless, British governmental involvement in international football proved more common in games involving England, especially as the other home associations were far more hesitant in playing non-British teams.

The imperial and Irish dimensions of British sport, having been fully covered in the writings of J.A. Mangan, among others, occupies only a marginal role in this work, especially as association football's imperial impact fell far short of its spread elsewhere.[150] Nor will domestic sport, including its contribution to fitness, health, leisure and recreation, attract much attention, except, say, to examine the manner in which the post-1937 'National Fitness' initiative highlighted the inter-relationship of the domestic and international dimensions. Research, though making limited use of oral testimony, has been based primarily upon public records, the private papers of politicians and officials, the archives of both FIFA and the four British footballing associations, and the press. Unfortunately, British government archives serve sport in an inconsistent manner, for key episodes either suffer from non-preservation of relevant papers or are covered vaguely, even ignored, therein.[151] Nor do the archives of the home football associations fill all gaps in public records. Relevant correspondence has seldom been preserved – significantly, FIFA archives often proved more useful on this aspect – while normally the minutes of meetings held by the various home associations are brief and unrevealing on both the reasons for decisions and any linkages with government departments; thus, 'the wishes expressed in Foreign Office correspondence often entered into FA policy without any direct reference to the source of the idea' (Polley).[152]

Therefore, the key objective is to examine how far during the period 1900–39 association football, viewed in the broader international sporting context, became part of the 'diplomatic repertoire' of British governments, and particularly to test the validity of assertions that, for governments, sport – to quote Colin Tatz – 'is always serious ... it is a medium of and for ideology, prestige, status, nationalism, internationalism, diplomacy and war. It is about and inclusive of politics.'[153] As such, the monograph will give substance to the policy frameworks outlined in the writings of Lincoln Allison, Barrie Houlihan, Martin Polley, and Trevor Taylor, among others.[154] Of course, today, there is nothing original in either exposing the naivety or testing the historical accuracy of official statements regarding governmental non-interference and the continued autonomy of British sport; indeed, 'showing the naivity [*sic*] of such a distinction is fast becoming a sport is its own right'.[155]

NOTES

1. Chris Smith, 19 Sept. 1997, Department of Culture, Media and Sport Press Release DCM 50/97 (http://www.culture.gov.uk).
2. Laurence Martin and John Garnett, *British Foreign Policy: challenges and choices for the 21st century* (RIIA/Pinter, London, 1997), pp.46–7.
3. House of Commons Foreign Affairs Committee, 4th report, 1986–87, *Cultural Diplomacy: observations by the government*, quoted Martin and Garnett, p.46.
4. Library, Trinity College, Cambridge University (hereafter TC), Lord Butler of Saffron Walden Papers (RAB), speech by Richard Butler, 23 May 1938, RAB K4/8; Sir Arthur Willert, 'National Advertisement', *The Fortnightly* (January 1939), 7.
5. PRO, 'Some notes on the "Cultural Relations" of Great Britain in the Mediterranean', C.G. Hardie, 3 June 1936, to British Council, BW34/8.
6. PRO, 'British cultural propaganda in the Mediterranean area', Kenneth Johnstone, 10 Oct. 1936, BW2/85.
7. Figures quoted for 1936 were France, 82.25m. francs; Italy, 69.2m. lire. No amount was given for Germany.
8. Philip Taylor, *The Projection of Britain: British overseas publicity and propaganda* (Cambridge University Press, Cambridge, 1981), pp.52–3; Mariel Grant, *Propaganda and the Role of the State in Inter-War Britain* (Clarendon, Oxford, 1994), pp.4–5, pp.32–47.
9. Andrew Steed, 'British propaganda and the First World War', in I. Stewart and S.L. Carruthers (eds), *War, Culture and the Media: representations of the military in 20th Century Britain* (Flicks Books, Trowbridge, 1996), p.36.
10. PRO, memorandum, Arthur Yencken, 17 Sept. 1927, FO395/423/P995; Sterling Memorial Library, Yale University, New Haven (hereafter Yale), Sir Arthur Willert Papers (MG720), memorandum, Willert, 30 July 1925, MG720/3/88.
11. PRO, minute, Sir Malcolm Robertson, Chairman, British Council (1941–45), 22 July 1941, BW2/85.
12. PRO, minute, G. Villiers, 1 June 1922, FO371/8360/W4530.
13. Willert, 1–2.
14. PRO, memorandum, 'Cultural Propaganda', R. Leeper, 18 June 1934, FO395/505/P1887.
15. Taylor, *Projection of Britain*, p.84; PRO, memorandum, Johnstone, 10 Oct. 1936, BW2/85; Yale, minute, Willert, 2 Jan. 1934, MG 720/14/56.
16. PRO, Johnstone, 10 Oct. 1936, BW2/85.
17. PRO, memorandum, Yencken, 17 Sept. 1927, FO395/423/P995.
18. Taylor, *Projection of Britain*, p.292.
19. Willert, 3–4.
20. Sir Stephen Tallents, *The Projection of England* (Faber, London, 1932). See also, PRO, 'The Projection of Britain', 1946, encl. FO953/1216/P1011.
21. Donald C. Watt, 'The European Civil War', in W.J Mommsen and L. Kettenacker (eds), *The Fascist Challenge and the Policy of Appeasement* (George Allen & Unwin, London, 1983), pp.3–18.
22. PRO, Sir J. Simon to HM representatives overseas, 6 July 1934, FO395/505/P1887.
23. PRO, minute, R. Vansittart, Permanent Under-Secretary of State, 19 June 1934,

FO395/505/P1887.
24. PRO, 'Cultural Propaganda', R. Leeper, 18 June 1934, FO395/505/P1887.
25. H.P. Croom Johnson, to C. Bridge, 15 Nov. 1937, quoted Taylor, *Projection of Britain*, p.161.
26. PRO, Leeper, 18 June 1934, FO395/505/P1887.
27. PRO, Lloyd to Eden, 22 Dec. 1937, T1/907/S35581/1; Willert, 2.
28. Lord E. Percy to Eden, 8 June 1937, quoted Frances Donaldson, *The British Council: the first fifty years* (Jonathan Cape, London, 1984), p.56.
29. W. Guinness, 1 June 1920, quoted Taylor, *Projection of Britain*, p.88; Churchill Archives Centre, Cambridge University (hereafter CAC), Lord Lloyd Papers (GLLD), Lloyd to Sir Thomas Inskip, 19 Dec. 1938, GLLD 19/7; CAC, Churchill Papers, R. Boothby to W. Churchill, 9 Sept. 1938, Chartwell, 2/331, folio 50.
30. PRO, Eden to Simon, 23 Dec. 1937, T161/907/S35581/1; minute, Rowland Kenney, 19 Feb. 1931, FO395/448/P334.
31. Neville Chamberlain to Lloyd, 17 Nov. 1937, quoted Taylor, *Projection of Britain*, p.168; PRO, minute, Chamberlain, 29 May 1938, PREM1/272, f.26, Leeper, 18 June 1934, FO395/505/P1887; Michael Stenton, 'British propaganda and raison d'état, 1935–1940', *European Studies Review*, 10 (1980), 47–53; Willert, 1–2, 5–6.
32. PRO, S. Hoare to Kennard, 8 Nov. 1935, FO395/529/P3900; Lloyd to Eden, 22 Dec. 1937, T161/907/S35581/03/38/1.
33. Taylor, *Projection of Britain*, p.87.
34. Ibid., pp.125–6; Philip M. Taylor, *Munitions of the Mind: war propaganda from the ancient world to the nuclear age* (Patrick Stephens, Wellingborough, 1990), pp.180–7.
35. CAC, Lord Noel-Baker Papers (NBKR), P. Noel-Baker to D. Lowe, 19 Aug. 1928, NBKR 6/14; David J. Whittaker, *Fighter for Peace: Philip Noel-Baker 1889–1982* (William Sessions, York, 1989), p.30.
36. Tallents, pp.14–15, p.40.
37. See *Evening Standard*, 29 Nov. 1935.
38. FA, Spanish Football Association to FA, 23 Dec. 1930, encl. ISC, 12 Jan. 1931, minute 9, 1930–31.
39. Geoffrey Green, *The History of the Football Association* (Naldrett Press, London, 1953), pp.196–202. During 1934, Motherwell, representing the SFA, played three tests during its South African tour: *Alan Breck's Book of Scottish Football* (Scottish Daily Express, Glasgow, 1937), p.33.
40. FIFA, Minutes of 26th FIFA Congress, London, 27–28 July 1948, p.2.
41. Sir Stanley Rous, 'Reflections on the 100th Anniversary of the Football Association', *FIFA Official Bulletin*, 39/40 (Nov. 1963), 464.
42. FA, F.J. Wall to A.S. Hutchinson, Home Office, 10 July 1923, encl. Council, 7 July 1923, minute 16, 1923–24.
43. PRO, Simon, Notes of TUC Deputation, 2 Dec. 1935, encl. TUC to Home Office, 16 Dec. 1935, HO45/16425/688144.
44. 'Football and international politics', *The Times*, 2 Jan. 1929.
45. *The Scotsman*, 1 Jan. 1929; *The Times*, 2 Jan. 1929.
46. Cecil Deal, 'Madrid merryground', *Daily Express*, 2 Dec. 1935; Teresa Gonzalez Aja, 'Spanish sports policy in republican and fascist Spain', in Arnaud and Riordan, pp.101–4.
47. PRO, E. Rennie to Marquess of Curzon, 20 Jan. 1923, FO371/9297/N996.
48. Murray, pp.84–5; Nathan D. Abrams, 'Inhibited but not "crowded out": the strange fate of soccer in the United States', *International Journal of the History of Sport* (hereafter *Int.J.Hist.Sport*), 12 (1995), 1–17.
49. *FIFA Official Bulletin*, 24 (Dec. 1958), 104.
50. *The Times*, 12 June 1982.

51. FIFA, Minutes of 11th Congress of FIFA, Christiania, 27–28 June 1914, p.6.
52. The IFA's isolationist stance was emphasised by the Republic of Ireland's fixture list, including its participation in the 1934 and 1938 World Cups.
53. Rous, *Reflections*, 464.
54. *Daily Express*, 24 May 1938; W. Capel-Kirby and Frederick W. Carter, *The Mighty Kick: romance, history and humour of football* (Jarrolds, London, 1933), p.236.
55. Modern Manuscripts Room, Bodleian Library, Oxford University (hereafter BL), Simon Papers (MS Simon) Sir John Simon, speech, 21 March 1934, encl. MS Simon 120, folios 1–2. See also Siegfried Sassoon, *Memoirs of a Fox-Hunting Man* (Faber & Faber, London, 1960 edn), p.194.
56. *The Bulletin* (FA), 1 (May 1939), 1.
57. Alan Tomlinson, 'Going Global: the FIFA story', in A. Tomlinson and G. Whannel (eds), *Off the Ball: the football world cup* (Pluto Press, London, 1986), pp.83-4; Murray, p.52.
58. James Douglas, 'Games we have taught the world', *Daily Express*, 3 Jan. 1929.
59. PRO, W. Ebor, Archbishop of York to BOA, 14 May 1935, FO371/18864/C4324.
60. George G. Graham, *Scottish Football through the Years* (*Scottish Daily Record and Evening News*, Glasgow, 1947), p.21; Walter Bensemann, 'Tutti Frutti', *World's Football (FIFA)*, 40 (Nov.–Dec. 1933), 194.
61. Graham, p.21.
62. Harold Perkin, 'Epilogue. Teaching the nations how to play: sport and society in the British Empire and Commonwealth', in J.A. Mangan (ed.), *The Cultural Bond: sport, empire, society* (Frank Cass, London, 1992), p.217; Rous, *Football Worlds*, p.62.
63. *The Times*, 2 Jan. 1929.
64. PRO, T.H. Preston, Turin, to Consular Dept., 30 Nov. 1928, FO370/289/L7516.
65. Wall, quoted, *Daily Express*, 1 Jan. 1929; Wall, p.219.
66. Wall, p.223.
67. Dave Russell, *Football and the English: a social history of association football in England, 1863–1995* (Carnegie, Preston, 1997), pp.122–3.
68. Quoted, Richard Holt, *Sport and the British: a modern history* (Clarendon Press, Oxford: 1992 edn), p.205. See J.A. Mangan, 'Prologue. Britain's chief spiritual export: imperial sport as moral metaphor, political symbol and cultural bond', in Mangan, *The Cultural Bond*, p.1.
69. Martin Polley, *Moving the Goalposts: a history of sport and society since 1945* (Routledge, London, 1998), pp.35–6.
70. *The Times*, 2 Jan. 1929.
71. Ivan Sharpe, 'Football on the Continent', *Football World*, 10–11 (Aug.–Sept. 1939), 2.
72. Bastin, p.146.
73. Philip Goodhart and Christopher Chataway, *War without Weapons* (W.H. Allen, London, 1968), p.149.
74. PRO, Sir H. Montgomery, The Hague, to Hoare, 7 Dec. 1935, FO371/19647/W10632.
75. PRO, Sir R. Graham, The Hague, to Lord Curzon, 12 July 1921, FO371/7087/W7671.
76. Ibid.
77. PRO, minute, D. Moss, 11 Sept. 1946, FO371/59326/R12016.
78. PRO, Kenney, News Dept., to Bridge, British Council, 3 Dec. 1937, BW34/8.
79. PRO, O. Jennings, British Council, to Rous, FA, 23 Dec. 1937, BW34/8.
80. PRO, Thomas Snow, Berne, to E. Bevin, 14 Aug. 1946, FO371/60490/Z7470.
81. Peter McIntosh, *Sport in Society* (Watts, London, 1983 edn), p.187.

82. PRO, memorandum, Yencken, 17 Sept. 1927, FO395/423/P995.
83. *The Scotsman*, 1 Jan. 1929.
84. J.A. Mangan, ' "Muscular, militaristic and manly": the British middle-class hero as moral messenger', *Int.J.Hist.Sport*, 13 (1995), 33–6.
85. Sharpe, *Forty Years*, p.68.
86. Encl. Sir Howard Kennard, British ambassador, Warsaw, to R. Leeper, 26 May 1936, FO371/20462/W5343.
87. *FA*, Council, 22 Feb. 1926, minute 9, 1925–26; Football Association of Wales, Cardiff (hereafter FAW), Council, 30 April 1919, minute 28, 1915–22; *Annual Report 1924–1925* (FAW, 1925), p.1.
88. Nicholas Fishwick, *English Football and Society, 1910–1950* (Manchester University Press, Manchester, 1988), p.150; Russell, p.121.
89. *Manchester Guardian*, 14 Jan. 1933. Significantly, one footballer's memoir, published in 1996, exploited this aspect: Alan Hudson with Ian Macleay, *The Working Man's Ballet* (Moon over Miami Productions, Sheffield, 1996).
90. *Annual Report 1924–1925* (FAW, 1925), p.1; FAW, Council, 29 Aug. 1939, minute 4967, 1939-40.
91. Russell, pp.120–1; Fishwick, pp.106–9.
92. Hapgood, p.43; Tommy Lawton (with Roy Peskett), *Football is my Business* (Sporting Handbooks, London, 1946), p.79.
93. National Archives (Archives II), College Park, Maryland, USA, Records of the United States State Department (hereafter USA), W.E. Dodd, Berlin, to State Dept., 5 Dec. 1935, RG59, Box 4248, 741.062/106.
94. PRO, Dugdale, 28 Oct. 1944, FO371/42026/Z7169.
95. See Steed, pp.22–3.
96. Lord Decies, 'Sport can kill war', *World's Football*, 37 (1933), 154 (formerly published, *Sunday Graphic and Sunday News*, 19 March 1933).
97. BL, Geoffrey Dawson Papers (MS Dawson), G.W. Johnson, New Jersey, to G. Dawson, 15 Oct. 1936, MS Dawson 79, folio 7. See Victor Peppard and James Riordan, *Playing Politics: Soviet Sport Diplomacy to 1992* (Jai Press, Greenwood, CT, 1993), p.5.
98. Letter, *The Times*, 12 Jan. 1956.
99. CAC, 'International Sporting Exchanges', 15 Dec. 1954, NBKR 6/12/1.
100. Georg Xandry, DFB, quoted, *Daily Mail*, 3 Dec. 1935; Richard Holt and J.A. Mangan, 'Prologue: heroes of a European past', *Int.J.Hist.Sport*, 13 (1996), 4, 10.
101. Tomlinson, p.83
102. Quoted, E.A. Montague, 'The Olympic Games', *Manchester Guardian*, 11 March 1938.
103. Stephen G, Jones, *Sport, Politics and the Working Class: organised labour and sport in interwar Britain* (Manchester University Press, Manchester, 1988), p.168.
104. Philip Baker, 'The Olympic Games', *The Empire Review* (May 1924), 559–63; P.J. Noel-Baker, 'International sport and international good understanding. Great Britain, Germany and the USA', *British Olympic Journal* (Autumn 1926), 46–7; Allen Guttmann, *The Olympics: a history of the modern games* (University of Illinois Press, Urbana, 1992), p.40. He began to use Noel-Baker in place of Baker during the early 1920s.
105. CAC, Draft letter, Baker, 3 April 1924, NBKR 6/22/1; Philip J. Baker, 'The Olympic Games – a retrospect', *The Independent*, 113 (30 Aug. 1924), 128–30.
106. Lord Noel-Baker, 'Stockholm, 1912' in Lord Killanin and John Rodda (eds), *Olympic Games* (Macdonald and Jane's, London, 1979), pp.62–3; CAC, Noel-Baker to J. Rodda, 14 May 1974, NBKR 6/37/1.
107. CAC, Noel-Baker to A. Bushnell, New York, n.d. (7 Feb. 1951), NBKR 6/13/2.

108. P. Noel-Baker, 'Olympic Games Memories', *Midland Daily Telegraph*, 18 Aug. 1928.
109. Whittaker, p.12.
110. George F. Allison, *Allison Calling: a galaxy of football and other memories* (Staples, London, 1948), p.142.
111. FAW, Jimmy Hogan, *Wales-England Match Programme, Cardiff, 22 October 1938*, 1937–39. See also F.N.S. Creek, *Association Football* (Dent, London, 1937).
112. Stanley Rous, 'Football as an international sport', *FIFA Official Bulletin*, 3 (1953), 2.
113. Decies, 154.
114. PRO, quoted, minute. A. Andrews, Research Dept., 17 Aug. 1950, FO371/85129/C5369.
115. Brian Glanville, *Soccer Nemesis* (Secker & Warburg, London, 1955), p.97.
116. Winston Churchill, 'Sport is a stimulant in our workaday world', *News of the World*, 4 Sept. 1938 (re-published *Sunday Dispatch*, 31 Aug. 1941).
117. George Orwell, 'The Sporting Spirit', *Tribune*, 14 Dec. 1945, in Sonia Orwell and Ian Angus (eds), *The Collected Essays, Journalism and Letters of George Orwell, vol.4: In Front of Your Nose, 1945–1950* (Secker & Warburg, London, 1968), p.42.
118. Derek Birley, *Playing the Game: sport and British society, 1910–45* (Manchester University Press, Manchester, 1995), p.30.
119. Quoted, David Bull, 'Politicians as Football Fans – incredible!', in David Bull and Alastair Campbell (eds), *Football and the Commons People* (Juma, Sheffield, 1994), p.2.
120. Kenneth Clarke, 'Forest first and foremost', in Bull and Campbell, p.68.
121. Bull, *Politicians as Football Fans*, p.7.
122. Lord Wilson, 'Foreword' in David Miller, *Stanley Matthews: the authorised biography* (Pavilion, London, 1989), p.vii. Cf. Blair, 19.
123. John Major, 'A blue on the blues', in David Bull (ed.), *We'll Support you Evermore* (Duckworth, London, 1992), p.212, p.219.
124. Ibid., p.213.
125. Blair, 19.
126. Nick Hornby, *Fever Pitch* (Gollancz, London, 1992); Ed Barrett, 'The rise and rise of the new fan', *Sunday Times*, 23 March 1997; Janie Lawrence, 'Supporters' club', *The Independent*, 29 March 1997.
127. PRO, minute, Jain Aitken, 29 June 1948, FO924/708B/LC2225.
128. Whittaker, pp.12–14, pp.29–30, p.199.
129. CAC, Noel-Baker to Bushnell, n.d. (7 Feb. 1951), NBKR 6/13/2; note by Noel-Baker, 7 Nov. 1959, NBKR 6/10/3.
130. University Library, Cambridge University (hereafter CU), Viscount Templewood Papers, Files X3, XVII-12, Sports 1938–59.
131. Fishwick, p.137.
132. Ibid.
133. BL, Simon's Diaries and Notebooks, 24 Aug. , 30 Sept. 1936, MS Simon 7, folios 54–7; Lord Horne to Simon, 30 Sept. 1937, MS Simon 84, folio 141. For his appointments diaries, see BL, MS Simon 30–31.
134. BL, Simon's Diaries and Notebooks, 30 March 1935, MS Simon 7, folio 25.
135. CAC, Sir Alexander Cadogan Papers (ACAD), draft chapter for autobiography, ACAD 7/1.
136. Fishwick, p.137.
137. Chamberlain, who attended Rugby School, played rugby, but 'disliked cricket and thought games overdone': Keith Feiling, *Neville Chamberlain* (Macmillan, London, 1946), pp.9–11. Robert Graves, *Goodbye to All That* (Penguin Books,

Harmondsworth, 1960 edn), pp.37–41.
138. CAC, Sir Hughe Knatchbull-Hugessen Papers (KNAT), Sir Hughe Knatchbull-Hugessen to Cadogan, 4 Nov. 1936, KNAT 2/39. One of the more blatant examples is in: BL, Sir Francis Wylie, formerly secretary of Rhodes Trustees, to Dawson, 1 Aug. 1941, MS Dawson 82, folio 86. See also Colin Tatz, 'The corruption of sport', in Geoffrey Lawrence and David Rowe (eds), *Power Play: essays in the sociology of Australian sport* (Hale & Iremonger, Sydney 1986), p.61.
139. TC, memorandum, Richard Butler, n.d. (June–Aug. 1939), RAB G10/28; Borthwick Institute of Historical Research, University of York, Papers of the Earls of Halifax (hereafter York), note, Lord Halifax, Dec. 1957, A4 410 7. 15a.
140. York, Lord Halifax, 'A record of events connected with Anthony Eden's resignation, February 19th–20th 1938', A 410. 11. 1, p.5.
141. Clarke, 'Forest first', p.68.
142. Holt, 'Sport and history', 231.
143. Houlihan, *Sport and International Politics*, p.152.
144. *Annual Report 1925–26* (FAW, 1926), p.1.
145. Murray, p.22; Tony Mason, 'Land of Sport and Glory' (review article), *History*, 82 (1997), 353.
146. See Alan Bairner 'Football and the idea of Scotland', in Grant Jarvie and Graham Walker (eds), *Scottish Sport in the Making of the Nation: ninety minute patriots?* (Leicester University Press, London, 1994), pp.9–26; H.F. Moorhouse, 'One state, several countries: soccer and nationality in a "United Kingdom"', *Int.J.Hist.Sport*, 12 (1995), 70–2.
147. Alexander Grant and Keith Stringer, 'Introduction: the enigma of British history', in Alexander Grant and Keith Stringer (eds), *Uniting the Kingdom?: the making of British History* (Routledge, London, 1995), p.3; Bernard Crick, 'The English and the British', in B. Crick (ed.), *National Identities: the constitution of the United Kingdom* (Blackwell, Oxford, 1991), pp.90–104.
148. Martin and Garnett, pp.17–20; Holt, *Sport and the British,*, p.262; Winston Churchill, 'England, My England!', *Answers* (12 Aug. 1933), 3–4 (reprinted *Sunday Dispatch*, 21 April 1940).
149. PRO, Consular Report, n.d. (May 1938), FO395/568/P2054.
150. Murray, pp.75–80.
151. See also Polley, 'Foreign Office and International Sport', p.ix.
152. Ibid., p.xxiv; Christopher Andrew interviewing Rachel Newnham, 'Making History: 3', *BBC Radio Four*, 14 Dec. 1996; Christopher Andrew, 'Secrets of our national game', *The Guardian*, 26 Nov. 1996.
153. Houlihan, *Sport and International Politics*, p.209; Tatz, p.61. For a concise survey of the use of sport by governments, see Barrie Houlihan, *Sport, policy and politics: a comparative analysis* (Routledge, London, 1997), pp.61-5.
154. See: Lincoln Allison, 'Sport and politics', pp.1–26 and Trevor Taylor, 'Sport and international relations: a case of mutual neglect', pp.27–48, in Lincoln Allison (ed.), *The Politics of Sport* (Manchester University Press, Manchester, 1986); Trevor Taylor, 'Sport and world politics: functionalism and the state system', *International Journal*, XLIII (1988), 531–53; Lincoln Allison (ed.), *The Changing Politics of Sport* (Manchester University Press, Manchester, 1993); Houlihan, *Sport and International Politics*; Houlihan, *Sport, Policy and Politics*; B. Lowe, D.B. Kanin and A. Strenk (eds), *Sport and International Relations* (Stipes, Champaign, IL, 1978); Polley, *Moving the Goalposts*; Arnaud, *Sport – a means of national representation*, pp.3–13.
155. Barrie Houlihan, *The Government and Politics of Sport* (Routledge, London, 1991), p.5; Green, pp.503–4.

3

Conquering the World through Football:
1900–18

AN 'ONRUSHING FORCE' IN BRITAIN AND BEYOND

The IFA's *Annual Report 1903–04* reminded readers about the rapid advance, even primacy, of the sport for which it was responsible: 'The game has increased in popularity, going steadily onwards, gathering new adherents every day, and conquering new districts, until it would appear there is nothing that can stem the onrushing force of Association Football as the popular game in town and country'.[1] An even faster period of growth occurred during the next decade, as demonstrated most vividly by 'the enormous increase in the popularity of the game' (SFA) in Scotland.[2] In April 1906, the Scotland-England match, played at Hampden Park (Glasgow), attracted the first-ever 100,000-plus attendance, but by 1914 even this figure was exceeded by a crowd of 127,000 yielding gate receipts approaching £7,000. Reasons for growth, whether measured by the number of players or spectators, go beyond the scope of this study, but the need for 'a new urban identity' and sense of 'belonging', identified by Mason and Holt as key factors explaining support for local clubs, are relevant in terms of raising questions about the link between Britons and their respective national teams.[3] For example, was British football 'too self-absorbed' in club loyalties and league rivalries to give itself wholeheartedly to the national cause, especially as compared to cricket?[4] If 'professional football helped flesh out a distinctive sense of place within the wider framework of national competition', did international football perform the same role in the broader international context, given the competitive, insecure conditions characterising the pre-1914 period?[5] How far did the rapid growth of the media promote football's image as the national game?

Similar expansion occurred across the Channel, where FIFA reported (1908–9) that the game was 'flourishing', and becoming 'more popular … all over Europe'.[6] At the 1909 FIFA Congress, held at Budapest, Daniel Woolfall, the first British president of FIFA (1906–18), summarised the game's history: 'Formerly football was considered the national game of

50

some countries, now this sport had become the game of the world'.[7] Football's post-1900 'phenomenal' (Carl Hirschman, FIFA's Secretary-Treasurer: 1906–32) rate of growth, warranting its tag as the 'world's game', ensured that FIFA's initial European orientation was qualified increasingly prior to 1914 by the advent of Latin American (e.g. Argentina, Chile) and other non-European (e.g. South Africa, USA) members.[8] Nor did the pace of expansion diminish in succeeding decades, and by 1950 FIFA presented itself as both the 'largest sporting organisation in the world' and 'the UNO (United Nations Organisation) of the footballers' (see Figure 3.1, Table 3.1).[9]

FIGURE 3.1
BRITISH FOOTBALL AND FIFA MEMBERSHIP

TABLE 3.1
FIFA MEMBERSHIP

1904	1910	1914	1920	1927	1931	1938	1950
6*	18	24	20	37	42	51	73

* Several accounts give 7, the number of associations represented at the inaugural meeting.

Source: FIFA Handbook, 9th edn (FIFA, Zurich, 1950), p.5.

51

Despite the enduring strength of the amateur ethic, one distinctive feature of the British scene concerned the fact that – to quote the FAW – 'professionalism is on the increase'.[10] By 1914, the FA claimed *circa* 7,000 professionals, even if only some 2,500 players were engaged exclusively in football.[11] Numbers proved much lower in the other home countries, but the general trend was upwards; for example, in Scotland, the total peaked at 1,754 players, employed by 90 clubs, during the 1913–14 season.[12] In Wales, where rugby emerged as the major sport, numbers rose from 160 to 431 professionals during the period 1900–14.[13] From this perspective, the SFA observed that 'A sport in the past, Association Football must in the future be reckoned with as a business pastime'.[14] Certainly, professional players were often suspected of treating football as a job of work rather than a game, so that those paid for playing for their country were adjudged, unfairly, as less likely to be moved by the national interest as compared to the power of the purse.[15] Indeed, football's apparent lapse from amateurism – in reality, even the FA's registered professionals proved a small proportion of the claimed one million plus players – led certain schools to switch to its allegedly purer rugby union variant, while encouraging official British perceptions of the game to adopt a negative tone. In many respects, this problem came to a head during the early months of the First World War when British football was accused of placing commercial considerations above the national interest. There were also early rumblings of what was to become a serious problem during succeeding decades, that is, the reluctant release, even non-release, of players selected for internationals, particularly for Ireland and Wales, such as on account of the narrow domestic vision of clubs, the premium placed on league and cup success, and the rival pretensions of football associations and leagues.[16]

During and after the 1880s, the formal recognition of professionalism, in conjunction with their assumption of responsibility through the IFAB for the laws of the game, established the way in which the four British associations led the world of association football. They were also to the fore in the development of international football, which came to represent a lucrative source of revenue.[17] The first-ever England-Scotland international, played in 1872, provided the basis for the home international championship (1884–1984), which, for Britons, represented the pinnacle of world football. Internationals versus non-British sides developed later for England, much later for the other three associations; indeed, one major work published on the British game in 1906 defined 'international football' as comprising only the home internationals to the exclusion of matches against non-British countries.[18] England's first full international against a non-British side is formally recorded as occurring in June 1908, but several

52

amateur internationals had been played already during the 1900s (see Table 3.2). Foreign visitors included a German representative team (1901), Holland (1907) and France (1908), while England teams travelled to Paris (1906), The Hague (April 1907), Berlin and Brussels (April 1908).[19]

TABLE 3.2
ENGLAND'S AMATEUR INTERNATIONALS BEFORE 1914

1901	Germany*
1906	France (Paris)
1907	Holland (The Hague and Darlington)
1908	France (Ipswich), Belgium (Brussels), Germany (Berlin), Sweden (Gothenburg, London Olympics), Holland (London Olympics), Denmark (London Olympics)
1909	Germany (Oxford), Holland (Amsterdam and London), Belgium (London), Switzerland (Basle), France (Gentily), Sweden (Hull)
1910	Belgium (Brussels), Switzerland (London), France (Paris), Denmark (Copenhagen), plus South African tour (May-August)
1911	Belgium (Brussels), France (Paris), Germany (Berlin), Holland (Amsterdam), Switzerland (Berne), Denmark (London)
1912	Holland (Hull), Belgium (Brussels, Swindon), Hungary (Stockholm Olympics), Finland (Stockholm Olympics), Denmark (Stockholm Olympics)
1913	France (Paris), Germany (Berlin), Holland (The Hague, Hull)
1914	Belgium (Brussels), Denmark (Copenhagen), Sweden (Stockholm)

* Not a recognised international.

In 1899, a FA representative team played matches in Berlin, Karlsruhe and Prague as part of a tour arranged by Frederick Wall, the FA Secretary, and Walter Bensemann.[20] Reportedly, the FA, viewing players as 'missionaries of sport', accepted its duty as the longest-established football association to perform an evangelical role, regardless of the possibility of pecuniary loss.[21] Despite pressure to cancel the tour because of Germany's position regarding the escalating South African crisis, this 'missionary enterprise' went ahead as planned. Pleasure at the outcome – the FA team, scoring 39 goals and conceding only two goals, returned undefeated from the four-match tour – led the FA to present commemorative badges to players.[22] Subsequently, several participants performed a prominent role in international footballing affairs. For example, C. Wreford Brown returned to Germany in May 1938 as the member-in-charge of the England team, while Dr Ivo Schricker, who also played in London in 1901, became active in the affairs of both the DFB and FIFA. Some three decades later, shortly before travelling to London to watch England play Germany, Schricker, then Secretary of FIFA (1932–51), informed Rous, Wall's replacement, that he was looking forward to returning to the Tottenham ground where he had played an English amateur XI in September 1901: 'This was the first official match of a FA team against Germany in England' (see Table 3.3).[23]

TABLE 3.3
ENGLAND VERSUS GERMANY, 1900–54

1901	England Amateurs	12	Germany	0*	(London)
	England Professionals	10	Germany	0*	(Manchester)
1908	Germany	1	England	5**	(Berlin)
1909	England	9	Germany	0**	(Oxford)
1911	Germany	2	England	2**	(Berlin)
1913	Germany	0	England	3**	(Berlin)
1930	Germany	3	England	3	(Berlin)
1935	England	3	Germany	0	(London)
1938	Germany	3	England	6	(Berlin)
1954	England	3	West Germany	1	(London)

*   Not generally listed as internationals.
**   Classified as amateur, not full, internationals.

England's first-ever full internationals versus foreign teams were played against Austria at Vienna on 6 and 8 June 1908 (see Table 2.3, Chapter 2), that is, during the 1908 FIFA Congress. Further tour matches, attracting crowds of 6,500 and 12,000, were played versus Hungary and Bohemia respectively. During 1907–8, correspondence exchanged about England's foreign fixtures in 1908 focused in part upon the level of these games. Whereas amateur matches were arranged against Belgium and Germany for April 1908, Austria, Bohemia and Hungary requested a representative team composed of England's best players, whether professional or amateur.[24] For its part, the FA secured guarantees about coverage of expenses, no Sunday games, and fixtures arranged against only national, not club, teams.[25] Four decisive wins, plus a goal tally of 28 goals for and 2 against (see Table 2.3, Chapter 2), appeared to validate the assumed primacy of British football, even if mitigating circumstances might be advanced for Austria, which played three internationals on successive days.[26] One year later, England visited Budapest and Vienna yet again (Table 2.3, Chapter 2), but the margin of victory proved slightly smaller. A modest profit of *circa* £250 – this arose from attendances of 10,000, 13,000 and 3,000 – offered an early indication of the fiscal potential of close season overseas tours.[27]

Excepting these two tours, prior to 1914, England's full internationals were confined to the home international championship, even if the period saw a growing number of amateur internationals, including those played as part of the 1908 and 1912 Olympics. Generally speaking, England's record, marked by two successive Olympic triumphs, reaffirmed impressions regarding the high standing of British football. The 1908 Olympics, held at London, attracted only five foreign teams (including France A and France B), but gave FIFA an opportunity to reaffirm the game's right to a place in the Olympics as well as to give partial substance to its hopes of organising an international tournament.[28] In 1907, the FA, displaying a more outgoing attitude than that for which it is often credited, accepted the BOA's invitation to take charge of a British football team at the Olympics, and even decided to present a challenge trophy for the gold medallists. In the event, the reluctance of the other home associations to become involved for a range of fiscal and other reasons meant that Britain was represented by an 'England' side organised and funded by the FA. On 24 October 1908, England, playing Denmark, won the Olympic final 2-0 as well as the FA's trophy![29]

Nor did England avoid the occasional reverse, most notably, in 1910, when a draw against Belgium was followed by its first ever defeat (1-2) by a foreign team, that is, Denmark. Nevertheless, in 1912 a second successive Olympic title in a competition entered by 11 European countries helped to maintain the impression of British footballing leadership, especially as a 4-2 win in the final brought both the Olympic title and revenge against Denmark.[30] Subsequently, England remained undefeated until June 1914, when Denmark gained yet another famous victory. Despite a preparedness to travel to Amsterdam, Berlin, Budapest, Copenhagen, Prague and Vienna, among other continental European cities, the FA, citing transport, player availability and other problems, was reluctant to visit the more distant countries, like Australia. A FA representative team tour to South Africa (May–August 1910) proved the exception.[31] In practice, club sides, offering another dimension to British international football, proved more adventurous in terms of not only regularly crossing the Channel but also going further afield, such as to Poland, Portugal, Russia, Canada, the USA and Latin America.[32] As a result, in December 1903, the FA, faced by the rapid growth in club requests to tour overseas, decided to formalise procedures in terms of specifying prior approval and the arrangement of fixtures against only properly organised clubs linked to recognised national footballing associations.[33]

By contrast, the fixture lists of the other three home countries were characterised by the complete absence of fixtures against foreign national sides, even following affiliation to FIFA. In this vein, the SFA's refusal to accept invitations to play in, say, Brussels (1905) or Prague (1913) typified a relatively isolationist course extending into the late 1920s.[34] By contrast, it adopted a more supportive approach towards club tours overseas, most notably during 1913 and 1914, when Celtic, Edinburgh Civil Service, Hearts, Queen of the South, Rangers and Third Lanark received approval to play in a range of countries (e.g. Denmark, Finland, Russia and Portugal), provided the teams were members of the appropriate national FIFA-affiliated association.[35]

The four British football associations, controlling the game within their respective countries, operated independently of each other, but came together to organise the home international championship and, acting through the IFAB, provide the laws of the game.[36] Initially, little interest was taken in broader organisational developments affecting the game. Exhibiting what has been described as 'indifference, bordering on contempt', they proved significant absentees from the meeting, held in the Rue Saint Honoré, Paris, on 21 May 1904, when delegates from Belgium, Denmark, France, Netherlands, Spain, Sweden and Switzerland met to establish FIFA, and elected Robert Guérin (France) as its first president.[37] The British associations proved reluctant to recognise the need for such a body, as demonstrated by the FA's delays in responding to a Dutch proposal, dated 8 May 1902, for the creation of an international association designed to promote the sport, organise an international championship, and unify the laws of the game.[38] The proposal originated from Carl Hirschman, whose role in arranging foreign fixtures made him realise the value of some over-arching international organisation.[39] For him, the support of the game's senior national association seemed an essential prerequisite for progress. But the FA, delaying its reply, pushed Hirschman's patience to the limits, while allowing his proposal to be overtaken by a French initiative for the convention of what became FIFA's founding assembly. Despite rationalising its tardiness in terms of the need to consult the other home associations, the FA was clearly unenthusiastic about an international body adjudged liable to qualify the power and influence of the British associations, particularly concerning the laws of the game.[40] Overlooking the manner in which British primacy in other spheres of life (e.g. industrialisation) had been challenged, even overhauled, in recent decades, the FA, like the other home associations, found it difficult to accept anything other than Britain's traditional leadership role.

In the event, FIFA's existence, in conjunction with a desire to 'give all Continental associations the full benefits of their many years' experience' as well as to safeguard British control over the laws of the game, soon prompted a change of position. In any case, contrary to accusations of 'contempt', 'indifference' and 'monumental ... insularity', the FA, when excusing itself from the inaugural congress, agreed to discuss future modes of cooperation with FIFA representatives the following year.[41] In April 1905, this meeting, held at Crystal Palace (London) on the eve of the England-Scotland game, cleared the way for FA membership, while providing the basis for further informal exchanges (e.g. on definitions of amateurism) during the Brussels Congress of Sport and Physical Education (June 1905).[42] Upon his return from Brussels, Wall reported both the strong desire of continental associations for British participation and the unfavourable impressions conveyed about the British game by recent club visitors to the continent. In fact, his advocacy of the need for action, including the despatch of teams 'under our control', provided one stimulus for the subsequent development of England's international programme.[43]

Whereas the FA was soon admitted to FIFA (1906), the applications of the other home associations became embroiled in an ongoing controversy about eligibility consequent upon FIFA's one member one country rule (Figure 3.1, Table 3.1).[44] This problem – was Britain entitled to one or four members? – had been raised already at the FIFA congress in 1906, when Austria objected to the affiliation of Bohemia, a province within the Austro-Hungarian Empire.[45] FIFA, returning to the application in 1908, refused Bohemia membership.[46] Inevitably, applications received from the IFA and SFA by the 1908 FIFA Congress were interpreted within this context, as evidenced by the objections voiced by the Austrian, French, German and other delegates; for example, the German delegate, fearing an unwelcome precedent, pointed to the possibility of 26 German state applicants. The FA, reiterating that the IFA and SFA were 'entirely independent' and 'not under its jurisdiction', failed to sway enough doubters, and the resulting 7-6 affirmative vote fell short of the requisite two-thirds majority. The matter was raised briefly at the 1909 FIFA Congress, when Sweden reaffirmed the advantages of having such 'important bodies' within FIFA.[47] But, the problem was only resolved in 1910, when Congress, acting on a Dutch-Swedish compromise proposal, adopted a resolution unanimously supporting the admission of the IFA, SFA and FAW (Table 3.1), while simultaneously declaring that membership was restricted to associations recognised as controlling football in their respective countries, with 'only one Association' being recognised in any country.[48]

Naturally, the delay caused some irritation on the part of the British associations, even if the membership question did in some way work to their advantage, particularly in 1908 when FIFA, acknowledging the FA's control over both amateur and professional football in England, refused membership to the rival English Amateur Football Association.[49] Conversely, the federation's rules meant that the FA, having sought to help the game overseas by allowing affiliation by a range of overseas associations (e.g. Argentina, Chile, New Zealand, North America, NSW and West Australia), was forced to discontinue formal organisational links as each country assumed membership of FIFA (e.g. Argentina 1912).[50]

Daniel Woolfall, whether speaking as its second president (1906–18) or national delegate, frequently acknowledged FIFA's 'great benefit' to the game and the fact that it more than 'justified its existence', at least as judged by the FA's limited view of its role.[51] For the British associations, FIFA provided a convenient and useful organising framework fostering regular contacts between national associations for the discussion of common problems, the arrangement of next season's international fixtures, and the encouragement of a uniform approach to the laws of the game, among other matters. There was also the key point made by the FA's representatives, who used their report on the 1906 FIFA Congress 'to impress upon the Council the importance of Continental football, and the necessity for the Football Association to be thoroughly conversant with the organizations operating in other European countries'.[52] But membership, despite being generally adjudged advantageous and cheap (annual subscription of two guineas, i.e. £2.10), was perceived to restrict its freedom of action. The FA, pointing to its lengthy history, assumed that it knew best: 'members must have the greatest liberty in making regulations in their own countries'.[53] Other British associations echoed this line; indeed, one of the strongest statements emanated from H. McLauchlan, who informed the 1913 FIFA Congress that the SFA would 'never submit the control of the game to the Federation'.[54] By contrast, the DFB, seemingly reflecting the authoritarian character of German politics, proved the most vocal advocate of an alternative approach viewing FIFA as 'the supreme power in all matters concerning international football', that is, the 'unrestrained governing body in International Football'.[55]

In the short term, the major clash concerned control over the laws of the game, which had been drafted by the British-controlled IFAB since the 1880s. Several members, led by Germany, advocated FIFA control as a function of their all-embracing vision of the federation, whereas the British associations, claiming that any change would be contrary to the best interests of the game, proved reluctant to allow any outsider, even FIFA, a voice in the question. Baseball (USA), cricket (MCC) and golf (St Andrews) were cited by the FA as part of its advocacy of the *status quo*: 'it was universally recognised that the home of a game had the right to make the laws for such game'.[56] Unsurprisingly, in 1912, the IFAB stated that the 'time was not ripe' for any change, but the FA, appreciating the risks of intransigence, adopted a more realistic position.[57] As a result, in April 1913, the IFAB, guided by lengthy debates at two recent special meetings held at Wrexham (22 February 1913) and London (4 April), decided to admit what one IFA representative described as 'those Continental people' to the IFAB.[58] But, this timely concession, though heading off an immediate clash with continental associations as well as the threat of FIFA's emergence as a rival law-making authority, proved relatively minimal in the sense that the British associations retained control over the laws of the game. FIFA was allowed representation on the IFAB, but the British associations, accounting for four-fifths of the votes, ensured their continued primacy through the stipulation that alterations required a four-fifths' majority! One early consequence of FIFA's admission came in June 1914, when the IFAB met abroad (i.e. in Paris) for the first time ever.[59]

Against this background, R. Hefner, addressing the 1913 FIFA Congress on behalf of the DFB, complained that some members seemed more equal than others: 'Every time that efforts were made to build up the Federation, the continental Associations were placed by England before a wall, stopping every progress'.[60] H. Walker (FA) vigorously denied the accusation: 'There was no country with a keener desire in that respect, no country had spent more money and ability to promote the interests of the game. This was not an opinion but is shewn by facts in the past.' In some respects, this clash offered another dimension to pre-1914 Anglo-German relations, even if the controversy might be interpreted in part as merely the growing pains of a new organisation in which the British and German footballing associations, operating in contrasting domestic political environments, occupied influential positions.

One project on which FIFA achieved little progress concerned the proposal for *'une coupe internationale'*. Despite opting for Switzerland as the host country for 1906, setting out its format (i.e. four groups with winners proceeding to semi-finals), and dividing teams into four groups (the 'British Isles' were listed as the first group), the 1907 Berne Congress effectively shelved the scheme.[61] Here, Woolfall, marking the FA's first congress appearance, sounded a somewhat sceptical note, when suggesting that an international tournament seemed premature because of the recent foundation of many national associations, the absence of FIFA-affiliated bodies in several countries, and the lack of uniformity in the laws of the game.[62] For him, a more stable organisational foundation was required to allow the proposal's successful implementation. Hefner (DFB) agreed, albeit for reasons linked largely to logistical problems arising from the competing demands of national championships. In the event, the project made no further progress prior to 1914, except in the sense that the Olympic Games, run by the International Olympic Committee (IOC), came to be interpreted by members as offering a framework within which not only to organise a world championship for amateur teams but also for FIFA – to quote the FA – 'to show its powers there'.[63]

The early months of 1914 saw the finalisation of arrangements for a close season tour of Austria-Hungary during May and June 1914 by England's full national side – these fixtures were suggested initially at the 1913 FIFA Congress – as well as the confirmation of amateur internationals for the 1914–15 season.[64] However, England's tour, replicating those made in 1908 and 1909, never took place. At first sight, it seems tempting to ascribe cancellation to the deteriorating international situation, especially as Austria performed a central role in events culminating in the outbreak of war in July 1914. By contrast, England's amateur internationals played in June against Denmark and Sweden at Copenhagen and Stockholm respectively went ahead in June as planned, while bringing about yet another defeat (0-3) by Denmark. FA minutes fail to provide a conclusive answer, but suggest that, despite escalating international tensions, the FA was prepared even at a late stage (i.e. 24 April) to go ahead with the Austro-Hungarian tour, as evidenced by the selection of both the official-in-charge and 17 players.[65] However, question marks were still being raised about logistics, for the FA, having accepted a three-match tour (27 May: Vienna; 30 May: 'Hungarian provincial town'; 1 June: Budapest), rejected proposals for an additional match, even to the extent of stating that, in such circumstances, it would feel 'unable to send a team this year'.[66] This interpretation, favouring a non-political explanation, is further supported by the fact that as late as 28 June (i.e. date of the Sarajevo assassination) the FA confirmed an amateur international against Germany in Berlin on 2 April 1915.[67]

THE ROLE OF THE BRITISH GOVERNMENT

Nor is there any evidence of government intervention in the FA's decision to cancel its 1914 close season tour. Naturally, the FA, like any other non-governmental sporting body, found it difficult to operate in the wider world outside of the government's foreign policy framework, even if the Foreign Office, confronted by a novel development, lacked clear and coherent guidelines, let alone any policy, concerning the growth of international sport. As a result, the topic, dealt with invariably at the official rather than the ministerial level, was treated in a pragmatic and reserved fashion, with intervention occurring upon only an infrequent *ad hoc* basis. By contrast, a seemingly more visible approach towards sport was adopted by certain members of the royal family through patronage (e.g. the FA) and attendance at major events, like the 1914 FA Cup Final or the 1908 London Olympics.[68] Of course, royal involvement, albeit often reflecting genuine personal enthusiasm, represented another element in the monarchy's efforts to adapt to a more democratic world by gaining credit from the 'governed'.[69]

Members of the Foreign Office, though often possessing personal sporting interests cultivated at school and university, exhibited a general reluctance to take sport seriously in the policy sense, as evidenced by the *laissez-faire* attitude adopted towards successive Olympic Games.[70] In June 1914, the Foreign Office, looking back for precedent in the light of Theodore Cook's demands for a more activist approach, reaffirmed the apparent lack of official involvement regarding past Olympics. One exception was the 1906 Athens Games, held between the 1904 and 1908 Olympics, for which Lord Desborough (BOA Chairman) and R.C. Bosanquet (Director, British School at Athens) were officially designated British representatives.[71] Unsurprisingly, less elitist sports, particularly an allegedly professional game like association football, were treated with indifference and disdain by officials deeply imbued through their schooling with the amateur ethic.

Reviewing the government's role regarding the 1908 London Olympic Games, a 1914 Foreign Office study concluded that 'there is no correspondence in the archives relative to this meeting'![72] The event, attracting competitors from 19 countries, proved perhaps the largest and most representative international sports meeting held to date, while the presence of several teams supported by public subsidies (e.g. France) established that many governments took the Olympics seriously for extra-sporting reasons.[73] By contrast, the British government proved more reticent, particularly as regards the provision of public funding or the use of the Foreign Office to issue invitations to participate in the Games. Subsequently, Cook, who proved active during 1908–9 in complaining about public apathy and governmental indifference towards the Olympics, stated that official support amounted to nothing more than the attendance of two ministers at a dinner party.[74] To some extent, the reported lack of archival references, as mentioned above, might seem to validate his critique, even if Cook, like the 1914 departmental study, failed to credit certain actions possessing a broader significance. In particular, the London Olympics, linked to a prearranged Franco-British Exhibition of Science,

61

Arts and Industry, saw several cases of practical assistance to French competitors (e.g. facilitating the importation of armed weapons for shooting events) viewed as reinforcing the 1904 entente, even if the episode's political impact paled into insignificance by comparison with the more substantial contributions to Anglo-French relations provided by ongoing military conversations or diplomatic support in the 1905–6 Moroccan Crisis. Similarly, recent improvements in Anglo-Russian relations in the wake of the 1907 entente were signified by, say, an insistence that, despite their nationalist pretensions, Finnish competitors at the London Olympics were required to compete under the Russian flag. For officials, a more enduring Olympic image concerned press reports about 'angry scenes' between competitors normally centred upon allegations of biased refereeing and frequently involving Americans.[75] Reports of confrontations helped to lodge in the departmental memory negative images offering convincing reasons for non-intervention in an activity adjudged likely to foster international disharmony. In future, the Foreign Office was to prove unwilling to jeopardise international relations for the sake of sport.[76]

The 1912 Stockholm Olympic Games prompted little change in the attitude of the British government, whose minimal role comprised principally *ad hoc* responses to specific Swedish enquiries (e.g. separate representation of colonies and dominions). However, subsequently, Britain's relatively disappointing overall performance prompted a broad debate about the government's role in arresting decline and helping to 'win back primacy'.[77] By implication, British competitors were adjudged to have done well in previous Olympics in spite of, rather than because of, the government's position. Although the BOA acknowledged rising standards elsewhere, there remained a widespread assumption that Britain, having originated, developed and performed well in so many sports, should remain the dominant force in football and other sports. Public controversy, frequently triggered by Olympic incidents, focused on the appropriate balance between playing the game for its own sake and the political imperative of sporting success as proof of national dynamism. Following the 1912 Stockholm Games, R.C. Lehmann, responding to criticisms that 'we are a nation of slackers, unable, for want of the proper spirit, to hold our own in the games by which the strength and manhood of a race are built up', articulated the problem: 'The danger is rather that we should attach too much importance to games … What matters is, not so much the winning or the losing, but the spirit in which the game itself is played.'[78] For Lehmann, the fact that great significance was attached to something of 'minor importance' transformed sport from its original recreational purpose into 'a department of foreign policy' capable of causing serious international controversy.

Lehmann provoked Philip Noel-Baker (then described as Philip J. Baker) to undertake one of his early excursions into the politics of sport. Having organised the 1911 universities athletics match between Cambridge, Harvard, Oxford and Yale and competed in the 1500 metres final at the 1912 Olympics, Noel-Baker dismissed press reports of Anglo-American clashes as little more than 'pure invention' for the sake of a 'silly newspaper quarrel' pursued by journalists ignorant of Olympic sports.[79] Defending the 'much-abused Americans' against Lehmann and others, Noel-Baker pressed the view – this became a persistent theme of his thinking and writing in future decades – that the Olympic movement, far from causing ill will, exerted a far more positive impact on relations between states and peoples: 'I don't think a single competitor came away from Stockholm without a warm corner in his heart for Sweden and a strong respect and liking for the people against whom he ran'.[80] He sought to turn Lehmann's attack to his advantage:

> Mr. Lehmann taunts us with trying to make the Olympic Games a 'branch of foreign policy'. I think we might do worse. I don't want to attach an absurd importance to athletics, but, seriously, it seems to me that international contests do provide a sort of international rivalry that is sane and healthy and desirable .... International meetings are good for the cause of athletics ... Is it so fantastic to believe that the provision of a sane intercourse and a sane rivalry of nations will help in breaking up the absurd fabric of 'routine thinking' on which the present system of international relations rests?

The months preceding the outbreak of the First World War witnessed a further phase in this debate in the wake of exchanges conducted between the Foreign Office and the War Office about the release of army officers to participate in the pentathlon at the 1916 Berlin Olympics. The Foreign Office, reaffirming its negative mindset, exhibited what became its typical lack of enthusiasm for international sport in general and the Olympics in particular: 'these games usually lead to much international ill-feeling'.[81] Neither the Foreign Office nor the War Office saw any significant grounds for intervention, even if British participation in the event depended on military personnel. One input derived from Sir Edward Goschen, the British ambassador in Berlin, who reminded London about the political dimension of German sport; indeed, reportedly Kaiser Wilhelm II had refused permission for riders to travel to London for international equestrian tournaments unless they were 'absolutely certain of winning'.[82]

Goschen offered a revealing piece of advice: 'I think the reason given by the Emperor holds good for the British Army in the present case'. Goschen's intervention, albeit causing no change of course, led the Foreign Office to urge the War Office to keep the matter under review.[83]

The 1916 Olympics were brought to the government's attention again in May 1914, when Theodore Cook, a member of both the BOA and IOC, visited the Foreign Office to discuss a forthcoming IOC meeting (June 1914). Of course, Cook, like the IOC's other British members (i.e. Lord Desborough, Reverend R.S. de Courcey Laffan), represented himself, not the British government, but he urged the Foreign Office to adopt a more coherent and supportive approach towards international sport because of its 'international political significance' and the serious interest taken by other countries therein.[84] Cook, maintaining the pressure, contacted the Foreign Office again the following month to highlight areas for action, including public funding, the release of military personnel, the award of honours to leading personalities (e.g. de Coubertin), and official hospitality. Cook, referring to a central foreign policy theme, reminded the Foreign Office that Germany, when agreeing to host the Olympics, specified the importance of British participation: 'any misunderstanding might produce incalculable consequences upon the general cordiality which should exist between the two countries'.[85]

The Foreign Office assumed initially that Cook, who was currently editor of *The Field* and a former international fencer, was speaking for the BOA – eventually it transpired that he was acting upon his own initiative – and gave serious thought to his approach. However, the department's response, influenced by the seeming lack of precedent for intervention, merely reaffirmed the government's existing cautious and reserved approach towards international sport. Eyre Crowe, writing as Assistant Secretary of State, saw no need to move far or fast in the direction favoured by Cook, even if his response illuminated both elitist misgivings about professional sport and misinformation about the Olympics:

> I do not think we ought to be rushed in a matter of this kind. There is much diversity of opinion even in this country about these games. Many sensible people consider them to be pure advertisement of professional sportsmen. If the govt. is to take them up officially, it must be after a deliberate decision. It is not a Foreign Office question at all, and cannot be decided by Sir E. Grey.[86]

Crowe, endorsing Robert Vansittart's minute to the effect that 'the matter did not seem one which the F.O. c^d decide', instructed 'no action'.[87] Soon afterwards, Vansittart, currently an assistant clerk in the Western department but destined to perform a central role in the international politics of British sport during the late 1930s, informed Cook that the government saw 'no particular reason' to support British participation in the Olympic pentathlon.[88] Despite, or perhaps because of, the international situation, their exchange glossed over the Anglo-German dimension. At the same time, the Foreign Office, denying departmental liability, sought to push responsibility for sport elsewhere, such as to the Prime Minister (honours) or the Board of Education.

FOOTBALL GOES TO WAR

The assassination of the Austrian Archduke Franz Ferdinand at Sarajevo on 28 June 1914 sparked off a train of events escalating into a major war involving most of the great powers, including Britain, which declared war on Germany and Austria on 4 and 12 August 1914 respectively. Inevitably, escalating international tension overshadowed the 1914 FIFA Congress, which met under Woolfall's presidency at Christiania (Norway) on 27–28 June 1914. Matters discussed included the 1916 Olympic football tournament and the location (i.e. Brussels) of the 1915 Congress. However, delegates, overriding previous exhortations to avoid politics, used the closing session to adopt unanimously a Swiss resolution, sponsored on behalf of the International Peace Office, to 'support any action which tends to bring the nations nearer to each other and to substitute arbitration for violence in the settlement of all the conflicts which might arise between them'.[89]

FIFA's peace resolution – paradoxically, it was adopted on the same day as the archduke's assassination at Sarajevo – was soon overtaken by events, which severely disrupted both domestic and international football. One initial impact affected Corinthians, a leading amateur club noted for its missionary visits to continental Europe, South Africa (1897, 1903), Canada/USA (1906), and Brazil (1910, 1913). In July 1914 Corinthians set out on yet another Brazilian tour, but were forced to return from Rio de Janeiro within days of arrival because of the declaration of war.[90] Nor were the British footballing associations unaffected by war. Despite initial hopes of a short, sharp war 'over by Christmas', the First World War soon raised serious question marks about the continuation of football in Britain, particularly given the media and parliamentary campaign focused on 'the scandal of professional football': 'Drink, gambling, professional football – here in the extreme was the conspicuous consumption of the energies of young men eminently eligible for the trenches – came under heavy fire'

(Marwick).[91] Both the FA and FAW responded by pointing to the game's 'very large place in the organised life of the nation', including its contribution to public morale, recreation and leisure, and recruitment.[92] For J.C. Clegg, the FA chairman, 'total suspension would be mischievous rather than good'.[93] At the same time, the football associations, attempting to disarm critics, appealed to the patriotism of those involved in the game to support the war effort, such as through the release of professional footballers for the army, the use of grounds for drill and recruitment, the purchase of War Loans, and contributions to war charities (e.g. Prince of Wales Relief Fund). What particularly irritated them was the singling out of association football for criticism: 'football, which is essentially the pastime of the masses, is the only sport which is being attacked'.[94] In November 1914, a *Times* editorial, displaying a strong antipathy towards professional sport, gave substance to their complaint: 'British sports and British games have done our race a service which other nations have emulated too late and freely acknowledge on the field today. Except, however, in this one solitary instance of professional football, they have long since fallen into their proper places as a pastime and a training, not as a business or a trade.'[95] Whatever the football authorities did or offered by way of explanation failed to halt pressure to suspend a game allegedly more concerned to make money than to support the war; indeed, one *Times* letter writer even went as far as to accuse football spectators of contributing towards a German victory![96]

The SFA, inclining from an early stage to a more conciliatory stance, experienced growing difficulty in keeping in line with the other home associations. On 17 November 1914, the SFA, concerned about escalating media, official and public pressure, requested a conference of the British associations to discuss the future of wartime football.[97] On 30 November, Clegg, preparing for this conference, visited the War Office, where H.J. Tennant, Under-Secretary of State, acknowledged what British football had done already for the war effort. Disclaiming any desire for the entire stoppage of the game, he pressed the need to do something more, like halting cup competitions, to appease public opinion.[98] On 3 December, the conference of the British associations, held at London, was adjourned to allow Clegg to have another meeting with Tennant, who now proposed the cancellation of both cup matches and home internationals in spite of counter-arguments about the alleged deleterious impact on recruitment. However, the London conference, though acknowledging the need for a gesture, was able to agree upon only the cancellation of home internationals for the current season: 'This meeting recommends that except as regards the International Matches it is not right that football should be stopped, or suspended. Further, the meeting is of opinion that to deprive the working people of our country of their Saturday afternoon recreation would be unfair, and very mischievous.'[99]

But this resolution did not go far enough for the SFA, whose delegates, having reserved its right to independent action, used an MP's good offices to arrange a meeting with Tennant on the following day. Tennant, handing over a written statement, welcomed the SFA's acceptance of 'the view of the War Office ... viz., the abandonment of both the International Matches and the Cup Ties': 'I recognise the difficulties of a complete cessation of professional football, but ... I do not consider that when so many homes are bereaved and so many brave men are laying down their lives for our country the full programme of amusement which we welcome in times of peace is in accord with public sentiment or with the cruel realities of this devastating war.'[100] Naturally, the FA was far from pleased with the unilateral action of the SFA, which, having requested the London conference, had acted contrary to its resolutions. Mutual recriminations and accusations of 'breach of faith' were accompanied by claims that events 'must affect the friendly relations and confidence which have previously existed between the Associations'.[101] In the event, the rift soon subsided, and was followed by expressions of regret about the misunderstanding and hope of harmonious future relations.[102]

The FA Cup Final, played at Old Trafford (Manchester) on 24 April 1915, went ahead as scheduled, but in April 1915 the impact of political, commercial (e.g. falling attendances) and other pressures led to the cancellation of the following season's league programme alongside the previously agreed suspension of home internationals. Even so, 'it was inconceivable that soccer would end entirely, or that it would cease to be played competitively and watched by at least some supporters'.[103]

CONCLUSIONS

Keeping FIFA and other countries in their place

During the pre-1914 period, FIFA continued to develop in terms of both its role and membership, while enjoying a somewhat ambivalent relationship with its British members. The latter, retaining an arrogant belief in British footballing superiority and leadership, preferred to go their own way, and particularly to protect themselves from unwelcome interference in *their game* by relatively new and allegedly uninformed foreign associations operating through an international framework created by continental countries: 'English football remained proud and insular ... At heart the English felt football was their property and were disinclined to cooperate with foreigners.'[104] Nor was the situation any different for Irish, Scottish or Welsh football.

However, faced by the reality of FIFA's existence, the British associations soon came to appreciate the merits of joining FIFA, most notably to ensure that this evolving organisation was kept in its place and developed in an acceptable manner. Also, they were encouraged, even flattered, by their continental counterparts to believe that FIFA would benefit from membership of the long-established British associations. Woolfall's election to FIFA's presidency (1906–18) reaffirmed the FA's high international standing, while helping British efforts to preserve the IFAB's control over the laws of the game as well as to contain the German-inspired campaign to boost FIFA's powers *vis-à-vis* members. One other change symbolic of British influence occurred in 1907, when English replaced French as FIFA's official language.

In this manner, membership of FIFA tended simultaneously to reinforce and qualify British football's isolationist tendencies. Of course, there was no guarantee that Britain's footballing hegemony would prevail indefinitely, especially as other countries became more competitive, even better, at playing the game as well as more experienced in the workings of FIFA. 'Splendid isolation', having been undermined already during the 1890s and 1900s as a foreign policy strategy, was to prove equally inappropriate in the world of sport, even if sections of British opinion continued to believe in the divine right to victory and control over the game by the country responsible for giving most games to the world. Nevertheless, in August 1914, D. Campbell, the SFA president, sounded the alarm bell: 'there is no doubt that the class of men who are taking the control of the game upon the Continent, etc. are apt scholars and may not be content to remain in that position very long'.[105] More seriously, on the field itself, Denmark, though defeated by England in both the 1908 and 1912 Olympic finals, undermined images of British invincibility by two victories over England's amateur XI before 1914. Elsewhere, British teams travelling overseas – some experienced the occasional defeat (e.g. Celtic: 1907; Sunderland: 1909) – often returned with revised views about standards in other countries.[106] For instance, in 1912, Swindon, a Southern League side which had reached the 1910 and 1912 FA Cup semi-finals, returned unbeaten from Argentina and Uruguay. Sam Allen, Swindon's Secretary-Manager, enthusing about the 'really good, clever, fast' teams, reported that 'the standard of play was much higher than we had been led to expect when we were in England ... Many of the men who have played in the more important teams out here could easily earn a living in England as professionals.'[107]

FIFA's lack of progress with its project for an international tournament meant that, for the time being, international matches offered the best 'test' of the actual playing strength of individual countries, even if their proliferation and one-off nature meant that – to quote the Russian delegate (R. Fulda) – 'one never knew which (i.e. team) was the best'.[108] However, during the pre-1914 period, England's excellent record against foreign teams in both full and amateur internationals (see Table 2.3, Chapter 2; Table 3.2) – Ireland, Scotland and Wales had yet to look beyond the home international championship – plus control over the IFAB inspired confidence in British footballing hegemony and – to quote one FA Council member – 'the general inferiority of Continental football'.[109] Moreover, at a time when the game was still played at the amateur level in most countries outside the British Isles, this primacy was seemingly validated by two successive Olympic titles, given FIFA's preparedness, as signalled at the 1914 Congress, to recognise future Olympic finals as the *de facto* amateur championship of the world.[110]

Throughout its initial decade, FIFA, rejoicing in its non-governmental nature and repeatedly urged by members to act 'entirely independent of politics' (Hungary), found it difficult to divorce international football from political considerations, especially as FIFA's one country, one member rule focused attention on the political status of applicants for membership, as highlighted by Bohemia's complaints about the interposition of non-footballing considerations.[111] Prior to 1914, the only real exception concerned the British associations, whose independence was measured in footballing, not political, terms! At the same time, members frequently saw FIFA as serving a broader interest extending beyond the world of football; for example, FIFA's *Annual Report, 1908-09* articulated international football's role in helping to 'strengthen the bonds of friendship between the sporting people of the various nations'.[112] Certainly, this objective was often echoed at FIFA congresses, such as at Dresden in 1911, when Gottfried Hinze, the president of the DFB, expressed the hope that 'by the international intercourse the bonds of friendship between the nations would become firmer'.[113] Perhaps, FIFA's most overt political move occurred in June 1914, when Congress adopted the Swiss peace resolution.

Posing sporting questions for British governments

The growth of contests between teams representing different countries in an ever broader range of sports alongside the emergence of transnational sporting bodies, like the IOC (1894) and FIFA (1904), explained why the decade or so preceding the First World War proved a formative period in the development of international sport. Naturally, these developments posed questions for British governments, whose *laissez-faire* attitude contrasted with evidence of official intervention in, say, France or Germany, during an era whose obsession with Social Darwinism, national efficiency and racial virility meant that all forms of international competition, not excluding sport, were being taken extremely seriously. Increasingly, international sport was seen as institutionalising national rivalries; thus, during the 1908 Olympics, 'the British press and public came to feel their "racial virility" was on trial' (Holt).[114]

Nevertheless, prior to 1914, in Britain 'the game was kept free from overt political interference' (Murray).[115] Bensemann, impressed by its determination to go ahead with its 1899 German tour, saw the FA as establishing from the start the principle that, at least in Britain, 'sport has nothing to do with politics'.[116] Even so, the FA soon came to realise its inability to divorce itself from politics, if only as a consequence of FIFA's membership requirements. At the same time, British governments, though fostering images about the autonomy of sport, found it equally difficult to steer clear of what was treated as a peripheral, low priority topic.[117] As a result, occasional sporting episodes, perceived as posing political questions, offered British governments, acting principally through the Foreign Office, the opportunity variously to foster and reinforce relations with Austria (e.g. support British representation at the 1910 Vienna Field Sports Exhibition) or France (e.g. 1908 Olympics; presence of the French Consul at the 1914 Scotland-England football game), avoid adverse impacts on Anglo-German relations (e.g. military participation in 1916 Olympics), or help trade (e.g. the Franco-British Exhibition of Science, Arts and Industry linked to the 1908 London Olympics).[118] In general, the government's role was unenthusiastically supportive rather than deliberately obstructive, even if there remained an enduring reluctance to spend public money on sport. The £5,000 Treasury grant, allocated in 1910 at the request of both the Foreign Office and Board of Trade, to ensure British representation at the Vienna Field Sports Exhibition, was the exception that proved the rule.[119]

British governments exhibited an emerging awareness of sport's propaganda potential, with particular regard to national images fostered by displays of sporting or unsporting behaviour, participation or non-participation in specific events, and success or failure on the sports field or track.[120] However, lack of evidence renders it difficult to assess how far official circles actually appreciated the intangible benefits accruing to Britain's material interests and prestige on a wider stage from the global expansion of football and other games 'made in Britain', as suggested in 1913, when the DFB, commemorating the FA's golden jubilee, pointed to the way in which 'your sport has influenced our football life'.[121] Association football, having been taken up in Germany during the 1880s, attracted growing support within society as a whole and the lower ranks of the armed services in particular; thus, 'the new sport of the soldier' occupied a prime place in Hans Donalies' *Sport und Militar* handbook published in 1911.[122] As a result, it must be assumed that the growth of association football in Germany, in conjunction with frequent amateur internationals played between the two countries (Table 3.3), the employment of British coaches (e.g. Steve Bloomer, Fred Spikesley), and British influence on club names (e.g. 'Britannia' of Berlin), impacted in some way or another on Anglo-German relations. Naturally, any impacts, including England's good record in internationals against Germany (i.e. three wins of 5-1, 9-0, 3-0, and one 2-2 draw), should be viewed in perspective, given frequent FA–DFB disagreements within FIFA, occasional *Turner* denunciations of German efforts to emulate British and other foreign examples, Anglo-German commercial and other rivalries, the two countries' drift towards war, and the internment of British football coaches working in, say, Austria (e.g. Jimmy Hogan) and Germany consequent upon the outbreak of war.[123]

Playing the game in war

The First World War highlighted the manner in which sports governing bodies, like the British football associations, operated within the domestic and international political context.[124] Wartime realities soon led the FA to cancel forthcoming amateur internationals arranged for 1914–15, including those versus France and Germany.[125] Eventually, the home international championship was also suspended – to quote the FAW – 'at the request of the War Office'.[126] Indeed, this episode, illuminating the extent of government interference in wartime sport, led the football associations to feel the need to publicise the fact that 'football has not shirked its duty under abnormal conditions' in spite of, say, *Punch*'s depiction of the football results as 'Shirkers' War News' (January 1915).[127] By way of illustration, the football associations, whose income was seriously reduced by the loss of gate receipts from home internationals, pointed to the money provided for war relief charities, the footballs sent to troops at the front, the large numbers of footballers enlisted in the armed forces, and players killed in the war.[128] Symbolically, perhaps, the more interesting development concerned the War Office's commandeering of the FA's headquarters building located at 42 Russell Square![129]

Moreover, it soon became clear that the 1916 Berlin Olympics, together with its football tournament designated by FIFA as the world amateur championship, would have to be cancelled. Events in which the German government proved a prime mover meant that, despite having built a new stadium, Berlin had to wait a further two decades before hosting the Olympic Games. Berlin was deprived also of the opportunity to host the 1916 FIFA Congress. Whereas Noel-Baker regretted that 'the Kaiser's general staff all blotted out the ardent hopes which had begun to blossom at Stockholm', Cook responded patriotically to events: 'The "British team" is certainly on its way to Berlin; but in a very different sense from what was contemplated even so lately as in June last'.[130]

For many, war came to be interpreted as a glorified football match, an analogy given substance by the frequent use on the front line of a football kick-off to symbolise going 'over the top'.[131] *The Illustrated London News*' coverage of one incident, centred upon the East Surrey Regiment on the first day of the Battle of the Somme (1 July 1916), brought the practice to national prominence, while inspiring the *Daily Mail*'s 'Touchstone' to follow Henry Newbolt in illuminating the linkage between playing the game and the 'great game of war'.[132]

> On through the hail of slaughter
> Where gallant comrades fall,
> Where blood is poured like water,
> They drive the trickling ball.
> The fear of death before them
> Is but an empty name;
> True to the land that bore them
> The Surreys play the game!

For the press, the episode's intrinsic interest was accentuated by the fact that it represented a rare instance of good news from the Somme. Subsequently, the footballs allegedly used to 'kick-off' the advance were returned to the regimental depot at Kingston upon Thames, where Colonel Treeby employed footballing analogies, albeit those derived from rugby, to claim that war was 'being won by our football heroes today. Our men have played and are playing the game. We are still in the scrum, it is true, but the ball is being carried forward, and we doubt not in God's good providence the goal for which we are fighting – the goal of freedom, justice, and lasting peace – will soon be won.'[133] Playing the game would ensure victory. In this manner, sport offered the natural metaphor and source of inspiration for politicians and the military educated at sports-mad public schools. Nor should football's wartime role in maintaining morale be underestimated, as

72

evidenced by Sassoon's practice of reading 'Football news' to his men while awaiting action.[134] For many troops in the trenches, football proved 'The Burning Question':

> Three Tommies sat in a trench one day,
> Discussing the war in the usual way,
> They talked of the mud, and they talked of the Hun,
> Of what was to do, and what had been done,
> They talked about rum, and – 'tis hard to believe –
> They even found time to speak about leave,
> But the point they argued from post back to pillar
> Was whether Notts County could beat Aston Villa.[135]

Looking ahead

The 1914–18 First World War proved a difficult time for association football in Britain. Accusations of disloyalty hurt, while colouring official perceptions about sport in general and professional football in particular. Certainly, the War Office's intervention, in conjunction with persistent parliamentary and press criticism during 1914–15, made the footballing authorities extremely sensitive about their wartime role. Looking back in 1919 on a long attritional struggle from which Britain had emerged eventually on the winning side, the SFA glossed over the game's wartime problems, when claiming some credit for victory: 'There is no doubt that athleticism, particularly football, was an important factor in carrying the war to a successful issue'.[136] Moreover, the intransigent attitude adopted by the British football associations during the immediate post-war period towards contacts with, let alone fixtures against, the defeated powers, must be partly ascribed to continued sensitivity about their wartime image, including the consequent need to appear more patriotic, even jingoistic, than the British people as a whole.[137]

NOTES

1. Irish Football Association, Belfast (hereafter IFA), *Annual Report 1903–4* (IFA, 1904), p.1, 1903–9; *Annual Report 1909–10* (IFA, 1910), p.2, 1909–24.
2. Scottish Football Association Museum Trust, Hampden Park, Glasgow (hereafter SFAMT*), Annual Report 1905–6* (SFA, 1906), p.3; *Annual Report 1907–8* (SFA, 1908).
3. Holt, *Sport and the British*, pp.166–70; Tony Mason, *Association Football and English Society, 1863–1915* (Harvester Press, Brighton, 1980), p.234, p.247; Richard Holt, 'Contrasting nationalisms: sport, militarism and the unitary state in Britain and France before 1914', *Int.J.Hist.Sport*, 12 (1995), 46.

4. Holt, *Sport and the British,* p.273.
5. Ibid., p.168.
6. FIFA, Annual Report 1908–9, 30 May 1909, encl. Minutes of 6th Congress, Budapest, 30–31 May 1909, p.6.
7. FIFA, Minutes of 6th Annual FIFA Congress, Budapest, 30–31 May 1909, p.1.
8. *FIFA Handbook, 1927 edn* (De Bussy, Amsterdam, 1927), p.v; Frederick Wall, *Fifty Years of Football* (Cassell, London, 1935), p.219.
9. FIFA, Minutes of 23rd Annual FIFA Congress, Berlin, 13–14 Aug. 1936, p.8; *FIFA Handbook 1950, 9th edition* (FIFA, Zurich, 1950), p.vii; 'Half a century of history: the FIFA is 50 years old', *FIFA Official Bulletin,* 7 (Sept. 1954), 11.
10. FAW, *Annual Report 1912–13* (FAW, 1913), p.2; Wray Vamplew, *Pay Up and Play the Game: professional sport in Britain, 1875–1914* (Cambridge University Press, Cambridge, 1988).
11. FA, Consultative Committee, 31 Aug. 1914, 1914–15.
12. SFAMT, *Annual Report 1903–4* (SFA, 1904), p.1; *Annual Report 1913–14* (SFA, 1914), p.1.
13. FAW, *Annual Report 1900–1* (FAW, 1901), p.1; *Annual Report 1912–13* (FAW, 1913), p.2; *Annual Report 1913–14* (FAW, 1914), p.1.
14. SFAMT, *Annual Report 1903–4* (SFA: May 1904), p.3.
15. Mason, *Association Football,* p.230. Of course, players received far less than the astronomic sums paid today. Also, the game was 'singularly unbusinesslike' in the sense that a desire for a winning team often took precedence over profit: see Steve Ickringill, 'Amateur and professional: sport in Britain and America at the turn of the twentieth century', in J.C. Binfield and J. Stevenson (eds), *Sport, Culture and Politics* (Sheffield Academic Press, Sheffield, 1993), p.39.
16. FAW, Council, 15 Oct. 1902, p.68, 1899–1906; FA, Council, 9 June 1909, minute 22, 1909–10; ISC, 10 March 1913, 1912–13.
17. FAW, AGM Report, 23 Aug. 1911, p.543, 1909–11; Wall, pp.138–9. Home internationals were proportionally less significant financially for the FA, but even its international account accounted for *circa* 40–50 per cent of its budget.
18. W. Unite Jones, 'International Football', in Alfred Gibson and William Pickford (eds), *Association Football and the Men who Made it: volume 4* (Caxton, London, 1906), pp.103–15.
19. FA, Council, 24 May 1901, minute 26, 11 Nov. 1901, minute 22, 1901–2; ISC, 12 Oct. 1906, 1906–7; Council, 2 Aug. 1907, 1907–8.
20. Heiner Gillmeister, 'The first European soccer match: Walter Bensemann, a twenty-six year old German student, set the ball rolling', *The Sports Historian,* 17 (1997), 1–3; Walter Bensemann, 'Missionaries of Sport', *World's Football,* 37 (1933), 151–2; FA, Council, 28 Aug. 1899, minute 17, 13 Nov. 1899, minute 14, 1899–1900. Subsequently, Bensemann was involved in the creation of the DFB and the founding of *Der Kicker.*
21. Bensemann, *Tutti frutti,* 194; Rous, *Reflections,* 464; Wall, p.51, p.55; Murray, pp.64–5.
22. Gillmeister, 2-3, indicates 38 goals for, 4 against. Bensemann claims that *Corinthians,* a leading amateur club which had already represented the FA before (e.g. against Wales), made this tour for the FA, even if this point is not supported by the club's histories: B.O. Corbett, *Annals of the Corinthian Football Club* (Longmans, Green, London, 1908); F.N.S. Creek, *A History of the Corinthian Football Club* (Longmans, Green, London, 1933), p.28; FA, Council, 26 Feb. 1900, minute 16, 1899–1900; Green, pp.192–3.
23. FIFA, Schricker to Rous, 20 Nov. 1935, England 1932–57.

24. FA, ISC, 4 Nov. 1907, 9 Dec. 1907, 27 Jan. 1908, 3 Feb. 1908, 9 March 1908, 1907–8.
25. At this time, the FA paid professionals ten guineas (i.e. £10.50) per match: FA, Council, 19 April 1907, minute 19, 1906–7.
26. Austria, which played England on 6 and 8 June 1908, beat Germany 3-2 on 7 June.
27. FA, ISC, 23 April 1909, 1908–9; Council, 30 Aug. 1909, minute 3, 1909-10. For attendance figures, see Ron Hockings and Keir Radnedge, *Nations of Europe: a statistical history of European international football, 1872–1993, vol. 1* (Articulate, Emsworth, 1993); Capel-Kirby and Carter, pp.86–7.
28. Günther Furrer, Paulo Godoy and Joseph Blatter, *FIFA 1904–1984* (FIFA, Zurich, 1984), p.66.
29. FA, Council, 19 April 1907, minute 15, 1906–7; Council, 4 Oct. 1907, minute 6, 1907–8; FAW, Council, 14 Aug. 1907, minute 275, p.290, 1906–9; Capel-Kirby and Carter, pp.83–4.
30. FA, Council, 13 March 1911, minute 17, 1910–11; FAW, Council, 13 Dec. 1911, minute 782, p.556, 1909–11; FIFA, F. Wall to C. Hirschman, 5 May 1911, Jeux Olympiques, 1912–32; IFA, Council, 9 Jan. 1912, 1909–24.
31. FA, ISC, 1 Oct. 1909, 17 Jan. 1910, 1909–10. The FA team, playing 23 games, won the three test matches 3-0, 6-2, 6-3. A South African invitation was rejected in 1913: FA, ISC, 1 Sept. 1913, 1913–14.
32. Tony Mason, *Passion of the People?: football in South America* (Verso, London, 1995), pp.15–26.
33. FA, Council, 10 Nov. 1902, minute 29, 1902–3; Council, 14 Dec. 1903, minute 12, 1903–7; Green, p.198. For examples of club requests: FA, Council, 24 May 1901, minute 26, 11 Nov. 1901, minute 22, 24 Feb. 1902, minutes 36–37, 1901–2; Consultative Committee, 9 Feb. 1903, minutes 38–39, 25 March 1903, minutes 26–27, 1902–3.
34. SFAMT, Tenth meeting of Committee, 30 Nov. 1905, Acc.9017/8, 1899–1905; Council, 18 Nov. 1913, Acc.9017/10, 1913–14.
35. SFAMT, Meeting of Office-Bearers, 8 May 1913, minute 3, Council, 7 April 1914, minute 175, Emergency and Finance Committee (hereafter EFC), 22 April 1914, minute 12, Acc.9017/10, 1913–14; Council, 7 May 1914, minute 8, Acc.9017/11, 1914–15. See Bert Bell, *Still Seeing Red: a history of Third Lanark A.C.* (Glasgow City Libraries and Archives, Glasgow, 1996), pp.135–6.
36. FA, Council, 7 March 1910, minute 8, 1909–10.
37. Tomlinson, pp.84–5; Furrer, Godoy and Blatter, p.58.
38. FA, Council, 30 May 1902, minute 17, 1898–1903.
39. The following section is based on C.A.W. Hirschman, 'Notes sur la Fondation de la F.I.F.A.', in *FIFA 1904–1929* (de Bussy, Amsterdam, 1929), pp.141–5; Green, pp.196–202; Furrer, Godoy and Blatter, p.58.
40. FAW, Council, 24 Sept. 1902, minute 6, 1899–1906.
41. FIFA, Minutes of 1st Congress, Paris, 21–23 May 1905, p.1; Green, p.197; Wall, p.219; William Pickford, *A Few Recollections of Sport* (private printing, Bournemouth Guardian, Bournemouth, 1938), p.110; Young, *History of British Football*, p.160.
42. FIFA, Minutes of 2nd Congress, Paris, 10–12 June 1905, p.1; FA, Report of International Conference, Berne, encl. Council, 20 July 1906, minute 14, 1906–7; FAW, Council, 31 May 1905, p.168, 1899–1906.
43. FA, Report by F. Wall, June 1905, 1905–6.
44. SFAMT, 2nd Meeting of Committee, 13 Aug. 1907, Acc.9017/9, 1905–8; FAW, Council, 14 Aug. 1907, minute 274, 1906–9.

45. FIFA, Minutes of 3rd Congress, Berne, 3–4 June 1906, pp.2–3.
46. FIFA, Minutes of 5th Congress, Vienna, 7–8 June 1908, pp.3–4.
47. FIFA, Minutes of 6th Congress, Budapest, 30–31 May 1909, p.2.
48. FIFA, Minutes of 7th Congress, Milan, 15–16 May 1910, pp.4–5; IFA, Council, 10 January 1911, 1909–24.
49. FIFA, Minutes of 5th Congress, Vienna, 7–8 June 1908, p.3.
50. FIFA, Minutes of 9th Congress, Stockholm, 30 June–1 July 1912, p.4.
51. FIFA, Minutes of 6th Congress, Budapest, 30–31 May 1909, p.1.
52. Green, p.201
53. FIFA, Minutes of 8th Congress, Dresden, 4–5 June 1911. See also Minutes of 10th Congress, Copenhagen, 31 May–1 June 1913, p.1.
54. FIFA, Minutes of 10th Congress, Copenhagen, 31 May–1 June 1913, p.5.
55. FIFA, Minutes of 8th Congress, Dresden, 4–5 June 1911, p.4; Minutes of 10th Congress, Copenhagen, 31 May–1 June 1913, p.5.
56. FIFA, Minutes of 9th Congress, Stockholm, 30 June–1 July 1912, p.7. Note the Dutch riposte that none of the three sports cited possessed international federations.
57. FAW, IFAB, 8 June 1912, 1911–15; FIFA, Minutes of 9th Congress, Stockholm, 30 June–1 July 1912, p.2, p.7.
58. FIFA, IFAB to FIFA, 10 April 1913, encl. Minutes of 10th Congress, Copenhagen, 31 May 1913, p.5; FAW, IFAB, 14 June 1913, 1911-15; SFAMT, Council, 12 Aug. 1913, minute 24, Acc.9017/9, 1908–13; IFA, Council, 12 April 1913, 1909–24.
59. FAW, IFAB, 13 June 1914, 1911–15.
60. FIFA, Minutes of 10th Congress, Copenhagen, 31 May–1 June 1913, pp.4–6.
61. FIFA, Minutes of 2nd Congress, Paris, 10–12 June 1905, p.3; Furrer, Godoy and Blatter, p.66.
62. FIFA, Minutes of 3rd Congress, Berne, 3–4 June 1906, p.2.
63. FIFA, Minutes of 8th Congress, Dresden, 4–5 June 1911, pp.4–5; Minutes of 11th Congress, Christiania, 27–28 June 1914, pp.3–4.
64. FIFA, Minutes of 10th Congress, Copenhagen, 31 May–1 June 1913, p.9; FA, Council, 24 April 1914, minute 11, ISC, 1 Sept. 1913, 12 Jan. 1914, 2 Feb. 1914, 1913–14.
65. FA, ISC, 30 March 1914, 24 April 1914, 1901–19. Colclough's selection depended upon release from Crystal Palace's Danish tour.
66. Ibid.
67. Ibid.; FIFA, Minutes of 11th Congress, Christiania, 27–28 June 1914, p.9.
68. Memorandum on Olympic movement, 2 June 1914, encl. Theodore Cook to Vansittart, 2 June 1914, FO371/2186/24954.
69. David Cannadine, 'The context, performance and meaning of ritual: the British monarchy and the "invention of tradition", c.1820–1977', in Eric Hobsbawm and Terence Ranger (eds), The Invention of Tradition (Cambridge University Press, Cambridge, 1983), p.133, pp.160–2; John Hargreaves, Sport, Power and Culture: a social and historical analysis of popular sports in Britain (Polity Press, Cambridge, 1986), pp.83–4; Mason, Association Football, p.240.
70. Martin Polley, ' "No business of ours"?: the Foreign Office and the Olympic Games, 1896–1914', Int.J.Hist.Sport, 13 (1997), 97.
71. Edward Parkes, memorandum, 6 June 1914, FO371/2186/24954.
72. Ibid.
73. Polley, Foreign Office and International Sport, p.7; Polley, 'No business of ours?', 102.
74. Polley, 'No business of ours?', 100–5.
75. The Sportsman, 4 July 1908.

76. Polley, 'No business of ours?', 102, 105.
77. Ibid., 106–7; *Report of the Olympic Games of 1912 in Stockholm,* quoted, Polley, *Foreign Office and International Sport,* pp.16–17.
78. CAC, R.C. Lehmann, 'Spread of Games: are we a nation of slackers?', n.d., NBKR 6/22/1; P.J. Baker, 'Olympiads and the noble English press', *The Granta,* 26 (23 Nov. 1912), 88–9.
79. Philip J. Baker, 'Olympiad and Liars', *The Outlook,* 19 Oct. 1912, 355–6, 359 (CAC, NBKR 6/22/1).
80. Baker, *Olympiad and Liars,* 359; Baker, *The Olympic Games,* 560.
81. PRO, minute, R. Sperling, 11 March 1914, FO371/1988/10779.
82. PRO, Sir E. Goschen, British ambassador in Berlin, to Lord Grey, 17 April 1914, FO371/1988/17138
83. PRO, Eyre Crowe, to Secretary, Army Council, 23 April 1914, FO371/1988/17138.
84. PRO, T. Cook to Foreign Office, 15 May 1914, FO371/1988/22388.
85. PRO, Cook to Vansittart, 2 June 1914, FO371/2186/24954.
86. PRO, minute, Eyre Crowe, n.d. (5 June 1914), FO371/2186/24954.
87. PRO, minutes by R. Vansittart and Eyre Crowe, 8, 10 June 1914, FO371/2186/24954.
88. PRO, minute, Vansittart, 11 March 1914, FO371/1988/10779; minute, Vansittart, 20 May 1914, FO371/1988/22388.
89. FIFA, Minutes of 11th Congress, Christiania, 27–28 June 1914, p.10.
90. Creek, *History of Corinthian FC,* p.32, pp.64–7, pp.77–80, pp.87–9; Corbett; Mason, *Passion of the People,* pp.19–25.
91. Sir George Young, 28 Nov. 1914, quoted Trevor Wilson, *The Myriad Faces of War* (Polity Press, Cambridge, 1986), p.164; Arthur Marwick, *The Deluge: British society and the First World War,* 2nd edn (Macmillan, London, 1991), p.90, p.186.
92. FAW, AGM, 19 Aug. 1914, 1911–15; Mason, *Association Football,* pp.251–5; Colin Veitch, 'Play up! Play Up! And Win the War', *Journal of Contemporary History,* 20 (1985), 363–78.
93. FA, Consultative Committee, 31 Aug. 1914, 1914–15.
94. FAW, Council, 10 Sept. 1914, minute 1498, 1911–15; Report, encl. Council, 12 Oct. 1914, minute 6, 1914–15; Birley, pp.71–3.
95. *The Times,* 25 Nov. 1914, quoted Mason, *Association Football,* p.252.
96. A.T. Pollard, *The Times,* 7 Nov. 1914, quoted Mason, *Association Football,* p.251.
97. SFAMT, EFC, 8 Nov. 1914, Acc.9017/11, 1914–15; IFA, Council, 17 Nov. 1914, 1909-24.
98. FA, Report of the War sub-committee adopted by Council, 7 Dec. 1914, Further Report of the War sub-committee, 8 Jan. 1915, 1914–15.
99. IFA, Council, 12 Jan. 1915, 1909-24; FA, Reports of the War sub-committee, 7 Dec. 1914, 22 Jan. 1915, 1914–15; SFAMT, Delegates' further report on War and Football, 26 Jan. 1915, Acc.9017/11, 1914–15.
100. SFAMT, H.J. Tennant to SFA's delegates, 4 Dec. 1914, encl. Council, 15 Dec. 1914, minute 95, Acc.9017/11, 1914–15.
101. FA, Report of the sub-committee, 22 Feb. 1915, 1914–15; SFAMT, Council, 2 Feb., 16 March 1915, Acc.9017/11, 1914–15.
102. SFAMT, correspondence encl. Council, 25 May 1915, minute 3, 3 Aug. 1915, minute 20, Acc.9017/12, 1915–16.
103. Birley, p.74; Murray, pp.72–4.
104. Holt, *Sport and the British,* p.273.
105. SFAMT, Council, 11 Aug. 1914, minute 13, Acc.9017/11, 1914–15.
106. Murray, p.66.

107. Quoted, Mason, *Passion of the People*, pp.20–1.
108. FIFA, Minutes of 11th Congress, Christiania, 27–28 June 1914, pp.3–4.
109. Pickford, *Recollections*, p.109.
110. FIFA, Minutes of 11th Congress, Christiania, 27–28 June 1914, pp.3–4; SFAMT, Council, 11 Aug. 1914, minute 13, Acc.9017/11, 1914–15.
111. FIFA, Minutes of 4th Congress, Amsterdam, 19–20 May 1907, p.2; Hungarian Football Association to FIFA, 20 Dec. 1909, encl. Minutes of 6th Congress, Budapest, 30–31 May 1909.
112. FIFA, minutes of 6th Congress, Budapest, 30–31 May 1909, p.6.
113. FIFA, Minutes of 8th Congress, Dresden, 4–5 June 1911, p.1.
114. Holt, *Sport and the British*, pp.273–5; Baker, 'Olympiads and the noble English press', 87; Polley, 'No business of ours?', 100, 104–5.
115. Murray, p.49.
116. Bensemann, 'Missionaries of Sport', 151–2.
117. Polley, 'Foreign Office and International Sport', pp.21–2.
118. For the Austrian episode, ibid., pp.19–21; SFAMT, EFC, 22 April 1914, minute 8, Acc.9017/10, 1913–14.
119. Polley, 'Foreign Office and International Sport', pp.20–1.
120. Ibid., pp.15–17.
121. FA, DFB to FA, n.d. (Nov. 1913), Consultative Committee, 1 Dec. 1913, 1913–14.
122. Richard A. Woeltz, 'Sport, culture, and society in late Imperial and Weimar Germany: some suggestions for future research', *Journal of Sport History*, 4 (1977), 300.
123. Ibid., 298, 302–3; Mason, *Association Football*, p.120, p.218; Capel-Kirby and Carter, pp.73–5; Murray, p.58.
124. Furrer, Godoy and Blatter, p.70; Green, p.288
125. FA, ISC, 24 April 1914, 12 Oct. 1914, 1914–15.
126. FAW, *Annual Report 1914–15* (FAW, 1915), pp.1–2.
127. SFAMT, *Annual Report 1914–15* (SFA, 1915), p.5.
128. Ibid., p.5; FAW, *Annual Report 1914–15* (FAW, 1915), p.2. For 1914–15, the FAW reported a deficit of £357.
129. Green, pp.286–7.
130. CAC, Noel-Baker to Bushnell, n.d. (7 Feb. 1951), NBKR 6/13/2; Theodore Cook, 'Public World and Public Duty', *The Field*, 15 Aug. 1914, in Theodore Cook (ed.), *Kaiser, Krupp and Kultur* (John Murray, London, 1915), p.45.
131. Holt, *Sport and the British*, p.276.
132. 'The Surreys play the game!: kicking footballs towards the German trenches under a hail of shells', *Illustrated London News*, 29 July 1916, pp.134–5; *Daily Mail*, 12 July 1916; Ruth Elwin Harris (ed.), *Billie. The Nevill Letters, 1914–1916* (Julia MacRae, London, 1991), pp.198–205. Note that Harris gives the incorrect date for the *Illustrated London News* article.
133. Harris, pp.203–4.
134. Sassoon, p.286; Jean Moorcroft Wilson, *Siegfried Sassoon, the Making of a War Poet: a biography (1886–1918)* (Duckworth, London, 1998), p.222.
135. Anon, 'The Burning Question', *The B.E.F. Times*, 1 Nov. 1917. In W. Gibson's 'Breakfast' (1917), shells screech overhead, while troops discuss whether Hull would beat Halifax.
136. SFAMT, *Annual Report 1918–1919* (SFA, 1919), p.7; Capel-Kirby and Carter, pp.70–80.
137. On post-war Britain, see Clarke, pp.98–102.

4

Responding to 'New Developments' in
International Sport after 1919

During September 1919, *The Times*, prompted by the post-war commencement of the league programme, praised the wartime contribution of football, whose status as the favourite sport of the armed forces meant that it had done 'more than anything else to revive tired limbs and weary minds'.[1] Such praise contrasted with the hostility directed at the game by this newspaper, among others, during 1914–15. Within this context, the SFA, like its fellow associations, welcomed the war's successful conclusion and the prospect of a 'just and lasting peace', while taking the opportunity to remind the general public about football's contribution to the war effort.[2] In this vein, throughout the inter-war years, the football associations continued to press their game's prominent place in British society alongside its contribution to harmonious international relationships; for example, in 1926, the FAW used its 50th anniversary to claim that 'the Association game has become firmly cemented as part of the National Life of our great Empire – health-giving in its effects – peace-making in its whole heartedness'.[3] Looking back towards the close of the decade, *The Times*, reiterating its more supportive view of the game, reminded readers that international football matches 'did much to foster a friendlier outlook on either side'.[4] Whether or not such attitudes were shared by British governments remains to be seen, particularly given the relatively sceptical official position taken prior to 1914 about sport's 'peace-making' capacities.

Following their wartime suspension, neither league programmes nor the home international championship were resumed until 1919–20, even if victory internationals, played between the home countries during 1919 to acknowledge 'the great part which football played in winning the War', fostered impressions of a return to normalcy and helped to replenish the football associations' depleted bank balances.[5] One reported peacetime consequence, at least in Wales, was a rapid deterioration in player behaviour; thus, whereas cases of misconduct were 'practically nil' during 1914–15, the first post-war season ushered in more cases of player and spectator misconduct than ever before![6]

PRESENTING A 'TRUE' PICTURE OF POST-WAR BRITAIN

In October 1919, James Headlam Morley, the Foreign Office's historical adviser, reviewed the News Department's responsibility for the presentation of Britain's role as a leading liberal democracy to a world audience: 'we cannot ignore the importance of using legitimate means for influencing this opinion'.[7] His lengthy and wide-ranging survey, stressing the need to counter the 'untrue picture' promoted elsewhere, overlooked the contribution of sport to external images of Britain, but this was scarcely surprising, given its peripheral position in departmental thinking prior to the war. Nor did war transform the Foreign Office's negative view of the Olympics, as reaffirmed by Eyre Crowe in May 1920: 'I hope that in future years, we may keep H.M.G. out of these sporting events'.[8]

However, despite official prejudices, during the next decade, the Foreign Office came gradually to recognise international sport's relevance to its responsibilities, most notably the fact that it was too important to be left to sporting bodies. In particular, it became clear that the quality of performance by British teams against foreign competition, at least in the more popular sports, influenced the nature of the 'picture' presented by Britain to overseas audiences. Victories on the football field, especially if achieved in a sporting manner, came to be seen increasingly as helping to encourage and reinforce positive national images, whereas defeats, like unsporting behaviour, exerted detrimental impacts.[9] As a result, the government's preferred non-interventionist approach, like its emphasis upon the autonomy of non-governmental sporting bodies, was qualified increasingly by a preparedness to take action in appropriate instances in order to protect and enhance Britain's interests in the wider world.

BRITISH FOOTBALL'S POST-WAR OSTRACISM OF THE DEFEATED POWERS

The most obvious manifestation of the intrusion of political factors in international sport during the period following the First World War was the initial ostracism of the ex-enemy countries. Germany's initial exclusion from major post-war conferences and the League of Nations was paralleled by its non-receipt of invitations to participate in the 1920 and 1924 Olympic Games; in effect, the IOC, though a non-governmental body, was unable to avoid the pressures from members responding to the pressures of war and the immediate post-war world.[10] As a result, German revisionism, though rooted primarily in resentment at both defeat and the harsh, 'dictated' nature of the 1919 peace treaties, was further encouraged by the second-rate status assigned to the country in the world of sport. Indeed, sporting isolationism, it might be argued, impacted even more heavily upon German public opinion.[11]

Wartime enmities took time to dissolve, and FIFA, having struggled on through the war, was soon faced by serious divisions between members about the resumption of international football. The British associations, operating within a victorious nation prominent in the conduct of war and peacemaking, adopted an unyielding position, as acknowledged by FIFA's official history: 'After a long, bloody war, wounds had not yet healed. Many delegates, particularly the English, did not yet want to accept yesterday's foes.'[12] Indeed, their strength of feeling in support of a ban on matches against the Central Empires (i.e. Austria, Germany, Hungary) was illustrated by not only its extension to include any association allowing teams to play those from the defeated states but also the threat to leave FIFA failing its adoption.

Obviously, the British position was largely a function of international political realities, but lack of archival evidence renders it impossible to assess how far the proposed ban resulted from government pressure. More likely, it proved the consequence of decisions made by sports administrators living through a post-war period dominated by patriotic attitudes forged through memories of a long and bloody war from which few families emerged without serious personal loss. In many respects, their approach might be interpreted as reflecting the application to international football of the sort of retributive slogans (e.g. 'Hang the Kaiser', 'Squeeze Germany 'til the pips squeak') articulated during the campaign for the British general election held in December 1918. Members of the football associations could be expected to share in the generally unsympathetic tone of British opinion towards Germany as well as to support efforts to contain future German power through relatively harsh peace terms.[13] To some extent, they were following the line mapped out by the IOC, whose recent meeting at Lausanne (April 1919) had effectively ensured the exclusion of the defeated states from the 1920 Olympics. Thus the IOC, though failing to infringe Olympic principles by specifically excluding the defeated states, had given the host country control over invitations, and naturally Belgium, having been occupied by German troops throughout the war, could hardly be expected to invite Germany. [14]

The basic British position was mapped out in June 1919, when the FA Council, prompted by a communication from the BOA about the 1920 Olympics, touched on future relations with the defeated powers.[15] As usual, the relevant minutes are brief, but clearly the FA did not relish the prospect of playing ex-enemy states when defending the Olympic football title: 'The

Football Association declined to have any association with the Central Powers'. Of course, at this time, when the Versailles peace treaties were awaiting signature and memories of war remained fresh, British feelings were 'strong against playing games, or joining with the Central Powers' (Pickford).[16] In September, the FA's Consultative Committee, guided by consultations with FIFA and the other home associations, announced that 'the Football Association could not entertain any association, official or unofficial, with the Central Empire's Associations'.[17] Moreover, unless the latter were excluded from membership, the FA threatened to withdraw from FIFA, possibly creating a rival 'Federation of National Football Associations'. Subsequent exchanges, reinforced by a meeting held on 15 November, secured the support of the other British associations, and this strict line provided the basis of the instructions for British delegates attending the Brussels Conference in December 1919.[18]

On 28–29 December 1919, delegates representing the FA and IFA – they acted also for the SFA and FAW – joined those from Belgium, France, Luxembourg, Netherlands and Switzerland at Brussels, where they were instrumental in securing agreement to ban relations with associations representing the 'Central Empires' or any association having relations therewith.[19] The Brussels Conference, making continued membership contingent on FIFA's adoption of the ban, widened the existing split, for already several members (i.e. Denmark, Finland, Netherlands, Norway, Spain, Sweden and Switzerland), meeting at Amsterdam on 29 November 1919, had objected to the proposal.[20] For this reason, the Dutch and Swiss representatives, stating that they lacked powers, dissented from the decision. The Brussels Conference was notified also of further opposition emanating from both Italian and Scandinavian members. In particular, the latter, having met recently at Gothenburg, upheld their right to play any country regardless of their wartime role.[21]

Despite being confronted by evidence of substantial support for a more conciliatory stance, the British football associations refused to change course.[22] Eventually, in April 1920 the FA, expressing disappointment with the position taken by other members, informed the FAW, IFA and SFA of its decision to leave FIFA because it was 'not prepared to be identified with any Federation'.[23] As usual, the other British associations followed suit in an episode emphasising yet again the FA's leadership role. Subsequently, the decisions adopted at Brussels were embodied in an agreement, dated 11 October 1920, covering only the four British associations, Belgium, France, Luxembourg and Spain.[24] Its practical impact was vividly illustrated in spring 1921, when Aberdeen, Dumbarton and Edinburgh Civil Service, though allowed to play close season games in Denmark and/or Norway, were refused permission by the SFA to arrange games in Sweden because of an international played against Austria in March 1921.[25]

Footballing practicalities soon exposed the unreality and unforeseen bureaucratic complications of a restriction imposed for non-sporting reasons. For example, in 1921 Rangers, having requested permission to play in Denmark, had to undertake a time-consuming set of enquiries to establish not only that no Danish team had played or planned to play the Central Powers but also that any post-war or forthcoming Danish opponent fulfilled this condition.[26] Similarly, the FA's plans to arrange an amateur international versus Norway were thwarted by the latter's inability to pledge not to play any team, like Sweden, which had played the Central Empires. As a result, in April 1921, the FA, influenced by further representations from the Scandinavian associations, proposed removal of the ban on fixtures against associations guilty of playing one of the Central Empires.[27] Despite indicating its willingness now to play Norway or tour Scandinavia, the FA failed to arrange any fixture.[28] Events moved on again, when 'altered circumstances', presumably defined to mean the further moderation of British hostility towards the defeated powers alongside a renewed dose of footballing realities, led the FA to propose the complete removal of the ban. Following agreement by the other home associations, British teams were allowed henceforth 'to play against any country, including the Central Empires', as evidenced within weeks when the SFA approved Aberdeen's request to play in Vienna in June 1922.[29] However, several years elapsed before England and Scotland played a full international against one of the Central Empires. Inevitably, the eventual removal of a prohibition, whose introduction prompted their withdrawal in 1920, was perceived generally to clear the way for British re-affiliation to FIFA, even if this step was delayed until 1924.[30] By contrast, in April 1923, the IOC, reaffirming the line taken during 1919–20, decided that it was still inappropriate to invite Germany to the 1924 Olympics.[31]

Despite members' protestations that it had 'nothing to do with politics and met only for the interests of sport' (Fischer, Hungary), FIFA's first post-war congress, held at Geneva in May 1923, was unable to avoid the game's political dimension.[32] Indeed, Bonnet (Switzerland) reminded fellow delegates that, despite British football's change of course, the continued refusal of some associations to play ex-enemy countries thwarted the game's contribution to a peaceful world. By way of response, Delaunay, denying French discrimination in a way implying guilt, reserved the right of members to select opponents 'not for political but only for sporting reasons'.[33] Clearly, the problem remained, as evidenced in 1926, when the Hungarian delegate renewed his complaints about the 'political tendencies' displayed by certain associations.[34]

A CHANGE OF COURSE IN BRITAIN TOWARDS SPORT?
THE 1920 OLYMPIC GAMES

The forthcoming 1920 Olympics served to trigger off not only moves by British football to ostracise the defeated states but also another chapter in discussions about the British government's attitude towards international sport; in fact, at one stage, a major change of course appeared imminent.

In October 1919 Baron Moncheur, the Belgian ambassador in London, invited the British government to be represented officially at the forthcoming 1920 Olympic Games to be held at Antwerp. For once, the Foreign Office proved surprisingly receptive, particularly as compared to the generally hostile position assumed towards such questions prior to 1914. Admittedly, it stressed the need for the agreement of the BOA, but unsurprisingly the latter, having made abortive efforts prior to 1914 to solicit greater governmental interest in the Olympic movement, was only too pleased to go along with the proposal, thereby allowing the British government to give an affirmative response to the Belgian embassy.[35] Nor soon afterwards did the Foreign Office – it advanced 'no objections on political grounds' – oppose the Prince of Wales' assumption of the BOA's presidency.[36] Once again, this enquiry arrived at a time when minutes, describing the proposal as both 'admirable' and likely to encourage 'our team', indicated that the Foreign Office was exhibiting an unusually sympathetic attitude towards international sport.[37]

Subsequently, in April 1920, the Belgian government, claiming that individual countries were represented already through the Olympic movement, withdrew its invitations for the presence of official delegations. This reversal was welcomed by the Foreign Office, which seized the opportunity to escape from what was now described as an 'embarrassing' commitment undertaken in response to 'injudicious', 'very rash', and 'inexcusable' decisions made the previous October without adequate consultations or reference to previous departmental practice.[38] Indeed, the error was adjudged sufficiently serious to render those responsible eligible for censure, except that the guilty person, Ernest Lebuman, no longer worked for the department. In this manner, it soon transpired that any apparent transformation in attitude represented less an actual switch of course but merely the consequence of bureaucratic shortcomings on the part of a clerk on temporary assignment. For a brief period, this administrative sloppiness continued, as demonstrated by the fact that the Foreign Office's letter to the BOA was sent mistakenly to the FA!

In 1920, the BOA's usual problems in financing British participation were aggravated by the manner in which post-war conditions hampered private subscriptions. Several government departments, including the Admiralty, Foreign Office, Ministry of Transport and War Office, were approached for help by the BOA through an appeal pamphlet prefaced with a quote from Lord Lee of Fareham, the Minister of Agriculture and Fisheries: 'this is a matter in which our national pride, to say nothing of our international credit, is deeply concerned'.[39] But the Foreign Office, reaffirming its pre-war line, was unmoved by such sentiments. In this vein, perhaps the most outspoken outburst emanated from Gerald Villiers in response to the local consul's proposal that the British community living in Belgium should be asked to raise £30,000 to facilitate participation at Antwerp: 'At the present moment, when ex-officers are starving in the streets of London, and men, women and children dying like flies of starvation and typhus in Central Europe, it seems to me somewhat anomalous to raise large sums of money to decide who can run fastest or jump farthest'.[40]

On 30 June 1920, the Foreign Office's 'negative' response to a parliamentary question about the provision of a government subsidy for the British team, though reflecting in part the impact of traditional Treasury parsimony and post-war fiscal pressures, derived also from a continued reluctance to recognise any policy grounds justifying public funding of international sport.[41] Even so, in July 1920, the Foreign Office agreed to a request from Noel-Baker, a member of the Olympic team, to enable British competitors obtain their visas by post rather than in person from the Belgian embassy. But, there were strict limits to its involvement, for the Foreign Office, having secured the embassy's approval for the procedure, was unwilling to do more than act as a kind of post office.[42] There was *no question* of the government meeting even the nominal visa fee of 1/3d (i.e. £0.07½p). Similarly, the government refused to follow the Belgian lead by arranging travel concessions for British competitors *en route* to Belgium.[43] One exception to this minimalist strategy occurred when the Foreign Office, notified about the planned despatch of warships by the French, Italian and other governments by way of support for the Olympic regatta events, responded favourably to requests from British diplomats in Belgium for a similar gesture. Subsequent inter-departmental exchanges, centred upon the propaganda advantages of showing the flag, culminated in eventual Admiralty agreement to send HMS *Cordelia*, even if actual fulfilment was foiled by yet another instance of administrative confusion about dates.[44]

Naturally, the 1920 Olympics represented a further focus of attention for the football associations, most notably the FA, which hoped for a successful defence of its Olympic title. As happened before the First World War, participation was left to the FA, whose FIFA-related problems failed to prevent British entry. Although the Central Empires were not invited to Antwerp, the BOA approached the FA, given the possibility that potential opponents might have played one or more of the defeated powers since the war. Surprisingly, the FA, denying that entry prejudiced its general stance towards the Central Empires, reassured the BOA that it would play any national team, even one representing an association which had played matches with the ex-enemy powers since the war![45] At the same time, the Olympics provided a good example of British sporting politics, for the FA, emphasising its independence, opted to make its own accommodation arrangements in Antwerp rather than to take up the BOA's offer of facilities.

At Antwerp, the British Olympic team, securing third place in the unofficial league table, performed creditably. But, unlike the 1908 and 1912 Olympiads, football was not a British success story in 1920, when a first round defeat (1-3) by Norway illuminated the game's rapid progress elsewhere, undermined traditional images of invincibility, and set the scene for further challenges to British footballing hegemony.[46] In addition, the defeat of England's amateurs, prompting an awareness of the ability of other countries to call on all registered players for the Olympics, made the FA increasingly sensitive about the case for a strict definition of amateurism, thereby preparing the ground for another controversy explaining the absence of British football teams from the 1924 and 1928 Olympics. In turn, between 1925 and 1939 the FA confined England's amateur internationals to the home counties.

BRITISH GOVERNMENTS AND INTERNATIONAL SPORT IN THE 1920s

For British governments, international sport remained still a peripheral, low priority sphere of activity. Following a brief indication of a change of course during 1919–20, traditional departmental attitudes, reaffirmed by expressions of concern about the resumption of international sport so soon after a lengthy and bloody conflict, soon reasserted themselves. As a result, officials, displaying little sympathy for or appreciation of international sport's political utility, adjudged it prudent to have as little to do with the BOA and other sporting bodies. Negative images predominated, so that major sports events were viewed as 'always the source of international friction'; thus, Eyre Crowe's dismissal of the Olympics as 'an international farce' was complemented by Villiers' complaint that 'the Games, far from promoting international amity, sowed discord and dissension'.[47] Similarly, the Reverend Laffan, a member of both the BOA and IOC, was dismissed contemptuously by Eyre Crowe as an 'idle parson'!

86

Observations, drafted within this negative mindset, overlooked the manner in which participation in the 1920 Olympics helped British relations with other countries, including its wartime ally, Belgium. Departmental myopia even resulted in the surprising conclusion that, despite the host government's reputed desire for British involvement, no permanent harm would be caused to relations with Belgium should the lack of public funding prevent participation.[48] Nor did the Foreign Office fully acknowledge the Olympics' propaganda value, such as in terms of either giving 'new' (e.g. Finland) and small (e.g. Belgium) states international visibility or illuminating recent imperial advances through the presence of teams from Australia, Canada, Egypt, India, New Zealand and South Africa.

In many respects, positions adopted in the 1920s provided the basic framework guiding the response of British governments to international sport during succeeding decades. Despite their overlapping nature, five themes can be identified for the sake of study, even if it is debatable whether collectively they represented a clear and coherent British policy towards international sport in general and international football in particular:

a) Regardless of their preferred position, British governments were made increasingly aware of, and affected by, what one embassy described as 'new developments' overseas consequent upon the growing politicisation of sport.

b) International sport acquired an acknowledged potential as a form of propaganda capable of transmitting to a global audience impressions of national power, leadership and values.

c) Sport offered a visible, seemingly non-political, way of initiating, developing and consolidating political, economic, cultural and other links with foreign countries.

d) Major international sporting events, most notably, the Olympics, continued to attract negative images on the part of British governments, which gave an unsympathetic, often critical, hearing to advocates of international sport as a force for multilateral cooperation.

e) British governments, albeit willing to perform a minor role, avoided substantial involvement in international sport, most notably any action adjudged liable to establish an unwelcome fiscal commitment or to infringe impressions regarding the separation of politics and sport in Britain.

(a) 'New developments' overseas

Throughout the decade, governmental indifference towards international sport was challenged repeatedly by reports from consular, diplomatic and military staff overseas establishing its policy priority and growing politicisation in, say, Belgium, Finland, France, Germany, Italy, the Netherlands or the Soviet Union.[49] Frequently, staff moved on to advocate a more active British approach on the subject. Unsurprisingly, the responses of policy-makers in London proved lukewarm and low-key, even if there occurred over time a kind of drip-feed effect resulting in occasional bursts of activity, most notably during 1928–29. By contrast, certain British local authorities, treating overseas practice as possibly worthy of emulation, demonstrated a more sympathetic approach, as evidenced during 1929–30 when a delegation from Liverpool visited Germany to review the impressive public provision of sports stadia and swimming baths.[50]

Naturally, reports revealed varying degrees of government intervention in sport elsewhere. Inevitably, the problematic course of Anglo-Soviet relations – diplomatic relations, having been disrupted by the 1917 Bolshevik Revolution, were not resumed until 1924, but were soon terminated again in 1927 until 1929 – made British governments and sports bodies, excepting left-wing organisations, like the British Workers' Sports Federation (BWSF), sensitive about the communist regime's seemingly overt exploitation of sport.[51] For instance, Rennie, writing from Helsinki in 1923 about 'new developments', warned the Foreign Office that 'it was hardly to be expected that this possible field for propaganda would escape the attention of international militant Communists'.[52] The fact that propaganda was frequently 'concealed under so praiseworthy a disguise' implied that international sporting events might have far-reaching, unforeseen, and unwelcome political implications. Subsequently, reports about the *Spartakiad* (February 1928), a winter sports festival held in Norway under the auspices of the Moscow-based Red Sport International (RSI), reinforced official perceptions about the instrumental role of sport.[53] The episode also confirmed departmental prejudices, as demonstrated by expressions of hope that the RSI's 'dreadful' left-wing influence would not spread further west.[54]

Writing in 1930, Alexander and Parker concluded that 'the whole German nation is striving towards a new ideal – physical fitness and beauty'.[55] The Nazi regime's notorious politicisation of sport renders it easy to gloss over the growing expertise in 'modern propaganda methods' (Arthur Willert), and particularly the already substantial level of intervention in sport undertaken in Weimar Germany by political, military, religious and social organisations: 'Every social caste and political party, from the conservative to the communist, devotes much time and attention to the athletic and sport phases of its organisation. Both proletarian and monarchist leaders insist that the athletic field is the best recruiting and training ground for their young members ... Partisan groups have learned that youth can be captured on the athletic field for a political party or religious organization.'[56] Unsurprisingly, there was also an international dimension arising from attempts to enhance the Weimar regime's credibility to domestic and external audiences through sporting success:

> Perhaps the test need never come again on the field of battle, but it is coming many times on the athletic field, and there will be many a sharp fight for Olympic laurels if German athletes continue to make the record gains they have achieved in the last few years ... The victory of a German champion in a foreign country assumes an importance of national scope and becomes an occasion in which it is the patriotic duty of every fellow countryman to rejoice.[57]

Victories on the sports field or in the swimming pool were perceived to offer, to quote one German-based American consul, 'the best propaganda the Reich can have', most notably, by securing 'more notice' elsewhere than the usual forms of diplomatic pressure.[58]

In this vein, one perennial focus for British policy-makers concerned the extent to which German sporting organisations possessed a revisionist role, given the manner in the country's post-war sporting ostracism encouraged links with both the *Reichswehr* and the campaign to revise the allegedly harsh and dictated 1919 peace treaties.[59] For instance, Hans Grimm's *Volk ohne Raum* (1926), acknowledging sport's role in promoting the health of both individuals and nations, pushed a revisionist message complaining about Germany's lack of space, and the fact that 'colonial land is as necessary for a people as a sports ground is for a school'.[60] During the late 1920s, the rapid growth of horse-riding clubs, known as *Reitervereine*, aroused the suspicions of the allies, who monitored the situation closely through the Inter-Allied Rhineland High Commission (IARHC). However, in 1927, Belgian and French calls for the *Reitervereine*'s dissolution were opposed by the British government in the light of embassy advice about the club's contribution to health and physical recreation as well as the German 'predilection for doing everything in organised bands and in distinctive clothing'.[61] The *Reitervereine*, having survived this initial attack, totalled some 2,500 clubs by 1930, when the imminent evacuation of the allied zone of occupation, in conjunction with further evidence (e.g. carbine practice) of German treaty infringements, prompted renewed Franco-Belgian pressure for a ban.

Once again, the British representative on the IARHC dissented, even to the extent of interpreting the imminent end of occupation as grounds for inaction, not renewed restrictions.[62] Neither the Foreign Office nor the War Office detected any breach warranting action against the 'innocent' equestrian societies; indeed, the War Office presented the *Reitervereine* as a 'natural' development akin to fox-hunting in Britain.[63] Captain Herbertson, writing from the IARHC at Wiesbaden, acknowledged the clubs' martial implications (e.g. for the cavalry), but 'doubted very much if this purpose were any more fulfilled than by the physical fitness attained by membership of football and athletics clubs, which assisted the early provision of infantry capable of taking the field'.[64] In April 1930, Herbertson, speaking to a French commissioner, offered an illuminating summary of British thinking:

> After the war the German Government had perceived that in the absence of conscription the only way to keep the manhood of Germany physically fit was by encouragement of every form of outdoor exercise and sport. As a result, every small town and village in Germany had its hockey, football and tennis ground. In a certain sense, the farsightedness of the German Government could be termed preparation for war, and the presence of riding clubs was merely one branch of this policy. No objection could be made to Germany's desire to improve her national physique, nor could objection be taken to the riding clubs.[65]

Another insight into official perceptions occurred during 1928–29, when the British government was drawn into exchanges about German involvement in the formation of an international rifle sports association and a forthcoming shooting contest at Berlin (February 1929). The fact of the British Society of Miniature Rifle Clubs' approach was of interest in itself, given its implicit recognition of the proposal's politico-military significance. Once again, neither the Foreign Office nor the War Office saw any reason to object in principle to the proposal, at least 'so long as the ostensible aims of the German clubs are purely sporting'.[66] Nevertheless, the society was reminded about the need to respect the disarmament clauses of the Versailles Treaty (e.g. article 177), most notably to ensure that any contest involving German competitors remained a purely civilian event. Moreover, the Foreign Office, drawing attention to the international association's apparent concentration on Britain, Denmark, Germany and Sweden, pressed for a broader membership extending to include Belgium and France, among other countries. Soon afterwards, in March 1929, the British embassy in Berlin forwarded evidence that German rifle clubs were infringing their 'purely sporting' status through links with the nationalist movement.[67] Even so, the Foreign Office, albeit exhibiting some disquiet, felt disinclined to change course and merely instructed the embassy to monitor future developments.[68]

In this manner, the lighter touch adopted by British governments towards German sporting developments, especially as compared to Belgium and France, reflected broader policy differences about the post-war treatment of Germany. The British emphasis upon appeasement prompted the adoption of not only a more moderate attitude, including the deferment of action against alleged infringements of the peace treaties, but also a more forthcoming policy accelerating the restoration of Germany to a position of equality in both the political and sporting senses.[69] There was also an economic dimension, for the growing popularity of rifle shooting as a sport benefited Anglo-German trade; thus, the export of British rifles and targets to Germany was matched by British reliance on German cartridges.[70]

(b) Transmitting national values to a wider audience

Successive Olympic Games reaffirmed the manner in which host governments, whether Belgium (1920), France (1924) or the Netherlands (1928), utilised the event in part as a platform for national projection directed at both domestic and foreign audiences. Nor were they alone in exploiting the Olympic movement. For instance, British representatives based at Helsinki drew the Foreign Office's attention to Finland's use of the Antwerp Olympics as a platform for asserting its recently acquired independent status.[71] Participation, and particularly Olympic medals, offered states visibility on the world stage alongside an effective focus for domestic opinion.

Within this framework, the Foreign Office, like the War Office, was apprised by British representatives overseas of the manner in which, *in their view*, international sport benefited from the participation of British teams in terms of not only raising overall standards but also projecting national values, like fair play and 'that spirit of sportsmanship, which is the tradition of their race' (King George V), to a wider audience.[72] Of course, the transmission of values is in effect a euphemism for propaganda, even if any impacts prove both long-term and unquantifiable. Nevertheless, reports from overseas representatives frequently presented sport as a 'very valuable field for British propaganda'.[73] For example, during the early 1920s, the British legation at the Hague claimed a noticeable improvement in Dutch attitudes towards Britain because of not only the government's more moderate strategy towards Germany, particularly as compared to France, but also international sport. In particular, the Diamond Sculls event at the 1921 Henley regatta was 'a factor producing good feeling' towards Britain.[74] In this case, the action of Jack Beresford, who slowed down when van Eycken, his Dutch opponent, encountered early difficulties, aroused widespread goodwill and favourable publicity for British sportsmanship on the part of 'all sections of the community', especially as the Dutch oarsman went on to victory. Reportedly, guests, attending a celebratory banquet held at Delft, where van Eycken attended university, sang the British national anthem and resolved to send Beresford a congratulatory telegram.[75]

More controversially, overseas representatives often pressed the broader benefits of British participation. For example, in 1922 the legation at The Hague pointed to the beneficial presence of a British fencing team at a six-nation military tournament held at Scheveningen. Despite finishing last, its presence was deemed extremely successful from the point of view of cultural propaganda. For Lieutenant-Colonel Temperley, the military attaché at The Hague, the team, conforming to the best traditions of British sport, raised 'the whole tone of the meeting': 'The superb sportsmanship and bearing of our team created a deep impression upon the other teams and the spectators'.[76] Temperley also mentioned the adverse reaction of the Dutch to the heavy-handed Germanophobia exhibited by two generals accompanying the French team. Whether or not Temperley assessed the situation correctly remains questionable – for instance, was he seeking to excuse the team's last place? – but his report was read with interest in London. For once, even the Foreign Office, glossing over the team's placing, reacted favourably to an international sporting occasion, which appeared to exert favourable impacts within and beyond the Netherlands. Even Villiers, whose dismissal of the 1920 Olympics as an arena for discord indicated his lack of enthusiasm for international sport, found the Scheveningen report 'pleasant reading'.[77]

(c) Demonstrating the tone of relations with other regimes or countries

Following the First World War, the ostracism of the defeated powers and the Soviet Union highlighted sport's role in offering a visible, seemingly non-political, way of demonstrating disapproval of any specific regime or country. Conversely, as Noel-Baker asserted regarding the 1920 Olympics, it could also help to 'reknit' international relations after a long period of conflict.[78] In this vein, British representatives serving abroad, pointing to its instrumental use for the initiation, development, and consolidation of political, economic and cultural links with the respective countries in which they were based, sought to convince policy-makers to treat sport more seriously. For example, in 1922, Lieutenant-Colonel J. Melvill, the British military attaché at Madrid, recommended the despatch of an army football team as a gesture of support for Spain during its Moroccan troubles, even if the damage caused to British prestige by recent footballing visitors, in conjunction with the rising standard of Spanish football, led him to point also to the need for a strong team: 'it will take our best team to beat them'.[79] Soon afterwards, Rennie, the British minister in Helsingfors, articulated the benefits accruing to Anglo-Finnish relations from football matches played between local teams and crews from visiting British ships.[80]

During the 1920s, Germany's improved international standing resulted from the Dawes Plan (1924), signature of the Locarno Treaty (December 1925), entry to the League of Nations (September 1926), and concessions on reparation and occupation arrangements. British governments, though still retaining doubts about German revisionism, were more inclined to force the pace than their Belgium and French counterparts. In turn, these politico-economic advances provided a supportive framework for German advances in other spheres. Inevitably, international sport, having played its part in post-war retribution, contributed to Germany's restoration to the comity of nations, such as through participation in the 1928 Olympics and international fixtures in athletics, football and other sports. From this perspective, the British government's responsibility for any specific sporting advance was more a matter of influencing the overall international context rather than of actually pressing any sports association towards a particular course of action. Nevertheless, the continued primacy of the German question in international politics, alongside Britain's leading role therein, gave an extra edge to Anglo-German sporting contacts.

The resulting transformation in Germany's status, though highlighted most vividly by the 1928 Olympics, was reflected by the increased frequency of Anglo-German sports contests. Thus, the appearance of German athletes at the 1926 AAA's championships held at Stamford Bridge, London, paved the way for further fixtures, such as in August 1927, when the Achilles club won a triangular match held at Berlin.[81] Similarly, British football teams, having initially confined themselves to military teams based in the occupied zone, moved on to play German clubs; for example, in May 1924, Arsenal's close season tour involved TSC 99 Düsseldorf, FC Preussen Berlin, Sp.Vgg. Fürth, Stuttgart Kickers, Cologne Sportklub 99, and a Hamburg XI.[82] Eventually, Scotland and England played full internationals in Germany in 1929 and 1930 respectively.

(d) International sport's friction potential

As happened prior to 1914, embassy and media reports about the Olympics exerted perhaps the principal impact upon official thinking about international sport, most notably its potential as a source of friction. In this sense, Temperley's Scheveningen report, though covering a non-Olympic event, constituted a rare example of good news.

During the 1920s, media coverage of the Olympics continued to focus on crowd problems and incidents in athletics, boxing and rugby football, among other sports.[83] Frequently, the media, refusing to confine itself to mere sports reporting, moved on to debate politics and sport. For example, in 1924, *The Times* correspondent, writing from Paris, argued that, if the Olympics were to become a force for international stability, other governments should follow the British model: 'all nations must learn equally to regard sport and politics as two separate and independent spheres'.[84] *The Times*, believing that the problem warranted a leading article entitled 'No More Olympic Games', claimed that the Olympic movement had failed the 'first real test under the new order': 'Miscellaneous turbulence, shameful disorder, storms of abuse, free fights, and the drowning of National Anthems of friendly nations by shouting and booing, are not conducive to an atmosphere of Olympic calm ... The peace of the world is too precious to justify any risk – however wild the idea may seem – of its being sacrificed on the altar of international sport.' Despite its apolitical message, this editorial implicitly acknowledged that international sport both reflected and affected international politics.

Of course, there were alternative viewpoints. Once again, Noel-Baker, currently Cassell Professor of International Relations at London University (1924–29), offered his usual insider's commentary upon the basis of his captaincy of the British track team for both the 1920 and 1924 Olympics. Prior to the Paris Olympics, he had already welcomed German participation in a recent French cycle race as beneficial to international relations.[85] Nor was his long-standing belief in international sport's positive qualities undermined by the 1924 Olympics. *The Times*' readers, among others, would have been surprised by his assertion that 'during this week in Paris, there has been no single incident that even the most malevolent of critics could magnify or distort': 'These games have shown once and for all that the Olympic atmosphere and Olympic traditions promote not ill will, but friendship, not international friction, but mutual respect and admiration'.[86] For Noel-Baker, the event was newsworthy for sporting reasons linked to, say, several record-breaking performances, the 'excellence of the American contingent', and the 'astonishing' progress of Finnish sport. Any 'problems' were dismissed as merely the product of the usual press distortions and exaggerations.[87]

Noel-Baker, pointing to his father's pre-1914 chairmanship of the Anglo-German Churches Council, took a close interest in Germany's post-war rehabilitation, and an appreciation of sport's 'broader political importance' led him to welcome its eventual return to the Olympics.[88] Naturally, he proved only too willing to illuminate the 'spirit of comradeship through sport', as symbolised in 1926 by the first post-war participation of German athletes in the AAA championships held at London.[89] Peltzer's 880 yards victory over Douglas Lowe, Britain's 800 metres olympic champion, suggested the country's sporting potential. More significantly, the spontaneous welcome and applause given German athletes encouraged Noel-Baker to interpret the event as part of the post-Locarno 'work of international reconciliation' healing the wounds of war: 'That spirit passes from the runners to the crowds, from the crowds to the nations whom they represent'.

Naturally, the 1928 Amsterdam Olympics, the largest yet, with over 3,000 competitors from 44 countries, including Germany, encouraged Noel-Baker to claim that 'the Olympic movement (with the help of the British Empire) had taken sport around the world'.[90] Significantly, Germany, re-entering the Olympics determined to reassert more than its sporting reputation, finished second to the USA in the unofficial league table, thereby accentuating Britain's fall to eleventh place. Once again, Noel-Baker, albeit conceding a few flash-points, recorded widespread evidence of the Olympic spirit: 'Who can doubt that such a movement as this for the promotion of International Sport, under the best possible conditions, is a movement that may do much for the promotion of that good understanding among the nations upon which peace depends?'.[91] British governments had yet to be convinced.

(e) A minimal sporting role

In 1922 Gerald Villiers, responding enthusiastically to Temperley's Scheveningen report, acknowledged the benefits of favourable publicity for which 'the British taxpayer has paid nothing'.[92] In this vein, a perennial theme centred on the reluctance of governments to allocate public funding for international sport, as demonstrated by their repeated unresponsiveness to the BOA's appeals for funding, travel concessions and other forms of financial help.[93] Moreover, their parsimonious approach, even respecting modest requests, contrasted vividly with the more receptive attitudes found elsewhere. For example, in July 1925 the British government refused to follow its French, German and Italian counterparts in sponsoring prizes and trophies for a Swiss international gymnastic tournament. Instead, the Foreign Office, playing down alleged propaganda advantages, merely used the occasion to reiterate criticisms of the way in which French governments seemed always to find money for everything except repayment of war debts.[94] Nor was it impressed by the British consulate's reference to a precedent dating back to 1891; indeed, officials, having consulted past files, took pleasure in denying the existence of any such precedent.

In many respects, this minor episode, centred on gymnastics sponsorship, epitomised a long-standing departmental obsession concerning the reluctance to allocate even modest sums of public money to sport for fear of creating an unwelcome and potentially costly precedent. However, ultimately, negative reactions followed on naturally from the fundamental desire of British governments to steer clear of international sport, excepting the performance of a minimal functional role.[95] In turn, the BOA, increasingly reconciling itself to the government's stance, acted in a manner reinforcing images of both its own apolitical character and the government's neutrality in sporting matters. Regarding the 1924 and 1928 Olympics, the Foreign Office confined itself largely to practical questions, such as securing permission for British military competitors travelling to Paris to pass through France and Belgium in uniform without passports, assisting British spectators, or supporting VIP ticket requests.[96] But, there was one exception in 1924, when departmental support for the Paris embassy's proposal for the attendance of Prince Henry at the Olympics proved more political than practical; thus, this 'highly desirable' move was adjudged likely to help Anglo-French relations at a time when the Ruhr occupation, among other developments, caused serious differences.[97]

CONCLUSION

Reports about the activities of, say, German riding and rifle clubs brought home yet again to members of the Foreign Office 'new developments' in continental Europe, where governments proved far from reticent about the use of sport as a tool of policy. Increasingly, events established that international sport did not take place in an international political vacuum. In many respects, the Foreign Office, having deferred action prior to 1914, was unprepared for the politicisation of sport increasingly characteristic of post-war Europe, thereby explaining the prevalence of pragmatic responses and the continued absence of any real policy overview.[98] Despite the relative lack of departmental time and thought devoted to sporting questions, reports about varying but growing levels of government intervention in sport elsewhere were read, commented upon, and attracted responses. In turn, critiques about the Olympics or the *Spartakiad* established the manner in which pre-existing personal and official prejudices were reaffirmed as part of the process of understanding current events. The extent to which this process encouraged a reappraisal of the preferred British non-interference approach remains uncertain, but clearly news of overseas developments fostered a continuing reappraisal of the relatively relaxed attitude adopted by British governments towards international sport.

NOTES

1. *The Times*, 25 Sept. 1919.
2. SFAMT, EFC, 27 Nov. 1918, minute 96, Acc.9017/15, 1918–19; *Annual Report 1918–1919* (SFA, 1919), p.3.
3. *Annual Report 1925–26* (FAW, 1926), p.1.
4. *The Times*, 2 Jan. 1929.
5. SFAMT, EFC, 19 Feb. 1919, minute 125, 2 April 1919, Acc.9017/15, 1918–19; *Annual Report 1919–20* (FAW, 1920), p.7; FA, Council, 11 June 1919, minute 11, 1914–20.
6. *Annual Report 1914–15* (FAW, 1915), p.2; *Annual Report 1919–20* (FAW: 1920), p.7.
7. PRO, memorandum, J.W. Headlam Morley, 28 Oct. 1919, FO371/4382/619.
8. PRO, minute, Eyre Crowe, 27 May 1920, FO371/3647/199995.
9. PRO, minute, Clifford J. Norton, 2 Jan. 1929, FO395/434/P4.
10. PRO, Lord Downham, BOA, to Sir S. Greville, Comptroller and Treasurer to Prince of Wales, 15 Nov. 1919, FO371/3647/162352; David B. Kanin, 'The Role of Sport in International Relations' (unpubl. PhD dissertation, Fletcher School of Law and Diplomacy, Tufts University, 1976), p.52.
11. Young, *Britain and the World*, pp.65–80. Resentment was still being expressed in German sporting quarters in the mid-1930s: CAC, L. Montefiore to Noel-Baker, 29 Nov. 1935, NBKR 6/54.
12. Furrer, Godoy and Blatter, p.70.
13. SFAMT, Council, 13 Aug. 1919, minute 87, 5 Nov. 1919, minute 147, Acc.9017/16, 1919–20; FAW, Emergency Committee, 3 July 1919, minute 50, 21 Nov. 1919, minute 121, 1915–22; Richard Holt, 'Interwar sport and interwar relations: some conclusions', in Arnaud and Riordan, p.212.
14. Guttmann, *The Olympics*, pp.37–8; Per Olof Holmäng, 'International sports organizations 1919–25: Sweden and the German question', *Int.J.Hist.Sport*, 9 (1992), 456–8.
15. FA, Council, 2 June 1919, minute 15, 1914–20; Holmäng, 458–60.
16. Pickford, *Recollections*, p.111; Green, pp.304–7.
17. FA, Consultative Committee, minute 10, 1 Sept. 1919, 1914–20.
18. IFA, Council, 26 Aug. , 4 Nov. 1919, 1909–24; FA, Emergency Committee, 3–15 Dec. 1919, minute 71, 1914–20.
19. *The Times*, 1, 13 Jan. 1920; *New York Times*, 9 Feb. 1920; SFAMT, EFC, 14 Jan. 1920, minute 6, Council, 11 Feb. 1920, minute 182, Acc.9017/16, 1919–20; IFA, Council, 13 Jan. 1920, 1909–24; FA, Consultative Committee, 12 Jan. 1920, minute 10, 1914–20.
20. FA, ISC, 12 Jan. 1920, 1919–21; SFAMT, EFC, 24 Feb. 1920, minute 1, Acc.9017/16, 1919–20.
21. SFAMT, Council, 11 Feb. 1920, minute 182, Acc.9017/16, 1919–20.
22. SFAMT, EFC, 14 Jan. 1920, minute 6, 17 March 1920, minute 2, Acc.9017/16, 1919–20.
23. FA, ISC, 23 April 1920, 1919–21; SFAMT, Office-Bearers Meeting, 19 May 1920, minute 35, Council, 11 Aug. 1920, minute 81, Acc.9017/17, 1920–21.

24. FA, ISC, 11 Oct. 1920, 1919–21; SFAMT, Council, 17 Nov. 1920, minute 142, Acc.9017/17, 1920–21; FAW, Emergency Committee, 16 Dec. 1920, minute 484, 1915–22.
25. SFAMT, EFC, 15 April 1921, minute 13, Acc.9017/17, 1920–21; Office-Bearers Meeting, 11 May 1921, minute 20, Acc.9017/18, 1921–22.
26. SFAMT, EFC, 22 March 1921, minute 3, Acc.9017/17, 1920–21.
27. SFAMT, EFC, 28 April 1921, minute 14, Acc.9017/17, 1920–21; Council, 7 Dec. 1921, minute 139, 1 Feb. 1922, minute 154, Acc.9017/18, 1921–22; FA, ISC, 22 April 1921, Council, 2 July 1921, minute 17, 1921–22.
28. FA, ISC, 3 Oct. 1921, 27 March 1922, 1919–22; ISC, 26 March 1923, 1922–23.
29. FA, ISC, 21 Nov. 1921, Council, 20 Feb. 1922, minute 8, 1921–22; SFAMT, Council, 1 Feb. 1922, minute 154, Council, 29 March 1922, minute 191, Acc.9017/18, 1921–22; *Annual Report 1921–22* (SFA, 1922), p.5; FAW, Consultative Committee, 26 May 1921, minute 693, Meeting of Office-Bearers, 19 Dec. 1921, minute 960, 1915–22.
30. FA, ISC, 10 March, 25 April 1924, 1923–24.
31. Paula Welch, 'Paris 1924' in J.E. Findling and K.D. Pelle (eds), *Historical Dictionary of the Modern Olympic Movement* (Greenwood Press, Westport, 1996), p.64.
32. FIFA, Minutes of 12th Congress, Geneva, 20–21 May 1923, pp.4–6.
33. Ibid., p.11. France played Hungary, Austria, and Germany in 1924, 1925 and 1931 respectively.
34. FIFA, Minutes of 15th Congress, Rome, 2–3 May 1926, pp.12–17.
35. PRO, Foreign Office to Baron Moncheur, 23 Oct. 1919, FO371/3647/142777.
36. PRO, L. Oliphant to Greville, 16 Dec. 1919, FO371/3647/162352.
37. PRO, minute, E. Lebuman, 13 Nov. 1919, FO371/3647/162352.
38. PRO, minute, Charles Tufton, 6 April 1920, FO371/3647/189349; minutes, Lord Hardinge, n.d. (May 1920), Marquess of Curzon, 29 May 1920, FO371/3647/199995.
39. Richard de Courcey Laffan, *The Olympic Games at Antwerp. VIIth Olympiad* (BOA, n.d.), frontispiece, quoted, Polley, *Foreign Office and International Sport*, pp.38–9.
40. PRO, minute, G. Villiers, 10 March 1920, FO371/3647/183849.
41. C.B. Harmsworth, Parliamentary Under-Secretary of State of Foreign Affairs, *Hansard (Commons)*, 5th ser. *CXXXI*, 464, 30 June 1920; PRO, minute, C. Howard Smith, 29 June 1920, FO371/3647/206914.
42. PRO, Foreign Office to Baker, 27 July 1920, FO371/3647/208247.
43. PRO, Tufton to Moncheur, 25 March 1920, FO371/3647/186747.
44. PRO, Admiralty to Under-Secretary of State, Foreign Office, 9 July 1920, FO371/3647/201804.
45. FA, ISC, 22 Dec. 1919, 2 Feb. 1920, 1919–21.
46. Capel-Kirby and Carter, p.85.
47. PRO, minute, Eyre Crowe, 7 April 1920, FO371/3647/189349; minutes, Tufton, Eyre Crowe, 10 May 1920, Villiers, 27 May 1920, FO371/3647/199995.
48. Ibid.
49. PRO, Annual report 1922, encl. Ernest Rennie, Helsingfors, to Foreign Office, 20 Jan. 1923, FO371/9297/N996; Sir Odo Russell, Holy See, to Sir Austen Chamberlain, 11 May 1928, FO371/12957/C3647.
50. For reports, including descriptions about modes of organisation and sport's ability to reach German youth, see: BL, Conservative Party archives, records of Conservative Research Department (CRD), CRD 1/60/8. One memorandum, dated 20 July 1934, noted that Liverpool's implementation of a German-inspired stadium complex was foiled by the depression: CRD 1/60/2 folio 10, pp.9–10. American consulates offered information on the construction of stadia, such as the one built in Cologne on the site

of old forts demolished as part of the Peace Treaties' disarmament provisions: USA, M. Taylor, American vice-consul in Cologne, to State Dept., 22 Sept. 1923, RG59, Box 9671, 862.4063/2.

51. Stephen Jones, 'The British Workers' Sports Federation: 1923–1935', in A. Krüger and J. Riordan (eds), *The Story of Worker Sport* (Human Kinetics, Leeds, 1996), pp.102–11.

52. PRO, Rennie to Foreign Office, 20 Jan. 1923, FO371/9297/N996.

53. PRO, F.O. Lindley, Oslo, to A. Chamberlain, 28 Feb. 1928, FO371/13299/N1339.

54. PRO, minutes, Laurence Collier and Leigh Smith, 8 March 1928, FO371/13299/N1339.

55. Thomas Alexander and Beryl Parker, *The New Education in the German Republic* (Williams & Norgate, London, 1930), pp.84–93; USA, M. Taylor, American vice-consul in Cologne, to State Dept., 22 Sept. 1923, RG59, Box 9671, 862.4063/2.

56. Alexander and Parker, p.91; J.G. Dixon, 'Physical education as moral education in Germany', in P. McIntosh (ed.), *Fair Play: ethics in sport and education* (Heinemann, London, 1979), pp.37–67; Woeltz, 306; PRO, Lord D'Abernon, Berlin, to Foreign Office, 12 May 1926, FO371/11280/C5624; minute, Arthur Willert, head of News Dept., 24 Aug. 1931, FO395/455/P2102.

57. Alexander and Parker, pp.93–4.

58. USA, H. Claiborne, US Consulate, Frankfurt am Main, to State Dept., 27 August 1927, RG59, Box 9671, 862.4063/4.

59. In May 1926, the Prussian authorities dissolved several sporting associations (e.g. *Werwolf Wiking, Sportverein Olympia)* suspected of planning a right-wing coup: see PRO, D'Abernon to A. Chamberlain, 12 May 1926, FO371/11280/C5624.

60. Quoted, Woeltz, 299.

61. PRO, British embassy, Berlin, June 1927, quoted, Capt. T. Herbertson, IARHC, Wiesbaden, to Arthur Henderson, 5 March 1930, FO371/14372/C1882.

62. PRO, Orme Sargent to Tyrrell, Paris, 7 April 1930, FO371/14372/C2601.

63. PRO, Orme Sargent to War Office, 21 March 1930, FO371/14372/C1882; Owen O'Malley, Foreign Office, to Herbertson, 31 March 1930, War Office to Foreign Office, 27 March 1930, FO371/14372/C2427; Orme Sargent to W. Tyrrell, Paris, 7 April 1930, FO371/14372/C2601.

64. PRO, Herbertson to Henderson, 5 March 1930, FO371/14372/C1882.

65. PRO, Herbertson to Henderson, 7 April 1930, FO371/14372/C2781.

66. PRO, minute, M.H. Huxley, 9 Jan. 1929, Orme Sargent to War Office, 12 Jan. 1929, FO371/13628C172; Orme Sargent to Lt.-Gen. Sir Alfred Codrington, 22 Jan. 1929, FO371/13628/C471.

67. PRO, Chancery, Berlin, to Central Dept., 13 March 1929, FO371/13628/C1969.

68. PRO, Chancery, Berlin, to Central Dept., 25 March 1929, FO371/13628/C2319.

69. Despite its close identification with the late 1930s, the term 'appeasement' was often employed by British ministers (e.g. by Austen Chamberlain, Foreign Secretary: 1924–29) as a description of policy during the 1920s. Young, *Britain and the World*, pp.88–96.

70. PRO, G. Lyall, Consul, Berlin, to British embassy, 25 Feb. 1929, encl. in British embassy, Berlin, to Central Department, 13 March 1929, FO371/13628/C1969.

71. PRO, Rennie, Helsingfors, to Foreign Office, 20 Jan. 1923, FO371/9297/N996.

72. Harold Abrahams (ed.), *The Official Report of the IXth Olympiad, Amsterdam 1928* (BOA, 1929), p.vii, quoted Polley, *Foreign Office and International Sport*, p.63.

73. PRO, Sir R. Graham, The Hague, to Lord Curzon, 12 July 1921, FO371/7087/W7671.

74. PRO, Sir Christopher Marling, The Hague, to Curzon, 23 Feb. 1922,

FO371/8360/W1911.
75. PRO, Graham to Lord Curzon, 12 July 1921, FO371/7087/W7671.
76. PRO, memorandum, Lt.-Col. A.C. Temperley, 23 May 1922, encl. Marling to Curzon, 29 May 1922, FO371/8360/W4530.
77. PRO, minute, Villiers, 1 June 1922, FO371/8360/W4530.
78. CAC, Noel-Baker to Bushnell, n.d. (7 Feb. 1951), NBKR 6/13/2; Noel-Baker to J. Rodda, 29 July 1974, NBKR 6/37/1.
79. PRO, Lt.-Col. J. Melvill to Director of Military Intelligence, War Office, 7 Jan. 1922, sent to Foreign Office, 7 Jan. 1922, FO371/8390/W294. Complaints made in 1921 are mentioned in the 1921 Foreign Office Index, but the relevant document (W5091/5091/41) has not been preserved.
80. PRO, Rennie to Foreign Office, 20 Jan. 1923, FO371/9297/N996.
81. *Westminster Gazette*, 30 Aug. 1927. The Achilles team included Lord Burghley.
82. Fred Ollier, *Arsenal: a complete record, 1886–1992* (Breedon, Derby, 1992), pp.407–8.
83. Peter J. Beck, 'Politics and the Olympics: the lesson of 1924', *History Today*, 30 (July 1980), 7–9.
84. *The Times*, 22 July 1924.
85. Noel-Baker, *The Olympic Games*, 559–63; Whittaker, p.27.
86. Noel-Baker, *Olympic Games retrospect*, 128–30. On Britain and the games, see Philip Baker, 'Britain and the Olympic Games', *Daily News*, 19 July 1924; Noel-Baker, 'Olympic Games Memories'.
87. See CAC, Noel-Baker to J. Rodda, 31 July 1974, NBKR 6/37/1. In 1982, Noel-Baker, who shared a room at the 1924 Olympics with Harold Abrahams, expressed irritation about the mix of fact and fiction characteristic of Hugh Hudson's 'Chariots of Fire' (1981) film about the event: CAC, Noel-Baker to Arthur Porritt, 24 May 1982, NBKR 6/54.
88. CAC, draft letter by P.J. Baker for 'Dear Sir', 3 April 1924, NBKR 6/22/1. Noel-Baker's father was also MP for East Finsbury.
89. Noel-Baker, 'International sport and international good understanding', 46–7.
90. Noel-Baker, in *IX Amsterdam 1928*, quoted Polley, 'Foreign Office and International Sport', p.62. See also P.J. Baker, 'The NUS and International Sport', *NUS Scene*, 3 April 1928.
91. CAC, Noel-Baker, 'Olympic Games Memories'. Note the text of his radio broadcast: CAC, 8 March 1927, NBKR 8/17/3.
92. PRO, minute, Villiers, 1 June 1922, FO371/8360/W4530.
93. Harmsworth, *Hansard (Commons) 5th Ser.* CXXXI, 464, 30 June 1920; PRO, minute, C. Howard Smith, 29 June 1920, FO371/3647/206914.
94. PRO, minute, Villiers, 20 July 1925, FO371/11103/W6868.
95. PRO, Foreign Office to C.G. Cazalet, 21 July 1925, FO371/11103/W6868.
96. PRO, Chancery, Paris, to Western Dept., 25 June 1924, 4 July 1924, FO371/10542/W5357; British embassy, Brussels, to Foreign Office, 11 July 1924, FO371/10542/W5907; W. Selby to Earl Granville, The Hague, 28 June 1928, FO370/285/L4100; minute, D.J. Scott, 22 June 1932, FO369/2295/K7486.
97. PRO, Marquess of Crewe, Paris, to Ramsay MacDonald, 4 April 1924, Eyre Crowe to Lord Stamfordham, 9 April 1924, FO371/10542/W2911; Young, *Britain and the World*, pp.76–8.
98. Polley, 'No business of ours?', 110.

5

'Football by Order of the Foreign Office'?
The 1920s

POST-WAR FOOTBALLING POLITICS

For British football, international politics was often taken to mean relations with other football associations and FIFA rather than with the British government. In this regard, the four British associations, which tended to act in unison within and outside the IFAB as far as international football was concerned, experienced a somewhat fluctuating post-war relationship with FIFA. Withdrawal in 1920 and re-entry in 1924 were followed by yet another departure in 1928. In this manner, the 1920s established football's ability to generate its own political pressures both within and between different sporting bodies, as evidenced by the competitive and cooperative features characteristic of relations between not only British football and FIFA but also clubs and football associations; the four home associations; and the latter and their foreign counterparts. Nor was British football unaffected by Olympic politics, as evidenced by exchanges between the football associations and the BOA as well as between FIFA and the IOC.

Internationally, the FA, helped by tradition, size and wealth, proved the most influential British association. Generally speaking, the FAW, IFA, and SFA, though not always in agreement, were prepared to accept, even welcome, its leadership concerning, say, FIFA membership, relations with other associations, participation in the Olympics and World Cup, and definitions of amateurism. Sooner or later, its lead was followed by its Irish, Scottish and Welsh counterparts, even if there occurred occasional sharp points of difference, as happened over wartime football in 1914 or the release of players by clubs for internationals. Conversely, there existed perennial resentment about being seen to follow the FA, as evidenced by the IFA's complaints articulated at the IFAB in June 1931: 'The Irish F.A. had followed the lead of England for many years. When England asked them to join the F.I.F.A. they did so; and when England wanted them to come out they did so. Again they rejoined at England's request, and again withdrew; and they might be asked to rejoin, for all he knew. They were getting suspicious of England.'[1]

In essence, the IFA's complaint proved a function of the Irish problem consequent upon partition. Henceforth, football in the Republic of Ireland came under the jurisdiction of a new body, the Football Association of Ireland (FAI), whose membership application, supported by the government's Ministry of Foreign Affairs, was accepted by FIFA in 1923 (see Table 2.1, Chapter 2).[2] However, the IFA, refusing to recognise its southern counterpart, adopted a confrontational line, most notably by upholding its traditional claim to select players from the whole of Ireland. The resulting controversy, as reflected also in disputes about nomenclature and the FAI's claim to a seat on the IFAB, preoccupied the British football associations, the IFAB, and FIFA throughout the inter-war period. Intensive efforts to resolve the problem proved abortive, and the issue, complicated by Irish politics, dragged on until the early 1950s, when the IFA, 'finally forced to recognise the political reality of a divided Ireland', dropped its claim to select players from the Republic.[3] In the meantime, pending agreement, the British associations, meeting at Liverpool in September 1925, decided against playing either the Republic of Ireland's national team or FAI-affiliated clubs.[4] As a result, the FAI, though always entering the Olympics and the World Cup (excepting 1930), experienced considerable difficulty in arranging fixtures; thus, only 11 internationals – these included Olympic matches – had been played by 1932![5] No match against England was played until 1946.

BRITISH FOOTBALL'S ISOLATIONISM

For much of the inter-war period, international fixtures against foreign teams continued to be arranged by British associations in a pragmatic manner, usually on either an individual basis or, more usually, as part of a close season tour. Eventually, during 1937–38 the FA adopted a longer-term strategy, but war soon foiled its implementation.

During the 1920s, international fixture lists offer revealing insights into the thinking of the British football associations, whose separatist histories and policies failed to prevent common traits, most notably their adoption of a somewhat myopic attitude treating an 'international match' as basically a home championship fixture. Foreign internationals were never accorded the same priority as the home international championship.[6] Inevitably, such isolationist thinking, based on a strong concept of Britishness, a belief in the fundamental superiority of British football, and the primacy of domestic league programmes, explained also their joint opposition to the Ministry of Labour's proposed relaxation of rules preventing the employment of alien players by British teams.[7]

102

Historically, the FA, often accepting a kind of missionary role, proved by far the most outgoing British association in terms of its willingness to face foreign opposition, but even its approach proved essentially reactive, that is, either accepting, deferring or rejecting foreign invitations, rather than proactive in the sense of taking the initiative in such matters. Only one foreign team (Belgium) played in England during the 1920s. For most of the decade, England's fixture list possessed a rather familiar appearance (see Table 2.3, Chapter 2), for, excepting one trip to Stockholm, England ventured no further than Antwerp, Brussels, Luxembourg or Paris. Invitations from Austria, Germany, Hungary, Italy, Spain, Switzerland as well as the Republic of Ireland were considered, but rejected until 1928–29, when the FA, having added Spain to a 1929 close season tour of Belgium and France, agreed to play Austria and Germany the following year.[8] By contrast, English amateur and league clubs became regular travellers to continental Europe and beyond – one contemporary account depicts West Ham as regular travellers 'promoting peace through the medium of the playing field' – but, despite numerous invitations, club visits to Latin America (e.g. Plymouth: 1924; Chelsea: 1929) or the dominions were rare.[9]

The other British associations possessed more limited geographical horizons. For example, it was not until 1929 that Scotland, having already played 140 'internationals', took on a non-British team (Table 2.3, Chapter 2). Paradoxically, in January 1917 the SFA, responding to New Year greetings from its French counterpart, welcomed the prospect of *re-establishing* (author's emphasis) fixtures after the end of war in spite of the fact that hitherto Scotland, albeit a member of FIFA, had never played France.[10] Moreover, for most of the next decade, the SFA continued to reject invitations for both full and amateur (e.g. France, Iceland, Norway) internationals.[11] It was only during 1928–29, when the FA began to look beyond north-western Europe for opponents, that the SFA showed signs of a change of position; thus, in 1928, a proposed close season tour to Austria, Czechoslovakia and Hungary attracted the normal refusal, but for the first time was rejected by majority, not the usual unanimous, decision.[12] One year later, the SFA, passing over invitations from Austria and Spain, agreed to undertake its first ever continental tour in May 1929 to the Netherlands, Norway and Germany. Although the SFA's *Annual Report* presented this change of course as a 'response to renewed invitations', it coincided with a change of key personnel, most notably, the advent in September 1928 of a new secretary, George Graham, in place of John K. M'Dowall, who had held the position since 1882.[13]

Scotland, boasting successive wins over England (March 1928: 5-1; April 1929: 1-0) and having won the 1928–29 home international championship with a series of impressive victories, was clearly the strongest British side at the time of commencing its first tour in May 1929. The tour opened with two victories in matches against Norway (Bergen: 7-3) and an Oslo XI (Oslo: 4-0) before crowds of 4,000 and 12,000 respectively.[14] The 24-person tour party – the latter, comprising only 14 players, was top-heavy with officials – then moved onto Berlin, where 42,000 spectators witnessed a 1-1 draw. A 2-0 win over the Netherlands in its final match, allowing Scotland to return home undefeated from its inaugural continental tour, prompted the SFA to express pleasure at the way in which the team 'upheld the prestige of Scottish football and the Association'.[15] More importantly, for Scotland, 'the continent was no longer an untried bogey'.[16]

As happened south of the border, Scottish clubs exhibited a far more outgoing attitude, and throughout the 1920s received the SFA's approval for foreign tours conducted within and beyond continental Europe, subject to conditions restricting fixtures to properly affiliated clubs. For example, in 1921, Aberdeen, Celtic, Dumbarton, and Rangers, among other applicants, received permission to make close season tours principally to Denmark, France and Norway, although Third Lanark, undertaking a 25-match tour of Canada and the USA, went even further afield.[17] Aberdeen, Hibernian, Motherwell, Queen's Park, 'and Third Lanark, among others, emerged as frequent travellers to an ever-wider range of countries, including Austria, Czechoslovakia, Germany, Iceland, the Netherlands, Poland, Portugal, South Africa, Spain and Switzerland. Transatlantic applications, as submitted by Third Lanark (Canada/USA: 1921; Argentina: 1923), Motherwell (Canada/USA: 1926; South America: 1928), Rangers (USA/Canada: 1928) and Kilmarnock (USA/Canada: 1930), remained less common. Eventually, in December 1929, the proliferation of applications led the SFA to adopt more formal procedures requiring prior sanction, the confirmation of fixtures at least one month before departure, the restriction of opponents to clubs (i.e. not representative teams) except in the colonies and dominions, the non-reinforcement of opposing teams, and the provision of a post-tour report.[18] Nor were these mere paper procedures, as evidenced the following year when Kilmarnock was severely censured for playing unscheduled matches on its North American tour.[19]

The FAW and IFA proved far less forthcoming respecting foreign internationals. However, the IFA, which failed to play a single full international against a non-British team during the whole inter-war period, arranged a three-match Norwegian tour (May 1922) as well as amateur internationals versus France (1921, 1928) and South Africa (1924).[20] Despite the IFA's resentment about France's cancellation of a return match scheduled for Easter 1922 – reportedly, this was prompted by French concern about 'the present political situation in Belfast and district' – another Irish team travelled to Paris in 1928, when France's 4-0 victory avenged its previous defeat (1-2).[21] Rejection of several invitations (e.g. 1925: Sweden; 1927: Spain) contributed to Wales' blank record for internationals versus foreign countries in the 1920s, excepting an amateur international played against a visiting South African side in 1924.[22] Nevertheless, the FAW approved club applications, principally to France and Scandinavia, although both Cardiff (1924: Berlin, Leipzig, Prague and Vienna) and Swansea (1927: Spain) received permission to go further afield.[23]

The football associations' archives offer minimal guidance regarding the actual reasons for individual decisions regarding invitations involving national sides, for minutes merely give outcomes, whether acceptance, deferral or rejection. However, it seems difficult to avoid acknowledging the way in which geographical and logistical considerations impacted upon the thinking of committee members and officials. For example, geography appears relevant when explaining why the FA, having ruled out Italy and Switzerland, confined England's 1927 close season tour to Belgium, France and Luxembourg.[24] Of course, for the IFA, even a match in nearby France proved an arduous and tiring undertaking, for its team, having travelled to Stranraer from Larne, still faced a lengthy rail/sea journey to Paris. Nor should one forget the lingering legacy of both the war and the post-1919 ban; thus, invitations from Austria, Germany and Hungary were rejected for most of the decade, even by the FA which had sent England teams to these countries prior to 1914.

For the smaller associations, further constraints arose from the difficulty of selecting a strong team, given their reliance on players employed outside their area of jurisdiction. Indeed, in 1928 the problem of securing the release of 'cross-channel' players (i.e. employed by clubs in England, Scotland, Wales) led the IFA to select only Irish-based players for the team to play France. The FAW faced similar obstacles, as revealed by its official history:

> The Welsh F.A. had so many ups and downs in early days that the rulers were unable to accept the financial and other responsibilities attached to overseas tours. Consequently, the Association could not copy the example of England in sending teams abroad until a few years after the First World War … The English F.A. had been sending teams to the British Dominions beyond the seas for a considerable period, and in addition the work of carrying the Soccer torch to Continental countries

to promote international friendships had proceeded steadily. Limited resources prevented the F.A. of Wales from taking a prominent part in these European missionary enterprises.[25]

Frequently, the British associations, albeit agonising for months, even years, about financial arrangements, player availability and tour schedules, displayed greater willingness to despatch representative (as opposed to full international) teams to Australia, Canada, New Zealand and South Africa. A long-standing missionary desire to promote the game in the face of the challenge from other sports reinforced traditional imperial sentiments, even if serious logistical problems meant that it took some time to process any invitation. For instance, the FA's 1925 Australian tour – this lasted from 4 April to 3 September – was under consideration for several years, especially as initial enquiries about player availability (e.g. to Oxford and Cambridge universities) revealed seemingly insurmountable difficulties.[26] Excepting the IFA, the other home associations also ventured forth to the empire during the inter-war years but far less regularly (see Table 5.1).[27] Both the SFA and FAW, having refused repeated invitations, agreed to send representative teams to Canada in 1927 and 1929 respectively, while the fact that over half of its tour party played for English clubs gave substance to the FAW's reluctance to accept such invitations.[28] In general, imperial tours proved a one-way process, but there were occasional exceptions, most notably, in 1924 when South Africa visited Britain; in fact, the amateur international played versus South Africa at Colwyn Bay represented Wales' first-ever game and victory (1-0) against a non-British team.

FA, FAW and SFA representative teams, though falling short of full international strength, returned from the dominions with seemingly impressive records in terms of both results and scores; for instance, the SFA team returned from Canada in 1927 having scored 111 goals and conceded 19 goals.[29] One distinctive feature of Australasian and South African tours concerned the arrangement of a series of cricket-type test matches. Unlike cricket, British teams normally experienced little difficulty in emerging with a clean sweep of test victories (Table 5.1), which reflected the relative weakness of the game in the dominions as much as British footballing primacy.

Foreign matches were seen by both the British football associations and club managements as serving a complex range of motives, such as to foster contacts with other associations and peoples, promote the spread of the national game, consolidate its status as the world game in the face of the challenge from other sports, establish the quality of British football, give players a working holiday, and take advantage of an extra out-of-season source of revenue. For clubs, the profit motive represented a significant

TABLE 5.1
BRITISH REPRESENTATIVE TEAM TOURS TO THE DOMINIONS, 1910–39

Place	No. of tests	Tests	
		Won	Lost
South Africa			
1910 (FA)	3	3	0
1920 (FA)	3	3	0
1929 (FA)	3	3	0
1939 (FA)	3	3	0
Australia			
1925 (FA)	5	5	0
1937 (FA)	3	1	2*
New Zealand			
1937 (FA)	3	3	0**
Canada			
1926 (FA)	0***		
1927 (SFA)	0		
1929 (FAW)	0***		
1931 (FA)	0***		
1935 (SFA)	0***		
1939 (SFA)	0***		

*   Combined with New Zealand.
**   Combined with Australia.
*** Combined with USA.

factor, but even individual football associations came to realise the fiscal potential of overseas tours by national sides. For example, during 1923–24 net receipts from England's internationals versus France and Sweden fell short of those from the Scotland game (£2,900), but still made a substantial contribution (i.e. £450 and £730 respectively) to the FA's international account (£9,461).[30] By 1929–30, when the two accounts were more in balance (general account: £17,170; international account: £16,283), the Scotland match remained predominant – net proceeds were £9,923 – with £1,490 and £782 being received from tour matches played at Madrid and Paris respectively.[31] Even 'missionary' tours to the dominions became increasingly dominated by financial considerations, whereby the British associations sought at least to cover their expenses.

Despite occasional media reports implying official intervention, British governments steered clear of the fixture-making process, even if they took an escalating interest in the manner in which certain matches had been or should be carried out by British teams. Nevertheless, government policy,

107

like media and public attitudes, was not entirely irrelevant in the sense of providing the broader policy framework within which the British football associations were able to follow their own inclinations, as evidenced by their fluctuating post-1919 contacts with the defeated powers or the continued lack of fixtures with the Soviet Union.

BRITISH FOOTBALL AND FIFA: GOING TO WAR OR PEACEFUL COEXISTENCE?

In 1924, Jules Rimet (FIFA president: 1921–54) expressed pleasure about the way in which the return of the four British football associations restored impressions of normalcy, while reaffirming FIFA's 'universal character'.[32] Following their withdrawal in 1920, FIFA sought to facilitate the return of the British associations by alleviating their unease about its often stated claim to 'control and develop the Sport as an International game'. Wall apprised FIFA of the central issue: 'Are we to assume that this control includes the control of the Laws of the Game and the individual Associations forming the Federation?'.[33] 'We have long established Laws of the Game and Rules of the Associations which are suitable to our wishes and requirements ... We do not desire to interfere with the action of other Associations who may not agree with all our Rules, nor do we desire that they should interfere with ours.'

A conference, held at London on 21 December 1923, was used by FIFA to reassure the British delegates, who recommended re-affiliation, subject to a series of conditions stressing non-interference in the internal management of and inter-relationships between the home associations as well as exemption of home internationals from FIFA's recently introduced levy (one per cent) on gate receipts.[34] Although British membership was resumed in 1924, key issues, most notably, FIFA's power *vis-à-vis* members and its definition of amateurism, remained unresolved, so Britain's return proved no more than a fleeting episode. Indeed, the 1924 FIFA Congress, responsible for approving the readmission of the British associations, was held at Paris alongside the Olympic Games, whose football tournament went ahead without any British team because of the allegedly shamateur status of certain entrants.[35] From the footballing point of view, the tournament, attracting another record entry, culminated in the triumph of Uruguay, whose 3-0 victory over Switzerland before some 40,000 spectators, capped a series of impressive results (7-0, 3-0, 5-1, 2-1).[36] More importantly, Uruguay's status as world amateur champions signalled Latin America's emergence as a major force in world football.

For British football, the Olympics were more significant because of the renewed emphasis upon the amateur principle. Professionalism had yet to spread far beyond Britain, and elsewhere divisions between amateur and professional footballers often proved somewhat blurred, with many 'amateurs' suspected of being 'very well paid'![37] The topic figured regularly on the agenda of FIFA, whose members gave varying answers to the central questions:

- Was amateur football characterised increasingly by a veiled professionalism in conflict with Olympic principles?
- Was the growing trend towards broken time payments (for loss of pay and other expenses) for footballers realistic, given the increased demands made for training and tours?
- Should amateurism be defined in a strict manner, and hence differentiated sharply from professionalism, as advocated by the British associations on the basis of past experience?
- Was professional football 'a good thing' or 'no longer sport' (M. Henninger, Switzerland)?[38]

The British associations occupied an increasingly isolated position, as shown in 1927 when the FIFA Congress, held at Helsingfors, paved the way for a FIFA–IOC agreement allowing football players receiving 'broken time payments' to participate in the 1928 Amsterdam Olympics. On 28 October 1927 the four British associations, meeting at Liverpool, described players receiving broken time payments as 'professionals', who 'cannot be admitted' to the 1928 Olympics.[39] This concession, albeit made reluctantly only for football by the IOC in the face of Dutch and FIFA pressure to prevent the exclusion of teams from countries allowing such payments, also angered the BOA, and on 12 November, it called a meeting – the FA, like other sporting bodies, was represented – to express strong disapproval about a concession adjudged detrimental to the Olympic principle.[40]

Naturally, the unyielding position of the British associations ruled out entry to the 1928 Olympic football tournament. More seriously, questions were raised yet again about British membership of FIFA, and on 17 February 1928, the four home associations, meeting at Sheffield, resolved on yet another British withdrawal, news of which hit Rimet 'like a thunderbolt'.[41] Although the actual breach was occasioned by their refusal to accept FIFA's definition of amateurism, the fundamental problem proved a function of the British football association's conservatism and insularity, as epitomised in their 'opinion that they should be free to conduct their affairs in the way their long experience has shown them to be desirable'.[42] Despite stressing a desire to maintain friendly and correct relations in future

109

with FIFA, their rationale for withdrawal reaffirmed a somewhat arrogant belief that they still knew best: 'the great majority of the Associations affiliated with La Federation Internationale de Football Association are of comparatively recent formation, and as a consequence cannot have the knowledge which only experience can bring'. From this perspective, broken time payments proved the last straw, as William Pickford told Hirschman: 'We have nothing against the FIFA, but our people here prefer to manage their own affairs in their own way, and not be entangled in too many regulations'.[43] Wall, describing FIFA as 'too unwieldy', echoed such views.[44]

Strong anxieties about FIFA's apparent encroachments upon British football in general and the rights of the IFAB in particular had been accentuated by a resolution adopted by the 1925 Prague FIFA Congress to the effect that it considered FIFA as 'the highest authority on all football matters, and that it cannot accept the interference or guidance of anybody else in such matters'.[45] Reservations about the draft proposal itself led the British associations to absent themselves from the Prague Congress, that is, within one year of their readmission.[46] Nevertheless, excepting the FAW, they were represented at an unofficial meeting, held at Brussels on 12–13 March 1926, when FIFA representatives made intensive efforts to bridge points of difference as well as to play down the implications of the Prague resolution.[47] British delegates confessed themselves satisfied with Rimet's assurances – significantly, the British associations, present for the first time since resuming membership in 1924, attended the 1926 FIFA Congress held at Rome – but the clash set a marker for future reference.[48] In the event, FIFA's conciliatory gestures proved abortive, and in May 1928 Rimet regretfully notified the FIFA Congress that British 'withdrawal was a fact'.[49] Also, he took the opportunity to assert how 'abnormal' it would be for the British associations to place themselves permanently 'outside universal football', an observation given added force by FIFA's ever-increasing membership (see Table 3.1, Chapter 3) and the fact that congress boasted yet another record attendance (i.e. 30 members).

For the next three years, exchanges, presented as being conducted 'for the advantage of the game', sought to find either a basis for British re-admission or, failing that, a *modus vivendi* allowing continued FIFA representation on the IFAB as well as matches between teams from the British and FIFA-affiliated associations. However, these contacts, failing to yield much by way of meaningful negotiation, merely revealed the seemingly unbridgeable gulf dividing the two sides; indeed, exchanges of correspondence largely concentrated on routine matters, like the lack of response to a previous proposal or difficulties over meeting dates.[50]

Unsurprisingly, the London conference, held on 19 November 1928 between the British associations and FIFA, did little more than outline points of difference.[51] Admittedly, delegates agreed on a mechanism (i.e. joint committee) to take the dispute forward, but, as Rodolphe Seeldrayers (a FIFA vice-president) informed the 1930 FIFA Congress, matters drifted; indeed, it proved difficult even to schedule meetings.[52] Nor was FIFA, which wanted to preserve its technical character dealing with the laws of the game, prepared to accept British proposals to use the IFAB as a forum for footballing politics.[53]

By contrast, private correspondence conducted between Hirschman and, say, Pickford, indicated the prevalence of cordial relations at the personal level, while enabling both sides to sound out alternative ways forward.[54] Even so, the British associations, though prepared to play their part in keeping the line open to FIFA, assumed that exchanges would not lead to re-entry; thus, Pickford, reviewing the prospects prior to the 1928 London conference, warned Hirschman: 'Don't expect too much', for 'at present membership of FIFA is not practical'.[55] Peaceful coexistence, not re-entry, proved the prime goal for the British associations, whose prime anxiety to preserve their authority vis-à-vis FIFA was complemented by a willingness to maintain friendly relations and fixtures with FIFA-affiliated associations. Certainly, they shrank from conflict, as stressed by Pickford: 'We must not go to war. War is always wrong, except in self-defence.'[56] For its own part, FIFA, albeit frequently irritated by the vacillations and apparent intransigence of the British associations as well as occasional bitter anti-FIFA outbursts, played along in the sense of hoping for the resumption of the 'old relations' with 'those who had founded and developed the game'.[57] Certainly, FIFA, pressed by members fearing the 'most disastrous consequences' for the game, tried to keep open the door to Britain, especially as Scandinavian members proved reluctant to enforce FIFA rules (i.e. those prohibiting matches with non-members) against British teams; for example, the Norwegian football association refused to stop Ayr's close season tour scheduled for summer 1928.[58]

Eventually, in June 1929, the British associations, coming together informally at the close of the scheduled IFAB meeting, drafted the 'Heads of Agreement', that is, a series of conditions setting out the basis on which they would consider rejoining FIFA. Basically, these points, replicating those specified for re-entry during 1923–24, were designed to protect them from FIFA interference in both their inter-relations and internal management as well as to continue the exemption of home internationals from FIFA's gate levy. But, FIFA, albeit prepared to modify its statutes to meet British demands, raised objections to certain conditions, most notably

111

the proposed IFAB-based disputes procedure, given its domination by the four British associations.[59] On 7 January 1931, the British associations, meeting at Liverpool, resolved not only to refuse any modification to their original demands but also to draw exchanges to a close on the basis of their future willingness to act with FIFA and play teams from FIFA-affiliated associations, 'but not again become Members of the Federation'.[60] This decision, having been ratified by individual associations, was communicated to FIFA.[61] A few months later, Rimet, emphasising the time given to the negotiations, informed the 1931 FIFA congress that 'much progress had not been made and no results obtained'.[62] Nevertheless, he expressed hopes of their eventual return in the wake of the forthcoming revision of FIFA's statutes designed to readjust the power balance between the federation and members in a way favoured by the British associations; thus, 'in the future the Federations should be a union of independent Associations governing themselves without any interference from the Federation'.[63]

Unlike the early 1920s, British withdrawal was not reversed within a few years, for the rift lasted until 1946–47. Nevertheless, the 1930s saw the development of what both Wall and Rous described as 'very cordial relations' between the British associations and FIFA, for whom the IFAB provided a regular formal point of contact. Unlike between 1920–23, FIFA retained IFAB membership after 1928. Moreover, the continuation of matches between British teams and FIFA members, in conjunction with the federation's repeated efforts to secure British entry to the World Cup, was complemented by the British associations' refusal to allow fixtures against non-members of FIFA. Regular exchanges of information were reinforced by representation at each other's matches.[64] Thus, FIFA was represented regularly at internationals played in Britain (e.g. 1932: England/Austria; 1933: Scotland/Austria; 1935: England/Germany), while representatives from the British associations attended FIFA's Central Europe versus Western Europe match played at Amsterdam in June 1937 as well as the 1938 World Cup final at Paris. Perhaps, the most vivid example of collaboration occurred in 1938, when FIFA agreed to field a team to celebrate the FA's 75th anniversary. In many respects, during the 1930s, the British associations, albeit reluctant to accept the perceived restraints of membership, acted almost as if they still belonged to FIFA. As McBride stated, 'if we are not with you in membership, we are with you in spirit. The British Associations will be most loyal.'[65] FIFA members seemed equally prepared to indulge this fiction; thus, their tolerance, even deference, offers a revealing insight into the esteem and 'exceptional position' (Seeldrayers) accorded to British football, as exemplified by Fischer's (Hungary) depiction of the British associations as 'our leaders and our advisers'.[66]

Today, British football's lengthy separation from FIFA, like non-entry to the World Cup, seem difficult to understand from the footballing point of view, even if the reasons for withdrawal and non-participation seemed to make sense at the time. Even so, hindsight has often prompted more critical perspectives; for instance, Rous observed that 'Our isolation was in no sense splendid. It was a matter for regret and a constant cause of difficulty.'[67] Macleod, writing at the time of the SFA's centenary, argued that 'In the long run we lost out because of these disputes ... The inheritance was ours to have and we gave it away.'[68]

PROTECTING BRITISH PRESTIGE THROUGH
INTERNATIONAL FOOTBALL

Public records are not very helpful in indicating whether FIFA debates about its powers or amateurism were followed by, let alone attracted the interest of, British governments. Perhaps, policy-makers, who proved dismissive of both the authority of the British football associations and the values of the professional game, might have adopted a more sympathetic attitude towards British football if they had followed developments more closely. For example, the football associations' attempts to prevent FIFA becoming too powerful would have struck a chord in official circles, given persistent British government efforts to resist the 1924 Geneva Protocol and other proposals intended to transform the recently founded League of Nations from an intergovernmental to a supranational organisation. For British governments, the League was viewed as 'us', its most powerful members, rather than 'it', an autonomous international actor.[69] Nor did officials, whose thinking was distorted by the professional game, give credit to the manner in which the British associations upheld a strict definition of amateurism, even at the cost of withdrawal from FIFA and non-participation in the 1924 and 1928 Olympic football tournaments. One decade later, the FA, claiming over one million amateur footballers, still felt able to claim that 'ours is really an amateur association with a mere platoon of professionals'.[70]

Officials, overlooking the predominantly amateur status of the FA's membership and the fact that rugby players also caused problems, were influenced principally by reports of unsavoury incidents involving British footballers engaged on overseas tours, especially as the British and foreign media tended to exaggerate their impact. Throughout the 1920s, the Foreign Office and, to a lesser extent, the War Office received a steady stream of complaints from British representatives based in continental Europe about the unsatisfactory performance and conduct of British footballers both on and off the field in, say, Portugal (1926), Denmark (1926) and Germany (1927, 1928).[71] Visiting British teams, attracting adverse media and official comment during their German tours, included Burnley, Cowdenbeath, and West Ham.[72]

One of the more illuminating episodes occurred in summer 1927, when Lord Kilmarnock (Earl of Erroll), the Inter-Allied Rhineland High Commissioner based at Coblenz, complained to the War Office about the poor standards of play and behaviour displayed by British footballers visiting the occupied zone (i.e. occupied by British troops to secure the disarmament clauses of the Versailles Treaty) in recent seasons.[73] 'Somewhat unrestrained' evening amusements, among other reasons, were adjudged to have exerted a deleterious impact upon results, and, even worse, had attracted adverse comment in the German press. An enclosure from W.P. Akerman, who was attached to the British Army on the Rhine (BAOR), recalled previous complaints about visiting football and rugby teams, while pointing to national images projected through sport: 'the average German, although he may dislike us, admires us in the field of sport and tries to take examples from us'.[74] Inevitably, the First World War, like the subsequent allied military occupation, gave an added political edge to any Anglo-German encounter, especially as the British football associations had assumed a prominent role in the initial post-war ostracism of German football.[75] Lord Kilmarnock, pointing to the underlying *political considerations,* urged that the matter be taken up with the footballing authorities: 'The significance is wider (than the occupied territory) and affects British prestige in general. The Germans have always looked up to us as leaders of sport, and now that they themselves are beginning to attach importance to prowess in games, the maintenance of our prestige is perhaps of even more interest than before.'[76]

The War Office, inclining to the view that the problem was a matter for sporting bodies, not the government, forwarded Kilmarnock's complaints to the Foreign Office, where Kenney summarised departmental practice: 'On previous occasions, when such complaints have been received it has been decided that nothing could be done, except to request H.M. representatives aboard to get in touch with managers of visiting teams and urge restraint'.[77] Initially, the Foreign Office, echoing the War Office line, held the FA and Rugby Football Union 'entirely responsible' for visiting clubs, since this stance pushed the blame elsewhere, excused the need for official action, and, perhaps most important of all, reaffirmed impressions about the separation of politics and sport in Britain. However, the News Department, fearing unwelcome implications for Britain's image and interests in the wider world, questioned the continued prudence of the usual

114

laissez-faire approach: 'the *evil* is apparently becoming a serious one'.[78] Although the prime focus was placed upon misbehaviour on and off the field, the Foreign Office was not entirely unconcerned about match results. Defeats to foreign teams were generally believed to reflect badly upon the quality of British football as well as foreign impressions of Britain, given the News Department's acceptance of the view that, for any sphere of activity – to quote Arthur Yencken – 'it is still true that success is by far the best form of propaganda'.[79] By implication, victory was adjudged important, particularly if a win was achieved with style and fair play. The worst scenario was to lose, while causing trouble on or off the field.

As a result, the Foreign Office's strong aversion to intervention, or to appear guilty thereof, was countered increasingly by an acceptance that 'it would however be well if something could be done to deal with it', since the problem was 'not confined to Germany alone'.[80] But what form should this 'something' take? By way of background, departmental exchanges sought to explain both the cause and nature of the problem. Officials failed to disguise elitist preferences: 'the basis of the trouble lies in the professionalisation, wh. has overtaken sporting effort in this country'.[81] Sporting bodies, it was asserted, did 'not seem to care so long as they can make money'. This rather harsh interpretation, inherited as part of the departmental memory and inculcated by the public school education common to most entrants to the Foreign Office, was deeply ingrained in official circles during the inter-war period.[82]

Despite believing that it possessed a reasonable understanding of both the causes and nature of the problem – this was adjudged 'of sufficient importance to be considered seriously enough' – the Foreign Office remained uncertain about the way forward: 'it is not easy however to know how best to deal with it'.[83] Officials considered a range of possibilities, including formal and/or informal contacts to remind football associations about the impact of international matches upon British interests and prestige; the exertion of varying forms of direct pressure on the associations respecting team composition, performance, conduct, and tour management; instructions to British representatives abroad to exercise a controlling, even restraining, influence upon visiting teams; advance notification by the football associations of overseas fixtures to enable meaningful inputs on the part of both the Foreign Office and British representatives abroad; and employment of the media to exploit the sensitivity of sporting bodies to public criticism. In certain cases, progress seemed problematic, given the fact that most international matches were played by national and club teams during the close season period, when players were tired and stale after a lengthy and demanding season. League priorities, including the uneasy relationship between the FA and Football League, meant that it was easier to identify the problem than to suggest a solution.

Moreover, the search for an appropriate response was handicapped by an appreciation of the political risks arising from intervention. The traditional independence of the footballing authorities, including the widely acknowledged separation of politics and sport in Britain, fostered a recognition on the part of the Foreign Office of the need to 'move cautiously and avoid specific complaints or we may be faced with … a most unwelcome press agitation'.[84] For this reason, the Foreign Office preferred hints and nudges to more direct action: 'Any sort of official action by us *vis-à-vis* the governing bodies would be sure to arouse resentment and might easily lead to a demand for chapter and verse. We shall however endeavour to find some way of conveying some sort of hint to the governing bodies in the hope that it will produce the desired result.'[85] In any case, the Foreign Office, albeit remaining fundamentally ignorant about their nature, composition, and rivalries, possessed a relatively unsympathetic opinion of the football associations, 'who are all tarred with the same brush', that is, their obsession with the profit motive.[86] Indeed, the presumed monetary preoccupation of professional footballers, in conjunction with their likely unresponsiveness to arguments linking sporting success and good conduct to favourable national images, was adjudged to limit the effectiveness of official pressure exerted on either governing bodies, clubs or players. In turn, lack of confidence in their ability to control clubs fostered the view that it was 'hopeless' to contact the football associations.

The Foreign Office, having considered the pros and cons of various options, inclined to a two-pronged strategy based largely on suggestions made during the course of private informal exchanges with the football associations complemented by media pressure, most notably, by priming one of the News Department's 'tame' journalists to highlight the damage caused to British prestige by 'incompetent or ill-balanced teams' playing overseas.[87] Foreign Office files, though reasonably full on the discussions about possible strategies, provide little guidance about action, except in the sense that the 1927 departmental index and subsequent file references hinted at the nature of the government's response.[88] For example, looking back in 1933, Orme Sargent recalled that, on one occasion, 'we asked a sporting correspondent to do his best to bring home to the football authority the importance of sending a good team'.[89] In this case, it is difficult to establish whether he was referring to actual events during 1927, for which archival evidence is absent, or is recalling some other episode, perhaps incorrectly. As a result, it is difficult to offer more specific coverage of the outcome, except in the sense that discussions provided the foundation for more substantial official action the following year.

'ORGANISING VICTORY' FOR FOOTBALL TEAMS VISITING CONTINENTAL EUROPE

During the late 1920s, reports about sport from British representatives abroad continued to make occasional inputs to the policy-making process. In fact, one contribution, which was leaked to the press and complicated by misreporting and entanglement with the German question, sparked off a media controversy suggesting the advent of a more interventionist approach towards football. In the event, the episode, failing to shake long-standing views about the separate worlds of politics and sport in Britain, soon subsided, even if the Foreign Office emerged from the affair determined to avoid any repetition of such an unwelcome and embarrassing public debate.

The controversy's partial focus on the German question renders it desirable to look back briefly to the mid-1920s, when Germany's restoration to the comity of nations was accompanied by rapid advances in the sphere of international sport, as outlined earlier. Significantly, within weeks of the formal signature of the Locarno Treaties (1 December 1925), the DFB sent the FA New Year's greetings for 1926![90] During the early 1920s, the eventual resumption of football matches between British and German sides, at least at club level, resulted in speculation about moving on to amateur and full internationals, given the reasonably positive response to British visitors. For example, in May 1928, one German commentator, responding to West Ham's visit to Munich, presented football as 'a sport that draws together and binds sportsmen into friendship. Through its medium may the people of your nation and mine learn to forget, and in forgetting the bitterness of the past may we come a big step nearer to building a happy future of friendship, peace and healthy rivalry.'[91] In January 1927, the SFA's rejection of a German invitation for an amateur international resulted from its reluctance to play non-British sides *per se* – during the 1920s, invitations from other countries (e.g. Belgium: 1926, 1927; France: 1922; Norway: 1922, 1923) were also rejected – rather than anti-German sentiments.[92] Significantly, the SFA's subsequent change of position regarding overseas fixtures led to Germany's inclusion on Scotland's inaugural continental tour in 1929.[93] Although Scotland had proved itself during 1928–29 as the strongest British footballing nation, historic reasons meant that an England fixture remained the DFB's priority objective.[94] However, in December 1928 the FA, citing 'existing commitments' (i.e. England's close season tour to Belgium,

France and Spain plus a FA tour to South Africa) rejected invitations to play Austria, Germany, Hungary and Norway in 1929, but apprised the DFB of its preparedness not only to visit Germany in May 1930 but also to arrange a return match in London.[95]

Despite this satisfactory outcome from the point of view of Anglo-German footballing relations, the initial stages became a matter for media controversy, for the question became entangled, at least in the minds of the British press, with what was in fact an entirely separate issue. In turn, succeeding exchanges offer the historian one of the best-documented episodes linking international politics with sport. The affair began in November 1928 when Thomas Preston, the British consul in Turin, submitted a report to London about Italian football. Recent Italian media speculation about a forthcoming England-Italy match, possibly at full international level, led Preston to contact the Foreign Office because of his assumption that the FA, like the British government, was relatively uninformed about not only the high standard of football in many parts of continental Europe but also its perceived extra-sporting significance. He emphasised the 'enormous' popular interest and the 'different mental angle' adopted by continental countries towards football: 'It might be argued that sport is sport and that it does not matter so much who wins; this is all very well with matches with our colonial teams, but not so with continental teams'.[96] For Italians, an international game was far more than a mere football match: 'it is an event of international importance'.

British football's difficulties with FIFA about the amateur/professional divide gave particular relevance to Preston's comment that, despite being classified as amateurs, leading footballers in Italy, like those in many other European countries, were seemingly able to live exclusively from their footballing earnings, which reportedly amounted to the equivalent of £900–£1,200 *per annum*.[97] If so, Italy's 'very well paid' amateurs were far better paid than their *professional* counterparts in England, where the maximum weekly wage was £6. Yet, 'amateur' status rendered all Italian players eligible for the Olympics, where third place in the 1928 Amsterdam Olympic football tournament – Italy lost 2-3 in the semi-finals to Uruguay, the eventual gold medallists – established the high quality of Italian football. Preston, stressing the expectation that 'we give them a good game', urged the Foreign Office to advise the FA that, if contemplating a fixture, it should make itself aware of Italy's 'first-class' quality. Only 'the strongest and best professional combination' should be fielded against Italy's 'amateurs'. England's amateur team would not be good enough. Significantly, Spain, which inflicted the first-ever defeat on England in a full international in 1929, lost 1-7 to Italy in the 1928 Olympics.

Unsurprisingly, within the Foreign Office, Preston's advice fostered the usual minutes in favour of staying on the sidelines of sport. In any case, officials, lacking information about England's international schedule or the FA's future plans, had no idea whether an Italian fixture was under consideration, since this represented an inevitable by-product of the way in which the British football associations operated independently of government. As a result, Preston's exhortations highlighted a fundamental difficulty concerning politics and football in Britain, that is, the fact that the Foreign Office learned of games only *after the event*, that is, when embassy, consular and press reports about problems reached London, and any damage to Britain's image and interests was complete. This sequence ruled out any opportunity for the Foreign Office to offer either advice on proposed fixtures or pre-tour briefings designed to limit the potential for trouble.

Capewell, echoing traditional lines of departmental thinking, proved pessimistic about the FA's ability to overcome the tension between footballing and national priorities: 'I don't suppose the Football Association will go out of their way to get the best possible team sent out'.[98] However, Stephen Gaselee, recalling occasional contacts on the topic with the footballing authorities in the past, saw no reason why Preston's information and advice should not be passed on to the FA, even if 'it is not quite a subject for a formal F.O. letter'.[99] As a result, following intra-departmental exchanges, on 7 December 1928, the Foreign Office despatched a 'semi-official' letter warning the FA about the improving quality of continental European football in general and Italian football in particular. Action was suggested, not demanded: 'Do you think that it would be possible to get a hint passed to the right quarter – the organisers of the England team – that it is worth their while to send a really strong side?'.[100] In addition, the Foreign Office, taking up Preston's point about the 'different mental angle' adopted towards international matches in continental countries and quoting from his communication, drew the FA's attention to the manner in which player misconduct abroad 'disgraced' not only themselves but also club and country.[101]

Despite hoping to remain immune from charges of intervening in sport for political purposes, the Foreign Office's behind-the-scenes moves were soon picked up by the press. On 31 December 1928, the *Daily Express* headlined the story in sensational terms: 'Football by order of the F.O.: English teams *must* win abroad'.[102] Frederick Wall, describing the note as a 'general request', was quoted as expressing astonishment about the government's sudden interest in the game: 'British sportsmen will be surprised to learn that the British Foreign Office is assisting in the task of organising victory for English football teams which visit the Continent'.

According to Wall:

> Far greater importance attaches to these fixtures than is generally
> supposed. It may surprise many to learn that the British Foreign Office
> takes a keen interest in the matter, and urges us to play only our first-
> class teams on the continent, as it regards it as essential that British
> prowess should be well maintained. In other words, our Continental
> friends respect us more when we lick them than when they lick us.[103]

The *Daily Express*, supporting the autonomy of British sport, criticised
what were described as the government's absurd, even childish, attempts to
link international fixtures with 'abstract considerations' of 'British
prowess'. Comment, pointed mistakenly towards an England-Germany
game, revealed also only a partial knowledge of the situation.

> The Foreign Office has done some queer things of late, but few as queer
> as its attempt to regulate 'soccer' football matches between England
> and Germany on a 1914–18 basis. The view of the Whitehall mandarins
> seems to be that unless our footballers were fairly certain of winning
> British prestige would receive an irreparable blow, the peace of Europe
> would be endangered, and Sir Austen Chamberlain would have to do
> whatever Herr Stresemann told him.[104]

Results of matches played between British and German teams were
deemed unimportant 'so long as the game was cleanly and stoutly played'.
'Could anything be sillier or more futile? It does not matter in the least
whether we beat the Germans at "Soccer" or are beaten by them. But it does
matter a great deal that we should be free and willing to meet them in
"friendly strifes and rivalries of peace".' Nor did the *Daily Express* confine
itself to footballing matters, for it moved on to articulate support for
improved Anglo-German relations in general, including the removal of the
'ridiculous' army of occupation.

By contrast, *The Times*, acknowledging the game's spread throughout
Europe in an editorial entitled 'Football and International Politics',
reminded readers about football's politicisation in many other countries:
'No appearance of, say, Frenchmen in Germany or of Czechs in Austria,
can be wholly devoid of political meaning to the onlookers. International
politics are very deeply rooted in the minds of the average European'.[105] By
implication, 'European' was defined to exclude Britons. *The Times* echoed
Preston's views about the 'different mental angle' of continental crowds,
who saw football teams as representing their country in far more than a
footballing sense. If British teams were repeatedly and decisively beaten by
continental opposition, *The Times* feared that people might assume that 'the

race which produced them must be decadent'. Therefore, to quote *The Scotsman*, another participant in this media controversy, British teams should be of 'best quality' and capable of giving a 'worthy display' whatever the circumstances.[106]

Naturally, the Anglo-German dimension ensured that this press flurry did not escape the attention of the media in Germany, where initial expressions of disappointment about the FA's rejection of the DFB's invitation soon gave way to expressions of pleasure about – to quote, Dr Georg Xandry, the DFB's Secretary – 'the greatest compliment' paid to the quality of German football by 'the world's greatest masters of football'.[107] Likewise, Otto Nerz, the DFB's chief coach, employed the opportunity to point to the good results secured in recent inter-club fixtures by 'German pupils' against 'the masters' of the game.[108] Nor did the affair escape the attention of other countries. Significantly, in the USA, a *New York Times* editorial, headlined 'Diplomats and football', noted the use of 'diplomatic' channels to transmit a 'friendly tip' to London about the strength of foreign football.[109] Speculation about the dangers of the game becoming a 'football of diplomats' – this was adjudged likely to arouse public indignation – prompted the editorial to question whether the British Foreign Office might be confusing the Football League with the League of Nations!

Within official circles, it was suspected that reports about government intervention were leaked to the press through the FA, most probably as the result of indiscretion on the part of Wall, and then exploited by the *Daily Express*' political editor. Even then, the latter, contrary to his claim of having checked the facts with the Foreign Office, exhibited only a garbled and incomplete version of events, since departmental contacts with the FA made no mention of either national prowess or an England-Germany fixture. As Norton complained, the *Daily Express*, having failed to discover the truth, 'unfairly twisted' the facts.[110] As a result, on 31 December 1928, the Foreign Office, seeking to correct the record as well as to safeguard its traditional reputation on sporting questions, issued a statement admitting contacts with the footballing authorities, including the despatch of a 'private' letter.[111] The Foreign Office, denying any reference to Germany in these exchanges, merely conceded the existence of a consular report about sport in 'a country other than Germany', but failed conspicuously to identify this 'country'. Subsequently, Wall, whose knighthood (1930) yielded perhaps an 'interesting' postscript, reinforced the government's line, when reaffirming that England's existing commitments ruled out a German fixture in 1929.[112] Finally, it is worth noting that, some two decades later, Thomas Preston, the initiating force in this controversy, participated in the Organising Group for the 1948 London Olympic Games.

CONCLUSION

During 1928–29 several British newspapers participated in this brief, albeit revealing, public debate about British football and politics. Even the *Berliner Tageblatt* and *New York Times* saw fit to express an opinion. Certainly, media interest, accentuating the episode's contemporary significance, proved extremely unwelcome to a somewhat embarrassed Foreign Office, which felt the need to issue a formal statement acknowledging that 'there seems to be some misunderstanding as to the nature of the interest which the Foreign Office takes in football matches'.[113]

During the 1920s, British governments lacked a clear and coherent approach, let alone a policy, towards sport in general and association football in particular. Nor was there any specific departmental or ministerial responsibility for the topic, except in the sense that departments were expected to deal with matters falling within their usual remit, as evidenced by the Foreign Office's lead role on international sport. However, the archives provide relatively few in-depth insights into departmental thinking; indeed, even allowing for the frequent non-preservation of seemingly relevant files, one is encouraged to believe that neither much time nor thought was devoted to the subject. Nevertheless, members of the Foreign Office received, read, digested, and responded to reports about sport sent by overseas representatives – witnessing developments elsewhere at first hand, they pressed the case for a more active and visible government role – even if the process often did little more than to reinforce existing viewpoints.

In general, the Foreign Office, inclining to a non-interference strategy, had to be pushed quite hard by overseas representatives to take action, and even harder to allocate public funding to international sport. Within this context, official attitudes, emerging within a framework defined largely by departmental precedent and personal prejudices strongly supportive of the amateur ethic, developed in a piecemeal, pragmatic manner. However, as the decade progressed, reports about the poor performances of many visiting British teams, the rising quality of football in continental Europe, and the enhanced politicisation of sport therein, forced officials to acknowledge the broader policy implications of international football, including its propaganda potential. Occasional episodes suggested an emerging appreciation of the fact that international football offered a low-cost, even no-cost, policy option capable of projecting favourable national images, reinforcing impressions of international normalcy, and promoting contacts with other countries. In particular, the Foreign Office increasingly acknowledged the merits of providing positive impressions of British football, as defined through results and/or player behaviour. Even so, for most of the decade, its role proved reactive, responding to problems reported by overseas representatives and the media. Rather than taking charge to ensure that forthcoming fixtures were undertaken in an appropriate and acceptable manner, the Foreign Office confined itself mainly to what might be called damage-limitation exercises. From this perspective, its communication sent to the FA in December 1928, though a relatively modest affair, proved significant in terms of qualifying the British government's usual position, for it involved the issue of a written warning about the 'first class' quality of Italian football, the need for the FA to take any forthcoming England-Italy fixture seriously, and the prudence of the despatch of the full international side in preference to an amateur eleven. Whether or not this more proactive approach would endure remained questionable.

Despite doubting the resolve and effectiveness of the football associations, the Foreign Office concluded that some good resulted from the *Daily Express* affair in terms of encouraging the FA to recognise international football's broader impact, most notably realising the 'harm' caused to national interests through the despatch of 'inferior (football) teams abroad'. Reportedly, Wall conceded that 'Obviously, it is right that Britain should be represented by her best players'.[114] But could the football associations resolve the key conundrum? Most complaints reaching London concerned club teams rather than national sides, as emphasised by Wall: 'Hitherto, our really representative sides have been successful on the Continent, but individual clubs who have toured Europe have not put up such good performances. We must be careful not to give our friends on the Continent a false impression of the quality of English football.'[115]

The fact that national sides prompted few anxieties might be interpreted in part as a function of the relative paucity of international fixtures against foreign teams, particularly as Ireland, Scotland and Wales proved reluctant travellers. Only England played foreign sides on a regular basis during the 1920s. Generally speaking, its performance in terms of results and player behaviour proved more than satisfactory (see Table 2.3, Chapter 2), even if during 1928–29 England inadvertently became the focus of the above-mentioned media controversy touching on Anglo-German relations. England was accustomed to overcoming continental opposition; indeed, its first-ever defeat in a full international by a non-British country did not occur until May 1929 on a close season tour, which started well with victories over France (4-1) and Belgium (5-1) but ended badly in Madrid with a surprise 3-4 reverse. This defeat, though failing to attract the level of media attention and national angst characterising England's loss to Hungary in 1953, prompted nonetheless a strong sense of shock at the way in which England's finest were 'well and truly whipped by Spain'.[116] Trevor Wignall, reporting from Madrid for the *Daily Express*, expressed typical British arrogance: 'I never thought I would live to see the day when eleven Spanish players humbled the might – more or less – of English soccer'.[117] To some extent, defeat was explained also in terms of a combination of factors, including three international matches in eight days, excessive travelling, the extreme heat of Madrid, and the fact that Spain was coached by Fred Pentland, a former Middlesbrough player.[118] The archives yield no evidence about Foreign Office thinking about this setback. Indeed, one speculates whether officials therein were even aware of the result of a football match played in a distant country during the more important cricket season, even if the interest of the British embassy in Madrid is mentioned in the literature.[119] No doubt England's defeat meant that the SFA, whose inaugural continental tour commenced soon afterwards, was even more pleased when Scotland returned undefeated. Although certain Scottish clubs (e.g. Cowdenbeath's 1928 German tour) attracted media criticism, the Foreign Office displayed even less interest in football outside of England, although it would have welcomed Scotland's successful inaugural overseas tour (May–June 1929), the Germany-Scotland fixture's contribution to Anglo-German relations, and the SFA's tightening up of formal procedures for clubs planning overseas fixtures (December 1929).[120]

Despite occasional challenges to traditional images, most notably, the *Daily Express*' 'Football by order of the Foreign Office' headline, British sport continued to be interpreted both within and outside Britain as largely separate from politics. Significantly, even Wall, though suspected of rocking the boat through a press leak, reaffirmed that the FA 'did not want to bring the Foreign Office into this matter'.[121] The *Berliner Tageblatt*, when commenting on the Foreign Office's statement issued on 31 December 1928, seemed happy to follow this line: 'The Foreign Office confirms the absurdity of the assumption that it regards it as its duty to give direct instructions to the British sports authorities. The Foreign Office has never been requested by the British Football Association to state its opinions with regard to matches between British and German teams, and has never taken any steps in this direction'.[122] However, the roots of the more active governmental role characteristic of the 1930s – even then, the level of intervention still fell far short of the international norm – can be traced back to the late 1920s, particularly given the departmental tendency to treat the late 1920s as a reference point. Moreover, unpleasant memories of the 1928–29 media debate strengthened official sensitivity about intervention in sport, or at least fostered an awareness of the need for any interference to be conducted in a clandestine manner.

The 1920s gave shape to what became one of British football's more enduring problems, that is, the club/country conflict. Sectional interests, most notably the clubs' quest for profit from close season tours and desire to give players an overseas break at the close of a hard season, took precedence. By contrast, flying the flag, and particularly enhancing the national interest through a good run of results achieved in a sporting manner, attracted low priority. Indeed, the manner in which star players boosted a tour's financial potential made clubs reluctant to release them for close season tours by national sides. As early as summer 1929, complaints were occasioned by close season tours involving Bolton (Spain), Huddersfield and Newcastle (Austria, Czechoslovakia, Hungary); indeed, the FA even convened a commission of inquiry regarding Newcastle's 'indifferent' display.[123] Subsequently, the Foreign Office's continued receipt of complaints about British clubs on tour throughout the 1930s revealed the limited impact of the pressure exerted hitherto by the government on the footballing authorities and of the latter on clubs.

NOTES

1. FA, Report on football in Ireland, n.d. (June 1931), 1931–32.
2. FIFA, Minutes of 12th Congress, Geneva, 20–21 May 1923, p.5.
3. IFA, Council, 7 Feb. 1922, 1909–24; International Committee, 25 Aug. 1931, 26 Jan. 1932, 2 March 1932, 5 April 1932, 26 April 1932, 1909–49; FIFA, Minutes of 26th Congress, London, 27–28 July 1948, pp.4–7; John Sugden and Alan Bairner, 'Northern Ireland: sport in a divided society', in Allison, *The Politics of Sport*, p.109; Moorhouse, 58–64; Green, pp.307–12; Peter Byrne, *Football Association of Ireland: 75 years* (Sportsworld, Dublin, 1996), pp.19–22, p.25.
4. IFA, Conference of Associations, 5 Sept. 1925, 1909–44; SFAMT, EFC, 23 Sept. 1925, minute 9, Acc.9017/22, 1925–26; FA, ISC, 3 July 1926, 1926–27. See also, J.T. Kelly, 'Football in the Free State', *Football World*, 4 (February 1939), 12.
5. FIFA, Minutes of 22nd. Congress, Rome, 24–5 May 1934, pp.6–7.
6. Author's interview with Sir Stanley Rous, 28 March 1980.
7. FA, F. Wall to C.A. Hirschman, 19 Oct. 1923, encl. Council, 22 Oct. 1923, 1923–24. On employing foreign players, see: ISC, 25 Aug. 1930, minute 11, 1930–31; FAW, Council, 10 Sept. 1930, minute 3330, 1928–31; Capel-Kirby and Carter, pp.121–2; Young, *History of British Football*, pp.182–3.
8. FA, ISC, 17 Dec.1923, 1923–24; ISC, 23 Feb. 1925, 1924–25; ISC, 10 Dec.1928, 1928–29.
9. Capel-Kirby and Carter, p.178; David Ransom, '1929 South American Tour', *Chelsea Historian*, 5 (Sept. 1996), 3, 13.
10. SFAMT, EFC, 17 Jan. 1917, minute 38, Acc.9017/13, 1916–17.
11. SFAMT, Council, 15 March 1922, minute 180, EFC, 14 April 1922, minute 117, Acc.9017/18, 1921–22.
12. SFAMT, EFC, 29 Feb. 1928, minute 87, Acc.9017/24, 1927–28; EFC, 6 Feb. 1929, minute 86, 20 Feb. 1929, minute 92, Acc.9017/25, 1928–29.
13. *Annual Report 1928–29* (SFA, 1929), p.4.

14. SFAMT, Continental Tour Officials, 6 Aug. 1929, Acc.9017/26, 1929–30. Oliver, who lists only one Norwegian game, gives a different score: Guy Oliver, *The Guinness Book of World Soccer: the history of the game in over 150 countries* (Guinness Publishing, Enfield, 1992), p.457.

15. *Annual Report 1929–30* (SFA, 1930), p.4.

16. Rod Macleod, *100 Years of the Scottish Football Association, 1873–1973* (Scottish Television, Glasgow, 1973), p.26.

17. See, for example: SFAMT, EFC, 13 Dec.1922, minute 55, Acc.9017/19, 1922–23; Bell, pp.136–8. SFA minutes, though informative on applications, are less forthcoming about whether proposed tours actually took place. Pending further research, it should not be assumed that all approved tours materialised; for instance, Ayr's proposed 1929 tour to Canada/USA failed to proceed.

18. SFAMT, EFC, 11 Dec.1929, minute 66, Acc.9017/26, 1929–30; Office-Bearers, 30 July 1930, minute 58, Acc.9017/27, 1930–31.

19. SFAMT, EFC, 30 Sept. 1930, minute 14, Acc.9017/27, 1930–31; Hugh Taylor, '*Go Fame': the story of Kilmarnock Football Club, 1869–1969* (n.d. [1969]), p.89, encl. Acc.9017/453.

20. IFA, 12 Feb. 1921, 25 March 1922, 1909–49.

21. IFA, Council, 7 March, 1 April, 6 June 1922, 1909–24; Council, 2 Nov. 1925, 10 Oct. 1927, 12 March 1928, 1909–44; International Committee, 28 Dec. 1927, 6 Feb. 1928, 1909–49; *Irish Football Association Ltd., Memorandum and Articles of Association, Laws of the Game, 1939–40* (IFA, Belfast, 1939), p.181.

22. FAW, Council, 12 March 1925, minute 2322, 1922–25; Council, 7 Sept. 1927, minute 2793, 1925–28.

23. FAW, Emergency Committee, 4 April 1924, minute 2002, 1922–25; Appeal Board, 29 April 1927, minute 2757, 1925–28.

24. FA, ISC, 28 March 1927, 1926–27.

25. *Football Association of Wales: 75th Anniversary 1876–1951* (FAW, Cardiff, 1951), pp.30–1.

26. FA, ISC, 1 July 1922, 1922–23; 14 Jan. 1924, minute 4, 1923–24.

27. IFA, Council, 26 Jan. 1926, 8 Oct. 1928, 1909–44.

28. SFAMT, Office-Bearers Meeting, 29 June 1921, minute 46, Acc.9017/23, 1921–22; *Annual Report 1928–29* (FAW, 1929), p.2; *FAW 75th Anniversary*, p.30. See also Peter Corrigan, *100 Years of Welsh Soccer: the official history of the Football Association of Wales* (Welsh Brewers Ltd., Cardiff: 1976), Chapter 5 (the book has no page nos.); *Football Association of Wales, Rules of the Association, Laws of the Game, Cup Rules, Season 1939–40* (FAW, 1939), pp.81–4.

29. SFAMT, Canada Tour Officials, 16 March 1927, Acc.9017/23, 1926–27; *Annual Report 1927–28* (SFA, 1928), p.5; W.G. Gallagher, 'Scotland Abroad', in A.H. Fabian and G. Green (eds), *Association Football, vol. 4* (Caxton, London, 1960), pp.107–8.

30. FA, Statement of Accounts 1923–24, 14 May 1924, 1924–25.

31. FA, Statement of Accounts 1929–30, 20 May 1930, 1930–31.

32. FIFA, Minutes of 13th Congress, Paris, 24–25 May 1924, pp.4–6; FA, Council, 2 June 1924, minute 10, 1924–25; SFAMT, Office-Bearers Meeting, 25 June 1924, minute 57, Acc.9017/21, 1924–25.

33. FA, Wall to Hirschman, 19 Oct. 1923, encl. Council, 22 Oct. 1923, minute 23, 1923–24.

34. Ibid.; SFAMT, EFC, 4 Jan. 1924, minute 63, Acc.9017/20, 1923–24; FIFA, Agenda of the 13th Congress, Paris, 8 May 1924, item 7; Green, pp.463–4.

35. FA, ISC, 1 Oct. 1923, Council, 22 Oct. 1923, minute 13, 1923–24.

36. Furrer, Godoy and Blatter, p.72.
37. PRO, T. Preston, British consul in Turin, to Consular Dept., 30 Nov. 1928, FO370/289/L7516.
38. FIFA, Minutes of 13th Congress, Paris, 24–25 May 1924, pp.8–10.
39. FA, Conference between UK Associations, Liverpool, 28 Oct. 1927, 1927–28.
40. FIFA, Lord Rochdale to Wall, 6 Oct. 1927, Correspondence Jeux Olympiques, 1912–32; FA, Meeting convened by BOA, 12 Nov. 1927, 1927–28.
41. FA, ISC, 12 Dec. 1927; Report of the Conference of UK Associations, 17 Feb. 1928, 1927–28; SFAMT, Council, 8 Feb. 1928, minute 185, Acc.9017/24, 1927–28; FIFA, Notes by Hirschman of London Conference, n.d. (Nov. 1928), Négociations avec les Associations Britanniques de Football, 1928–31 (hereafter Négociations 1928–31).
42. FA, Wall to Hirschman, n.d. (Feb. 1928), encl. Report of Conference of UK Associations, 17 Feb. 1928, 1927–28.
43. FIFA, W. Pickford to Hirschman, 25 Oct. 1928, 2 Nov. 1928, Wall to Hirschman, 20 Aug. 1928, Négociations 1928–31; Wall, pp.65–75, p.220; Pickford, *Recollections*, pp.111–15. Pickford was also a FIFA Vice-president, 1927–28.
44. Wall, p.244.
45. FA, J. Rimet to J. Clegg, 9 Nov. 1925, encl. Council, 14 Dec. 1925, 1925–26.
46. SFAMT, Office-Bearers Meeting, 6 May 1925, minute 17, EFC, 23 Sept. 1925, minute 9, Acc.9017/22, 1925–26.
47. FA Report of Conference at Brussels, 12–13 March 1926, 1925–26; SFAMT, EFC, 24 March 1926, minute 45, Acc.9017/22, 1925–26.
48. FIFA, Minutes of 14th Congress, Prague, 24–26 May 1925, p.8; Minutes of 15th Congress, Rome, 2–3 May 1926, p.4.
49. FIFA, Minutes of 17th Congress, Amsterdam, 25–26 May 1928, pp.8–10. In the case of the FAW, membership was cancelled because of alleged non-payment of debts covering its 1927–28 subscription and levy on the 1924 South Africa fixture. The 1927 Congress had already censured the FAW for non-payment of the levy.
50. For correspondence between FIFA and the British associations between 1928–31, see encl. in FIFA, Minutes of 20th Congress, Berlin, 22–23 May 1931, pp.17–27.
51. FIFA, Notes by Hirschman of London Conference, n.d. (Nov. 1928), Négociations 1928–31.
52. FIFA, Minutes of 19th Congress, Budapest, 6–7 June 1930, p.5.
53. FIFA, Hirschman to British football associations, 22 April 1930, Wall to Hirschman, 28 April 1930, Négociations 1928–31.
54. FIFA, Hirschman to Rimet, 29 Oct. 1928, Négociations 1928–31.
55. FIFA, Pickford to Hirschman, 25 Oct. 1928, Négociations 1928–31.
56. Ibid.
57. FIFA, Hirschman to Fischer, 10 Oct. 1928, Hirschman to Pickford, 22 Oct. 1928, Notes by Hirschman of London Conference, n.d. (Nov. 1928), Hirschman to British football associations, 23 Jan. 1929, Négociations 1928–31. For example, Ferguson (IFA) claimed that FIFA's circular about British withdrawal must have been written by 'a drunk'.
58. SFAMT, Office-Bearers Meeting, 16 May 1928, minute 30, Council, 23 May 1928, minute 43, 12 June 1928, minute 48, Acc.9017/25, 1928–29.
59. FIFA, Rimet to Hirschman, 3 March 1930, Hirschman to Rimet, 10 March 1930, Hirschman to British football associations, 24 Oct. 1930, Négociations 1928–31.
60. FIFA, Note of Conference of UK Associations, Liverpool, 7 Jan. 1931, Négociations 1928–31.
61. FAW, Council, 28 Jan. 1931, minute 3489, 1928–31; FIFA, C. Watson, IFA, 19 Jan. 1931, Wall to Hirschman, 21 Jan. 1931, G. Graham, SFA, to Hirschman, 22 Jan.

1931, T. Robbins, FAW to Hirschman, 10 Feb. 1931, Négociations 1928–31.

62. FIFA, Minutes of 20th Congress, Berlin, 22–23 May 1931, p.5.

63. Ibid., p.7, p.9; FIFA, Minutes of 21st Congress, Stockholm, 13–14 May 1932, pp.6–7; I. Schricker to Wall, 10 May 1932, 8 Feb. 1933, England correspondence, 1932–57.

64. FIFA, Wall to Schricker, 17 Feb. 1933, 11 Jan. 1934, S. Rous to Schricker, 22 Aug. 1934, England correspondence, 1932–57. For example, the FA, seeking to keep in touch with broader developments, subscribed to FIFA publications.

65. FIFA, Notes by Hirschman of London Conference, n.d. (Nov. 1928), Hirschman to British football associations, 23 Jan. 1929, Négociations 1928–31; Pickford, *Recollections*, pp.116–18; Rous, *Football Worlds*, p.92.

66. FIFA, Notes by Hirschman of London Conference, n.d. (Nov. 1928), Hirschman to British football associations, 23 Jan. 1929, Négociations 1928–31.

67. Quoted Bryon Butler, *The Official History of the Football Association* (Queen Anne Press, London, 1991), p.69; Glanville, *Soccer Nemesis*, p.23.

68. Macleod, p.31.

69. See Peter Beck, 'Was the League of Nations really a failure?: the "new diplomacy" in a period of appeasement', *History Teaching Review Yearbook of the Scottish Association of Teachers of History*, 9 (1995), 33.

70. William Pickford, 'How soccer is controlled', *The Listener*, 29 Sept. 1937, 657.

71. PRO, minute, L. Collier, 21 July 1927, Arthur Yencken to Earl of Erroll (Lord Kilmarnock), 12 Aug. 1927, FO395/423/P689. The Danish question is referred to in the 1926 Index of Foreign Office Correspondence (N468/468/15), but the papers have not been preserved in FO371/11749. Nor has document P473/472/150 (26) on Portugal been retained. See Capel-Kirby and Carter, pp.63–5.

72. *Daily Express*, 1 Jan. 1929.

73. PRO, Lord Kilmarnock, IARHC, Coblenz, to War Office, 6 July 1927, FO395/423/P689.

74. PRO, W.P. Akerman, BAOR, to Lt.-Col. R.S. Ryan, IARHC, 29 June 1927, encl. Kilmarnock to War Office, 6 July 1927, FO395/423/P689.

75. PRO, Rous, FA, to P. Noel-Baker, 15 Dec. 1945, FO371/46736/C10121.

76. PRO, Lord Kilmarnock to War Office, 6 July 1927, FO395/423/P689.

77. PRO, minute, R. Kenney, 14 July 1927, FO395/423/P689.

78. PRO, minutes, Kenney, 14 July 1927, Yencken, 18 July 1927, and Yencken to Erroll, 12 Aug. 1927, FO395/423/P689.

79. PRO, Yencken, memorandum on News Dept., 17 Sept. 1927, p.25, FO395/423/P995.

80. PRO, Yencken to Erroll, 12 Aug. 1927, FO395/423/P689.

81. PRO, minutes, J. Perowne, 20 July 1927, L. Collier, 21 July 1927, FO395/423/P689.

82. PRO, minute, Geoffrey Thompson, 24 Dec. 1929, FO395/434/P1900. Note subsequent British Council thinking: Lt.-Col. C. Bridge, Secretary-General, British Council, to R. Leeper, 12 July 1938, FO395/568/P2241.

83. PRO, Yencken to Erroll, 12 Aug. 1927, FO395/423/P689.

84. PRO, minutes, Yencken, 18 July 1927, Perowne, 20 July 1927, FO395/423/P689.

85. PRO, Yencken to Erroll, 12 Aug. 1927, FO395/423/P689.

86. PRO, minute, Collier, 21 July 1927, FO395/423/P689.

87. PRO, minutes, Ivone Kirkpatrick, 22 July 1927, Yencken, 29 Aug. 1927, FO395/423/P689; minute, Thompson, 24 Dec. 1929, FO395/434/P1900.

88. Hitherto, any resulting 'article' has proved untraceable in the archives or the press.

89. PRO, Orme Sargent to A.J. Dawe, Colonial Office, 5 April 1933, FO395/492/P673.

90. FA, DFB to FA 30 Dec. 1925, encl. Council, 11 Jan. 1926, minute 9, 1925–26.

91. Klipstein, quoted, Capel-Kirby and Carter, p.187.
92. SFAMT, Council, 26 Jan. 1927, minute 133, Acc.9017/23, 1926–27.
93. *Annual Report 1928–29* (SFA, 1929), p.4.
94. *Daily Express*, 31 Dec. 1928, 1 Jan. 1929.
95. FA, ISC, 10 Dec. 1928, 1928–29; ISC, 14 Oct. , 16 Dec. 1929, 1929–30; Wall to Dr Xandry, 14 Dec. 1928, quoted, *Daily Express*, 1 Jan. 1929;
96. PRO, Preston to Consular Department, 30 Nov. 1928, FO370/289/L7516.
97. Ibid.
98. PRO, minute, Henry Capewell, 6 Dec. 1928, FO370/289/L7516.
99. PRO, minutes, Gaselee, G. Ingrams, 6 Dec. 1928, FO370/289/L7516.
100. PRO, Gaselee to Wall, FA, 7 Dec. 1928, FO370/289/L7516.
101. PRO, minute, C.J. Norton, 2 Jan. 1929, FO395/434/P4; minute, Thompson, 24 Dec. 1928, FO395/434/P1900.
102. *Daily Express*, 31 Dec. 1928.
103. *Daily Express*, 1 Jan. 1929.
104. Ibid. Chamberlain and Stresemann were foreign ministers of Britain and Germany respectively.
105. *The Times*, 2 Jan. 1929.
106. *The Scotsman*, 1 Jan. 1929.
107. Quoted, *Daily Express*, 31 Dec. 1928, 1 Jan. 1929; *Berliner Tageblatt*, 3 Jan. 1929.
108. Quoted, *Daily Express*, 1 Jan. 1929.
109. *New York Times*, 2, 3 Jan. 1929.
110. PRO, minute, Norton, 2 Jan. 1929, FO395/434/P1900.
111. PRO, Foreign Office Statement, 31 Dec. 1928, FO395/434/P4; *Daily Express*, 1 Jan. 1929; *The Scotsman*, 1 Jan. 1929.
112. *Daily Express*, 1 Jan. 1929; Polley, 'Foreign Office and International Sport', p.68.
113. PRO, Foreign Office Statement, 31 Dec. 1928, FO395/434/P4.
114. PRO, minute, Norton, 2 Jan. 1929, FO395/434/P4.
115. Wall, quoted *Daily Express*, 1 Jan. 1929. Conversely, Arsenal, seeking to minimise the problem, advocated mid-week home internationals: SFAMT, EFC, 6 Nov. 1929, minute 49, Acc.9017/26, 1929–30. Even so, there were criticisms of the FA's selection procedures (e.g. by a large committee) and outcomes (e.g. too many players were tried in the 1920s): Niall Edworthy, *England: the official FA history* (Virgin, London, 1997), p.24.
116. *Daily Express*, 17 May 1929; *The Times*, 16 May 1929.
117. *Daily Express*, 10, 13, 17 May 1929.
118. Capel-Kirby and Carter, pp.95–6.
119. Murray, p.96.
120. SFAMT, EFC, 11 Dec. 1929, minute 66, Acc.9017/26, 1929–30; Office-Bearers, 30 July 1930, minute 58, Acc.9017/27, 1930–31.
121. Quoted, *Daily Express*, 1 Jan. 1929.
122. *Berliner Tageblatt*, 3 Jan. 1929.
123. Capel-Kirby and Carter, pp.63–5.

6

'"To Intervene in International Football, or Not to Intervene?", That is the Question': The Early 1930s

'SUPER CLASS' FOOTBALLING POWERS

Early in 1933 a Hungarian newspaper, *Pesti Naplo* (Budapest), published a ranking list of national football teams (Table 6.1).[1] England and Scotland, along with Austria and Italy, were placed in the 'super class' category, wherein Austria was assigned first place. This is not the appropriate place to assess the validity of a ranking scheme seemingly inspired by those employed for boxing and tennis.[2] Nor is there time to consider the resulting controversy concerning, say, the assignment of first place to a non-British team or the exclusion of the other home countries, especially as Wales went on to win both the 1932–33 and 1933–34 home international championships. To some extent, exclusion might be rationalised by their failure hitherto to play full internationals against non-British teams; in fact, Wales' first such match did not take place until later in 1933. The Republic of Ireland's omission seems more difficult to explain, since recent results against Belgium, Holland and Spain clearly warranted inclusion with at least a second class ranking. Finally, the listing's Eurocentrism, viewed alongside the results of the 1930 World Cup, emphasises the need to take full account of Latin American football.

However, what is relevant here is the way in which the proposal, implying both rising continental standards and a foreign demand for such rankings, challenged traditional perceptions of British footballing supremacy. Indeed, the first place assigned to Austria's 'wunderteam' showed that Britain's 'super class' status could no longer be taken for granted, even if, as will be seen, the actual results of games between the top four countries provided encouragement for those believing in England's continued claim to global footballing hegemony. One year later, the World Cup tournament offered perhaps a more meaningful guide, at least regarding global rankings, but even then the non-entry of British teams and Uruguay qualified its comprehensiveness.

TABLE 6.1
PESTI NAPLO'S EUROPEAN FOOTBALL RANKINGS, 1933

Super class		Second class	Third class
1.	Austria	Hungary	Yugoslavia
2.	Scotland	Switzerland	Romania
3.	England	Czechoslovakia	Norway
4.	Italy	Spain	Portugal
	5.	Holland/Germany	Poland
	6.	France	Bulgaria
	7.	Belgium/Sweden	Greece
		/Denmark	
		8. Finland	
		9. Turkey	
		10. Luxembourg	

Source: *Pesti Naplo* (Budapest, 1933), quoted Capel-Kirby and Carter, *The Mighty Kick*, p.81.

BRITAIN MOVES TWO STEPS FORWARD AND ONE STEP BACK ON EUROPE

FIFA, increasingly overriding what Rimet described as 'its initial European orientation', continued to grow in membership (see Table 3.1, Chapter 3) and influence. However, like many members, it failed to escape the impact of the 1929 economic depression; thus, it experienced a serious and sudden financial crisis – this prompted Hirschman's resignation – which was resolved largely with Dutch help.[3] The economic downturn, severely affecting gate receipts at home and abroad, exerted adverse impacts upon the income of both British clubs and the football associations, as recognised by the FA's 1931 Canadian tour report:

> It is regretted that owing to the continuance of industrial depression, and in a minor degree to weather conditions, there will be a serious financial loss to the Dominion F.A. as a result of the tour. The gate receipts of the 1926 tour were $52,444 as compared with $24,017 upon the present tour – a decrease of about £5,700. The expenses of the present tour will also exceed those of 1926.[4]

Of course, dominion tours, unlike those made elsewhere, were seldom conducted with the prime aim of making a profit, but this extract offers a vivid illustration of the conditions.

During the early 1930s, the FA displayed an ever more outgoing attitude towards international football (see Table 2.3, Chapter 2), but the extent of any change should not be exaggerated, given continuing non-membership of FIFA, non-entry to the World Cup, and a marked reluctance to venture beyond continental Europe. However, excepting 1932, when the FA rejected invitations from Austria, Belgium, Hungary and Switzerland, close season continental tours became the norm, while a foreign team was invited to England each December with effect from 1931.[5] The long-standing belief in the FA's responsibility for developing the game elsewhere and making contact with other associations – FIFA no longer provided a forum for this objective – was reinforced increasingly by an appreciation of the fiscal benefits of close season tours and one-off friendly internationals. Despite the depression, the FA's revenue for the international account (i.e. receipts from both home and foreign internationals) increasingly matched that for the general account (e.g. 1929–30: general account, £17,170; international account, £16,283).[6] Net receipts of, say, £719 or £2,143 from mid-season internationals played in London against Spain (December 1931) and Italy (December 1934) respectively paled against those for England-Scotland fixtures, but still compared favourably with those for internationals against the other home countries.[7]

Scotland, departing at last from its long-standing insular course, began to play continental sides in 1929 (see Table 2.3, Chapter 2). Following the success of its inaugural overseas tour, the SFA, faced with several invitations (e.g. Czechoslovakia, Hungary, Spain), repeated the experience the following year by arranging fixtures in France (Scotland won 2-0) and Belgium (subsequently cancelled by the Belgian football association) for May and September 1930 respectively.[8] One year later, the SFA, anxious to respond to several 'most pressing invitations' and tempted by the prospect of profit, agreed to visit Austria, Italy and Switzerland.[9] In the event, this 1931 close season tour proved less successful in terms of results – one victory over Switzerland (3-2) was outweighed by two heavy defeats by Austria (0-5) and Italy (0-3) – but yielded a modest profit (£491). Another visit to Paris in 1932 produced a 3-1 win, but marked the end of Scotland's close season continental tours until 1937. There seems no obvious reason for this five-year gap, whose impact was partially qualified by the fact that the SFA, seeking to follow the FA's example as well as to respond to pressure from clubs (e.g. Hearts, Rangers), brought Austria and Germany to Scotland in December 1933 and October 1936 respectively. Also, in 1935 the SFA sent a representative team to North America (eight matches in Canada, four in USA). Players returned 'exhausted', but the tour proved relatively successful, for a 100 per cent match record was supplemented by a profit of *circa* £1,000.[10] Moreover, the visit was adjudged to represent good propaganda for British football in North America, while enabling the SFA to make contact with Scottish exiles living across the Atlantic.[11] As usual, Scottish clubs proved more adventurous; for example, Motherwell, one of the more successful Scottish sides during these years (league champions in 1931–32, and always in the league's top three between 1926–27 and 1933–34) visited South Africa in both 1931 and 1934, when it lost only one of 31 games.[12] Significantly, during 1931–32, the SFA, seeking to protect the quality of the national side in the wake of difficulties in securing Celtic and Rangers' players for its May 1931 tour, made approval of club proposals conditional henceforth on the ability to 'call on its full strength', that is, players selected to represent Scotland should be released from either the whole or part of any club tour.[13]

Northern Ireland and Wales continued their more isolationist courses, even if in February 1933 the FAW, having sent a team to Canada in 1929, arranged Wales' first ever full international against a foreign country, that is, France, while sending an amateur side to Norway, where two games, including one international (won 2-1), were played.[14] Undefeated since December 1931, Wales travelled to the continent for the first time in May 1933. Wales, having been recently crowned home international champions (1932–33), only managed to draw (1-1) with France, even if the FAW welcomed the profit (£680), particularly given the manner in which the severe impact of depression in Wales meant that receipts from home internationals yielded the 'only income at our command'.[15] Even so, Wales, venturing no further than Paris yet again six years later, played only one more foreign team in the 1930s, despite several invitations (e.g. Austria, Belgium, Hungary).[16] More recently, Peter Corrigan, pointing to its successful run in the 1930s (home international champions: 1932–33, 1933–34, 1936–37, joint champions: 1938–39), claimed that if Wales had entered the World Cup and played more foreign sides, 'perhaps the Welsh tales of glory would have resounded with greater feats'.[17] Repeated refusals to enter the World Cup seem incomprehensible today, but Wales' inability to beat France, combined with its inexperience against foreign opposition, suggests that Corrigan's assertion should be kept in perspective.

As happened during the 1920s, Northern Ireland never played a single non-British team during the decade. Invitations were considered from time to time, but, as with a French offer in 1934, various obstacles, including the IFA's refusal to play on Sundays and player availability, impeded progress.[18] Nevertheless, the IFA approved foreign fixtures for clubs, such as for Belfast Celtic to play Fussball Klub Austria in December 1935. Meanwhile, the Republic of Ireland, denied the opportunity to play British teams, highlighted its northern rival's insular course through entry to the 1934 and 1938 World Cups and matches against a range of foreign teams, including Belgium, Germany, Hungary, Netherlands, Spain and Switzerland. Paradoxically, in 1936 Germany's visit to Dublin even brought the IFA into contact with the DFB, whose players and officials received hospitality *en route* to play the Republic of Ireland.[19]

A MORE SYSTEMATIC BRITISH APPROACH TOWARDS CULTURAL PROPAGANDA

The 'British Committee for Relations with Other Countries' met for the first time in December 1934, but was soon renamed the British Council with instructions 'to make the life and thought of the British peoples more widely known abroad; and to promote a mutual interchange of knowledge and ideas with other peoples'.[20] These moves for 'advertising our culture' reflected official acceptance of the case for a more active and effective cultural propaganda strategy intended to promote 'closer cultural relations between Great Britain and foreign countries'.[21] In particular, it was deemed 'of great importance that this country's affairs sh^d be presented to foreign peoples in the most favourable light possible' at a time 'when misunderstanding and misinterpretation of this country's position is likely to be frequent' because of propaganda conducted by other states.[22]

Despite figuring in Tallents' thinking, sport was not specifically mentioned in the Council's mission statement, whose elitist bias was shown by the focus on 'the study and use of the English language', assistance to overseas schools, and the provision of opportunities enabling other peoples to appreciate 'contemporary British work in literature, the fine arts, drama and music'.[23] This emphasis was reaffirmed by the Prince of Wales on 2 July 1935, when addressing the British Council's inaugural meeting: 'Of all the great powers this country is the last in the field in setting up a proper organisation to spread a knowledge and appreciation of its language, literature, art, science and education – that is to say, to let the world know what it owes to British achievements in these spheres'.[24] Nor did limited budgets (1935–36: £5,000) – Leeper complained from the start that the funding was 'far too little for our purpose' – facilitate efforts to extend the range of its work.[25] Nevertheless, during the late 1930s, sport did become part of its portfolio, thereby bringing the Council into contact with more popular forms of culture.

During the early 1930s, sport continued to be viewed in official circles as a peripheral government activity. For example, in February 1932, the lobbying efforts of Barnett Janner, MP for Whitechapel, made no impact upon the Treasury, which refused to waive visa fees for British competitors attending the World Union of Jewish Gymnasts and Sports Clubs.[26] But, there were occasional exceptions, most notably respecting the 1932 Los Angeles Olympics, which offered host and participating countries not only a major propaganda opportunity but also a welcome diversion from depression. Despite President Hoover's reputed lack of enthusiasm for sport, the USA government, issuing invitations through the State Department and missions abroad, identified itself closely with the event.[27] As usual, the British government took minimal interest in – to quote, Wentworth Gurney, the British consul in Los Angeles – 'these confounded games', but an anxiety to ensure that the consulate was not placed at a disadvantage in providing hospitality during this 'special occasion' led to the award of the princely sum of £50 for additional expenses![28] Even then, the lack of any official British involvement with the event prompted departmental concern in case auditors queried the rationale for the supplementary grant.[29]

Meanwhile, the Foreign Office continued to receive regular reports from overseas representatives in Europe, Latin America and Asia acknowledging closer links between politics and sport in a wide range of countries, most notably, in Germany, where Hitler's advent to power (January 1933) transformed the situation in the manner outlined in the next chapter. Reportedly, in Hungary, another defeated power seeking to revise the 1919 peace treaties, public funding, official hospitality, and ministerial attendance at football internationals established the 'deep interest in sport' of a government, which continually exposed sporting visitors 'to the view that Hungary is a much ill-treated land'.[30]

Japan proved a major source of anxiety for British policy-makers throughout the 1930s. Within this context, Sir Francis Lindley, who became British ambassador in Tokyo in 1931, recorded the rising popularity of Western sports in Japan since his previous diplomatic posting therein two decades earlier, before moving on to point to the potential of 'well-placed' cultural propaganda, including sport, to support more traditional diplomatic efforts to improve Anglo-Japanese relations.[31] Soon afterwards, the invasion of Manchuria (September 1931) vividly indicated the escalating extent of Japan's territorial ambitions alongside its willingness to ignore the peacekeeping efforts of the League of Nations. At the same time, Japan, leaving behind its generally disappointing Olympic record, used the world stage provided by the 1932 Olympics to demonstrate substantial sporting advances. At Los Angeles, Japan, whose team was second in size only to that of the USA, achieved unparalleled success, most notably in swimming, and a medals tally of seven golds, seven silvers and four bronzes provided a sound basis for its successful bid for the 1940 Olympics.[32]

Despite growing unease about Japan's threat to its Far Eastern and Pacific interests, the Manchurian crisis failed to lessen the British government's desire to keep open the line to Tokyo. Naturally, diplomatic measures received priority, but at first sight sport offered alternative possibilities. However, Lindley, pointing to baseball's popularity as proof of American influence, painted a 'gloomy sketch' of the current popularity of British sports, like cricket, which seemed in a 'less satisfactory condition' as compared to the 1900s.[33] Nor did there seem much British contact with Japanese football, whose national association (founded 1921) joined FIFA in May 1929.[34] Japan, whose opponents were confined largely to China, the Dutch East Indies and the Philippines, played relatively few internationals, most of which were lost.[35] In fact, its military gains in Manchuria during the early 1930s contrasted with the lack of success normally experienced by Japan on the football field against China; thus, prior to 1930, when the two teams drew 3-3 in Tokyo, all five games resulted in easy Chinese victories.[36] The Japanese Football Association, priding itself on its strict approach to amateurism, entered the 1936 Olympic Games, but a first round victory over Sweden was followed by 0-8 loss to Italy, the eventual gold medallists.[37]

From the footballing point of view, the distinctive feature of the Los Angeles Olympics was the game's absence from the schedule. At first sight, this might be excused by football's relative lack of appeal in the USA, but in reality it proved a matter of sporting politics. During 1927–28 FIFA-IOC disagreements appertaining to broken-time payments had been papered over to safeguard the football tournament at the 1928 Amsterdam Olympics, even if certain parties, most notably, the BOA and the British football associations, shared the IOC's strong reservations on the matter.[38] Subsequent negotiations failed to produce a *modus vivendi*, and eventually in April 1931, the IOC, meeting at Barcelona, excluded football from the 1932 programme.[39] Inevitably, the post-mortem conducted at FIFA's 1931 Congress was employed by delegates to articulate a range of concerns resulting from exclusion. Was football 'an inferior Olympic sport' (Dr Pelikan, Czechoslovakia)?[40] Was the game 'not pure enough' (Pelikan) for the Olympics because of the increasingly 'camouflaged' nature of most teams (Dr G. Randolph Manning, USA), or was Rimet correct to present football as both more honest and realistic than other sports in taking account of contemporary realities?[41] How would relations between the IOC and FIFA develop in the future? A revealing insight about sporting politics was offered by Pelikan: 'We must not go to the International Olympic

Committee; but if they want football in the programme, the International Olympic Committee must come to us'. By contrast, the United States Football Association (USFA), having welcomed the Los Angeles Games as providing the opportunity for a much needed 'demonstration', even showcase, for the game in the USA, complained about FIFA's 'lamentable' lack of effort to keep football in the Olympics.[42]

NO 'RED JERSEYS' ALLOWED IN BRITAIN

More recently, James Riordan commented light-heartedly on the possible consequences of the tsarist regime's failure to promote football as a recreation for the urban populace in pre-1917 Russia: 'The British diplomat Robert Bruce Lockhart, who was in Russia during World War 1 ... regarded the introduction of soccer ... in Russia as "an immense step forward in the social life of the Russian workers and, if it had been adopted rapidly for all mills, history might have been changed" '.[43] If soccer had been spread more quickly in Russia, Riordan suggested that 'the Whites might have won on the playing fields of Moscow what they lost in the Reading Room of the British Museum'! In the event, the Bolsheviks' success in 1917 posed several questions for the world of football, while limiting the opportunities for British footballers to take the field in Moscow.

Prior to 1930, the rare instances of political intervention in British sport occurred behind-the-scenes because of the government's reluctance to draw attention to any bridges built occasionally between the allegedly separate worlds of politics and sport. From this perspective, 1930 offered an exceptional case, which not only became the subject of parliamentary and media attention but also went beyond the usual official preoccupation with results and player behaviour. More significantly, given the more sympathetic attitude displayed towards the Soviet Union by the Labour Party as compared to its conservative counterpart, the resulting ban on the entry of a Soviet football team came at the time of a Labour government (1929–31) led by Ramsay MacDonald.

In many respects, this episode, though largely explicable in terms of the difficult Anglo-Soviet relationship, or rather, non-relationship, proved a function of the manner in which Soviet sport was integrated into the all-pervasive socialist state in order to suit its varying needs, whether these be 'health, hygiene, defence, patriotism, integration, productivity, international recognition, even nation-building'.[44] Inevitably, this 'functionalised' approach meant that physical culture and sport were far too important to be left to non-political bodies.[45] On 13 July 1925, the Communist Party, acknowledging their instrumental role in building 'socialism in one country', issued its first authoritative pronouncement on the subject.

> Physical culture must be considered not only from the standpoint of public health and physical education but should also be utilised as a means to rally the broad working masses around various Party, Government and trade union organisations through which the masses of workers and peasants are drawn into social and political life ... Physical culture must play an integral part in the general political and cultural training and education of the masses.[46]

'On the Tasks of the Party in Physical Culture' became – to quote James Riordan, the leading authority on Soviet sport – 'the definitive statement on the role of sport in Soviet society to which all subsequent policy statements were to refer'.[47] Another revealing insight – in 1930, this was even quoted in parliament by Samuel Clynes, the Home Secretary – was provided in December 1929 by a resolution adopted by Young Communist International: 'The Young Communist League organisations must pay particular attention to the sport unions of the working class youth. In these unions they must crystallise the basic kernel for strike pickets, proletarian self-defence, workers' fighting committees and Red Guards, people for work in the imperialist armies. They should utilise sport organisations for the military training of the working class youth.'[48] Soon afterwards, in April 1930, the establishment of the All-Union Physical Culture and Sports Council, possessing responsibility for operational direction, planning and funding, provided a *de facto* ministry of sport at the head of a hierarchical structure facilitating further changes.

For the Soviet Union, international sport was limited in terms of frequency, countries involved, and type of contact.[49] Inevitably, western domination of international sports organisations meant that Soviet non-membership of, say, FIFA and the IOC was an inevitable consequence of its difficult relationship with the major powers during the period following the 1917 Bolshevik Revolution. Despite occasional attempts to re-establish sporting contacts with neighbouring countries, most notably Finland and Sweden, for political, commercial and other reasons, there existed a self-imposed exclusion resulting in non-participation in 'bourgeois' events, like the Olympics, alongside a preference for alternative 'contacts between worker-athletes of the Soviet Union and other countries' intended to fortify 'the international workers' front'.[50]

Like all spheres of Soviet life, the nature, objectives and organisation of sport within socialist society attracted considerable domestic debate. The belief that, 'in play, as in work, collectivisation is stressed rather than individual excellence', led one leading faction, the *'Proletkultists'* (Proletarian Cultural and Educational Organisation), to view football as a harmful bourgeois influence, particularly as compared to the collectivist values fostered by labour gymnastics or the annual physical culture parades.[51] Despite the subsequent disbanding of 'bourgeois' clubs and/or their takeover by factory or trade union clubs, association football not only survived as the country's leading sport but also became a major instrument of soviet diplomacy.[52] Generally speaking, external footballing contacts operated within the framework of communist internationalism, as evidenced by occasional visits conducted by teams representing the BWSF and other left-wing organisations or foreign tours by Soviet factory sides to Estonia, Finland, Germany, Norway and Sweden in 1923. Non-membership of FIFA, emphasising Soviet isolation from the world of international football, explained the virtual absence of international matches. Only two fixtures are formally recorded – two fixtures against Turkey during 1924–25, with both resulting in Soviet victories (November 1924: 3-0, Moscow; May 1925: 2-1, Angora) – but other 'internationals' were rumoured to have taken place.[53]

British governments kept a watching brief over sporting developments in the USSR, but attitudes were determined as much by speculation and anti-communist prejudice as hard evidence.[54] Lack of regular contacts meant that international bodies, like FIFA, and individual football associations, excepting perhaps that based in Turkey, possessed minimal knowledge about the organisation and standard of Soviet football, even if occasional visits by Hirschman, the FIFA Secretary, among others, provided evidence of progress.[55] Even George Sinfield, looking back from the 1950s to a period when he proved an active communist force in the BWSF, acknowledged a lack of information about, say, Soviet footballing standards in the 1920s, excepting the occasional insights provided by British visitors to the country.[56]

In 1927, the British government became involved in a proposed BWSF football tour to the Soviet Union. Unsurprisingly, exchanges between the Foreign, Home and Passport Offices, pointing to the BWSF's communist affiliations, focused on the tour's propaganda implications.[57] In the event, the Passport Office, advised by the Foreign and Home Offices as well as Scotland Yard, issued passports for the whole party, excepting two 'known communists'. Apparently, the Soviet authorities, selecting a strong eleven, expected any British team to be of high quality, as suggested when the BWSF side, watched by a crowd of 35,000, was crushed in the opening match.[58] Even so, Sinfield, implying that the England national team could be expected to win with ease, adjudged the Soviet team as only roughly equivalent to 'senior amateur standard' in Britain. More importantly, to quote Stephen Jones, 'the tour gave ordinary workers – railwaymen, woodworkers, and furniture workers – as *Young Worker* (27 August 1927) wrote, "the opportunity to see the Workers' State for themselves" '.[59]

The British government intervened more decisively and publicly in another Anglo-Soviet footballing question in 1930, when the BWSF invited a Soviet factory football team to participate in Red Sports Day in Britain. Despite their departure from FIFA in 1928, the British associations continued to refuse permission for fixtures against teams from non-FIFA members, like the USSR. However, the FA, lacking jurisdiction over the BWSF, was powerless in this case, even if affiliated clubs were apparently instructed to refuse permission for grounds to be used for any tour games.[60] The BWSF's application was dealt with by the British government primarily as a political question: given the recent troubled history of the Anglo-Soviet relationship, should Soviet footballers be given permission to enter Britain? Anglo-Soviet links, having been disrupted by the 1917 revolution, were resumed in 1924, only to be broken off again in May 1927 until December 1929. Subsequently, bilateral exchanges were strictly controlled by the British government, which was issuing entry visas in 1930 only to Soviet citizens involved in activities adjudged likely to benefit British trade in the wake of the recently concluded Anglo-Soviet Commercial Agreement (April 1930).[61]

Naturally, the Home Office took the lead in visa questions, but the destruction of relevant files means that relatively little documentary evidence remains for this episode.[62] However, in 1935 one official, looking back with the benefit of access to relevant documents, recalled the Home Office's conclusion that the visit would do more harm than good, and was deemed unlikely to benefit either sport or trade: 'the main object of the proposed visit of the Russian football team was propaganda, not sport'.[63] Foreign Office files, informed by inter-departmental exchanges, recorded Home Office fears about serious disorder at match locations, given the context of depression, worsening unemployment, and the involvement of the British Communist Party. Reports of communist-inspired propaganda (e.g. waving the Red Flag, singing the International) and trouble during the course of a Soviet team's visit to France made the Home Office 'apprehensive of all sorts of similar disturbances here'.[64]

Inevitably, the Foreign Office, having sought to keep the politics of international sport out of the public arena, expressed unease about the tabling of a parliamentary question on the proposed visit; indeed, one official exclaimed, 'What a question!'.[65] On 1 May, Samuel Clynes, responding as Home Secretary, justified the refusal of visas in terms of the overt politicisation of Soviet sport – he made the point by quoting the resolution adopted by Young Communist International mentioned above – alongside BWSF affiliation to the sports section of *Communist International*: 'In the absence of any evidence that the object of the proposed tour was for the purpose of genuine sport, I could not see my way to accede to the application'.[66] By implication, the Home Office might have accepted a visit intended for purely sporting reasons, but in practice this rationale seemed difficult to establish for any Soviet exchange. But some MPs, even those from the government's own side, were unimpressed; indeed, William J. Brown, who had recently resigned the Labour Whip, doubted whether the BWSF team's recent visit to Germany had brought revolution there one day nearer. Similarly, Ernest Brown (Liberal) offered a somewhat sarcastic query to the effect 'Does this team wear red jerseys, like Woolwich Arsenal?'.[67] Unsurprisingly, Clynes left this question unanswered.

This episode provided perhaps the clearest and most public example of government intervention in British football between 1900–39. In effect, MacDonald's Labour government, refusing entry visas for a Soviet team, prevented a sporting event on political grounds, even if some might quibble with the description of the proposed Soviet tour as a 'sporting event'. The rejection of visa applications enabled the British government to take a strong anti-Soviet stand in a relatively risk-free manner, for the Soviet government, though irritated, was unlikely to regard the ban as grounds for a serious rift or conflict. Although the outcome might be interpreted in part as a function of the Labour Party's antipathy towards the British Communist Party, the BWSF's initial approaches to the Home Office made about the tour during the closing months of Baldwin's Conservative Government (1924–29) elicited minimal encouragement.[68] Subsequently, it was only natural that the affair became a reference point both within and outside government circles. For example, in 1935 it was cited frequently as a precedent by left-wing and Jewish groups seeking to stop a forthcoming England-Germany football international. In reality, the two cases were not analogous.[69] Thus, in 1935, German players did not require visas to enter Britain. Nor were Anglo-German exchanges in 1935 being strictly regulated by the British government.

For a country espousing liberal values, the government's response might be interpreted as not only a gross over-reaction but also as evidence that 'the state and its governing institutions viewed sport as an expression of political values and allegiances'.[70] If nothing else, the affair, highlighting official sensitivities about any form of contact with the Soviet Union, emphasised the USSR's status as an international sporting recluse, especially as similar bans were imposed during this period by several other governments, like those in Austria, Czechoslovakia or Spain.[71] Furthermore, on 10 May 1930, Soviet isolation was reaffirmed when England took the football field against Germany for the first time since the First World War. By this date, Germany, having been specifically ostracised by the British football associations after the 1914–18 war and excluded from the 1920 and 1924 Olympics, was back in the mainstream of international sport. Football internationals against Scotland (1929) and England (1930) were played in successive seasons. The IOC and FIFA, meeting at Berlin in 1930 and 1931 respectively, held sessions in Germany for the first time since the war, and, soon afterwards, the award of the 1936 Olympic Games reaffirmed German rehabilitation. By contrast, the Soviet Union remained still a marginal player in the world of sport. In fact, at a time when the Olympic movement and international football were sweeping the world, Noel-Baker, among others, regretted that the Soviet Union remained 'a gap not being filled'.[72] Sinfield summarised the position clearly and concisely: 'no official British sporting organisation was prepared to touch Russia with a barge-pole'.[73] The position was equally true of international sports bodies.

WORLD FOOTBALL MOVES ON WITHOUT BRITAIN: THE 1930 WORLD CUP

The 1920s, albeit dominated by the usual one-off friendly internationals, saw occasional moves within both Europe and Latin America towards the arrangement of international football tournaments, which took their place as regional competitions for national sides alongside the British International Championship (1884–1984). More importantly, the late 1920s witnessed discussions resulting in what was to become the premier competition, FIFA's World Cup, which owed much to the organisational efforts of Jules Rimet, the FIFA president (1921–54), and Austria's Hugo Meisl. For FIFA, an international tournament had always been a prime objective dating back to its early days, but, excepting the Olympic football competition organised through the IOC, nothing materialised during the federation's early decades. Eventually, FIFA's desire to exercise direct control over any contest, in conjunction with the gradual advance of professionalism, provided the foundation for exploratory discussions held at its 1927 Congress about a competition open to all teams, including those relying wholly or partly on professional players.[74] One year later, the 1928 FIFA Congress decided to stage a world championship competition in 1930.[75] Potential hosts included Hungary, Italy, Netherlands, Spain, Sweden and Uruguay, but withdrawals eventually left the latter as the only

142

contender facing the 1929 Congress. As a result, despite Europe's long-standing influence over both FIFA and international football, the right to stage the inaugural World Cup was awarded to a Latin American member.[76] Even so, Argentina, pointing to Uruguay's successive Olympic successes (1924, 1928), the enormous development of football in Latin America, and the fact that 1930 marked the centenary of Uruguayan independence, gave strong support to the bid from its Latin American footballing rival.[77]

Uruguay's offer to meet participants' travel and accommodation expenses proved insufficient to ensure a significant European entry. Nor did invitations meet a sympathetic British response. In November 1929, Wall, acting upon a decision taken by the FA's International Selection Committee, sent a curt refusal to the Uruguayan football authorities: 'I am instructed to express regret at our inability to accept the invitation'.[78] The SFA, having already reacted negatively in January 1927 towards initial proposals for an international championship, followed the FA's line, even if, unlike its English counterpart, refusal was accompanied by polite appreciation for the invitation.[79] Nor is there any indication in minute books that the matter attracted much discussion, let alone any expression of interest on the part of the other British associations. No reasons for rejection were given in Wall's letter, but this negative outcome can be interpreted as perhaps a function of the FA's conservative and insular tendencies, and particularly its concerns about player availability, distance, the lengthy sea voyage, and tour duration. Frequently, non-membership of FIFA has been advanced as the prime reason for British non-participation in *FIFA*'s World Cup, but this failed to prevent their receipt of invitations.[80] Nevertheless, their recent defection, in conjunction with the lack of progress during 1928–29 by negotiations to settle points at issue, diminished the prospects of British entry in any FIFA competition.

Another influential consideration must have been Wall's recent correspondence with Chelsea about the problems, even dangers, encountered during the club's recent tour of Argentina, Brazil and Uruguay. On 31 July 1929, Colonel Charles Crisp, a Chelsea director, apprised the FA of a series of problems which 'hindered real football'. He mentioned 'non-observance of the laws of the game'; 'very bad refereeing'; 'badly controlled crowds' who 'dominate the play' and intimidate both players and referees; no charging of goalkeepers by players (this proved a feature of the British game); and the 'Latin temperament'.[81] Allegedly, one Chelsea player was punched by a spectator, while crowd trouble at the Boca ground in Buenos Aires resulted in not only the premature end of the match but also serious damage to the team's motor coach. Events prompted the *Buenos Aires Herald* to ask: 'When does football cease to be a game? What is the dividing line between a game and a conflict? ... We deplore the fact that Chelsea, with so sound a reputation for clean play in England, should have been the centre of disturbance and assault in Argentina.'[82] One can imagine the reactions of Wall, among other members of the FA, to the receipt of a World Cup invitation from one of the countries visited by Chelsea within weeks of reading Crisp's letter.

An understandable Uruguayan desire for England's participation for both footballing (i.e. the game's British origins, reinforcing the event's credibility as a *world* cup) and historic (i.e. Britain's long-standing links with South America) reasons led Roberto MacEachen, the Uruguayan *chargé d'affaires* in London, to lobby the Foreign Office and FA in favour of a change of mind. However, the Foreign Office's expressions of sympathy about the merits of British participation from the point of view of Anglo-Uruguayan relations did not extend towards an official disposition towards intervention. From this perspective, it suited the Foreign Office to rationalise inaction by pointing out that the footballing authorities were 'a law unto themselves'.[83] Despite being tempted to treat the tournament as a sideshow in a far away part of the world, departmental reservations were occasioned more by the usual anxieties about the adverse effects on British prestige of poor performances and conduct. Thus, it proved 'rather chary of seeking to promote the despatch of British football teams abroad, especially those composed of professionals, as we have had some unhappy experiences recently in Europe in which such teams had not only disgraced themselves, but had caused much disappointment to their opponents and their supporters'.[84] The fact that recent problems affected clubs, not the national team itself, was glossed over in such exchanges. Nor did the Foreign Office favour the despatch of an amateur side, given reports about the improving standard and quasi-professional status of many 'amateur' national sides.

In the event, British teams were not the only absentees from the inaugural World Cup tourney played at Montevideo in July 1930. A mere 13 countries participated, with only Belgium, France, Romania and Yugoslavia making the journey from Europe (see Table 2.2, Chapter 2). Most entrants derived from South America, with Mexico and the USA providing a Central and North American presence. None of Uruguay's rivals for hosting the competition accepted invitations. Nor, surprisingly, given their historic links with Latin America, did Portugal and Spain. Inevitably, both FIFA and Latin American associations expressed concern about the minimal European representation, even if both von Frenckell (a FIFA vice-president) and Bauwens (DFB) reminded members that FIFA was unable to compel entry by members.[85] American teams, that is, Argentina, Uruguay and the USA, dominated the semi-finals. Yugoslavia was the sole European survivor at this stage, but, despite scoring first, was beaten decisively (6-1) by Uruguay, which went on to become the first World Cup champions by defeating Argentina 4-2 in the final.

Patchy global coverage, combined with the absence of several major footballing powers (e.g. Austria, England, Germany, Italy, Scotland), means that the term 'World Cup' might be treated as a misnomer. For example, none of the four 'super class' footballing powers listed by *Pesti Naplo* in 1933 had participated in the 1930 World Cup, while Yugoslavia, the defeated semi-finalists, received only a third class ranking therein. Nevertheless, despite doubts about the tournament's credibility, Uruguay's victory should not be underestimated, particularly as it followed on from two Olympic football gold medals at a time when the amateur/professional divide proved somewhat blurred in both Europe and Latin America.[86] Uruguay, having defeated Italy in the 1928 Olympics, might still have won the World Cup, even with a stronger European entry. In the meantime, the 1930 World Cup reminded Europeans – patchy press coverage limited the size of the British audience – about the growth and quality of the game in Latin America in general and of *'rioplatense football'* in particular. Brazil, having finished second to Yugoslavia in its group, was still an emerging force. Moreover, the large crowds attending matches in the final stages – the final was watched by 93,000 spectators – established football's massive popular appeal in Latin America, a point shown graphically by the efforts made by thousands of Argentinians to cross the River Plate for the final.

Organisational deficiencies, like the tardy opening of Montevideo's Centenary Stadium and occasional incidents (e.g. one game ended several minutes early) prompted critics, but subsequent FIFA Congresses were employed by Rimet, among others, to praise the 'great success' of the competition, which established not only the federation's ability to organise such a tournament but also provided the league/cup format of what was to become a regular competition held every four years.[87] One unfortunate feature was an anti-Uruguayan campaign in Argentina, which involved the stoning of the Uruguayan consulate at Buenos Aires and the temporary severing of Argentine-Uruguayan football links.[88] Subsequently, memories of this episode contributed to the British Foreign Office's somewhat jaundiced view of Latin American football.

THE NOT SO CORDIAL *ENTENTE CORDIALE*

The Anglo-French relationship proved a central focus for international politics during the inter-war period. France also featured regularly in the fixture lists of British football, as demonstrated by the six internationals played against England between 1923 and 1929 (see Table 2.3, Chapter 2) and the fact that Wales' only two internationals played between the wars took place in Paris. Whether or not France, like Belgium, featured regularly for political reasons appertaining to wartime and post-war alignments and/or geographical proximity remains debatable. However, it is clear that France was not regarded by either the FA or British media as a strong footballing power, given England's string of impressive away victories (1923: 4-1, 1924: 3-1; 1925: 3-2; 1927: 6-0, 1928: 5-1; 1929: 4-1) in which it averaged over four goals per game; thus, in May 1929, even a 'very moderate' England team won easily on French soil.[89] Nor did France, which lost two of its three group games, reach the final stages of the 1930 World Cup tournament.

As a result, in May 1931 England, having given an 'outclassed' France a regular 'lesson in football' throughout the past decade, was expected to win easily yet again in Paris.[90] In the event, a reportedly under-prepared and over-confident team lost 2-5 in what was described as one of England's worst-ever displays. *The Times* summed up the sense of shock in a prophetic phrase: 'the pupils of other days turned the tables on their masters'.[91] In the long term, England's second-ever defeat to a foreign country appeared less significant, for in December 1933, France, playing a full international on British soil for the first time, was 'outclassed' by England, whose 4-1 win resumed a winning sequence continued in 1938.[92] Meanwhile, the extension of England's fixture list to include a wider range of countries meant that France featured less regularly therein, even if this was partially offset by visits made to Paris by Scotland (1930, 1932) and Wales (1933, 1939); in fact, France proved Wales' sole foreign opponent prior to the Second World War. Similarly, even the IFA, though arranging no full internationals against foreign countries during the inter-war period, played two amateur internationals against France (1921, 1928). In addition, 1930 saw the introduction of the annual Racing Club of Paris–Arsenal fixture played each November to mark Armistice Day, while raising money for the French war wounded.

To some extent, the impact of England's defeat in 1931 was accentuated by the fact that it came at a time of difficult Anglo-French relations, arising in part from a 'decided shift of British opinion away from France' attributed by Arthur Willert, the Foreign Office's Press Officer, to policy, racial, temperamental and other reasons.[93] Nor was the situation helped by the recent suspension of rugby internationals between France and the home countries because of British concern about shamateurism, the French club championship, and France's recent history of rough play.[94] As a result, in

March 1931 the British Rugby Football Union, representing the English, Scottish, Welsh and Northern Irish unions, suspended games against France with effect from the 1932–33 season until the 'control and conduct of the game had been placed on a satisfactory basis in all essentials'.[95] Naturally, the French rugby authorities, pointing to remedial measures, claimed that there was no longer a problem.[96] But, the British Rugby Football Union, arguing that French rugby had yet to prove that it was 'played in the right spirit and in accordance with the traditions of the game long ago laid down by the home unions', refused to reverse its decision until July 1939, thereby forcing France to look elsewhere for opponents, even including Germany (e.g. March 1935).[97]

Subsequently, members of the Foreign Office, looking back on this episode, were confirmed in their view about the merits of keeping politics and sport in separate compartments as far as possible. In turn, the generalising of past experiences led to an unfortunate blurring of official memories, as evidenced by subsequent references implying that the 1931 rupture in Anglo-French sporting relations affected association, not rugby, football.[98] It was almost as if the official mind, finding it difficult to associate unsporting behaviour with rugby and other amateur sports, only expected incidents in games played by those dreadful professional footballers.

MAKING POLITICS OF FOOTBALL?

England and Italy, two of the world's leading footballing powers, played each other three times during the 1930s, and England's excellent record – one win and two draws – against the 1934 and 1938 World Cup winners helped to reaffirm images of British footballing hegemony in spite of Scotland's 0-3 defeat by Italy in a less high profile game played in 1931.

Despite the British government's growing focus on the German problem during the 1930s, Italy proved an equally significant concern for policy-makers, given its principal role in the European Civil War and the manner in which Mussolini's restless foreign policy, most notably his involvement in the Spanish Civil War (1936–39) and invasions of Ethiopia (1935–36) and Albania (1939), threatened British interests in key strategic areas, like North Africa, East Africa and the Mediterranean. In particular, Italian ambitions exacerbated the fundamental problem confronting British policy-makers in the 1930s, that is, over-stretch resulting from the simultaneous threat posed to national interests by three potential aggressors (i.e. Germany, Italy, Japan) increasingly active in different parts of the world.[99]

147

Mussolini's Axis links with Hitler's Germany merely complicated the position, while reinvigorating the search for an Anglo-Italian agreement as part of British efforts to contain German power.

Anglo-Italian sporting contacts operated within a context defined also by Mussolini's totalitarian aspirations: 'Sports were lavishly subsidized and from the late twenties increasingly propagandized by the fascist regime'.[100] In 1929, the Sports Charter cemented links between the *Opera Nazionale Dopolavoro* (OND) and the Italian Olympic Committee, while the fascist regime's instrumental approach towards sport was typified by Mussolini on 28 October 1934, when addressing athletes after a mass parade celebrating the twelfth anniversary of his march on Rome: 'You Athletes of all Italy have particular duties. You must be tenacious, chivalrous and daring. Remember that when you take part in contests beyond our borders, there is then entrusted to your muscles, and above all to your spirit, the honour and the prestige of national sport. You must hence make use of all your energy and of your willpower in order to obtain primacy in all struggles on the earth, on the sea and in the sky.'[101] Their role, he asserted, was to epitomise 'the new race which Fascism, in its virile way, is forging and is tempering for all competitors'. Naturally, football's propaganda potential was fully exploited, given the national side's World Cup and Olympic achievements and the successes of club sides, like Bologna. For example, the latter's victory in the 1937 Paris Exhibition tournament was presented 'before the crowds of the whole world in the image of their nation' as a 'crystalline victory' for fascist Italy.[102] Team sports adopted the garb of fascism and nationalism, a trait reinforced by the use of language (e.g. '*calcio*' replaced 'football') and the adoption of a distinctive style of play (*il metodo*), based on an attacking centre half, to distance the Italian game from lingering British influences.[103] Inevitably, any England-Italy footballing encounter possessed a political edge, which was sharpened by the game's status as the national sport in both countries, their high footballing reputation, and the fact that contemporaries viewed, and were so encouraged to view, their fixtures as tests of primacy in the world of football. Thus, the 1934 England-Italy match, prompting one reporter to head his match report as 'The Battle of Highbury: From our War Correspondent, Highbury, Wednesday', encouraged some commentators to argue that the two countries went to war well before June 1940![104]

In December 1932, the FA, faced by several foreign invitations for its 1933 close season tour, selected Italy and Switzerland, while rejecting those from, say, Belgium, France or Hungary.[105] Once again, the FA, acting without reference to the British government, faced the Foreign Office with a difficult dilemma. Although it was entitled to arrange matches in a unilateral manner, previous contacts with the Foreign Office, most notably, during 1928–29, should have apprised the FA of the prudence of consulting the government about more politically sensitive fixtures.[106] In the event, the forthcoming game sparked off another set of official exchanges about the politics of international football in the wake of a communication from Sir Harry Luke, the Lieutenant Governor of Malta, reminding London about the importance for British prestige therein of a good performance by England. Malta neither belonged to FIFA nor played internationals, but football's rapid growth in popularity meant that the performance of British teams, particularly *vis-à-vis* those from Italy, constituted a substantial element in islanders' images of Britain. Luke, pointing to the propaganda value of an English victory, urged the Colonial Office to leave 'no stone unturned' when urging the FA to select the best possible team.[107] The Colonial Office, interpreting the matter as involving 'higher diplomacy', passed Luke's letter to the Foreign Office, which not only learned of the forthcoming fixture for the first time but also soon realised that more was at stake than a mere football match.

Recent form suggested a close match, but the reputed strength of Italian football, alongside recent results (i.e. Scotland, having lost to Italy in 1931, had recently beaten England), meant that a British win could not be taken for granted. Orme Sargent, the head of the Foreign Office's Central Department, admitted previous departmental interest in such matters: 'Our attention has frequently been drawn to the importance attached to sport in Italy and to the necessity for winning matches etc.'.[108] 'We have on several occasions in the past and, *indeed in this particular case*, done our best to encourage our people to send a first rate team to meet the Italian footballers.' But he introduced a note of caution: 'You will realise, I am sure, the hubbub there would be in the press if it should leak out that the Foreign Office, "for reasons of British prestige abroad", was bringing pressure to bear upon those responsible for the government of football! If this should ever become publicly known (*we very nearly had a case once*) and should then be telegraphed abroad, our position would be rather ridiculous.' Orme Sargent's retrospective reference highlighted the Foreign Office's anxiety to avoid a re-run of the 1928–29 media controversy arising from a rumoured England-Italy fixture, particularly given the risk of a FA-inspired press leak: 'Unfortunately, the Football Association here is not quite as intelligent in these matters as we should like them to be, and we are afraid to trouble them too much'.

Orme Sargent noted the previous use of officially inspired press articles, but advised against the need to do more for the present. By implication, he ruled out also the despatch of a letter of the type sent to the FA in December

149

1928, since overt, heavy-handed action was adjudged likely to cause as many, if not more, problems than an Italian victory. Charles Duff, whose line was seconded by Lindsay, minuted that 'the less we do to put diplomatic pressure on football, the better':

> Imagine the damage to our prestige, if it leaked out, that we had interested ourselves in this – in other words, if we had attempted to make politics of sport – and if afterwards our footballers were thoroughly beaten (which might easily happen as football is more seriously taken by foreigners than by English people). We shall lose far more in such circumstances than we are ever likely to gain by any representations we might make. *Let us leave sport clea[n].*[109]

The last phrase offers an interesting summary of the preferred departmental position, even if the writing renders it difficult to state conclusively that the final word was 'clean' rather than 'clear'. In the event, the Colonial Office accepted the cautious line favoured by the Foreign Office: 'We quite realise how careful one has to be about official intervention in matters of this sort'.[110] However, there is little or no documentary evidence about what actually took place, except Sargent's implied reference to the exertion of behind-the-scenes pressure, perhaps through Howard Marshall (1900–73), a sports journalist who worked for the *Westminster Gazette* and the *Daily Telegraph*, among other papers, during this period.[111] Nevertheless, *political reasons* led the Foreign Office to hope that not only would England win but also players would 'comport themselves properly off the football field as well as on', given probable impacts upon Britain's image in general and in the Eastern Mediterranean in particular, 'where anything to the discredit of the British team will be enormously magnified by the Italian propagandists'.[112] Once again, official preferences to steer clear of sport were challenged by the way in which events threatened to impact on national interests. No longer was it possible to feign indifference to, or display unawareness of, the political implications of any fixture, particularly one pitching a British national team against another representing a country where sport constituted a major part of its propaganda apparatus. In this case, regardless of the British position, the Italian government was bound to exploit the result as part of 'intensive' propaganda both at home and in other countries, like Malta, possibly as part of the Darwinian-type analyses feared by Perowne: 'a defeat w$^{d.}$ enable their propagandists to point triumphantly to the effeteness of the British race as compared with the Italians of today and give an enormous fillip to the Italianising influences in the colony [i.e. Malta]'.[113]

At the same time, officials, acknowledging both the FA's autonomy and the risks of public controversy, pressed the difficulties of intervention; indeed, the Foreign Office might well have done more in this case, but for its fear of publicity and the perceived difficulty of collaboration with the FA. In the meantime, the British government awaited the outcome of a game attracting greater media attention than most internationals. Nor did the match's broader significance escape the *New York Times*, which reported the Italian desire to 'prove that the Continental pupils have reached the level of the masters ... No other contest in the history of modern Italian sport has caused so much interest as the forthcoming match.'[114] Inevitably, there arose also the usual stories that Italy's 'amateur' footballers, having been warned by party officials about their conduct on the field, were being promised substantial pecuniary and other inducements for a win.[115]

The match itself, played at Rome on 13 May 1933, attracted some 50,000 spectators, including Mussolini and Sir Ronald Graham, the British ambassador.[116] Despite its perceived importance, the game proved a reasonably sporting, albeit far from distinguished, affair. For Walter Bensemann, 'it was not a very great game, because all the players seemed to be overcome by the importance of their task. The Italians had been told to avenge the Austrians' defeat in London and the Englishmen were trying to uphold the prestige of the old country.'[117] A 1-1 draw enabled both parties to draw some comfort from the result, even if at a later date England players, like Eddie Hapgood, indicated strong reservations about the encounter. Whether or not these opinions were held at the time or were intended merely to give retrospective colour to their books is uncertain. Hapgood, claiming that one clearance caught Mussolini 'just above his lunch', expressed the wish that it had been something more lethal than a football!'[118] The wartime context within which the book was published suggests that his 'wish' possessed elements of mythology rather than historical fact. In any case, as noted by Polley, footballers' biographies, often ghosted by a journalist with an eye for an interesting story rather than good history, were over-influenced by contemporary concerns and 'written for sports fans, for followers of the particular star, whose tastes are assumed to be sporting, not political'.[119] Reportedly, the England tour party, which was received by both Mussolini and the Pope, was shown considerable courtesy by the Italian authorities, but Wall did not relish the experience: 'as to myself, I have no desire to again be a guest of the Italian Football Association'.[120] Thus, in 1934, the FA, influenced by Wall's unpleasant memories of his visit, refused to accede to FIFA's request for switching the scheduled IFAB meeting from Cannes to Rome in order to facilitate attendance at World Cup games and functions.

By contrast, England's other tour fixture, played versus Switzerland at

Berne, attracted minimal official attention, thereby showing how the government focused selectively on the more politically sensitive fixtures. Clearly, British footballing contacts with, say, both Italy and the Soviet Union were treated as worthy of close official attention, but *political reasons* meant that a game against Italy was interpreted in a more sympathetic manner than one against the USSR. The Swiss game possessed less perceived foreign policy significance, even if England's decisive 4-0 victory over Switzerland, witnessed by Rimet, among other dignitaries, proved extremely good propaganda in terms of offering – to quote one informed spectator – an 'object lesson in heading, dribbling, passing, shooting and position play'.[121] Nor were political aspects entirely forgotten, for Sir Howard Kennard, the British minister in Switzerland, addressing the post-match banquet, offered some light-hearted comments about football's political potential: 'It might be better to have the differences of Europe settled by the Football Federation, who did things without any fuss or loss of time, than by Diplomatists, who seemed hampered by the weight of their own responsibility'.[122]

Despite its *laissez-faire* inclinations, the Foreign Office inclined at times towards a more interventionist approach regarding selected Anglo-Italian sporting encounters, most notably those involving rugby football. Perhaps the game's strict amateur status led officials to believe that the rugby union authorities and players would be easier to work with than their association football counterparts. Whereas association football was interpreted as a game for the masses in both countries, its rugby variant fitted in more easily with elitist perceptions of both amateur sport and cultural propaganda. Italian rugby was centred on the universities, and, according to the British embassy at Rome, there was no intention to extend the game to 'the people' until a tradition of clean and fair play was well established.[123] Against this background, in July 1933, the Foreign Office, welcoming any method of improving bilateral contacts between potential opinion-formers, proved more responsive than usual to an invitation, forwarded by the British embassy at Rome, for British participation in an international universities tournament scheduled to be held at Turin in September.[124] In the event, it was soon realised that the invitation arrived at the wrong time (i.e. during the university vacation) and too late to enable British participation.

Nevertheless, the early weeks of 1934 saw yet another attempt by the Rome embassy to solicit government support for a British visit, especially as the Italian universities team, coached by a former Oxford university captain and seemingly aware of France's unsporting reputation, wished to 'play British rugby, and not French rugby'.[125] However, in London, traditional attitudes, having been slightly relaxed the previous year, soon reasserted themselves:

I am very doubtful whether we sh^d ever take more than a vague interest in sport; there are so many 'snags'. Sporting events so often end with the creation of violent ill-will between the participants and among spectators, even in our own sporting country. Games between our people and Latins are frequently responsible for riots. Then, to take the Italian case, if they happen to win a game (and they work, almost fight, to do so) it merely proves to a vast assembly of people, including perhaps Il Duce and his supermen, that the Fascist system produces a finer type of homo sapiens than the decaying system of Parlty Govt. Football becomes a sub-section of the creed. Our sportsmen can never be very comfortable in such circumstances.[126]

Duff's minute, though betraying the usual prejudiced and negative departmental view, failed to disguise an implicit acceptance of sport, and particularly football, as propaganda capable of transmitting a Darwinian message. Nevertheless, Duff, whose cautious approach was seconded by Leeper, opposed intervention: 'I should be in favour of letting it [sport] work for itself, and avoid like the plague any attempt to glorify it into an activity of national or international importance; but I realise that sportsmen may not agree with this view'.[127] Nor, it seemed, would politicians and diplomats in most other European countries.

Within the Foreign Office itself, James Lambert, who had returned recently from a posting in Rome, proved a rare dissenter; thus, he advocated informal support for the rugby tour on the grounds that refusal might not only offend Italian interests anxious to maintain contact with Britain but also signify a fear of exposing national inferiority in a major British sport.[128] Duff, having been led to believe that amateur rugby players would be better behaved than professional footballers, softened his original line, but was over-ruled by Leeper, who returned a negative reply to Rome stating that sporting bodies should be responsible for their own fixtures.[129] Despite being confronted yet again by evidence of the way in which sport spilled over into international politics, the Foreign Office reaffirmed long-standing preferences: 'All the same we are not disposed to encourage sport as a means of propaganda'.

This episode, albeit having a negative outcome, was of historical interest in demonstrating yet again official British perceptions of sport's propaganda potential, the lack of consistency in government 'policy' consequent upon the pragmatic treatment of individual events, and the more sympathetic official approach adopted towards amateur and elitist sports, like rugby. In addition, Leeper's note, recalling Britain's 'far from happy' experience in regard to professional football, reaffirmed official prejudices when concluding that 'these contests have done more harm than good'.

'THE BATTLE OF HIGHBURY', NOVEMBER 1934

On 14 November 1934, Arsenal's ground provided the setting for the return match between England and Italy, which proved one of the more controversial internationals played on British soil. In the past, unsporting conduct on the field often possessed extra-sporting consequences, but in this case there appears to have been remarkably little political fallout in spite of the fact that it came at a time when a sharper focus was being placed upon the future shape of Anglo-Italian relations regarding, say, Germany, the Mediterranean and East Africa as well as the relative standing of the two countries in the world of football.

By the close of 1934, questions about footballing primacy, left unresolved by the drawn match one year earlier, had acquired an added importance because of Italy's recently acquired status of World Cup champions.[130] In particular, was Italy really the best team in the world, as suggested by both its 1934 World Cup triumph and excellent record (7 wins, 1 draw, 1 loss) since playing England in 1933? Or was England, a notable absentee from the 1934 World Cup competition hosted by Italy, still the game's leading force, despite a rather mixed record (5 wins, 3 defeats) following its visit to Rome? In fact, England's 1934 close season tour, undertaken just prior to the World Cup finals and coincidentally involving two of *Pesti Naplo*'s three leading second-grade teams, brought defeats to two teams, that is, Hungary (1-2) and Czechoslovakia (1-2), scheduled to participate in the World Cup a few days later. Whereas Hungary departed at the quarter-final stage, Czechoslovakia reached the final, where it lost to Italy in extra time. Admittedly, England – to quote one player – 'did not have a good team' on its 1934 tour but both Hungary and Czechoslovakia illuminated excellent positional play and skills.[131] Of course, British football represented more than just England. Scotland, albeit less active than England in terms of foreign internationals and another absentee from the 1934 World Cup, had already lost (0-3) to Italy in 1931, but partially retrieved its reputation in December 1933 when securing a 2-2 draw against Austria. Soon afterwards, Austria ended Italy's lengthy unbeaten run, even if the latter's 1-0 victory in the 1934 World Cup semi-finals brought revenge. The consequent failure of recent results to offer clear-cut answers to questions posed about the relative standing of leading footballing nations merely served to magnify the perceived significance of the England-Italy game.

At this stage, a brief examination of the 1934 World Cup, which was awarded to Italy by FIFA in 1932, offers a useful background to the Highbury fixture.[132] Mussolini, though reputed to be relatively unenthusiastic about football *per se*, welcomed the World Cup as a heaven-sent opportunity to impress domestic and external audiences with the qualities of the new Italy, as reflected through the high standard of Italian football and the efficient organisation of the tournament.[133] Perhaps the major challenge was to prove that the fascist regime was capable of organising an Italian victory. Despite the fact that a recent home defeat (2-4) by Austria (February 1934) ended an eight match unbeaten run, an Italian victory remained a strong possibility because of home advantage, the team's thorough preparations guided by Vittorio Pozzo, the usual monetary and other inducements offered for footballing success, and the selection of Italian-based foreigners, like Monti, who had played for Argentina in the 1930 World Cup final![134]

Of course, it might be argued that Italy's prospects were considerably enhanced by the absence of British teams. In April 1933, Schricker, visiting Glasgow to represent FIFA at the Scotland-England game, sounded out the British associations about entry to the 1934 World Cup.[135] Conceding that the competition was essentially 'a matter of prestige', he claimed that entry would prove beneficial to global images of British football.[136] Informal conversations were followed up by correspondence and further personal exchanges, whenever the opportunity presented itself, such as at IFAB meetings or internationals. FIFA's anxiety to secure British participation even led Schricker to guarantee both England and Scotland direct admission to the finals proper – unlike other entrants, there would be no need to participate in preliminary matches – plus coverage of travel and accommodation expenses. Indeed, Schricker, detecting the SFA's fiscal worries, promised to arrange a continental tour in 1935 to accommodate its concerns. FIFA's *Official Bulletin* reinforced the pressure, for an article written by Walter Bensemann urged the British associations to 'come over and do their bit' for world football and bring for Britain 'a substantial win of prestige'.[137] But, these moves, albeit revealing the lengths to which FIFA was prepared to go to bring in British teams, fell on barren ground. Naturally, FIFA regretted the negative outcome, but further pressure – entry, Schricker reiterated, would offer 'a fine opportunity to make propaganda for British football' – brought no change of mind.[138] Once again, rejection letters failed to provide reasons for non-entry, whose impact was emphasised by the fact that both the FA and SFA decided to conduct close season continental tours in 1934.[139] As mentioned earlier, England even took on two participants a few days prior to the commencement of the World Cup finals, while the SFA, having rejected FIFA's invitation, decided at the same committee meeting to tour Scandinavia in 1934![140]

Another prominent absentee was Uruguay, the holders. Various reasons, including retaliation for the poor European representation at the 1930 tournament and a players' strike over professionalism, have been advanced to explain the absence of a country whose success in the January 1935 South American Championships – it defeated Argentina 3-0 in the final – suggests that it was a major loss.[141] Nevertheless, the 1934 World Cup, though dominated by European teams, proved far more credible than its predecessor in both footballing and geographical terms. Indeed, 31 entrants necessitated a 12 group qualifying tournament (1933–34) to produce 16 finalists, comprising 12 teams from Europe, two from South America, plus the USA and Egypt. Unlike 1930, the tournament's closing stages were dominated by European sides, since neither Argentina, Brazil, Egypt, nor the USA progressed beyond the first round. The semi-finals, involving Austria, Czechoslovakia, Germany and Italy, brought together an interesting mix of teams drawn from democracies and dictatorships. Italy's hard-fought win (1-0) over Austria was watched by 60,000 spectators at Milan, whereas at Rome a much smaller crowd witnessed Czechoslovakia's 3-1 victory over Germany; in fact, crowd figures for Germany's quarter-final (3,000), semi-final (10,000) and third-place matches (7,000) suggested limited popular interest on the part of Italians in things German at this time. By contrast, a capacity crowd of 55,000, including Mussolini, packed the stadium in Rome to watch the final, in which Italy, recovering from being a goal down, beat Czechoslovakia 2-1 to become World Cup champions. Czechoslovakia, playing neat constructive football, gave the home crowd several anxious moments, and Italy, equalising with only eight minutes to go, needed extra time and, some argued, rather robust play to secure victory.[142]

Inevitably, Italian propaganda proceeded to exploit the successful Roman Soccer Empire as epitomising the dynamic qualities of the fascist regime in general and the personal influence of *Il Duce* in particular. Significantly, Mussolini, normally sporting a yachting cap, attended most of Italy's games and often received the team afterwards.[143] Of course, there were other unheralded reasons for Italy's success. For example, Argentinian players performed a crucial role; thus, Guaita scored the only goal in the semi-final, while his compatriot, Orsi, was responsible for the late equaliser in the final. Nor should one overlook the impact of the gifts and other rewards, including, it was rumoured, 10,000 lire per player, promised to Italy's amateurs for reaffirming national footballing superiority![144]

Soon afterwards, Schricker sent the FA a report about the 'exciting' final played between Czechoslovakia and Italy, plus a set of commemorative World Cup stamps requested by Wall when they met at Cannes for the

IFAB.[145] However, the British media's characteristically insular attitudes meant that World Cup matches, rating no more than a few lines here and there, were largely ignored in the press; indeed, subsequently, one writer looked back somewhat disparagingly on this 'burlesque competition' held in Italy during 1934.[146] Nevertheless, the tournament and Italy's status as World Cup champions provided an interesting backdrop to the England-Italy match scheduled for November 1934, given the fact that the Italian football association operated under a regime, whose totalitarian pretensions invested such games with an extra-sporting significance: 'the government in Rome welcomed the opportunity to prove their country's superiority. It was strictly a political decision ... Italy officially feared no-one.'[147] The politico-sporting impact of World Cup success in a competition hosted and organised by the Italian authorities would be considerably boosted if England could be beaten for the first time on British soil a few months later.

Once again, the fixture represented the outcome of a decision made by the FA, not the Foreign Office, which, having been confronted by the fact of the match, became involved principally from the point of view of official representation. Both Sir John Simon, the Foreign Secretary, and the Foreign Office itself received invitations from the FA to attend the game and post-match banquet. Yet again, a relatively simple request prompted a wide-ranging discussion about principles and precedents in the light of the knowledge that dignitaries in attendance would include Prince Arthur of Connaught and Grandi, the Italian ambassador, accompanied by other embassy staff. Owen O'Malley, the head of the Southern Department, typified the departmental preoccupation with precedent alongside the lack of enthusiasm of officials for attending football matches: 'If we agree to be represented at this match, there will be a cast iron precedent for representation at all international football matches and the precedent may well spread to cricket, lacrosse, basket ball, ping pong & goodness knows what else. I think the F.O. will sooner or later regret this.'[148] Eventually, the precedent set by the 1932 England-Austria game, in conjunction with knowledge of Grandi's scheduled attendance, led the Foreign Office to decide upon formal ministerial representation at only the match, not the post-match banquet.[149] Subsequently, parliamentary business made the Foreign Secretary unavailable, but Simon took care to forewarn Grandi about his enforced absence.[150] Instead, the Foreign Office was represented by James Lambert, a member of the Southern Department with recent experience of a diplomatic posting in Italy.[151]

Sporting histories have ensured the enduring force of the game's descriptor as 'the Battle of Highbury', including its image as one of the roughest matches ever played on British soil.[152] Although one player felt that the press had over-sensationalised problems, the match proved, to quote one British diplomat, a 'less pleasant' affair characterised by a range of unsavoury incidents assumed to be a function of the high political and footballing stakes attached to the result.[153] Early English goals, in conjunction with the loss of one player through injury (no substitutes were allowed), forced Italy to resort to unsporting methods in order to retrieve the situation. As Stanley Matthews observed, 'they meant to win – at any price'.[154] Eddie Hapgood, who left the field for treatment for a broken nose, used his autobiography to complain, in suitably picturesque terms, about the difficulties of upholding high standards of sportsmanship 'when somebody closely resembling an enthusiastic member of the Mafia is wiping his studs down your leg, or kicking you up in the air from behind'!'[155]

A large crowd of some 50,000 people, including an estimated 5,000 visiting Italians, produced net gate receipts of over £2,143.[156] Italy, having fought back from 0-3 down, scored two second-half goals, but failed to equalise, thereby giving England the honour of becoming the first team to beat the 1934 world champions. Inevitably, Mussolini, when personally welcoming players back to Rome, blamed defeat on the injuries and, by implication, the tactics employed by England. However, Grandi, responding to the Foreign Secretary's apology for absence, presented Simon with a glowing account of both the game and the team's reception: 'It was a most exciting and interesting match and it would be impossible to speak too highly of the magnificent game played by the English team. It was football at its very best.'[157] Italian players returned home, he reported, 'greatly touched by the warm welcome and cordial hospitality'. Mussolini's reported comments indicate an alternative interpretation, especially as the crowd at Highbury, albeit pleased with England's victory in a 'most exciting and interesting' match, might suspect Grandi of being either excessively diplomatic or ignorant of the niceties of the game. Whether or not the 'Battle of Highbury' seriously disturbed the course of Anglo-Italian relations, most notably ongoing efforts to form what became the Stresa front, remains questionable at a time when Mussolini's eyes were turning towards Ethiopia. On 5 December 1934, a clash of Ethiopian and Italian troops at Wal Wal was to prove the point of departure for the eventual conquest of Ethiopia, even if military invasion did not commence until October 1935.

MATCH COMMENTARIES AS AN INSTRUMENT OF DIPLOMACY

For Asa Briggs, the historian of the BBC, the 1930s marked the golden age of broadcasting. This decade also saw an ever-closer alliance between radio and totalitarianism, as noted by Philip Taylor: 'During the inter-war years, the lofty BBC ideal that "Nation shall speak peace unto Nation" gradually gave way to the exploitation of broadcasting as an instrument of nationalistic expansion and aggressive diplomacy'.[158] However, even liberal democracies, like Britain, came to appreciate radio's invaluable contribution to national projection, since it was capable of reaching people in a way unhindered by constraints arising from illiteracy, territorial boundaries, or censorship.[159] Football, like boxing, was a major beneficiary from the growth of broadcasting; thus, match commentaries, though provided by the BBC principally for purposes of entertainment and public interest, performed a role in terms of imparting an aura of respectability to the 'people's game', strengthening football's status as the national sport, and reinforcing its domestic and external visibility, most notably by maximising the audience for any particular international fixture. But, sports broadcasting remained a novel development, as evidenced by contemporary debates concerning whether the wireless represented football's friend or foe.[160] Bans imposed by the Football League and the SFA contrasted with the slightly more relaxed approach adopted by the FA.

During 1933, this issue prompted the British government's intervention in the forthcoming Scotland-Austria fixture, whose historical significance is increased by the episode's focus on a home country other than England. Moreover, Austria's 'Wunderteam' was often regarded as one of the world's strongest sides, as suggested by its victory in the 1931–32 International Cup, the fact that it proved the only country to defeat Italy during the two-year period preceding the 1934 England-Italy match, and its top placing in *Pesti Naplo*'s ranking list (Table 6.1).[161] Club sides, like Rapid Wien, First Wien, and FK Austria, reinforced the country's reputation through victories in the Mitropa Cup (1930, 1931, 1933). Unsurprisingly, the national team's exploits attracted keen interest from all levels of Austrian society, which placed a high value on live match commentaries.[162] For example, in December 1932, when Austria played in London, England's unbeaten home record against foreign teams received perhaps its severest test to date.[163] At the same time, the radio broadcast reportedly brought the country to a virtual standstill.[164] Sessions of Austrian parliamentary committees were temporarily suspended, while many shops and offices closed to allow staff to listen to the commentary. Upon its arrival back in Vienna, Dollfuss, the Federal Chancellor, personally welcomed the Austrian team.[165] Significantly, the Austrian footballing authorities, expressing pleasure at the team's reception in Britain, acknowledged 'the still greatest English sporting nation'.[166] Meanwhile, Austria's impressive performance in defeat (England won 4-3) brought home to Britons the quality of the best foreign teams, perhaps even making the British media and public more 'inclined to accept the foreigner as a menace to Britain's football prestige'.[167]

Public records yield little or no light on the 1932 England-Austria game from the perspective of government policy, excepting a brief retrospective reference to the manner in which Foreign Office representation at the match set a precedent, such as for the 1934 England-Italy game. However, in November 1933, the British government was drawn into problems surrounding the broadcast of Austria's forthcoming international against Scotland scheduled to be played at Glasgow in December 1933. For Scottish football, the game, offering Scotland the opportunity to avenge its humiliating 0-5 defeat at Vienna a few years earlier, represented the first ever visit by a foreign national side. Three Austrian requests to broadcast the game were rejected by the SFA, which was described by one BBC spokesman as being 'radically prejudiced' against the mere idea of match commentaries.[168] Radio's relatively novel nature meant that fear of the unknown was compounded by selfish concerns about the adverse impact upon gate money. Certainly, the SFA was unconvinced by reassurances from the BBC, which not only denied any injurious consequences but also argued that broadcasting exerted a positive impact in terms of generating public interest and future income. Furthermore, the BBC, claiming fundamental rights of access, refused to pay as a 'matter of important principle': 'In common with other broadcast organisations (and the Press), we cannot agree to pay for the *right to broadcast* our own description of events'.[169] Naturally, this created problems for the Austrian broadcasting authorities, given their reliance upon facilities provided by the BBC, whose duty 'to provide programmes for British listeners' meant that 'we should not be justified in the interests of our own listeners in providing facilities for foreign programmes based on British events, which are denied to British listeners'.

The resulting impasse led the Austrian authorities to solicit government support in order to secure a breakthrough. Baron Frankenstein, the Austrian ambassador in London, though accepting the SFA's invitation to attend both the game and post-match banquet, expressed his government's disquiet about the lack of radio facilities.[170] In December 1933, Frankenstein, expressing regret about the seeming lack of progress on what Chancellor Dollfuss treated as a matter of 'great importance', urged official pressure to force a change of mind. As a result, the British government became involved in what was viewed officially as essentially a conflict of principle between the BBC and the SFA. Sir John Simon, the Foreign Secretary, acting through the Scottish Office, expressed the hope that something could be done on what he described as 'a matter of national importance' for Austria in the interests of good Anglo-Austrian relations as well as of Scottish tourism. Confronted by governmental pressure, channelled through the Scottish Office, the SFA relented, even if soon afterwards its refusal of the BBC's request to broadcast the 1934 Scottish Cup Final reaffirmed the pragmatic nature of this solution and its continued suspicion of the wireless.[171]

This episode was significant in marking a rare governmental intervention in Scottish football. Official discussions, though covering the usual matter of departmental representation, concentrated upon broadcasting. Despite being forewarned of the attendance at the match of a large number of Austrian supporters, the Foreign Office saw no grounds for action respecting what was becoming an emerging European-wide trend (Table 6.2). In the meantime, the match itself, ending as a 2-2 draw, helped to validate images about the general quality of British football. Needless to say, the Foreign Office, Scottish Office and the Austrian government were extremely pleased with the outcome, which prepared the way for further invitations for Austrian club visits to Scotland.[172]

TABLE 6.2
FOREIGN SPECTATORS IN BRITAIN, EARLY 1930S

1931	9 December	1,000 Spaniards (England)
1932	7 December	2,000 Austrians (England)
1933	29 November	`Large number' of Austrians (Scotland)
	6 December	4,000 French (England)
1934	14 November	5,000 Italians (England)
1935	4 December	10,000 Germans (England)

Source: M. Drummond to Newsam, 28 November 1935, HO45/16425/688144.

CONCLUSION: THE 'CONTINENTAL MENACE TO OUR FOOTBALL SUPREMACY'

The 1932 Los Angeles Olympics, among other events (e.g. International Horse Show at London, June 1934), reaffirmed the enduring force of the British government's non-interference strategy towards international sport, including its preference to perform no more than a minor role confined to official help with, say, customs, travel and visa arrangements.[173] The 1932 Olympics highlighted another continuity, that is, the strong reluctance to spend public money on international sport; thus, the award made to cover the British consulate's Olympic-related expenses was not only made grudgingly but also amounted to only £50. But, this period also posed new questions for the government, such as those relating to official representation at football matches and post-match banquets, the politico-legal (e.g. law and order) implications arising from the attendance of ever-increasing numbers of foreign supporters at internationals in Britain, and foreign requests for broadcasting facilities. The fact that other governments, like those in Austria and Italy, attached 'great importance' to such matters forced British governments not only to treat them seriously but also to take action. Generally speaking, Northern Ireland, Scotland and Wales rarely figured, if at all, in the government's discussions about the international politics of *British football*, especially as the tendency to conflate England with Britain was encouraged by the fact that during this period the other home countries played either fewer or no foreign internationals. For the wider world, 'England' remained the face of Britain in general and of British football in particular. From this perspective, the 1933 Scotland-Austria game possessed an added interest in terms of occasioning a rare case of official intervention in Scottish football.

The late 1920s and early 1930s were characterised by occasional foreign references to British decadence, as demonstrated by not only political and economic developments but also sport. Of course, in reality, decline is a relative term, and it might have been more accurate to acknowledge that, at least in the world of football, it was perhaps more a case of the game's advance elsewhere rather than of British decay, even if more frequent foreign victories over British teams, and particularly the disappointing results of many clubs engaged on close season tours, prompted media comment. For example, in 1932 press headlines – according to Capel-Kirby and Carter, these included 'Our Degrading Football. England's lost prestige' and 'How our crack teams let down Britain' – were occasioned by poor overseas performances by British clubs.[174] As one newspaper observed, defeats of leading teams, like Newcastle, the FA cup holders, and Everton, had broader consequences: 'it must be accepted that the results of these Continental matches, holiday games as they may be called, do matter. The prestige of British football is at stake ... The people who let British football down are letting Britain down. There is no question about that.'[175] There was less of a problem at the national level. England, though not always performing distinctively, continued to secure good results when it mattered, as demonstrated by its unbeaten record against Austria and Italy between 1930–34 (Table 2.3, Chapter 2). Occasional blips, like away defeats to Spain (1929) and France (1931), were soon reversed by decisive home victories; for example, Spain, having become the first foreign country to defeat England, was soon put in its place in 1931, when England triumphed 7-1. Similarly, England resumed its winning ways over France. Likewise, in December 1933, Scotland, overriding its disappointing results against Austria and Italy in 1931, partially retrieved its reputation through a draw with Austria.

Generally speaking, British football was still perceived by other countries as offering both a source of inspiration and a reference point for world standards; for example, writing in 1933, Hugo Meisl, Secretary of the Austrian Football Association, acknowledged a great 'debt to Britain' in Austria's rise to the first rank of world football.[176] 'Any football nation that puts up a good game against England, Scotland, Ireland or Wales has every reason to be proud. Take no notice of those who argue that Britain is decadent in sport. It is still the home of sport and sportsmanship, and it will be a sad day for the rest of the world when Great Britain ceases to take an active part in International sporting affairs.' But there were two sides to the story, as noted by Walter Bensemann after the 1933 Italy-England match: 'The Football Association has proved once more that there is life in the old dog yet, and Italy has shown that the great teams of the Continent, led by Connaisseurs [sic] like Hugo [i.e. Meisl] or Vittorio Pozzo, are on their way to assume supremacy'.[177] By implication, England was still at or near the top of world football, but needed to be alert in the face of the strong challenge from new powers, like Austria, Germany and Italy; thus, in 1932 England's famous and somewhat fortunate victory (4-3) over Austria, like its two hard matches against Italy (1933, 1934), established that continental opposition should no longer be underestimated. Indeed, during 1934, defeats by Czechoslovakia and Hungary vividly reaffirmed this point, while suggesting the growing strength even of teams categorised one year earlier as merely 'second class' by *Pesti Naplo*.

In part, the tremendous advance of football outside of Britain reflected the adoption of a more progressive and professional attitude towards the game in spheres like coaching, match preparations, and the design of football stadiums.[178] Paradoxically, the skills of British coaches were more valued abroad, such as in Austria, than in Britain, where neither national nor club sides seemed enthusiastic about using their services. For informed commentators, it was in these areas that the British game was being outpaced; thus, in 1933, Capel-Kirby and Carter, criticising the conservatism of an ageing footballing establishment, felt that a change of attitude, and particularly of personnel, was required to meet the foreign challenge: 'England is not moving as fast as the Continental countries, and … the supremacy of Britain is threatened'.[179] Prior to the England-Austria match in 1932, Sharpe witnessed Jimmy Hogan, the Austrian coach, using a blackboard for a tactical talk, a sight unlikely to be seen in an England dressing room.[180] Three years later, Hogan, whose footballing legacy was acknowledged by the Hungarians in the early 1950s, told a FA coaching course of the relatively static nature of the British game, particularly as compared to the rapid advance of the continental game in terms of skills, tactical play, and pre-match preparations.[181] Of course, this FA course, reflecting in part Rous' assumption of the secretaryship in place of Wall, was itself an innovatory, albeit somewhat belated, response to an often articulated problem.

Frequently, continental developments were interpreted as a consequence of the manner in which football and other sports were treated as 'national assets' worthy of state support.[182] Against this background, during the early 1930s, Capel-Kirby and Carter, having surveyed the European scene, trailed the possibility of a British Ministry of Sport, especially as the French Ministry of Physical Education was deemed to establish that such a move could provide a useful enabling framework allowing sporting bodies to operate more effectively without undue political interference. However, for Britons, 'the sound of the title, Ministry of Sport, conjures up visions of fussy top-hatted, old gentlemen, long past athletic activity, devoid of all knowledge of modern sport and its requirements, interfering with rules and regulations, and butting into arrangements of any sporting fixture of an International character'.[183] In any case, there were strict limits to what British governments either felt able or were prepared to do in the sphere of sport – a Ministry of Sport never reached the political agenda – as well as to what British football associations were prepared to accept. After all, their departure from FIFA in 1928 demonstrated strong hostility to any 'butting into' their affairs by any external body.

Meanwhile, both FIFA and member associations saw the growth of international football as serving the interests of the world game, as demonstrated when Schricker, FIFA's Secretary, expressed regret about Turkey's decision not to enter the 1934 World Cup: 'International encounters are a necessity for our sport: such matches are the best means to advance the standards of the game and the ability of the players'.[184] At the same time, international football was presented as helping to improve international relations, and frequent contemporary claims that 'Sport is still the best League of Nations' were encouraged by the fact that the period 1929–33 saw the first post-1918 full internationals between major combatants in the First World War; thus, Germany played Scotland (1929, Berlin: 1-1 draw), England (1930, Berlin: 3-3 draw), France (1931, Paris: France 1 Germany 0; 1933, Berlin: 3-3 draw), and Belgium (1933, Duisburg: Germany 8 Belgium 1).[185]

One interesting development, foreshadowed at the 1928 Olympics and the 1930 World Cup, concerned the rapid growth of sports tourism, as represented by the growth in the number of spectators travelling to watch their national team play in another country, whether it involved some 2–3,000 French spectators visiting Berlin (1933), 15,000 Germans watching their national team play in Paris (1935), or Austrians, Italians and Spaniards visiting Glasgow or London (Table 6.2).[186] For one British observer, this trend reinforced football's international political significance at a time when international travel remained still a minority activity: 'Such games as that between Germany and France at soccer in Berlin are as good as any League of Nations in fostering the spirit of tolerance and peaceful thinking among the nations'.[187] Lord Decies, a BOA vice-president and one-time Council member, moved on to argue that the formation of a European league for national sides, taking advantage of transport improvements, would help establish 'a real League of Nations': 'They would be united, as peoples – not merely through diplomatic channels or by scraps of paper that can be destroyed at will – by the firm bond of sportsmanship'. He felt that Austria's recent visit to England proved the point, for both players and supporters returned to Vienna as 'potential ambassadors for England'.[188]

> It is well to remember that if you play football with a man, box against him, row against him, or compete at any other sport where the best man should win, then you won't want to kill him, no matter what the politicians think about it. We want to foster a real brotherhood of man, and the best way to do it, in my view, is by encouraging the nations to meet each other in games ….
>
> A League of Nations, united by a common interest in sport, is a far greater safeguard of the peace of the world than any League that Pacts can produce – and one that will be infinitely less costly and less likely to split under stress.

Whether or not international football could succeed where political leaders and institutions had failed remains debatable, but such contemporary perceptions provided a foundation for post-1945 presentations of FIFA as the UN of football.[189]

But Lord Decies' views, albeit echoed by Noel-Baker, attracted little support in official British circles, where negative images of international sport predominated, as demonstrated throughout this chapter by official references to, say, 'these confounded games' and the belief that such international 'contests have done more harm than good'. Significantly, this period also witnessed the infamous 'bodyline' controversy in which cricket, having been interpreted traditionally as a cohesive imperial force,

165

threatened the friendly course of Anglo-Australian relations. From this perspective, in 1932 the English team, resorting to intimidatory short pitched bowling, seemed prepared to regain the Ashes at any price, even at the cost of ruining Britain's sporting reputation and losing a dominion.[190] If nothing else, the controversy, like the recent suspension of British rugby fixtures with France, highlighted the difficulty of keeping even cricket separate from politics; indeed, for Stephen Jones, it represented perhaps 'the most contentious' and 'best-known example of government intervention in inter-war sport'.[191] It also showed officials, ministers, the media and public opinion that unsporting conduct and international sports incidents were not the sole preserve of professional footballers. Nor was the growing tendency for large numbers of people to travel to support their respective national teams always viewed as necessarily trouble-free, and, as elaborated in the next chapter, in 1935, the predicted arrival of 10,000 Germans to watch the scheduled England-Germany international prompted considerable discussion and controversy in Britain because of fears of disorder and adverse impacts upon relations between the two countries.

NOTES

1. Capel-Kirby and Carter, p.81.
2. FIFA started a world ranking list in August 1993. The list, updated monthly and indicating how rankings are now determined, is available on FIFA's website: http://www.fifa.com.
3. FIFA, Minutes of 21st Congress, Stockholm, 13–14 May 1932, pp.4–5; Minutes of 22nd Congress, Rome, 24–25 May 1934, p.9.
4. FA, Report of Members in Charge, *Canadian Tour, 1931*, Aug. 1931, 1931–32.
5. FA, ISC, 25 Jan. 1932, minute 5, 15 Feb. 1932, minute 8, 1931–32.
6. FA, Statement of Accounts 1929–30, 20 May 1930, 1930–31.
7. FA, Statement of Accounts, 1930–31, 21 May 1931, 1931–32; Statement of Accounts 1931–32, 18 May 1932, 1932–33; Statement of Accounts 1934–35, 15 May 1935, 1935–36.
8. SFAMT, EFC, 11 Dec. 1929, minutes 61–2, Acc.9017/26, 1929–30.
9. SFAMT, EFC, 1 Oct. 1930, minute 21, Acc.9017/27, 1930–31; EFC, 22 July 1931, minute 5, Acc.9017/28, 1931–32; *Annual Report 1930–31* (SFA, 1931), p.5; Gallagher, p.108.
10. SFAMT, Office-Bearers Meeting, 26 June 1935, minute 13, EFC, 7 Aug. 1935, minute 27, Acc.9017/32, 1935–36; FIFA, G. Randolph Manning, chair, Foreign Relations Committee, USFA, to Schricker, 21 July 1935, USA correspondence, 1932–69; *Alan Breck's Book*, pp.107–22.
11. FIFA, Schricker to Manning, 18 June 1935, Manning to Schricker, 21 July 1935, USA correspondence, 1932–69; *Alan Breck's Book*, p.108.
12. *Alan Breck's Book*, p.33.
13. SFAMT, EFC, 19 Sept. 1931, minute 31, Selection Committee, 4 April 1932, minute 145, Acc.9017/28, 1931–32; Gallagher, p.108; Glanville, *Soccer Nemesis*, p.43.

14. FAW, Council, 21 Feb. 1933, minute 3814, 1931–33; *FAW 75th Anniversary*, pp.30–1.
15. *Annual Report 1929–30* (FAW, 1930), pp.1–3; *Annual Report 1933–34* (FAW, 1934), pp.2–3; *Annual Report 1934–35* (FAW, 1935), p.3; *FAW Rules of the Association*, p.83.
16. FAW, Council, 15 May 1933, 1931–33, *Annual Report 1932–33* (FA, 1933), p.2.
17. Corrigan, Chapter 6 (no page numbers).
18. IFA, Council, 30 Oct. 1934, 1925–44.
19. IFA, Council, 26 Nov. 1935, 5 Nov. 1936, 1925–44.
20. Taylor, *Projection of Britain*, p.153.
21. PRO, memorandum, Rex Leeper, 2 April 1931, FO395/446/P772; Taylor, *Projection of Britain*, p.150.
22. PRO, circular despatch by Lord Reading to missions abroad, 26 Sept. 1931, FO395/446/P2217.
23. Tallents, *The Projection of England*, p.14.
24. Quoted, Taylor, *Projection of Britain*, p.153.
25. Leeper to Vansittart, 14 March 1935, quoted Donaldson, p.41.
26. PRO, Leeper to Yencken, Berlin, 10 March 1931, FO395/446/P4; minute, C. Duff, 26 March 1931, FO395/446/P600, Treasury to Foreign Office, 17 Feb. 1932, FO372/2831/T2029; minute, M. Wright, 28 January 1932, FO372/2831/ T734.
27. D.B. Kanin, *A Political History of the Olympic Games* (Westview, Boulder, 1981), p.51; Allen Guttmann, *The Games Must Go On: Avery Brundage and the Olympic Movement* (Columbia University Press, New York, 1984), pp.60–1.
28. PRO, D. Scott, Foreign Office, to W. Gurney, 30 June 1932, FO369/2295/K7486.
29. PRO, minute, Scott, 22 June 1932, FO369/2295/K7486.
30. PRO, Sir George Knox, Budapest, to S. Hoare, 5 Dec. 1935, FO371/19647/W10610.
31. PRO, Sir F. Lindley, Tokyo, to A. Henderson, 23 July 1931, minute, N. Charles, 24 Aug. 1931, FO371/15521/F4555.
32. PRO, Sir Robert Clive, Tokyo, to A. Eden, 8 April 1936, FO370/510/L2912; E. Crowe, Dept. of Trade, to C. Orde, 16 July 1936, FO370/511/L4823.
33. PRO, Lindley to Henderson, 23 July 1931, FO371/15521/F4555; Gordon Daniels, 'Japanese sport: from Heian Kyó to Tokyo Olympiad', in Binfield and Stevenson, pp.180–4.
34. Yamone, 'Football Game in Japan', *Football World*, 2 (Dec. 1938), 20. One reported contact, albeit occurring later in the decade, came in April 1938 when Islington Corinthians, an amateur team engaged in a lengthy world tour, lost 0–4 in Tokyo: FIFA, note, Japanese Football Association, n.d. (1952), Japan correspondence, 1932–83; R.W. Pickford, 'The psychology of the history and organization of association football, Part. 2', *British Journal of Psychology*, XXXI (1940), 130.
35. For a list of results, etc.: FIFA, note, Japanese Football Association, n.d. (1952), Japan correspondence, 1932–83; *FIFA Handbook, 1935*, p.193.
36. Another Chinese victory (4-3) is recorded for 1934. The 1931 Manchurian Crisis suggests the historical value of further research on this fixture.
37. FIFA, Japanese Football Association to Schricker, 18 April, 31 May, 1 June 1938, Japan correspondence, 1932–83.
38. FIFA, Minutes of 16th Congress, Helsingfors, 3–5 June 1927, pp.8–9.
39. FIFA, Minutes of 19th Congress, Berlin, 6–7 June 1930, p.10; FIFA, Hirschman to USFA, 27 Oct. 1931, Correspondence Jeux Olympiques, 1912–32. Unlike FIFA, the IAAF (International Amateur Athletics Federation) took a tough stance on amateurism, and its suspension of Finland's Paavo Nurmi for accepting remuneration resulted in his exclusion from the 1932 Games: Guttmann, *The Games*

Must Go On, p.60.

40. FIFA, Minutes of 20th Congress, Berlin, 22–3 May 1931, p.14.
41. FIFA, Manning, USFA, to Schricker, n.d. (Aug. 1934), 5 Dec. 1934, USA correspondence, 1932–69.
42. FIFA, Minutes of 20th Congress, Berlin, 22–3 May 1931, p.13; Manning, USFA, to Schricker, n.d. (Aug. 1934), 5 Dec. 1934, USA correspondence, 1932–69.
43. James Riordan, 'Worker sport within a worker state: the Soviet Union', in Krüger and Riordan, p.46; R.B. Lockhart, *Giants Cast Long Shadows* (Methuen, London, 1964), pp.173–4.
44. Samuel S. Shipman, 'Sports in the Soviet Union', *Current History*, XLVII (1937), 81; James Riordan, *Soviet Sport: background to the Olympics* (Blackwell, Oxford, 1980), pp.3–4; Henry W. Morton, *Soviet Sport* (Collier, New York, 1963), pp.17–18.
45. James Riordan, 'The USSR', in J. Riordan (ed.), *Sport under Communism: the USSR, Czechoslovakia, the GDR, Cuba* (Hurst, London, 1978), p.18; Riordan, *Soviet Sport*, p.42; Morton, p.20; John N. Washburn, 'Sport as a Soviet tool', *Foreign Affairs*, 34 (1956), 496; Riordan, *Worker Sport,* pp.46–64.
46. Riordan, *Soviet Sport*, pp.30–3. Morton, p.22, has a different translation.
47. Riordan, *The USSR*, p.21.
48. Quoted, *Hansard (Commons)*, 5th ser. *CCXXXVIII*, 349–50, S. Clynes, 1 May 1930.
49. Riordan, *Soviet Sport*, p.115; Peppard and Riordan, pp.27–43.
50. Riordan, *The USSR*, p.21; James Riordan, *Worker Sport,* pp.62–3.
51. Thomas Woody, *New Minds. New Men?: the emergence of the Soviet citizen* (Macmillan, New York, 1932), p.478; Riordan, *The USSR*, pp.20–1; Norman Schneidmann, *Soviet Road to the Olympics* (Routledge, London, 1979), pp.20–4.
52. Riordan, *Soviet Sport*, pp.113–18.
53. FIFA lists a 4-2 win over Estonia, 18 Sept. 1923: *FIFA Handbook 4th ed* (de Bussy, Amsterdam, 1931), p.196. Compare Peppard and Riordan, pp.38–40, 100–1.
54. Jones, *Sport, Politics and the Working Class*, p.180.
55. Capel-Kirby and Carter, p.84.
56. George Sinfield, 'When our British players gave the Russians a shock', *Daily Worker*, 13 Nov. 1954. See Allan Findlay on 'the great work' of Soviet sport in 1920s: *Westminster Gazette*, 10 Aug. 1927.
57. PRO, minute, Gascoigne, 8 Aug. 1927, FO371/12606/N3771.
58. Sinfield. Sinfield's scoreline (1-11) differs from that (0-11) given by Jones, *BWSF*, p.105; Peppard and Riordan, p.41.
59. Jones, *BWSF*, p.105.
60. Jones, 'State intervention in sport', 172.
61. PRO, minute, F. Newsam, 3 Nov. 1935, HO45/16425/688144; *Hansard (Commons)*, 5th ser. CCXXXVIII, 349–50, 1 May 1930.
62. The relevant file (PRO, HO556038/6) has not been preserved.
63. PRO, minute, Newsam, 3 Nov. 1935, HO45/16425/688144.
64. PRO, minute, L. Baggalley, 28 April 1930, FO371/14883/N2923.
65. PRO, minute, C.H. Bateman, 1 May 1930, FO371/14883/N2923.
66. *Hansard (Commons)*, 5th Ser. CCXXXVIII, 349–50, 1 May 1930.
67. Ibid.; *New York Times*, 22 April 1930.
68. Jones, 'State intervention in sport', 171.
69. PRO, H. Barnett, Wood Green branch, NUR, to Foreign Office, 20 Oct. 1935, FO371/18884/C7175.
70. Jones, 'State intervention in sport', 172.
71. BL, memorandum, 20 July 1934, Appendix B, p.7, CRD 1/60/2 folio 10.
72. CAC, extracts from SCR (probably LSE Senior Common Room) talk by Noel-

Baker, 'Russia and Sport', 12 Feb. 1928, p.1, p.8, NBKR 8/7/2. The file has only an incomplete copy.
73. Sinfield.
74. FIFA, Minutes of 16th Congress, Helsingfors, 3–5 June 1927, p.13.
75. FIFA, Minutes of 17th Congress, Amsterdam, 25–6 May 1928, pp.6–7.
76. Furrer, Godoy and Blatter, p.72, p.76.
77. FIFA, Minutes of 18th Congress, Barcelona, 17–18 May 1929, p.2.
78. FA, ISC, 15 Nov. 1929, minute 2, 1929–30; Wall, FA, to Uruguayan Football Association, 30 Nov. 1929, encl. FO395/434/P1900.
79. SFAMT, Council, 26 Jan. 1927, minute 132, Acc.9017/23, 1926–27; EFC, 30 April 1930, minute 150, Acc.9017/26, 1929–30.
80. Compare, Clive Leatherdale (ed.), *Scotland's Quest for the World Cup: a complete record, 1950–1986* (John Donald, Edinburgh, 1986), p.1; Vic Duke and Liz Crolley, *Football, Nationality and the State* (Longman, Harlow, 1996), p.13; Russell, p.91; Fishwick, p.140.
81. Capel-Kirby and Carter, pp.162–4; Glanville, *Soccer Nemesis*, pp.87–8.
82. Ibid., p.170. Chapter 8, pp.225–7 below, provides evidence of official irritation about the unsporting play of Chelsea players on tour in Poland. Crisp accompanied the team therein.
83. PRO, A. Willert, head of News Dept., to Senor Don MacEachen, Uruguayan embassy, 3 Jan. 1930, FO395/434/P1900.
84. PRO, minute, G. Thompson, 24 Dec. 1929, FO395/434/P1900.
85. FIFA, Minutes of 19th Congress, Budapest, 6–7 June 1930, pp.4–6.
86. Capel-Kirby and Carter, pp.162–4; Murray, pp.129–31.
87. FIFA, Minutes of 20th Congress, Berlin, 22–3 May 1931, p.4; *New York Times*, 23, 24 May 1931.
88. Cottrell, pp.59–60.
89. *Daily Express*, 10 May 1929.
90. *The Times*, 10 May 1929, 7 Dec. 1933.
91. *The Times*, 15 May 1931; *New York Times*, 15 May 1931; Capel-Kirby and Carter, p.86.
92. *The Times*, 7 Dec. 1933.
93. PRO, W. Tyrrell, Paris, to Henderson, 17 Aug. 1931, Willert to Sir Charles Mendl, Paris, 17 Sept. 1931, FO395/455/P2102. Obviously, the lack of opinion polls renders it difficult to verify this assertion.
94. *Daily Telegraph*, 11 Feb. 1931; *The Times*, 21 Oct. 1931.
95. *The Times*, 3, 4 March 1931.
96. *The Times*, 4 March 1931.
97. *Daily Telegraph*, 17 May 1934; *The Times*, 25 March, 12 July 1939; *New York Times*, 25 March 1935.
98. PRO, minutes, R. Wigram, 18, 19, 21 October 1935, FO371/18884/C7348.
99. David Reynolds, *Britannia Overruled: British policy and world power in the 20th century* (Longman, Harlow, 1991), pp.126–33.
100. Victoria de Grazia, *The Culture of Consent: mass organisation of leisure in fascist Italy* (Cambridge University Press, Cambridge, 1981), p.170; Sharpe, *Forty Years*, pp.68–9; Angela Teja, 'Italian sport and international relations under fascism', in Arnaud and Riordan, pp.147–67. For Conservative party discussions on Italian sport, based on information provided by government departments and an Italian paper to the First International Recreation Congress (Los Angeles, 1932): BL, memorandum, 20 July 1934, Appendix B, pp.4–5, CRD 1/60/2 folio 10.
101. PRO, Sir E. Drummond, Rome, to Sir J. Simon, 9 Nov. 1934, FO371/18427/R6327.

102. Quoted Pierre Lanfranchi, 'Bologna: the team that shook the world', *Int.J.Hist.Sport*, 8 (1991), 336.
103. Ibid., 338–9.
104. Quoted Roy Peskett (ed.), *Tom Whittaker's Arsenal Story* (Sporting Handbooks, London, 1957), p.112; Glanville, *Soccer Nemesis*, p.88; Cottrell, p.76.
105. FA, ISC, 28 Dec. 1932, minute 6, 1932–33.
106. PRO, Preston, Turin, to Consular Department, 30 Nov. 1928, FO370/289/L7516.
107. PRO, H. Luke, Lt.-Governor, Malta, to Colonial Office, 9 March 1933, encl. A.J. Dawe, Colonial Office, to Orme Sargent, 15 March 1933, minutes by Duff, R. Lindsay, J.V. Perowne, Willert, March–April 1933, FO395/492/P673.
108. PRO, Orme Sargent to Dawe, 5 April 1933, FO395/492/P673.
109. PRO, minutes, Duff and Lindsay, 18 March 1933, FO395/492/P673.
110. PRO, Dawe to Orme Sargent, 6 April 1933, FO395/492/P673.
111. PRO, Orme Sargent to Dawe, 5 April 1933, FO395/492/P673. Nor have the author's searches at the PRO and the British Library's Newspaper Library revealed such an article.
112. PRO, minute, Perowne, 20 March 1933, FO395/492/P673.
113. Ibid.
114. *New York Times*, 14 May 1933. See also P.J. Bauwens, 'England-Italien', *World's Football*, 44 (15 Jan. 1935), 10–11.
115. PRO, minute, A. Noble, 22 May 1939, FO371/23785/R4193; Wall, p.11.
116. *The Times*, 15 May 1933; *New York Times*, 14 May 1933.
117. Bensemann, 'Missionaries of Sport', 153–4.
118. Hapgood, p.33. For more restrained views: Bastin, pp.115–19; Glanville, *Soccer Nemesis*, p.94.
119. Polley, 'Foreign Office and International Sport', p.xxvii.
120. Bastin, p.118; FIFA, Wall to Schricker, 26 Jan. 1934, England correspondence, 1932–57.
121. Bensemann, 'Missionaries of sport', 152.
122. Ibid., 153.
123. PRO, William McClure, Rome, to C. Norton, 19 July 1933, FO395/492/P1769.
124. PRO, Norton to McClure, 24 July 1933, minute, Duff, 25 July 1933, FO395/492/P1769.
125. PRO, McClure to Leeper, 13 Jan. 1934, FO395/515/P165.
126. PRO, minute, Duff, 19 Jan. 1934, FO395/515/P165. Agreed by M. Huxley and Leeper, 22, 23 Jan. 1934.
127. PRO, minute, Duff, 19 Jan. 1934, FO395/515/P165.
128. PRO, minute, J. Lambert, 25 Jan. 1934, FO395/515/P165.
129. PRO, minutes, Duff, 29 Jan. 1934, Leeper, 30 Jan. 1934, Leeper to McClure, 2 Feb. 1934, FO395/515/P165.
130. FA, ISC, minute 3, 5 March 1934, 1933–34.
131. Bastin, pp.120–2.
132. 'The Italian Football Federation: 75th anniversary', *Italy: Documents and Notes*, 23 (1974), 92; FIFA, Minutes of 21st Congress, Stockholm, 13–14 May 1932, p.10.
133. Furrer, Godoy and Blatter, p.258.
134. Hapgood, p.35; Murray, pp.93–9.
135. FIFA, Schricker to T. Robbins, FAW, 19 April 1933, Wales correspondence, 1932–63; G. Graham, SFA, to Schricker, 6 April 1933, Schricker to Graham, 19 April 1933, 15 June 1933, Scotland correspondence, 1932–65.
136. FIFA, Schricker to Graham, 15 June 1933, Scotland correspondence, 1932–65; Schricker to Wall, 25 May 1933, England correspondence, 1932–57.

137. Bensemann, 'Tutti frutti', 194.
138. FIFA, Schricker to Graham, 27 Nov. 1933, Scotland correspondence, 1932–65.
139. FIFA, Graham to Schricker, 28 Sept. 1933, Scotland correspondence, 1932–65; Wall to Schricker, 30 May 1933, England correspondence, 1932–57.
140. SFAMT, Council, 16 Aug. 1933, minute 65, Selection Committee, 5 Sept. 1933, minute 11, Acc.9017/30, 1933–34. Scotland's 1934 tour does not appear to have taken place.
141. Mason, *Passion of the People?*, p.43.
142. Cottrell, pp.74–5.
143. Ibid., pp.76–7.
144. Ibid. Reputedly, Orsi's transfer to Juventus was secured through a contract promising 8,000 lire per month, a house and a car with chauffeur: Eduardo P. Archetti, 'In search of national identity: Argentinian football and Europe', *Int.J.Hist.Sport*, 12 (1995), 206.
145. FIFA, Schricker to Wall, 12 June 1934, England correspondence, 1932–57.
146. *The Times*, 10 June, 20 June 1934; W. Schmid-Parker, 'Continental menace to our football supremacy', *Football Pictorial*, 12 Oct. 1935.
147. Cottrell, pp.75–6.
148. PRO, Stanley Rous, FA, to Paul Mason, Simon's Private Secretary, 26 Oct. 1934, Owen O'Malley, minute, 30 Oct. 1934, FO371/18439/R6262.
149. PRO, minute, Orme Sargent, 1 Nov. 1934, Mason to Rous, 3 Nov. 1934, minute by Mason, 7 Nov. 1934, FO371/18439/R6262. The relevant file on the Austrian match (C10134/10134/3, 1932) has not been preserved.
150. PRO, Grandi to Simon, 15 Nov. 1934, FO371/18439/R6262. Attendance is listed among Simon's official engagements: BL, Simon's appointments diary, 14 Nov. 1934, MS Simon 30.
151. PRO, minute, Perowne, 12 Nov. 1935, FO371/18884/C7566.
152. See, for example, Glanville, *Soccer Nemesis*, p.88; Jim Munro, 'An old rivalry with passion aplenty', *Sunday Times*, 5 Oct. 1997; Hapgood, pp.36–8; Matthews, pp.23–4. Compare Bastin, pp.113–14.
153. PRO, minute, Noble, 22 May 1939, FO371/23785/R4193.
154. Matthews, p.24.
155. Hapgood, p.37.
156. FA, Statement of Accounts 1934–35, 15 May 1935, 1935–36.
157. PRO, Grandi to Simon, 15 Nov. 1934, FO371/18439/R6262; *New York Times*, 15 Nov. 1934.
158. Taylor, *Projection of Britain*, p.189.
159. Ibid., pp.181–215; Asa Briggs, *The History of Broadcasting in the United Kingdom: Vol. II: the golden age of wireless* (Oxford University Press, Oxford, 1965), p.395.
160. Russell, pp.106–7.
161. John, pp.72–5.
162. PRO, Baron Dr G. Frankenstein, Austrian Legation in London, to Simon, 24 Nov. 1933, FO395/492/P2745; Murray, p.89.
163. Glanville, *Soccer Nemesis*, pp.54–60.
164. John, p.75
165. PRO, Frankenstein to G. Graham, SFA, 21 Nov. 1933, Frankenstein to Simon, 9 Dec. 1933, FO395/492/P2745. The Austrian team, playing as Vienna, then lost 2–4 to Arsenal: Glanville, *Soccer Nemesis*, pp.60–1.
166. FA, Hugo Meisl to FA, 4 Jan. 1933, encl. Council, 16 Jan. 1933, minute 6, 1932–33.
167. Capel-Kirby and Carter, p.87, pp.88–93.
168. PRO, G. Cock, BBC, to Frankenstein, 24 Nov. 1933, FO395/492/P2745; SFAMT,

171

Council, 20 Aug. 1930, minute 89, Acc.9017/27, 1930–31.

169. PRO, Cock to Frankenstein, 24 Nov. 1933, FO395/492/P2745.

170. PRO, Frankenstein to Simon, 24 Nov. 1933, FO395/492/P2745.

171. PRO, H. Hopkin, Foreign Office to D. Milne, Scottish Office, 23 Nov. 1933, FO395/492/P2745; SFAMT, Selection Committee, 13 Dec. 1933, minute 29, Council, 14 March 1934, minute 142, Acc.9017/30, 1933–34.

172. PRO, Simon to Sir Godfrey Collins, Scottish Office, 27 Nov. 1933, Frankenstein to Simon, 9 Dec. 1933, FO395/492/P2745. Rapid Wien played Hearts and Rangers in August 1934.

173. PRO, file FO370/455/L477 (1934).

174. Quoted, Capel-Kirby and Carter, pp.66–7.

175. Ibid.

176. Hugo Meisl, 'Our debt to Britain', foreword in Capel-Kirby and Carter, p.17.

177. Bensemann, 'Missionaries of Sport', 153–4.

178. Capel-Kirby and Carter, pp.46–9, pp.131–4.

179. Ibid., pp.237–8. Support for younger men was justified by pointing to the FA's octogenarian president (Clegg) and septuagenarian secretary (Wall). Herbert Chapman, the Arsenal manager, was another contemporary advocate of coaching: John Graves (ed.), *Herbert Chapman on Football* (Garrick, London, 1934).

180. Sharpe, *Forty Years*, p.49.

181. Quoted, Schmid-Parker, 'Continental menace', 18. For Hungarian praise, see *Daily Mirror*, 26 Nov. 1954; *Daily Worker*, 26 Nov. 1954.

182. Capel-Kirby and Carter, p.232.

183. Ibid., pp.52–4. On French politics and sport, see Pierre Arnaud, 'French sport and the emergence of authoritarian regimes, 1919–1939', in Arnaud and Riordan, pp.114–35.

184. FIFA, Schricker to Hamdi Emin, Turkish Football Federation, 26 Dec. 1933, Turkey correspondence, 1932–70.

185. Capel-Kirby and Carter, p.69.

186. Ibid., pp.230–1; Murray, pp.89–90; Lanfranchi, 340.

187. Decies, 154. For a match report stressing the political dimension, see René Lehmann, 'Allemagne-France', *World's Football*, 37 (April–May 1933), 154.

188. Decies, 154; Meisl, 'Our Debt to Britain', p.17.

189. SFAMT, Sir Charles Clegg, Notes of observations at London Conference, 19 Nov. 1928, Acc.9017/411; Capel-Kirby and Carter, p.239; Kennard quoted, Bensemann, 'Missionaries of sport', 153.

190. See Birley, pp.246–51; Holt, *Sport and the British*, pp.233–6.

191. Jones, 'State intervention in sport', 170.

7

'The Greatest ever Triumph of the "Keep Politics Out of Sport" Brigade'? England versus Germany, 1935

In November 1935 a *Football Pictorial* cartoon looked forward to the England-Germany international scheduled to be played on 4 December at Tottenham Hotspur's White Hart Lane ground. Despite being dwarfed by the German goalkeeper, an England forward scored by shouting 'heil' and slipping the ball past the goalkeeper whose arm had been raised automatically in the Nazi salute.[1] Inevitably, the fixture gained considerable visibility in both the footballing and political senses, especially as it resulted in what Sir John Simon, the Home Secretary (1935–37), described as the 'Nazi invasion' of London, it being the largest one-day influx of foreign visitors to date.[2] Moreover, controversies within and outside Britain about the forthcoming Berlin Olympics meant that the match was viewed in part as a 'test case' for the 1936 Games as well as yet another element in the Nazi 'cultural offensive ... to give British people a favourable impression of Germans'.[3]

Resulting media, official and other exchanges offer illuminating insights into the inter-relationship, or rather the alleged non-relationship, between politics and sport in Britain as well as the state of relations between two major powers at a time when Hitler's Germany, having been identified recently by the Defence Requirements Committee (February 1934) as Britain's 'ultimate potential enemy against whom our "long-range" defence policy must be directed', figured prominently in official British thinking.[4] Also, the fact that the episode is well covered in the archives enhances its value as a case study, given the way in which preceding weeks were characterised by a wide-ranging debate within and outside government about the politics of international football. Broadly speaking, discussion revolved around questions raised by Simon at the time: was the England-Germany match merely 'a game of football', or 'a sporting fixture with political implications'?[5] Or, as one newspaper asked readers: 'is it necessary to take your politics with you down to White Hart Lane Wednesday afternoon?'.[6] For the government, there were more specific concerns. Was the match primarily a matter of either law and order or international politics? In turn, did it fall within the sphere of responsibility of the Home Office or the Foreign Office? How should the government respond to pressures exerted by various individuals and groups seeking variously to support or stop the game? What might be the consequences for British domestic and foreign policy of either allowing or prohibiting the game? In particular, what impact would any resulting incidents or controversies exert upon Anglo-German relations? There were, of course, several other questions.

One of the *Daily Worker*'s least controversial assertions about this 'Nazi Football Stunt' was the claim that 'in Nazi Germany there is no sport apart from Nazi politics'.[7] The British government was generally well informed about developments in Germany, and naturally official perceptions regarding the political character of sport therein, including the fact that it functioned very differently from Britain, were boosted following Hitler's advent to the chancellorship in January 1933. Simon, whose previous post as Foreign Secretary (1931–35) had acquainted him fully with the German question, adjudged it vital to maintain 'in our own country a tradition that this sporting fixture is carried through without any regard to politics at all'.[8] Most British newspapers supported this line; thus, the *Daily Express*, seemingly forgetting what it had written seven years earlier about 'Football by order of the F.O.', used an editorial entitled 'Nazi Footballers' to observe that 'the affair, after all, is only a football game. It should not be turned into something that may have unhappy consequences.'[9] Subsequently, the fact that the game went ahead, or rather that the government failed to stop it, reinforced long-standing impressions about the autonomy of British sport. Certainly, the government's *apparent* decision not to intervene was capable of such an interpretation, as indicated by Simon Hoggart's presentation of the episode as 'the greatest ever triumph of the "Keep Politics Out of Sport" brigade'?[10] Non-interference remained the preferred strategy, but the British government found it impossible either to stand aside or to avoid treating the match as a political event.

As happened during the 1920s, sport, like most other topics, continued to be covered principally at the official level, for international sport was rarely perceived as serious enough to warrant ministerial, let alone Cabinet, intervention. But international conditions were creating new pressures. During the early 1930s, the escalating threat posed by Germany, Italy and Japan to Britain's global interests, in conjunction with the rapid growth of hostile propaganda, moderated British reticence towards national projection, as demonstrated by the creation of the British Council (1934–35).[11] For British governments, seeking to develop a more coherent response to the foreign challenge, it became increasingly difficult to ignore the propaganda potential of international sport, including its perceived role as an instrument of national advertisement for British power and values. Although the 1936 Berlin Olympics became the central focus for the politics–sport debate within Britain during this period, football internationals were no less important, particularly when England faced a national team from a country, like Germany, whose high footballing reputation was reinforced by the government's prominence for British policy-makers.

'UNPOLITICAL SPORTSMEN ARE UNTHINKABLE IN HITLER'S STATE'

Contemporary images about the apolitical nature of British sport were strengthened by the widespread acknowledgement of the contrast with England's opponents, Germany, where football, like other sports, performed a blatant political role, as reiterated in December 1935 by Sir Eric Phipps, the British ambassador in Berlin: 'the National Socialist Party are slowly but surely tightening their hold on German sport'.[12] Sport, he asserted, was subject to greater political control and exploitation in Germany as compared to either other countries or previous German history; thus, the process of *Gleichschaltung* (coordination) forced German sport into the National Socialist mould in pursuit of Hitler's totalitarian and expansionist aspirations: 'Under the Nazis the sporting contest became just another branch of the greater struggle – the creation of a "new" and "pure" Germany' (Woeltz).[13] State glorification was to the fore for a regime led by a politician believing in the power of propaganda to bring about a 'mental revolution' supportive of the regime: 'Propaganda, propaganda, propaganda. All that matters is propaganda.'[14]

> He [Hitler] decided however that it was the German people and not his plans which needed changing. A great deal was done and said from 1933 onwards to prepare them for war by glorifying the martial virtues, by explaining how much stronger Germany had become, by exciting indignation over injustices inflicted on Germany and Germans by other people.[15]

Decisive action, like Hitler's coups in walking out of the Disarmament Conference (October 1933), denouncing the disarmament clauses of the 1919 Versailles Treaty (March 1935) or reoccupying the Rhineland (March 1936), proved most effective, but significant contributions were made by other activities, not excluding sport, as highlighted by the 1936 Berlin Olympics.[16]

For Hitler's Germany, sporting success, including victory in high profile football internationals, seemed capable of presentation to domestic and external audiences as the product of a German nation composed of gifted Aryans and led by Hitler.[17] Working alongside political education, sport offered a subtle form of indoctrination used to inspire the people, and especially the youth, to believe in their often proclaimed racial superiority and role in the construction of a dynamic new order. Or, to quote one of Hitler's critics, German sportsmen and women, presented as 'soldiers of sport', were 'indoctrinated with grotesque conceptions of national prestige' to play their part in one of the most serious attacks to date on the notion that politics had no place in sport.[18] Unsurprisingly, sportsmen and women were placed under ever-increasing pressure to establish their political soundness in Germany's 'Neuordnung', as suggested by the German News Bureau's report that 'in the future, winners of athletic contests in the Third Reich may be only those who master National Socialist ideology and who make it known that not only in athletic contests but also in nationalistic life, do they stand up for that ideology'.[19] Reportedly, in July 1935, Dresden's Blau Weiss club was deprived of victory in the Middle German tennis championships because of the allegedly unsatisfactory replies given to local party officials by players, who were expected to 'show that they can hold their ground not only in sporting contests but in the national life'.[20]

In many respects, sport was viewed as a national asset strengthening the state through the psychological rearmament of the German people: 'the Nazis' glorification of teamwork, comradeliness and physical fitness was amalgamated with aggressive patriotism'.[21] Phipps frequently stressed sport's contribution to both social control and military strength: 'It is one of the more important objectives of Nazi policy to develop the health and strength of the nation, and sport is also valued for the unifying influence which it exercises on Germans of different classes and from different states'.[22] Colonel Hotblack, the British military attaché in Berlin, echoed this line, when reporting that the German army was impressed with sport's reputed value in giving the British 'stamina and good nerves in the last war'.[23]

From an early stage of his political career, Hitler, albeit no sportsman himself, demonstrated an appreciation of the political value of physical culture and sport. For example, in February 1920 the 25 articles adopted by the emerging National Socialist party included a recognition of the state's role in raising national standards of health and physical fitness through gymnastics and sport, with particular regard to the 'physical development of the young' (article 21).[24] Writing in Mein Kampf a few years later, Hitler linked 'healthy bodies' with national power: 'Physical culture must inoculate the individual with the conviction of his superiority and give him … those athletic skills which serve as a weapon for the defence of the nation'.[25] Inevitably, his advent to the chancellorship in January 1933 ushered in a stronger emphasis upon philosophical aspects, as exemplified by Bruno Malitz's *Die Leibesübungen in der Nationalsozialistischen Idee* (1933): 'There is one sentence in German sports which we, who are National Socialists, ... negate. The sentence is, "Politics do not belong in Sport". For the Nazi, "Politics belong in sports" ... National Socialism can look at sport only from the point of view of the unity of the nation ... Sport must be recaptured ... and used as a weapon for the genuine building of a nation ... We Nazis want to educate the people through sport.'[26] 'International propaganda reasons' were identified as also warranting wide-ranging government control, even regarding team selection, while Malitz's attack on alien, particularly Jewish, influences led into a critique of the way in which, say, German football emulated Austrian, English and Hungarian practice and employed foreign coaches.

Kurt Münch's *Deutschkunde über Volk, Staat, Leibesübungen: Hilfsbuch für die politische Erziehung in den Vereinen des deutschen Reichsbund für Leibesübungen,* a 413-page National Socialist 'education' manual published in late 1935, served as a political bible for German sport, a view encouraged by its use of catechism to inculcate the party message through questions of the 'Why must gymnasts and sportsmen fight Jewry?' format. Naturally, it offered a rather one-sided view of history, but British readers of translated extracts – in December 1935, these included Phipps and Vansittart – were left in no doubt about the Nazi regime's distinctive vision of sport, since, to quote the former, 'the political importance of sport is insisted upon throughout the book'.[27] Phipps cited a key section:

> Gymnastics and sport are thus an institution for the education of the body and a school of the political will in the service of the State. Unpolitical, so-called neutral gymnasts and sportsmen, are unthinkable in Hitler's state .... National socialism is on the road to creating a new sport, which is to be a German political education of the body. The consciousness of sport that it is to fulfil a German mission in the world, and the pride of the sportsman in being allowed to fight under the swastika as the outward expression of a strong German Reich, have won the respect of our foreign sporting comrades. Only a strong sporting institution, as strong in achievement and behaviour as the groundwork of the strong Fatherland, can win the friendship of the sportsmen of other countries. That is the natural reason for which German sport in National Socialist Germany now enjoys a greater measure of respect abroad.

Another British reader was Philip Noel-Baker – he relied on brief extracts published in the *Daily Herald* – who welcomed it as an 'important'

177

publication providing ammunition for the regime's critics, and particularly for the ongoing campaign against British participation in the Berlin Olympics.[28]

VON TSCHAMMER UND OSTEN AS *REICHSSPORTS FÜHRER*

In December 1935, the Berlin embassy, reaffirming previous reports, reminded London about the hierarchical nature of German sport: 'All sport and athletics in present day Germany are under the control of the *Deutsche Reichsbund für Leibesübungen*' (German Federal Association for Physical Culture).[29] This central authority, created in 1934 to develop 'the national consciousness in the spirit of the National Socialist State' through physical culture, was headed by Captain Hans von Tschammer und Osten (1887–1943, hereafter Osten), the *Reichssports Führer* (leader of German Sport: 1933–43). Procedures continued to evolve, but, basically, a four-fold scheme, based on the Reich, regional divisions (16), sub-regions, and clubs linked to schools, the army and municipalities, displaced the sporting role performed by labour, religious, non-Nazi political and other groupings in Weimar Germany. Its executive and administrative bodies formed part of the *Haus des deutschen Sport* (House of German Sport). The latter was located in Berlin's Reichssportfeld, which was described by a visiting British delegation in glowing terms as a 'Wonder of the World' offering an 'ever present inspiration and help to German athleticism' now and in the future.[30]

Osten, whose wartime hand injury is apparent in most photographs, often wore uniform, as if to establish the fact that he was more of a party official than a sports appointee. As *Reichssports Führer*, he codified the regime's instrumental approach to sport, which was subjected to 'the same process of drastic change that has been applied to our country's political constitution, its economy, its laws and all its other activities': 'When, therefore, a revolutionary change was effected in the organisation of German sports after the advent of the National Socialist Government, it was not intended to enthrone centralisation for its own sake, but rather to raise the biological standards of the whole nation, to safeguard its cultural aspects, and to restore social, religious and economic peace'.[31] Good team performances, upholding collective values, were welcomed as 'an area of development for soldierly qualities and for the education of national spirit': 'The military authorities are well aware that it will be a great advantage if every young recruit is good at his sports'.[32] Naturally, every opportunity was taken to extol German virtues; for example, in November 1935, when visiting Athens on Olympic business, Osten's hosts received – to quote the British minister therein – 'numerous dissertations upon Germany's role in Europe as the inheritor of the classical tradition of physical culture'.[33]

Osten, welcoming delegates to the 1936 FIFA Congress held at Berlin to coincide with the Olympics, articulated the 'importance of the most popular sport of football for the relations between the Nations'.[34] However, despite frequently pressing sport's role in improving international relations, football was often exploited for more divisive purposes, as evidenced by the use of victories to sing the praises of the new Germany, particularly as compared to other countries' shortcomings.[35] In practice, as Phipps reported, the government's approach to any specific fixture depended on a range of variables, including its perceived international importance, the sporting reputation of the opposition, and the political complexion (diplomatic, ideological, political) of the opposing team's government *vis-à-vis* Germany. By implication, any success against England in the national sport would be strongly valued for both footballing and political reasons.[36] Obviously, it was difficult for the British embassy to identify the actual demarcation of role between the *Deutscher Reichsbund für Leibesübungen* and the DFB, but clearly the government's control extended to cover the approval of international fixtures. Certainly, Osten, presenting the *Fuhrerprinzip* as the key to sporting success, proved intolerant of any public criticism of selection, such as occurred regarding the team picked to play Hungary in January 1934.[37] Indeed, the *Reichssports Führer*, having identified Germany's 'politically important tasks', threatened 'ruthless steps' against 'liberal' elements, as he described critics, even if British diplomats wondered how this threat could be made effective.[38]

Preceding pages, drawing on materials becoming available throughout the 1930s, offer a fuller picture than that available to the British government during the weeks leading up to the 1935 England-Germany game. Even so, by October–November 1935, the British government was already well informed about developments in Germany; in fact, it probably knew more about the sporting scene therein than in any other country, even if there was the associated problem of evaluating how far the regime's totalitarian pretensions were made effective.[39] Naturally, for British governments seeking to steer clear of sport, Anglo-German sporting relations posed tricky problems, for any kind of move, even inaction, was bound to be interpreted in political terms, especially as British critics of Nazi Germany, most notably, the labour movement, saw sport as a medium through which to propagate an anti-fascist message as well as to exert pressure upon Hitler's regime.

FOOTBALLING *FAIT ACCOMPLI*

Summer 1935 saw the finalisation of arrangements between the FA and DFB for a return fixture for that played at Berlin in 1930.[40] The latter, the first match played between the two countries since the First World War (see Table 3.3, Chapter 3), passed off without incident. Paradoxically, most problems occurred before the fixture was even agreed by the respective footballing authorities, that is, during 1928–29. Then, the coincidence of the FA's exchanges with the Foreign Office about Italian football and delay in accepting a DFB invitation resulted in mistaken press reports to the effect that the British government, fearful of the broader consequences of defeat, opposed a German fixture. The resulting media controversy was soon forgotten, but the episode reinforced long-standing Foreign Office fears about being seen to interfere in international sport, especially in cases involving a major power, like Germany.

In the event, in 1929, the FA, acting on its own volition rather than in response to government pressure, agreed to play Germany the following year. Naturally, England's reputation as a major force in the game, in conjunction with the international political significance of Anglo-German relations, ensured that the match aroused widespread contemporary interest. In Germany, where people seemed 'inclined to take their sports a little too seriously', England's visit was treated as the 'biggest sporting event' for years, perhaps even 'the great football battle for the supremacy of the world'.[41] By contrast, W. Schmid-Parker claimed, somewhat dubiously, that the match, played on 10 May 1930 before some 50,000 people, was treated by England as merely another international 'having no national importance at all'.[42] A clean and exciting game ended in a 3-3 draw. Sections of the British media, adopting a somewhat patronising tone, recorded the 'respectful' attitude displayed in Germany towards England's professional footballers, while assuming that England, having been reduced to ten men through injury, would have won if the team had remained at full strength throughout the match.[43] A few days later, England travelled on to Vienna, where its match against Austria ended goalless.[44]

Five years elapsed before the next England-Germany fixture, by which time Hitler's advent to power had transformed the position of German sport; thus, affiliation to the *Deutscher Reichsbund für Leibesübungen* made the DFB subject to a range of government controls, most notably, concerning fixtures.[45] By contrast, the British government was presented with the fixture, described as 'privately arranged without our knowledge' by the FA, as a *fait accompli*.[46] Obviously, the FA, despite possessing a considerable degree of autonomy, was unable to ignore international realities, but from this perspective the forthcoming fixture would have been seen by the FA – there exists no hard evidence for this claim – as conforming to the ongoing British search for détente with Germany, as highlighted recently by the government's acquiescence in Hitler's introduction of conscription (March 1935) in defiance of the Treaty of Versailles and the conclusion of the Anglo-German Naval Agreement (June 1935).

As a result, the British government was confronted with a situation which had developed initially without its knowledge, let alone its approval or under its control. Arrangements for the fixture, scheduled for Tottenham's White Hart Lane ground on 4 December 1935, were finalised by 27 August, but it appears that the government did not become aware of the fixture until *circa* 19 September, when the Home Office received a request from a German steamship company for permission to land supporters at Southampton. A further month elapsed before the game attracted the attention of the media, whose initial coverage concentrated on the negative reactions of various anti-fascist, Jewish, and left-wing groups towards the mere idea of entertaining a team seen as representing a regime guilty of serious excesses against the Church, Jews and the labour movement. The *Star*'s 'Jews Up in Arms' report, urging that the match 'must be stopped', typified the tone of initial reports.[47] Barnett Janner, then Liberal MP for Whitechapel and a long-standing champion of Jewish sporting interests (e.g. request for waiving visa fees for Jewish athletes competing in Palestine, January 1932), predicted a major protest campaign: 'the great mass of English football followers regard the Nazi persecution of Roman Catholics, churchpeople, and Jews as a violation of the rules of sportsmanship'.[48]

'THERE IS THE MAKING OF MUCH POLITICAL TROUBLE'

Representations for a ban on the fixture soon arrived at the FA as well as at the Foreign and Home Offices, among other government departments. They emanated from a diverse range of individuals and bodies, including the Trades Union Congress (TUC); individual trade unions, like the National Union of Railwaymen (NUR), Transport and General Workers Union, Electrical Trade Union, and National Union of Unemployed Workers; trade union branches (e.g. Wood Green branch of the NUR); political party branches (e.g. Barnsley and District Labour Party); trade councils (e.g. Southgate Trades Council); and other pressure groups (e.g. British Non-Sectarian League, Anti-Nazi Council). A general sense of solidarity with those persecuted by Hitler's regime was reinforced by fears about the game's use for the purposes of Nazi propaganda. Significantly, both the Wood Green NUR branch and Southgate Trades Council, among others, argued that the ban imposed on the entry of a Soviet football team in 1930 set a clear precedent for government intervention.[49] Nor was the situation helped by either Tottenham Hotspur's strong Jewish links or rumoured plans for German players, supporters and fascist sympathisers to march to the ground through Jewish residential areas, like Stamford Hill and Stoke Newington. Unsurprisingly, the local press (e.g. *Tottenham and Edmonton Weekly Herald*), like the *Jewish Chronicle*, was active in articulating the potential for disorder.[50]

Another initial complicating factor concerned press allegations that a Jewish footballer in a Polish team had been stoned to death by local Nazis at a match held recently at Ratibor, Upper Silesia.[51] Indeed, reports about a handbill and poster campaign directed at British football grounds to publicise the incident prompted a swift response from the German embassy in London, as evidenced on 16 October when Baron Marschall, the First Secretary, called at the Foreign Office to dispute the charges.[52] One day later, Prince Bismarck, the Counsellor, phoned to deny that there had been such a match, let alone any fatality. In this manner, the embassy, seeking to contain the impact of protests, implied the German government's desire to remove any obstacle to the fixture.

Clearly, the forthcoming match raised various policy issues for the British government, and, on 17 October 1935 the Foreign and Home Offices, represented by Ralph Wigram, head of the Central Department, and F.A. Newsam, Permanent Under-Secretary of State, respectively, met to consider the problem. In turn, this session provided the basis for what proved a regular series of inter-departmental exchanges, held normally at official level but occasionally drawing in ministers. Throughout, von Hoesch, the German ambassador, and other members of the German embassy remained in close and frequent touch with the Foreign Office, with the FA, police and Special Branch being consulted as required.[53] However, initial official exchanges, which concentrated upon the poster campaign, revealed substantial points of inter-departmental disagreement consequent upon differing policy priorities and varying perceptions of the problem. The Home Office, impressed by the legal difficulty of proving the threat of 'riot' and a breach of the peace, inclined to inaction.[54] By contrast, Sir Robert Vansittart, the Permanent Under-Secretary of State at the Foreign Office, expressed strong irritation about Home Office inertia towards the poster campaign: 'this is an intolerable attitude to take. We do not want incidents and yet no one will do anything to stop it.'[55] In particular, 'this kind of thing contributes to wider breaches of peace, and we must not take refuge behind red tape. Get the H.O. to do this.' The Foreign Office seemed particularly anxious to respond positively to German pressure by defusing the situation, as demonstrated on 18 October, when an unofficial press briefing was called to expose the 'fabrications' underlying media coverage of the Ratibor incident.[56] Significantly, the German embassy, having been forewarned about the briefing, expressed gratitude for such corrective action.

Even so, the Foreign Office, though acknowledging the extreme urgency of the question, remained reluctant to take the lead, and sought continually to push responsibility onto the Home Office; thus, Wigram, seconded by Vansittart, advised that it 'does not seem to be our (i.e. Foreign Office) affair'.[57] However, this non-committal stance failed to disguise the Foreign Office's awareness of the fixture's foreign policy implications, given the government's ongoing desire to improve Anglo-German relations through the accommodation of reasonable grievances against the peace treaties. Thus, the risk of unpleasant incidents on or off the field from allowing the match to go ahead, such as by either standing aside or dissuading the FA from postponement, had to be balanced against that of offending the German government through non-fulfilment of the fixture. Regardless of the actual reasons, a ban was bound to be seen in Germany as the result of government intervention, and hence would – to quote Wigram – 'not improve our relations with Germany', particularly given its implications for the politically more significant Berlin Olympics.[58] Risk evaluation was influenced in part by what Wigram referred to as the 'unfortunate experience' of a France-England international held at Paris some four years earlier, following which it was 'thought advisable not to hold these matches' for the time being.[59] In reality, he appears to have confused association football with its rugby union variant – the post-1931 Anglo-French rugby rift was mentioned earlier – but this failed to stop official attitudes being influenced by hazy and inaccurate memories of past events. Wigram minuted that 'on the whole, I am for caution'. Vansittart agreed, but fears about an 'unchecked Nazi influx' led him to request more information, such as about the expected number of visiting supporters and whether they would be wearing distinctive badges and uniforms.[60]

Hitherto, visiting spectators for football internationals had posed a minimal threat to law and order. The previous year's England-Italy game was still embedded in official memories as 'the Battle of Highbury', but trouble was confined to the pitch. Reportedly, the presence of some 5,000 Italian supporters caused no serious problems either in or around the ground, while further enquiries revealed that hitherto foreign supporters travelling to matches held in Britain or abroad (see Table 6.2, Chapter 6) had prompted no real disorder. Any problems had proved minor, as shown by the arrest of some 20 demonstrators when Germany played in Amsterdam during February 1935.[61] Vansittart was reassured by news that, on 17 March 1935, the France-Germany match, watched by some 15,000 Germans, passed without incident, in spite of the fact that it took place in Paris on the day following Hitler's announcement of conscription in breach of the Versailles Treaty.[62] Nevertheless, fears of unrest, even riots, consequent upon the presence of some 10,000 German spectators dominated the thinking of the Home Office, which appeared from an early stage – to quote Vansittart's reading of early exchanges – 'very anxious' to stop the match.[63] Even so, the Home Office, having studied the relevant papers, decided that the 1930 ban did not constitute a precedent because, unlike Soviet visitors in 1930, neither German players nor spectators required entry visas.

Vansittart, sensing that the Foreign Office was placed between Scylla and Charybdis, began to wish that the game had never been arranged: 'there is the making of much trouble here', even worse, '*political trouble*'.[64] A few weeks later, he went further, when complaining about the FA's freedom of action: 'Whether it was originally wise to fix the match may be questioned'.[65] However, the fact that the game had already been arranged and publicised forced the British government not only to assume that the match would take place but also to treat the fixture, at least in private, as far more than a sporting event, particularly as various pressure groups, pursuing their respective agendas, already viewed it through political spectacles.[66] The potentially serious policy implications, respecting both Anglo-German relations and law and order, led officials to bring in the responsible ministers at an early stage, even if the frequency and scale of their involvement was to be constrained by other preoccupations, most notably, the Ethiopian dispute and the forthcoming general election scheduled for 14 November 1935. Having met Simon, Sir Samuel Hoare, the Foreign Secretary (June–December 1935), welcomed the basic conclusion – 'we have agreed not to intervene. It is a Home Office affair' – but regretted that 'the H.O. don't like the test'.[67]

A MATTER OF LAW AND ORDER?

Initially, the anticipated presence of several thousand Germans in and around London remained the prime focus. Indeed, for Orme Sargent, 'what is objectionable is not so much the match but the fact that 10,000 Nazis are coming over to attend it'.[68] This comment illustrates also the official tendency to describe visiting spectators as 'Nazis', not Germans, especially as the state of the economy, in conjunction with exchange control, suggested that any exodus would have to be approved, even subsidised, by the German government.

Meanwhile, inter-departmental discussions, conducted primarily by Sir Russell Scott (Home Office), Vansittart, and Lord Trenchard, the Commissioner of Police, examined key points of difficulty, with particular regard to the dissemination of Nazi propaganda, the wearing of badges and emblems by German spectators, the prospect of demonstrations, and the avoidance of unmanageable burdens on the police. On 4 November, Trenchard reassured the Home Office that the police, following further consultations with the FA, felt able 'to keep control without over much difficulty', even if some spectators, including Germans, might find themselves in court.[69] The number of police assigned to the game was more than trebled (i.e. 700 instead of the usual 200), while German spectators were to be placed in a separate stand entered through a special turnstile. In addition, the government, taking advantage of the embassy's anxiety to minimise any threat to the match, secured German guarantees about the orderly and unprovocative behaviour (e.g. no swastika badges) of both players and spectators. To some extent, police assurances were influenced by the fact that, on 27 October, an anti-Nazi demonstration (i.e. not against the forthcoming fixture as such), addressed by Sir Walter Citrine (President of the Anti-Nazi Council, TUC General Secretary) and Clement Attlee (leader of the Labour Party), arranged at Hyde Park by the British Non-Sectarian Anti-Nazi Council, passed off in an 'orderly' fashion.[70] Nor did it attract the large numbers predicted, even if one believes press (20,000) rather than police estimates (4–5,000).

OFFICIAL REPRESENTATION AT THE MATCH

The Foreign Office re-evaluated its position yet again, when it received the usual FA invitation, dated 9 November, to attend both the match and post-match banquet. In the ensuing exchanges, law and order issues merged with those of international politics, especially as Osten, accompanied by members of the German embassy, was expected to attend both events.[71] Indeed, the *Reichssports Führer*, who had recently visited Athens to arrange for the carriage of the Olympic flame to Berlin, was felt likely to use his visit for discussions about British participation in the 1936 Games.[72]

Resulting exchanges yielded further evidence of the Foreign Office's

SCORING FOR BRITAIN

preoccupation with precedent; thus, Perowne, referring to departmental
representation at the Austrian and Italian internationals played in 1932 and
1934 respectively, ruled out attendance at the banquet because of the lack
of precedent.[73] Perhaps, the position regarding banquets might warrant re-
consideration, but for the time being Perowne, like Orme Sargent and
Wigram, saw 'no particular reason why the F.O. sh^d be represented ...
Official Governmental or F.O. representation on an occasion of this sort wh.
has been privately arranged without our knowledge is not strictly
necessary'. In particular, fears that the match might become the 'Battle of
White Hart Lane' – the 'Battle of Highbury' was still fresh in official
memories – and hence the subject of adverse press and parliamentary
comment, prompted caution about appearing to depart from the norm in this
case. Nor was Perowne enthusiastic about following precedent through
attendance at a match 'at wh. 10,000 badged Nazis are it is announced to be
present and at wh. ugly scenes are anticipated'. In any case, representation
only seemed worthwhile if undertaken by the minister himself, a possibility
ruled out by the fact that the opening of Parliament was scheduled for the
day prior to the match.

Vansittart conceded the force of counter-arguments, but concluded that
'We *should* be represented at the match'.[74] Hoare, though ruling out high-
level attendance undertaken by either Vansittart or himself, agreed, and the
FA was informed accordingly.[75] At the same time, the relatively novel
nature of government attendance at football matches in Britain, alongside
an appreciation of the practice's policy implications, suggested the need to
establish clear guidelines for the future. As a result, Vansittart issued
instructions for a departmental study of overseas practice concerning
official representation and/or attendance at international sporting
engagements. Of course, this study would take time, so that any report (see
Table 8.2, Chapter 8) would only become available some time after the
England-Germany game.[76]

'LET THE MATCH STAND'

By mid-November, the British government accepted that, on balance, it was
preferable to allow the match to take place. Nor did the general election –
this returned the National Government and brought no switch of minister at
the Foreign and Home Offices – prompt any change of course. Simon and
Hoare agreed that 'it is best not to seek to prevent the fixture taking place',
for 'it is not thought that there will be any real disorder and there should be
no difficulty in the police being perfectly able to maintain order, and the

match should proceed in an orderly way'.[77] Moreover, Home Office exchanges, acknowledging that 'It has not hitherto been the policy to attempt to interfere with the dissemination in this country of Nazi propaganda, though a close watch is kept upon it', revealed also a desire to avoid the appearance of giving way to outside pressure: 'It would be a mistake … to allow ourselves to be intimidated into refusing to allow this match'.[78]

Despite reassuring messages from the police, the Special Branch and the German embassy, Simon kept the matter under constant review, and continued privately to express 'grave anxiety' about an event adjudged liable to throw up all sorts of complications and to be exploited as 'a piece of political propaganda in the interests of the Nazis': 'Why should we approve of this Nazi invasion? Is it not extremely likely to lead to violent demonstrations in which the London Police will have to defend a lot of Germans against a protesting British crowd?'[79] In fact, Simon, pointing to the growing need to defend the match increasingly in terms of 'international policy', made another abortive effort to shift the burden of responsibility onto the Foreign Office.[80]

Meanwhile, the British government and the FA, assuming that the controversy had been settled once-and-for-all, continued preparations for the match; thus, inter-departmental discussions, concentrating primarily upon practical issues, continued uninterrupted throughout the election period. In the event, two further developments, that is, the escalation of TUC pressure and Hitler's reported interest in the fixture, re-opened debate, even if the game's imminence was adjudged to restrict the government's options. Ironically, on 18 November, that is, the very day that Hoare and Simon reaffirmed their non-intervention strategy, Sir Walter Citrine reminded the Home Office about the TUC's strong support for a ban.[81] 'Bitter feelings' aroused in Britain by Hitler's 'brutish intolerance' towards the labour movement led him to predict that the mere presence of the German team, accompanied by large numbers of swastika-carrying supporters, would cause both 'great public indignation' and a 'grave disturbance of the peace'. Even worse, government inaction would be interpreted as a 'gesture of sympathy' towards a regime condemned by most shades of 'democratic opinion'. TUC intervention, drawing attention again to the potential for trouble, reinforced Simon's unease about the presence of 'thousands of German Nazis who otherwise would not come here at all': 'This is far more important than other protests, and confirms my anxiety'.[82] But Hoare was unmoved: 'Let us, however, say as little as possible and interfere as little as possible'.[83] Reluctantly, Simon agreed; indeed, according to Hoare, TUC protests, far from prompting a change of course, merely 'confirmed us in the line that we had taken'.[84]

187

Moreover, as Wigram noted, 'there are other people here, who (as they have arranged it), presumably want it (i.e. the fixture) to take place'.[85] Hitherto, the government's preoccupation with protests had obscured the fact that within Britain various groups, including the FA and presumably a large proportion of the media and people, wanted the match to go ahead. In fact, the FA, though confronted by an even larger number of protests, did receive some letters of support, such as from one writer expressing hopes that it would not be coerced by those who would 'grind a political axe upon the grindstone of sport'.[86] At the time of the TUC protest, the press had yet to formulate a clear position towards the game, although at an early stage A. Leslie Knighton, the Chelsea manager, used his weekly newspaper column to assert the need to 'Keep Politics out of Football'.[87] Knighton, offering yet another example of ambiguity about politics and sport, saw the game as exerting beneficial impacts upon Germans and their policies: 'the broad effect of the game is for democracy, friendship and mutual understanding'! Moreover, the conduct of its London embassy suggested the German government's support for the fixture, and, on 20 November, Hoare, seeking to reassure Simon, summoned von Hoesch specifically to solicit German support. Having pointed to his government's reluctance to stop 'a genuinely athletic contest', he stated that 'There was deep and bitter feeling in London … it was essential that no risks should be taken'.[88] Von Hoesch's positive response – for instance, he promised no displays of Nazi insignia – was reinforced on 28 November, when Linnemann, the DFB president, used a radio broadcast to urge German supporters to behave themselves in London.[89]

The Foreign Office, pressing the law and order dimension in its dealings with both the FA and German embassy, reiterated Home Office responsibility: 'While, therefore, the question does not directly concern the Foreign Office, our feeling in the matter has always been that the only concern of the Government is as to whether or not the matter would mean a breach of peace'.[90] 'After all, the match is a private affair, arranged by private individuals, and it is not clear why the Government should interfere in an affair of that kind any more than in any other contact between private individuals and Germans, so long as it does not lead to a breach of the peace.' The Foreign Office, realising that it was a 'tall order' to interfere, was happy to maintain this line. After all, 'it is difficult, isn't it, to conceive a public statement in which we would say the match had not been put off because we were afraid of the effect in Germany'.[91] Certainly, German involvement accentuated the likely scale of any 'diplomatic incident', while the increased proximity of the match rendered it even more difficult to stop the game without arousing strong resentment in Berlin; indeed, Wigram proposed that this point, alongside embassy reassurances about the conduct of visiting spectators, might be made privately to Citrine.[92]

Another important development occurred on 28 November, when von Hoesch reported that Hitler, 'having personally considered the matter' in the light of Hoare's recent request, wanted to avoid trouble for the British government, even to the extent of accepting the withdrawal of the FA's invitation.[93] TUC pressure had clearly bought the issue to his attention.[94] In effect, the German government, though still hoping that the match would be played, placed the burden of decision on Britain. However, the Foreign Office, appreciating that at this late stage it would be impossible to avoid implying that the game had been cancelled for anything other than political reasons, still saw no reason to ask the FA to stop the game.[95] The Home Office agreed: 'From our point of view, it is not an official matter at all'.[96] For this reason, it was hoped that Hitler's recent message would not be published for fear of transforming this 'purely private and unofficial sporting engagement' into an 'official matter'.[97] But these entreaties failed to prevent coverage in the *Evening Standard*, among other papers.[98] As happened in 1928, the FA was suspected as the source of the leak.

Meanwhile, on 25 November, the FA's International Selection Committee picked the England team in its usual way, that is, without any apparent government interference in the process.[99] Presumably, the FA was conscious of the need for a good performance in such a high profile game, but there exists no documentary evidence on the point. Despite England's generally good record, the ever-increasing strength of continental football, in conjunction with occasional revelations of British fallibility, meant that the result could not be taken for granted. Although the actual quality of German football was unclear, a draw with England in 1930 and third place in the 1934 World Cup suggested that Germany was a major force in international football, even one of the strongest continental teams.[100] Certainly, it had the better recent record. Following Hitler's accession as Chancellor (January 1933), Germany won 23, drew three, and lost only three games. By contrast, England's results during the same period (nine wins, one draw, five defeats) were far less impressive. The Netherlands, having lost narrowly to both countries (2-3 to Germany, 0-1 to England) within the past year, offered a useful reference point.

Naturally, the German media devoted considerable attention to the forthcoming game, but few Germans spoke openly of the possibility of victory against England's experienced professionals.[101] German football had yet to go professional, and technically, all players, like those in, say, Italy, were amateurs. Several players, including Szepan, the captain, were categorised as clerks, while other occupations listed for those playing

England in 1935 included butchers and cobblers! Nevertheless, Germany took internationals very seriously, as evidenced by lengthy preparations based on a systematic coaching and selection scheme and the team manager's pre-match visit to London to check out players adjudged likely to represent England.[102] Inevitably, an Arsenal match (versus Brentford) was on Otto Nerz's schedule, given the number of its international players.[103]

THE TUC PLAYS POLITICS WITH FOOTBALL

On 29 November, Hoare and Simon, undertaking yet another review, still decided to 'let the match stand', especially as both the police and Special Branch saw 'no grounds for anticipating any serious disturbances'.[104] As a result, on 29 November Simon, reminding Citrine about the FA's autonomy, rejected TUC demands: 'I do not think that interference on the part of the Government is called for'.[105] Government approval for the fixture was neither required nor solicited:

> The introduction of political feeling into what should be a purely sporting contest is, as I am sure your Council will agree, most undesirable ... Wednesday's match has no political significance whatever, and does not imply any view of either Government as to the policy or institutions of the other. It is a game of football, which nobody need attend unless he wishes, and I hope that all who take an interest in it from any side will do their utmost to discourage the idea that a sporting fixture in this country has any political implications.

This reply, deliberately distancing the government from the game, was influenced by Newsam's response to points raised by Simon to the effect that 'the visit involves no such approval either express or implied, and the British Government attach no political importance at all to the visit'.[106] Significantly, a copy of both the TUC note and Simon's reply was passed on to the German embassy the same day.[107] Simon's communication, welcomed by most newspapers, was interpreted variously as a 'timely rebuke' and 'snub' to TUC meddling.[108] The *Evening Standard*, using Simon's cricketing interests to draw links with the Anglo-Australian body-line controversy, identified his prime responsibility: 'The decision whether the match shall be played or not rests with Sir John Simon, whose duty it is to ensure order at the match and freedom from undesirable demonstrations for the visiting German team'.[109] From this perspective, the British government had been successful in down-playing the game's foreign policy implications.

Nevertheless, Simon, seeking to conciliate the TUC, indicated his willingness to receive a deputation. As a result, on 2 December, an 11-person delegation, including Citrine himself, visited the Home Office. Unions represented included the Associated Electrical Union (AEU), Amalgamated Society of Locomotive Engineers and Firemen (ASLEF), Agricultural Workers Union, Mineworkers Federation, National Union of Clerks, and the NUR. Bromley (ASLEF) chaired the delegation, which was received by Simon, Lloyd, Scott, Newsam, and representatives from New Scotland Yard led by Colonel Maurice Drummond, the Acting Commissioner of the Metropolitan Police.[110] The latter's presence, in conjunction with the lack of Foreign Office representation, emphasised the law and order focus.

Bromley, speaking as both an 'old footballer' and long-time Arsenal supporter, emphasised the vital importance of keeping British football 'unpolluted' by politics, while Citrine, irritated by media criticism of the TUC's 'perfectly legitimate protest', denied that his organisation was introducing politics into sport.[111] Nor had this ever been its policy, as demonstrated in the past by the absence of protest against matches involving other countries attracting TUC disapproval because of their politics. However, the 'abnormal' situation in Nazi Germany, where the government controlled sport through a *Reichssports Führer*, warranted a change of course: 'The German football team is in an entirely unique and distinct position ... That team that will come over here to play is as directly representative of the Nazi Government as the ambassador in London here.' Moreover, 'the German Government has imported into sport politics so grossly that it is practically impossible for any sort of organisation which is not under the direct auspices of the Nazi Government to take part in sport'. Citrine, referring to the destruction of non-Nazi sports organisations, complained that both team selection and participation in sport were subject to political influences. As a result, the forthcoming game was more than a mere football match: 'It is a matter of national prestige with the Germans', or as Bromley added later, 'it is a football match between Britain, British football, and the German Government'. By allowing this politically significant game, the British government was making 'a gesture of sympathy' towards the Nazi regime. Significantly, Citrine, seemingly accepting that the match would not be stopped, ended his presentation on a sporting note by expressing confidence in an England victory. Other members made their contributions, but, generally speaking, what seemed objectionable was the use of the police and taxpayers' money to protect what Citrine described as 'a gang of organised bullies' alongside the risk of 'decent British, clean Trade Unionists getting battered by our police'.

Simon, displaying growing irritation at constant references to the likelihood of trouble, listened patiently, before restating his position: 'I agree with you entirely that the thing should be so handled that, as far as the Government concerned, it has got no sort of political implication'. After all, he observed, the FA, 'a quite independent body', arranged the fixture 'privately' without consulting the government: 'I think we have to keep up in our own country a tradition that this sporting fixture is carried through without any regard to politics at all'. Cancellation, as urged by the TUC, would require, and would be so interpreted as, the unwelcome intrusion of politics into British sport. Simon, supported by Drummond, made repeated, yet seemingly abortive, efforts to reassure the deputation about the police's ability to maintain order, but closing statements showed little meeting of minds. Thus, whereas Simon presented the match as a sporting occasion – 'Do not let us do anything *on any side* to make it a political question' – Citrine claimed that 'it has already been made political' to become an Anglo-German political contest expressed through football.

Predictably, the TUC attracted – to quote Valentine Lawford – 'a very bad press', excepting from a few papers, like the *Daily Worker* and *Daily Herald*.[112] Moreover, its intervention, drawing public and media attention to the game's broader implications, forced many newspapers not only to take a position on the match but also to phrase this in terms of the relationship between politics and sport in Britain. For example, *The Times*, attacking 'exaggerated' and 'imaginary' fears about the threat to law and order, complained that the TUC 'rather hysterically have lent themselves to the designs of those who would poison even sport with partisan intolerance': 'The event he [Simon] was asked to ban is a game of football, and a sporting fixture in this country has no political implication. So says every one.'[113] 'Their [delegation members] highly excited imaginations pictured an indignant populace identifying a football team and its supporters with the authors of dictatorship and the agents of the brutalities, which have disfigured the Nazi regime, and venting their spontaneous anger vicariously on unoffending visitors from the land of the outrages.' Likewise, the *News Chronicle* attacked the TUC for compromising its fundamental economic role by playing politics with sport, while the *Daily Mail*'s welcome to German visitors was accompanied by criticism of the TUC's 'clumsy' pursuit of sectional interests designed to 'stop all but Marxists playing on British grounds'.[114]

Despite its seeming lack of achievement, TUC intervention, prompting Hitler's involvement, did accentuate Simon's pre-existing anxieties, while causing him to reappraise his position yet again. From this viewpoint, TUC protests might have proved more influential at an earlier stage – Citrine justified tardy action in terms of his absence in Paris and the general election – since the game's imminence severely constrained the government's options. Even so, this setback failed to deter the TUC's ongoing campaign for British withdrawal from the 1936 Olympic Games.

SHOWING OFF LONDON

The presence of some 10,000 German supporters, arriving by ship and train and returning the same day, provided the British authorities with a major logistical challenge to be resolved without threatening law and order. Special traffic plans were drawn up by the police for match day, when over 280 coaches were scheduled to transport German spectators to the ground, while 'showing them London' according to a sightseeing schedule excluding sensitive areas, like Whitechapel.[115] Paradoxically, many of the German-speaking tour guides were provided by Jewish organisations – guides were specifically instructed to avoid politics – while catering arrangements were based on the Coventry Street branch of J. Lyons, a Jewish catering company. Even so, sightseeing arrangements were attacked by the *Daily Worker* as a provocative government effort to parade the Nazis' 'Hallelujah chorus' around the capital, whereas *The Star*, among other papers, welcomed an opportunity to show German visitors not only the quality of British football but also the real character of a country hidden from them by official censorship.[116] For a brief period, they were seen as having the chance of experiencing life in a free country, thereby establishing that the fixture, far from being just a law and order problem or a Nazi stunt, came to be seen by the British government and media as a major British propaganda opportunity.

Significantly, on 2 December, that is, the very day that the TUC deputation visited the Home Office, German players and officials, furnishing an early example of the use of air travel for international sport, arrived at Croydon airport, where they were met by Sir Frederick Wall and Stanley Rous, representing the FA, and von Hoesch, the German ambassador.[117] No British government ministers or officials were present, although members of Special Branch were assigned to protect the tour party, which included Osten, Dr Theodore Lewald, President of the Olympic Games Organising Committee, Carl Diem, the committee's secretary, and Herman Neef, a member of the Reichstag.[118] The presence of Lewald and Diem suggested the visit's likely use for Olympic business. Phipps, describing him as a 'pleasant' 'unassuming man' enjoying good relations with the embassy, believed that Osten, whose attendance indicated the high politico-sporting priority attached to the match in Germany, would 'make a good impression in English sporting circles'.[119]

Upon arrival, Otto Nerz, the team manager/trainer, went out of his way to distance the team from the government, even if anyone familiar with the nature of German sport would find it difficult to accept his claim that 'We are a private association, like your own Football Association. We have nothing to do with the German Government ... we have had no message from Herr Hitler.'[120] Similarly, Dr Xandry, the DFB's Managing Secretary, took up a theme already advanced by Osten in *Reichsportsblatt*: 'we are here as ambassadors of sport'.[121] Xandry, reiterating that 'this game has nothing whatever to do with politics', took refuge in nice phrases about being taught the game by England whose footballers were household names in Germany.[122] Reportedly, German footballers, whose comments to reporters were confined to the game, were under strict instructions to state *'keine politische Fragen'* (no political questions).[123] During the evening, they joined their English counterparts at the Windmill Theatre for the music hall, another form of popular British culture, but left at the interval for an early night.[124]

A POLITICAL, PSYCHOLOGICAL AND SPORTING SUCCESS

At the match itself, German players gave the Nazi salute during the playing of national anthems, but wore no party emblems.[125] England gained a relatively easy 3-0 victory in a sporting, albeit somewhat undistinguished, contest watched by *circa* 54,000 people, but transmitted to a much larger wireless audience at home and abroad.[126] Stanley Matthews, returning to the team for the first time since the 'Battle of Highbury', had a poor match, which he ascribed to the attentions of his German marker, Muenzenberg.[127] Although Matthews' memoirs glossed over extra-sporting aspects, the game's political dimension was reaffirmed at the post-match banquet, held at the Hotel Victoria in Northumberland Avenue. Here, Osten, addressing players and officials from both teams as well as representatives from the German embassy, welcomed the match's role in illuminating the 'blue sky' of Anglo-German sporting relations.[128] Significantly, Sir Charles Clegg, speaking for the FA, used the occasion to attack the TUC for interfering in matters 'outside their business': 'These TUC people, seem to forget that this is a sport – a sport free of political influence and, as far as I know, they well never succeed in dragging politics into the great game of football'.[129] As agreed, the Foreign Office was not officially represented.

On the next day, Simon, taking the opportunity to put the TUC in its

194

place, used a parliamentary answer to articulate the government's pleasure at the outcome: 'There will be general satisfaction that this sporting fixture has been carried through in the best spirit and without serious incident'.[130] The rumoured demonstrations failed to materialise, and only a few arrests were reported alongside the police's seizure of placards and a quantity of anti-Nazi literature outside the ground.[131] Perhaps the most serious problems centred on the difficulties experienced by press correspondents in getting access to a telephone to pass on their stories to the wider world. Reportedly, the *Frankfurter Zeitung*'s correspondent used a phone belonging to a local undertaker.[132]

Whether or not the absence of serious trouble proved a function of either careful official preparations, the large police presence, disunity in the ranks of groups opposed to the game, the hollowness of their campaign, or – to quote the *Manchester Guardian* – 'the instinctive humorous sanity of an English crowd', remains debatable.[133] Certainly, the structured and ordered nature of the crowd, like that at the Italy international one year earlier, reinforced football's claim to represent a major element of British national culture.[134] In the meantime, a higher than normal level of match expenses, amounting to £3,118 (cf. £464 and £604 for the 1934 Italy and Scotland games respectively), established the impact of extra policing and other costs, even if gate receipts of £4,986 meant that the fixture still yielded a good profit for the FA.[135]

Nor did the match itself end controversy. Following the game, several British newspapers, praising the government's non-interventionist position, renewed their attack on the TUC. Even so, *The Times*' editorial, entitled 'The Anglo-German Match: Sport and Politics', conceded that the politicisation of German sport rendered it difficult to treat it as a mere football game.[136] The TUC's efforts to solicit government intervention also attracted criticism in Germany, even if the attack in *Der Angriff*, the mouthpiece of Joseph Goebbels, the Minister of People's Enlightenment and Propaganda, was accompanied by recognition of the game's 'political significance': 'for Germany, it was an unrestricted *political, psychological and also sporting success*'.[137] Nor could it avoid mixing metaphors, when asserting that Germany, having found its strength again, was now 'quite capable of swimming by herself', and, unlike the TUC, had no need to make political capital out of a football match.[138] A similar ambiguity characterised other German newspapers. In particular, the *Berliner Börsen Zeitung*, which enjoyed close links with the Ministry of Foreign Affairs, took strong exception to *The Times*' description of German sport: 'No country has more categorically declined to connect sport with politics than the new Germany'![139]

Of course, these examples tell the historian more about the controlled nature of the press in a country where the Ministry of Propaganda issued secret weekly instructions specifying what was prohibited, what must be published, and the degree of prominence of published items.[140] Phipps, reaffirming the 'exaggerated' political importance attached to the game in Germany, felt that *The Times*' report was substantially accurate in identifying both the increasingly 'political character of the organisation of German sport' and the exploitation of international football for non-sporting reasons.[141] One week later, he forwarded extracts of *Deutschkunde über Volk, Staat, Leibesübungen* – extracts were quoted above – to London:

> The English Trades Union leaders whom Sir John Simon had good reason to rebuke a few days ago were wrong in protesting against an Anglo-German football match, but they were right if they merely meant to assert that there was no such thing as sport for sport's sake in Germany. There is in fact only sport for the sake of war, i.e. sport to increase physical fitness with an ultimate view to prowess in the field of battle, and this sport is obligatory for the entire male population.[142]

Perhaps the manual's earlier availability might have given critics a stronger case, but even then it is debatable whether the TUC's equally partisan view would have struck a chord with British opinion.[143]

For most observers, the game appeared to reinforce, rather than disturb, the course of Anglo-German relations, even if subsequent events established the major obstacles still hindering progress. Nevertheless, for the time being, the friendly and relatively trouble-free 'Nazi invasion' of London, in conjunction with the British government's refusal to bow to pressure for a ban, was interpreted generally as a boost to ongoing efforts at détente with Germany. Any threat to improved relations, as might have happened if the match had been either banned by the government or accompanied by serious incidents on and off the field, failed to materialise. According to *The Observer*, the German team returned home, leaving 'perfect peace in all London'.[144] Similarly, one British football correspondent, whose newspaper's letter of welcome to German players and supporters was reprinted on the front page of the German journal *Kicker*, expressed a common view when arguing that the 'feeling of friendship' created between the two countries through sport at varying levels of society had done more than 'years of diplomatic effort could ever have effected'.[145]

Therefore, the governments, media and football associations in both countries seemed generally pleased with the outcome. For Britain, reaffirmation of the national image for 'sportsmanship and fairness' in

German eyes was accentuated by understandable pleasure in an England victory. From this perspective, in retrospect, it seems fortunate that the match occurred when it did, since four defeats by Austria, Belgium, and Wales (twice) plus one draw (Scotland) meant that a further year passed before England registered another win. Meanwhile, upon their return to Hanover, German players were welcomed officially by Professor Glaser, the League Sport leader, who referred to their friendly reception in London, identified the great interest in the game, praised the team's performance, and rationalised defeat in terms of England's status as 'the acknowledged masters of the game'.[146] Subsequently, the DFB, writing to the FA, described the game as both 'propaganda for the football sport in general' and 'a special example of the friendly sports relations' prevailing between the two countries and their respective football associations.[147]

Significantly, within a fortnight, the SFA, seemingly impressed by events, invited Germany to Glasgow the following season. As a result, within a year, Germany returned to Britain in October 1936, when Scotland, the 1935–36 home international champions, triumphed 2-0 in a match, which, like most Scottish internationals, failed to figure in the British government's calculations.[148] From Glasgow, German players moved on to Dublin, where Germany suffered another defeat (2-5) in a return fixture for that played at Dortmund in May 1935 (Germany won 3-1) as part of the DFB's response to the FAI's complaints about its difficulty in arranging internationals.[149]

CONFUSING POLITICS AND SPORT

In a thoughtful, well researched study of the England-Germany match, Brian Stoddart concluded that 'the German grasp on the relationship between sport, culture and politics put at major disadvantage an English society anxious to deny that powerful interconnection'.[150] Indeed, even the *National Sozialistische Briefe*, glossing over the German situation, expressed the hope that British football would remain unaffected: 'it would be tragic if so great a country became the scene of a confusion of sport and politics'.[151] Of course, the position in Britain was never quite as black and white as implied by such statements. Despite carefully cultivated public images, in private, British governments had often proved somewhat interventionist towards international sport. Nor were they naive and uninformed about German sport. Admittedly some of the detail outlined earlier in this chapter arrived only after the England-Germany game, but by late 1935, the British government possessed enough material to compile a fairly accurate picture of the German scene, most notably, the way in which the international would prove far more than a mere one-off football match.

The Foreign and Home Offices, realising that any German international required official approval and support, speculated about the German government's position towards the forthcoming match. Would it be treated merely as a game of football testing the national side against the masters of the game? Or, more likely, was it a political move arising from the way in which German sport was integrated into the governmental structure? If so, what was the principal objective? In particular, was it seen as a test of power and rival ideologies in a broader sense, given Germany's espousal of an alternative political philosophy to Britain's liberal democratic values? Despite such uncertainties, there emerged an official consensus that the match was bound to be treated as part of a propaganda effort designed to propagate a favourable image of the dynamic new Germany. Simon, like the Foreign Office, was in no doubt when describing the match as 'a piece of political propaganda in the interests of the Nazis', for any victory would be employed to remind domestic and external audiences about the merits of the regime responsible for producing a team capable of beating England.[152] For Dodd, the US ambassador in Berlin, the match possessed a clear non-sporting objective: 'an international soccer match for which a German soccer team was sent to London was looked forward to here as an occasion on which the unifying influence of good sportsmanship could be made to serve Nazi political ends'.[153]

From an early stage, policy reasons led, even forced, the British government to intervene, even if in public its activities were concealed by the propagation of the usual *laissez-faire* images. Moreover, the blurred nature of departmental responsibility for sporting matters, as epitomised by the reluctance of either the Foreign Office or the Home Office to take the lead, ensured that pragmatism predominated. In general, the Home Office took the initiative, even if the international political dimension ensured that, contrary to departmental inclinations, the Foreign Office was unable to remain entirely in the background.[154] Indeed, the *Sunday Referee*, indicating scepticism about the official version, depicted the footballers as 'sportsmen propagandists' offering 'self-evident proof that the British Foreign Office and the German Foreign Office are agreed to promote friendliness between Germany and Britain. The British Foreign Office, having knowledge that the feeling in Britain is so strongly anti-German owing to the German Government's ruthlessness and lack of human understanding, feel that the drawing together of the two countries would not be better achieved than through a sporting event, hence the football match.'[155] This 'lively paragraph' – to quote Simon's description – was quoted by Citrine, when visiting the Home Office with the TUC deputation, even if it attributes a more proactive role to the Foreign Office than occurred in practice.

Throughout, the British government, emphasising the FA's non-governmental status, was anxious to avoid appearing to depart from tradition, as stated by Simon: 'we have to keep up in our own country a tradition that this sporting fixture is carried through without any regard to politics at all'.[156] As a result, the match went ahead in a way presented by the government, press and the FA as reaffirming the continued autonomy of sport in Britain. Significantly, the *Jewish Chronicle*, an active participant in the campaign to ban the fixture, typified the general assumption that the episode 'was a demonstration on the part of the British authorities of how to keep politics out of football'.[157] Nevertheless, carefully cultivated public images could not disguise the reality that even a decision not to intervene was made for *political* reasons, especially as the conditions of the time, most notably, the Nazification of German sport and the political factors underlying the British campaign to ban the game, rendered it difficult for any British government, even one favouring strict separation, to steer clear of international football. Even a decision not to intervene, as happened in this case, proved a function of a careful and continuing evaluation of domestic and international political considerations arising from, say, the police's confidence in preserving law and order, the Home Office's reluctance to be seen giving way to left-wing pressure, and the Foreign Office's view that, on balance, it would prove more advantageous and less harmful to Anglo-German relations to allow the match to go ahead rather than to prohibit it.

Moreover, this outcome followed lengthy and intensive discussions held at ministerial and official level, supplemented by various diplomatic (e.g. German embassy), police and non-governmental (e.g. FA) inputs on a wide range of practical issues (e.g. crowd arrangements, traffic plans, official representation at the match) approached primarily from a politico-legal, not sporting, point of view. Far from establishing the apolitical nature of international football in Britain, non-intervention reaffirmed its political character. Nor was the government's response out of line with its position regarding comparable sporting events, given its contemporary recognition of the prudence of a coherent approach towards such issues: 'We are at present, I understand, "damping down" adverse comment on the forthcoming Anglo-German football match on Dec. 4th. and there w^d. therefore seem some inconsistency in trying at the same time to stir up hate ab^t the Olympic games'.[158] Unsurprisingly, departmental exchanges, occurring at roughly the same time and involving the officials dealing also with the England-Germany game, evoked a similar range of comments about another sporting activity organised by a 'private body'.[159] From this perspective, the football international, acquiring an Olympic dimension, was viewed by the British government alongside the ongoing campaign conducted by Jewish, left-wing and other groups demanding British withdrawal from the 1936 Winter and Summer Olympics scheduled for Garmisch Partenkirchen (February) and Berlin (August) respectively.[160]

AN OLYMPIC 'TEST CASE'

During early November 1935, Phipps reminded the Foreign Office that Hitler, attaching great importance to the Olympics, was 'beginning to regard political questions very much from the angle of their effect on the Games'.[161] As a result, the football international, described more recently by Hart-Davis as a 'huge political trick' pulled by the German government, has been presented as a 'test case' needing to pass off without either incident or a ban to avoid any boost to the Olympic boycott campaign.[162]

Inevitably, the 1936 Olympics, having been awarded in 1932 to Germany, attracted controversy once Hitler's accession (January 1933) led to anti-Semitic and other measures adjudged generally to be both repressive and in breach of Olympic ideals. Nor did German reassurances to the IOC quell demands within Britain for either a boycott or the use of the Olympics as leverage in dealings with Berlin, such as to improve Anglo-German relations or to secure better treatment for German Jews.[163] Whether or not British withdrawal would seriously damage the event was questionable, but extravagant claims were made to justify action; indeed, one German exile felt it would strike a stronger blow against the Nazi regime than either political or military sanctions![164] Likewise, William Ebor, the Archbishop of York, among others, argued that the country's sporting reputation ensured that Hitler would take special notice of any British threat to the Games.[165]

Another prominent critic was Philip Noel-Baker, who failed to regain his seat at Coventry (MP 1929–31) in the November 1935 general election. Unlike the 1920s, when he viewed sport as an instrument for restoring Germany to the comity of nations, Noel-Baker presented Olympic sanctions as a way of containing the 'dangerous' threat posed by Hitler to two causes dear to his heart, that is, disarmament and the Olympic movement.[166] For him, sport offered an 'unparalleled' way of reaching the German people, especially the youth: 'our most powerful agent in combating it [i.e. Nazism] is the agent of sport'. Despite fearing that it was already too late to stop the Berlin Olympics, in November 1935 Noel-

Baker, collaborating with Harold Abrahams, the 1924 Olympics sprint gold medallist, and L. Montefiore, the *Manchester Guardian*'s athletics corespondent, decided on a two-pronged strategy. Thus, letters sent in his name to both *The Times* and *Guardian,* highlighting Germany's 'hideous excesses' against the Jews as justification for British withdrawal, would be complemented by Montefiore's articles on the 'Olympic Games in the New Germany' published in the *Manchester Guardian.*[167]

At one stage, the three men, guided by Montefiore's German contacts (e.g. Kurt Hahn), considered action to coincide with Osten's visit to London, but W.P. Crozier, the *Manchester Guardian*'s editor, advised them to steer 'clear of the trouble about the football match', especially as in his view their case benefited from evidence of clear breaches of IOC regulations.[168] Also, by this time, the campaign to ban the football match had been lost, and nothing would be gained through association. Indeed, *The Times*' strong attack on the TUC's stance towards the football international prompted Abrahams and Montefiore to advise that the moment was 'inopportune' for the proposed letter to *The Times*.[169] Noel-Baker, though praising the TUC's exposure of Germany's footballing politics, agreed, since British opinion seemed 'more pro-Nazi than it has been at any time'.[170] On 5 December, Crozier, regretting that the England-Germany fixture had been taken up so seriously, complained that 'the football match business does not help', while rescheduling the forthcoming Olympic publications, including his own supportive editorial, for 6–7 December, that is, to allow a few days to elapse after the football international.[171]

Active lobbying against both the England-Germany match and British participation in the 1936 Olympics meant that November 1935 witnessed official exchanges on both topics. Indeed, in many respects, the Olympic question, having been the subject of official discussions since 1934, provided a framework defining the British government's approach to the England-Germany game. Unsurprisingly, in 1934 the government's receipt of a German invitation for British participation in the 1936 Olympics prompted reaffirmation of 'the attitude of non-intervention in these Olympic events hitherto adopted by His Majesty's Government'.[172] The British government, stressing its inability to stop British competitors and spectators travelling to Berlin and Garmisch, informed the German government that the invitation was being passed for action to the BOA, which was – to quote the standard official British response to all enquiries from governments, embassies and sporting associations – 'a private organisation' responsible for British Olympic affairs.[173] 'The question of British participation in the Games is left entirely in the hands of the above

Association, a private organisation with which His Majesty's Government has no connexion, and there is no question of any official participation or assistance (financial or otherwise) being given to British team participants.'[174] Despite further lobbying by the TUC and other groups as well as continuing uncertainties about its appropriate course of action, the Foreign Office upheld this 'strict rule of abstention', which Vansittart reiterated in mid-November 1935: 'we had better keep out of all this'.[175]

Non-intervention, albeit partly rationalised in the usual uncritical terms related to the 'eternal bickering which goes on over them', rested also on precedent: 'For years past, we have carefully refrained from any action which might give rise to a suggestion of official support for our connexion with these Games. We have therefore studiously avoided communicating with the British Committee. This attitude we wish to maintain.'[176] In particular, there was the political difficulty of telling the BOA what to do. Government pressure in support of, say, an anti-German stance might become public, thereby exerting unwelcome impacts upon not only domestic images about the autonomy of sport but also Anglo-German relations.[177] Naturally, the Foreign Office realised that the Olympics were likely to become a 'predominantly Nazi beanfeast' designed to impress foreign countries, but remained anxious to avoid antagonising the German government about an event to which Hitler attached 'enormous importance'.[178] In London, the event was also perceived to offer a window of opportunity for Anglo-German détente, and hence in May 1936, Anthony Eden, Hoare's replacement at the Foreign Office, ruled that the government should follow the traditional practice of sending a British warship to the Olympic regatta in order to be 'well represented' therein.[179]

Otherwise, the British government confined its involvement to the usual minor practical matters, like arranging hospitality at the Berlin embassy during the Games or assisting German enquiries about heraldic designs of competing states.[180] At times, the Foreign Office flirted with the threat of withdrawal as a 'weapon' to influence German policy in more acceptable directions, but doubted the value of such leverage. In any case, Vansittart advised that sporting boycotts should be used 'very sparingly', especially as recent press reports suggested that the BOA would prove unreceptive to political interference.[181] For example, in mid-November 1935, Lord Aberdare, its chairman, used a letter to *The Times* to warn about being 'very careful before interfering with affairs in Germany', no matter how much one regretted the mis-treatment of Jews therein.[182] The BOA's sensitivity was acknowledged also by Montefiore, who complained that, whenever the German problem was raised, 'the tendency of the BOA is to say, "Oh well, that is a political question – nothing to do with us" '.[183] Nor did persistent lobbying prompt a change of course by the BOA, whose claim to be 'acting in the best interests of sport' has often been attacked as a defence of the indefensible.[184]

CONCLUSION

The 1935 England-Germany match forced the British government, media and opinion to give serious thought to the international politics of British sport. In particular, it posed awkward questions for those, like Orme Sargent, who believed that 'it is undesirable that the Foreign Office should be too closely associated with international football'.[185] Despite strenuous efforts to conform to such *laissez-faire* images, the mere act of non-intervention represented in reality the result of a complex decision-making process determined by a range of *political considerations*, including those arising from related debates about the 1936 Olympics. Even so, the British government, though confronted by a wide range of extra-sporting issues, most notably the uncertain nature of departmental responsibility for sport, still failed to employ the occasion to conduct a serious appraisal of its role *vis-à-vis* sport in general and international sport in particular. Meanwhile, the Foreign Office's commissioned study reviewing the practice of foreign governments towards sporting events promised to provide a possible basis for future action. The football international offered yet another example of meaningful British cultural links with Germany.[186] In particular, as noted by the American ambassador in Berlin, reports of the match, stressing England's 3-0 victory, were given 'much space' in the German press.[187] Certainly, the game secured more visibility as cultural propaganda than, say, more elitist contacts occurring at roughly the same time in the form of the exchange of visits by Sir Malcolm Sargent and the Berlin Philharmonic Orchestra. In many respects, the Berlin Philharmonic Orchestra's British tour caused more trouble, as demonstrated when one newspaper, exasperated by a Jewish boycott of performances, observed that, 'If you are going to allow politics to keep you away from music, it is time to give up politics'.[188]

Significantly, the match, having been utilised beforehand largely for anti-German propaganda by the TUC, Jewish and other groups, was exploited subsequently for a 'big Anglo-German demonstration', taking place between 4 and 11 December 1935, sponsored by the German Chamber of Commerce, among other organisations.[189] For example, the day following the match was chosen by Ernest Tennant to launch the Anglo-German Fellowship, whose first public function, a celebratory dinner, was

203

attended by Osten, Lewald and von Hoesch, as well as Lord Aberdare, chair of the BOA.[190] One speaker, Lord Mount Temple, accusing TUC leaders of not minding 'their own damned business', described the football international as the 'turning point' in relations between the two countries.[191] However, the Foreign Office, wondering how far such 'unrepresentative' Anglo-German groups really spoke for British opinion, was unimpressed: 'We can't stop their German propagandist efforts: and we can't stop a great many English people making approaches to Germany. It is being done every day'.[192] For Leeper and Perowne, those involved therein were deemed more likely to promote 'misunderstanding than the converse', while Vansittart doubted whether 'this lot' would go far.[193] Despite such official disclaimers, these events offered an illuminating *political postscript* to the football international.

Another interesting politico-sporting postscript was Hoare's resignation as Foreign Secretary only days after the England-Germany match. Acting on medical advice, Hoare had arranged to leave London on 7 December 1935 for a Swiss skating holiday, but was persuaded by Pierre Laval, his French counterpart, to break his journey in Paris to exchange views about the ongoing Ethiopian crisis. More seriously, he was induced to initial what became the Hoare–Laval Pact – this involved the cession of Ethiopian territory to Italy – whose rapid leakage to the press resulted in considerable public indignation in Britain against an agreement seen as rewarding the aggressor, betraying a small state, and by-passing the League of Nations. Nor did Hoare's Swiss holiday go any better: 'For months past I had been looking forward to the skating holiday in Switzerland. The sport that I loved above all others was to set me up after a long period of overwork. I had arranged for one of the best rinks in the Engadine to be ready for me before the usual time of opening, and everything was prepared for a few weeks of Swiss paradise.'[194] Hoare stepped upon the ice, but suffered yet another blackout, fell, and broke his nose. Meanwhile, the political storm unleashed by news of the pact forced his resignation from office, following which Hoare used sport, most notably, his quest for the Skating Association's gold medal, as one way of recovering from the crisis. 'For the time being, however, the intense concentration that is needed for advanced skating dispelled from my mind any mourning or morbid regrets that I might be nursing over my resignation. Except for a correspondence with Chamberlain and Baldwin, I avoided political contacts. When Hitler invited me to the winter Olympic sports at Partenkirchen, I at once refused.'[195]

One Briton who met Hitler – they met at a Davis Cup match in Berlin (1932) – was Fred Perry, Britain's leading tennis player, who described him as 'a little man surrounded by tall bodyguards and aides. With all those people around him I don't know how he managed to see a single ball being hit.'[196] Moreover, it is often forgotten that during 1935–36, Hoare, acting primarily in his capacity as President of the Lawn Tennis Association (LTA) but also emphasising the underlying national interest, made abortive efforts to dissuade Fred Perry from turning professional.[197] Once again, the episode proved illuminating for the historian, since Hoare's anxiety to protect national interests in the world of tennis, most notably, Britain's performance in the Davis Cup, was qualified by elitist reservations about professionalism and the perception that Perry was 'not one of us'!

NOTES

1. *Football Pictorial*, 2 Nov. 1935, p.5.
2. PRO, note, Sir John Simon, 18 Nov. 1935, HO45/16425/688144; *Daily Worker*, 9 Nov. 1935. For match accounts, see Duff Hart-Davis, *Hitler's Games: the 1936 Olympics* (Harper & Row, New York, 1986), pp.84–92; Brian Stoddart, 'Sport, cultural politics and international relations: England versus Germany, 1935', in N. Müller and J. Rühl (eds), *1984 Olympic Scientific Congress Official Report: Sport History* (Schors-Verlag, Niedernhausen, 1985), pp.385–412; Richard Holt, 'The Foreign Office and the Football Association: British sport and appeasement, 1935–1938', in Arnaud and Riordan, pp.53–8.
3. Hart-Davis, p.82, p.85; Arnd Krüger, 'The role of sport in German international politics, 1918–1945', in Arnaud and Riordan, p.87.
4. Anthony P. Adamthwaite, *The Making of the Second World War* (Allen & Unwin, London, 1977), pp.125–6.
5. PRO, Simon to W. Citrine, 29 Nov. 1935, HO45/16425/688144.
6. *Daily Express*, 29 Nov. 1935.
7. *Daily Worker*, 9 Nov. 1935.
8. PRO, notes of TUC Deputation, 2 Dec. 1935, HO45/16425/688144.
9. *Daily Express*, 29 Nov. 1935.
10. Simon Hoggart, 'When the Nazis came to Tottenham', *The Observer*, 14 March 1982.
11. Donaldson, pp.24–30; Taylor, *Projection of Britain*, pp.146–52.
12. PRO, E. Phipps to Hoare, 16 Dec. 1935, FO371/18884/C8362; Phipps to Hoare, 7 Dec. 1935, FO371/19647/10611; Woeltz, 295–312; John Hargreaves, 'The Political Economy of Mass Sport', *Bulletin of the Society for the Study of Labour History*, 32 (1976), 11; Alexander and Parker, pp.91–2; David Childs, 'The German Democratic Republic', in Riordan, *Sport under Communism*, p.75; Gerald Carr, 'The synchronization of sport and physical education under National Socialism', *Canadian Journal of History of Sport and Physical Education*, vol. 10 (1979) 15–26.
13. PRO, Phipps to Simon, 16 Jan. 1934, FO371/17758/C502; H. Livingstone, British consul, Leipzig, to Phipps, 4 March 1936, FO371/19922/C1534; CAC, Eric Phipps' diary, 25 April 1934, Sir Eric Phipps Papers (PHPP) 10/1, p.47; Woeltz, 310; Krüger, 'The role of sport in German international politics', pp.82–93.
14. Adolf Hitler (1923), quoted in Michael Balfour, *Propaganda in War: organisations, policies and publicity in Britain and Germany* (Routledge, Kegan & Paul, London, 1979), p.11, p.14.
15. Ibid., p.49.

16. Gerald Carr, 'Sport and party ideology in the Third Reich', *Canadian Journal of History of Sport and Physical Education*, 5 (1974), 7–9; Hans von Tschammer und Osten, 'German sport', in *Germany Speaks by 21 Leading Members of Party and State* (Thornton Butterworth, London, 1938), p.224.
17. PRO, Phipps to Hoare, 7 Dec. 1935, FO371/19647/W10611.
18. Alex Natan, 'Sport and politics', in J.W. Loy Jr, and G.S. Kenyon (eds), *Sport, Culture and Society: a reader on the sociology of sport* (Collier-Macmillan, New York, 1969), p.203; Carr, 'Synchronization of Sport', 32–5.
19. Osten, 'German sport', pp.225–6; PRO, memorandum, Heinrich Sorg, 5 June 1945, encl. H. Elvin to Eden, 16 June 1945, FO371/46742/C3507; *New York Times*, 21 Oct. 1935.
20. *The Times*, 25 July 1935; *New York Times*, 21 Oct. 1935.
21. Mandell, p.59, pp.287–8.
22. PRO, Phipps to Hoare, 7 Dec. 1935, FO371/19647/W10611; *The Times*, 25 July 1935.
23. PRO, minute, Colonel Hotblack, 19 Sept. 1935, encl. Chancery, Berlin embassy, to Central Dept., 21 Sept. 1935, FO371/18858/C6740.
24. Board of Education, *Educational Pamphlet no. 109: Physical Education in Germany; National Fitness: the First Stage* (National Advisory Council for Physical Training and Recreation, 1937), p.75.
25. D.C. Watt (ed.), *Hitler's Mein Kampf* (Hutchinson, London, 1969), p.497. See also, pp.370–3, p.401, p.411.
26. Carr, 'Sport and party ideology', 1–9; Bruno Malitz, *Die Leibesübungen in der Nationalsozialistischen Idee* (Verlag Fritz Eher, Munich, 1933), translation in, Committee on Fair Play in Sports, *Food for Thought* (Committee on Fair Play in Sports, New York, 1935), pp.4–5, pp.11–12.
27. PRO, Phipps to Hoare, 16 Dec. 1935, minute, R. Vansittart, 31 Dec. 1935, FO371/18884/C8362. Extracts are quoted from p.73, pp.334–5.
28. CAC, note, P. Noel-Baker, undated (1936), NBKR 6/54; *Daily Herald*, 31 Dec. 1935.
29. PRO, Phipps to Simon, 9 Jan. 1935, FO371/18866/C244; Phipps to Hoare, 7 Dec. 1935, FO371/19647/W10611; Board of Education, pp.36–9; Arnd Krüger, '*Sieg Heil* to the most glorious era of German sport: continuity and change in the modern German sports movement', *Int.J.Hist.Sport*, 4 (1987), 11–14; Arnd Krüger, 'The German way of Worker Sport', in Krüger and Riordan, pp.19–20.
30. Board of Education, p.42; Hapgood, p.29; Osten, 'German Sport', pp.224–5.
31. Osten, 'German sport', p.219, p.222; Hans von Tschammer und Osten, 'Sport und Leibesübungen im Nationalsozialistischen Staat', in H.H. Lammers and H. Pfundtner (eds), *Grundlagen Aufbau und Wirtschaftsordnung des Nationalsozialistischen Staates* Band 1, Gruppe 1 Beitrag 10a (Spaeth and Linde, Berlin, 1936), pp.2–3, p.6; PRO, minute, Leigh Smith, Aug. 1936, FO371/20449/W8826; Carr, 'Sport and party ideology', 1–5; USA, H.C. Foster, US Consulate-General, Berlin, to State Dept., 29 June 1936, RG59, Box 6791, 862.406/2.
32. Osten, 'German sport', p.227; Osten, 'Sport und Leibesübungen', pp.8–9; Carr, 'Sport and party ideology', 5; *Daily Herald*, 9 Jan. 1936.
33. PRO, S. Waterlow, Athens, to Hoare, 11 Nov. 1935, FO370/484/L7257.
34. FIFA, Minutes of 23rd Congress, Berlin, 13–14 Aug. 1936, p.2; Board of Education, p.34. On German football, see Christiane Eisenberg, 'Deutschland' in Eisenberg, *Fussball, soccer, calcio*, pp.104–15.
35. *New York Times*, 6 Aug. 1933; Osten, 'German sport', p.223. For a footballer's view

of the Nazi regime, see Alan Rowlands, *Trautmann: the biography* (Breedon, Derby, 1991), pp.21–31.

36. Henderson, quoted, Sharpe, *Forty Years*, p.73.
37. PRO, Phipps to Simon, 16 Jan. 1934, FO371/17758/C502.
38. PRO, minute, Willert, 23 Jan. 1934, FO371/17758/C502.
39. PRO, Sir R. Lindsay, British ambassador in Washington DC., to Hoare, 16 Aug. 1935, FO371/18866/C6172; D.G. Osborne to Hoare, 25 Oct. 1935, FO371/18866/C7400; Lindsay to Hoare, 13 Dec. 1935, FO371/18866/C8436; *New York Times*, 21 Oct. 1935.
40. FA, ISC, 26 Aug. 1935, minute 1, 7 Oct. 1935, minute 4, 1935–36.
41. Alexander and Parker, p.94; *The Times*, 12 May 1930. See also, Schmid-Parker, 'Continental menace'; W. Schmid-Parker, 'German invasion, Dec. 4', *Football Pictorial*, 19 Oct. 1935.
42. Schmid-Parker, 'Continental menace'; Schmid-Parker, 'German invasion'.
43. *Daily Express*, 12 May 1930.
44. *Daily Express*, 15 May 1930.
45. PRO, Phipps to Hoare, 7 Dec. 1935, FO371/19647/W10611.
46. PRO, minute, Perowne, 12 Nov. 1935, agreed by Wigram and Orme Sargent, 12–13 Nov. 1935, FO371/18884/C7566.
47. *The Star*, 15 Oct. 1935.
48. *News Chronicle*, 16 Oct. 1935.
49. PRO, H. Barnett, NUR, Wood Green branch, to Foreign and Home Offices, 20 Oct. 1935, H. Haigh, Secretary, Wood Green and Southgate Trades Council, to Foreign Office, 5 Nov. 1935, encl. FO371/18884/C7175.
50. Polley, 'Foreign Office and International Sport', pp.105–6.
51. *Manchester Guardian*, 3 Oct. 1935; *News Chronicle*, 16 Oct. 1935; PRO, Deutsches Nachrichten Bureau, 26 Sept. 1935, encl. FO371/18884/C7348.
52. PRO, minutes, Ralph Wigram, 16, 17 Oct. 1935, FO371/18884/C7348; Wigram to F. Newsam, 17 Oct. 1935, HO45/16425/688144; *News Chronicle*, 17 Oct. 1935.
53. PRO, Wigram to Newsam, 15 Nov. 1935, Wigram to E. Ovey, Brussels, 26 Nov. 1935, FO371/18884/C7604; A.S. Hutchinson, Simon's Private Secretary, to H. Seymour, 29 Nov. 1935, FO371/18884/C7975.
54. PRO, minutes, Wigram, 17, 18 Oct. 1935, FO371/18884/C7348; minute, Newsam, 17 Oct. 1935, HO45/16425/688144.
55. PRO, minutes, Vansittart, 17, 23 Oct. 1935, FO371/18884/C7348.
56. PRO, minutes, Wigram, 18, 19 Oct. 1935, C. Norton, 21 Oct. 1935, FO371/18884/C7348.
57. PRO, note, Wigram, 16 Oct. 1935, minutes, Vansittart, 17, 23 Oct. 1935, FO371/18884/C7348.
58. PRO, minute, Wigram, 18 Oct. 1935, FO371/18884/C7348; minute, Wigram, 21 Nov. 1935, FO371/18884/C7757.
59. PRO, minutes, Wigram, 18, 21 Oct. 1935, FO371/18884/C7348.
60. PRO, minute, Norton, 19 Oct. 1935, FO371/18884/C7348.
61. *New York Times*, 17, 18 Feb. 1935; Drummond to Newsam, 28 Nov. 1935, HO45/16425/688144.
62. PRO, minute, Vansittart, 22 Nov. 1935, FO371/18884/C7757; *New York Times*, 18 March 1935.
63. PRO, minute, Vansittart, 23 Oct. 1935, FO371/18884/C7348.
64. Ibid.
65. PRO, minute, Vansittart, 22 Nov. 1935, FO371/18884/C7757.
66. PRO, minute, V. Lawford, 25 Oct. 1935, FO371/18884/C7175.

67. PRO, minutes, Hoare, 23, 25 Oct. 1935, Vansittart, 23 Oct. 1935, FO371/18884/C7348; Wigram, 21 Nov. 1935, FO371/18884/C7757.
68. PRO, minutes, Wigram, 18, 21, 23 Oct. 1935, Norton, 19 Oct. 1935, Orme Sargent, 21 Oct. 1935, FO371/18884/C7348.
69. PRO, Sir Russell Scott to Vansittart, 4 Nov. 1935, HO45/16425/688144; minutes, Wigram, 18 Oct. , FO371/18884/C7348, 21 Nov. 1935, FO371/18884/C7757; Drummond, New Scotland Yard, to Home Office, 19 Nov. 1935, HO45/16425/688144.
70. PRO, minute, Seymour, 25 Oct. 1935, FO371/18878/C7372; Police report, 27 Oct. 1935, encl. McIver, Home Office, to Wigram, 12 Nov. 1935, FO371/18878/C7613; *The Times*, 28 Oct. 1935.
71. PRO, S. Rous, FA, to Foreign Office, 9 Nov. 1935, FO371/18884/C7566.
72. PRO, Waterlow, Athens, to Hoare, 11 Nov. 1935, FO370/484/L7257.
73. PRO, minute, Perowne, 12 Nov. 1935, agreed by Wigram and Orme Sargent, 12–13 Nov. 1935, FO371/18884/C7566.
74. PRO, minutes, Vansittart, 13 Nov. 1935, Hoare, 14 Nov. 1935, FO371/18884/C7566.
75. PRO, Wigram to Rous, 20 Nov. 1935, FO371/18884/C7566.
76. PRO, minute, Orme Sargent, 19 Nov. 1935, FO371/18884/C7566; Hoare to H.M. representatives abroad, 28 Nov. 1935, FO371/19647/W10098.
77. PRO, minutes, Simon, 18, 19 Nov. 1935, note by Hutchinson, 22 Nov. 1935, Drummond to Home Office, 19 Nov. 1935, HO45/16425/688144.
78. PRO, minutes, Newsam, 19 Nov. 1935, Geoffrey Lloyd, Parliamentary Under-Secretary of State, 6 Nov. 1935, HO45/16425/688144.
79. PRO, minute, Simon, 18 Nov. 1935, HO45/16425/688144; Scott to Vansittart, 20 Nov. 1935, FO371/18884/C7757.
80. PRO, note, Hutchinson, 21 Nov. 1935, HO45/16425/688144; minutes, Hoare, 23, 25 Oct. 1935, FO371/18884/C7348; minutes, Perowne, 12 Nov. 1935, Vansittart, 18 Nov. 1935, FO371/18884/C7566; minute, Hoare, 24 Nov. 1935, Vansittart to Scott, 27 Nov. 1935, FO371/18884/C7757; Hoare to Phipps, 20 Nov. 1935, FO371/18878/C7749.
81. PRO, Citrine to Home Office, 18 Nov. 1935, FO371/18884/C7757.
82. PRO, minute, Simon, 18 Nov. 1935, HO45/16425/688144; Scott to Vansittart, 20 Nov. 1935, FO371/18884/C7757.
83. PRO, minute, Hoare, 24 Nov. 1935, FO371/18884/C7757.
84. PRO, Hoare to Phipps, 20 Nov. 1935, FO371/18878/C7749.
85. PRO, minute, Wigram, 21 Nov. 1935, FO371/18884/C7757.
86. The FA has not preserved this correspondence, but it was referred to by Supt. Canning: PRO, Colonel M. Drummond, New Scotland Yard, to Newsam, 22 Nov. 1935, HO45/16425/688144.
87. *Evening Standard*, 16 Oct. 1935.
88. PRO, Hoare to Phipps, 20 Nov. 1935, FO371/18878/C7749; minute, Seymour, 28 Nov. 1935, FO371/18884/C7974.
89. *News Chronicle*, 29 Nov. 1935; *Daily Express*, 29 Nov. 1935.
90. PRO, Vansittart to Scott, 27 Nov. 1935, minute, Vansittart, 22 Nov. 1935, FO371/18884/C7757.
91. PRO, minutes, Wigram, 21 Nov. 1935, Vansittart, 22 Nov. 1935, FO371/18884/C7757.
92. Ibid.
93. PRO, minutes, H. Seymour, 28 Nov. 1935, Wigram, 29 Nov. 1935, FO371/18884/C7974.

94. W. Schmid-Parker, 'A splendid game without a single foul', *Football Pictorial*, 14 Dec. 1935; USA, W.E. Dodd, US ambassador, Berlin, to State Dept., 5 Dec. 1935, RG59, Box 4248, 741.62/106.
95. PRO, Vansittart to Scott, 27 Nov. 1935, HO45/16425/688114.
96. PRO, Hutchinson, Home Office, to Seymour, 29 Nov. 1935, FO371/18884/C7975.
97. Ibid.
98. *Evening Standard*, 29 Nov. 1935; *Evening News*, 29 Nov. 1935; *Manchester Guardian*, 30 Nov. 1935; PRO, minute, Seymour, 29 Nov. 1935, FO371/18884/C7975.
99. FA, ISC, 25 Nov. 1935, 1935–36.
100. Schmid-Parker, 'German invasion'.
101. Linnemann, quoted *News Chronicle*, 29 Nov. 1935.
102. See *Football Pictorial*, 12, 19 Oct. 1935, 23 Nov. 1935; *Daily Express*, 2 Dec. 1935. Already in 1927, one American consul reported that Germany's Olympic preparations, especially in football, 'smacks somewhat of professionalism': USA, H. Claiborne, Frankfurt, to State Dept., 27 Aug. 1927, RG59, Box 9671, 862.4063/4.
103. Author's interview with Rous, 28 March 1980; *Daily Worker*, 1 Nov. 1935.
104. PRO, minute, Vansittart, 29 Nov. 1935, FO371/18884/C7975; Supt. Canning to Drummond, 28 Nov. 1935, Home Office to Seymour, 29 Nov. 1935, Simon to Citrine, 29 Nov. 1935, HO45/16425/688144; *Jewish Chronicle*, 29 Nov. 1935, 6 Dec. 1935.
105. PRO, Simon to Citrine, 29 Nov. 1935, HO45/16425/688144.
106. PRO, minute, Newsam, 28 Nov. 1935, HO45/16425/688144.
107. PRO, minute, Seymour, 29 Nov. 1935, FO371/18884/C7975.
108. *Evening News*, 29 Nov. 1935; *Morning Post*, 30 Nov. 1935.
109. *Evening Standard*, 29 Nov. 1935.
110. PRO, notes of Deputation, 2 Dec. 1935, encl. TUC to Home Office, 16 Dec. 1935, HO45/16425/688144; Home Office, Press statement, 2 Dec. 1935; *Daily Herald*, 3 Dec. 1935. Surprisingly, the deputation's visit was not listed in Simon's appointments diary for this date: BL, MS Simon 31.
111. For examples, see *News Chronicle*, 28 Nov. 1935, *Daily Express*, 29 Nov. 1935, *Morning Post*, 30 Nov. 1935, *Daily Mail*, 30 Nov. 1935.
112. PRO, minute, Lawford, 3 Dec. 1935, FO371/18884/C7975.
113. *The Times*, 3 Dec. 1935.
114. *News Chronicle*, 6 Dec. 1935; *Morning Post*, 30 Nov. 1935; *Daily Mail*, 4 Dec. 1935.
115. PRO, Drummond to Newsam, 28 Nov. 1935, HO45/16425/688144.
116. *Daily Worker*, 30 Nov. , 2 Dec. 1935; *New York Times*, 5 Dec. 1935; *The Star*, 29 Nov. 1935.
117. *Daily Mail*, 3 Dec. 1935; *Morning Post*, 3 Dec. 1935; *New York Times*, 3 Dec. 1935.
118. *Daily Telegraph*, 3 Dec. 1935; PRO, Phipps to Hoare, 18 Nov. 1935, FO371/18884/C7737; Phipps to Hoare, 7 Dec. 1935, FO371/19647/W10611.
119. PRO, Phipps to Hoare, 18 Nov. 1935, FO371/18884/C7737; CAC, Phipps to Eden, 7 Jan. 1936, encl. PHPP 1/16 folio 5; Hart-Davis, p.66.
120. *Morning Post*, 3 Dec. 1935; *Daily Express*, 3 Dec. 1935.
121. PRO, Osten, quoted, Phipps to Hoare, 7 Dec. 1935, FO371/19647/W10611.
122. Quoted, *Daily Mail*, 3 Dec. 1935; *Morning Post*, 3 Dec. 1935.
123. *Daily Express*, 2, 3 Dec. 1935.
124. *News Chronicle*, 3 Dec. 1935.
125. *Jewish Chronicle*, 6 Dec. 1935.
126. *Daily Express*, 5, 6 Dec. 1935.

127. Matthews, pp.26–7.
128. Stoddart, pp.402–3.
129. Quoted, Sharpe, *Forty Years*, p.75.
130. Simon, *Hansard (Commons) 5th Ser.* CCCVII, 280, 5 Dec. 1935.
131. PRO, minutes, Jan. 1936, MEPO2/3084; *Jewish Chronicle*, 6 Dec. 1935; *Daily Express*, 6 Dec. 1935; Stoddart, pp.401–2.
132. Schmid-Parker, 'A splendid game'.
133. *Manchester Guardian*, 5 Dec. 1935.
134. Russell, p.120.
135. FA, Statement of Accounts 1935–36, 18 May 1936, 1936–37; cf. Statement of Accounts 1934–35, 15 May 1936, 1935–36.
136. *The Times*, 6 Dec. 1935.
137. *Der Angriff*, 5 Dec. 1935, quoted *The Times*, 6 Dec. 1935.
138. PRO, Phipps to Orme Sargent, 7 Dec. 1935, FO371/18884/C8128.
139. Ibid.
140. PRO, Phipps to Orme Sargent, 9 Dec. 1935, FO371/18884/C8235; CAC, Phipps' diary, 10 June 1936, PHPP 10/2, p.216.
141. PRO, Phipps to Eden, 7 Dec. 1935, FO371/18884/C8128.
142. CAC, Phipps to Eden, 10 Dec. 1935, PHPP 1/15 folio 63; PRO, Phipps to Hoare, 16 Dec. 1935, FO371/18884/C8362.
143. *News Chronicle*, 28 Nov. 1935.
144. *The Observer*, 8 Dec. 1935.
145. Schmid-Parker, 'A splendid game'.
146. *The Times*, 6 Dec. 1935.
147. FA, DFB to FA, no date, encl. ISC, 30 Jan. 1936, minute 8, 1935–36.
148. SFAMT, Selection Committee, 18 Dec. 1935, minute 22, 29 Jan. 1936, minute 25, Acc.9017/32, 1935–36; EFC, 26 Oct. 1936, minute 57, Acc.9017/33, 1936–37.
149. FIFA, Minutes of 22nd Congress, Rome, 24–5 May 1934, pp.6–7.
150. Stoddart, pp.388–9, p.405.
151. *National Sozialistische Briefe*, 29 Nov. 1935, quoted *Daily Telegraph*, 30 Nov. 1935.
152. PRO, minute, Newsam, 3 Nov. 1935, note, Simon, 18 Nov. 1935, HO45/16425/688144; minutes, Perowne, Wigram, 22 Nov. 1935, FO371/18884/C7737.
153. USA, Dodd, Berlin, to State Dept., 5 Dec. 1935, RG59, Box 4248, 741.62/106.
154. PRO, minute, Orme Sargent, 19 Nov. 1935, FO371/18884/C7566.
155. PRO, *Sunday Referee*, 1 Dec. 1935, quoted Sir Walter Citrine, Notes of Deputation, 2 Dec. 1935, encl. TUC to Home Office, 16 Dec. 1935, HO45/16425/688144, p.5, p.11. This issue of the *Sunday Referee* is currently unavailable for use at the British Library's Newspaper Library.
156. Ibid.
157. *Jewish Chronicle*, 6 Dec. 1935.
158. PRO, minute, Perowne, 13 Nov. 1935, FO371/18863/C7600.
159. PRO, minute, Orme Sargent, 15 Nov. 1935, FO371/18863/C7600.
160. PRO, minute, R. Kenney, 19 June 1936, FO371/19940/C4559; Frank Rodgers, Organising Secretary of Non-Sectarian Council, to Sports Clubs, Jan. 1936, encl. A. Tudor, Home Office, to Wigram, 15 Jan. 1936, FO371/19940/C306; Walter M. McLennan (Sir Walter Citrine), *Under the Heel of Hitler: the dictatorship over sport in Nazi Germany* (General Council, TUC, London, 1936).
161. PRO, Phipps to Orme Sargent, 7 Nov. 1935, FO371/18884/C7552.
162. Hart-Davis, p.82, p.85.

163. PRO, Waterlow to Simon, 29 May 1934, FO370/455/L3505; *The Times*, 7 Nov. 1935.
164. PRO, memorandum, Dr A. Yahuda, 15 April 1936, encl. FO371/19940/C4559.
165. PRO, Archbishop of York to BOA and Yacht Racing Association, 14 May 1935, FO371/18864/C4324.
166. CAC, Noel-Baker to Douglas Lowe, 4 Jan. 1931, NBKR 6/15/4 (Lowe was the 1924 800 metres gold medallist); Noel-Baker, 'International sport and international good understanding', 47. On his German sources: CAC, Hugh Dalton to Noel-Baker, 3 May 1933, P. Noel-Baker, Geneva, to E. Hunt, BOA, 22 May 1933, NBKR 6/15/2; Ben Pimlott (ed.), *The Political Diary of Hugh Dalton, 1918–40, 1945–60* (Jonathan Cape/LSE, London, 1986), p.175.
167. CAC, Noel-Baker to Ida Whitworth, 26 Nov. 1935, Noel-Baker to Montefiore, 30 Nov. 1935, NBKR 6/54.
168. CAC, W. Crozier to Noel-Baker, 2, 5 Dec. 1935, NBKR 6/54.
169. CAC, H. Abrahams to Noel-Baker, 3 Dec. 1935, Noel-Baker to Crozier, 4 Dec. 1935, NBKR 6/54. Noel-Baker's undated draft letter to the editor of *The Times* is enclosed.
170. CAC, Noel-Baker to Abrahams, 4 Dec. 1935, NBKR 6/54.
171. CAC, Crozier to Noel-Baker, 5 Dec. 1935, NBKR 6/54; 'Our Athletics correspondent' (i.e. Montefiore), 'Olympic Games in the New Germany', *Manchester Guardian*, 6–7 Dec. 1935; letter from Noel-Baker, editorial, *Manchester Guardian*, 7 Dec. 1935. The *Manchester Guardian* kept up the pressure: 'Germany puts on her best face for the Olympic Games', 22 July 1936.
172. PRO, minute, Boniface, 2 Feb. 1934, FO370/455/L600.
173. PRO, minute, Orme Sargent, 15 Nov. 1935, FO371/18863/C7600; minute, H. Capewell, 25 April 1936, Horace Seymour to Pedro Conde, counsellor at Spanish embassy, London, 30 April 1936, FO371/19940/C3137; *Hansard (Commons) 5th Ser.*, CCCX, 887, 23 March 1936.
174. PRO, minute, Sargent, 15 Nov. 1935, FO371/18863/C7600; minute, Capewell, 25 March 1935, FO370/484/L1833; Wigram to B. Heckstall Smith, Yacht Racing Association, 13 June 1935, FO371/18864/C4324; Foreign Office to Prince Bismarck, German embassy, 20 Feb. 1936, FO370/510/L580 (on use of carrier pigeons at the opening ceremony); minutes, Lawford, 24 April 1936, Capewell, 25 April 1936, Seymour to Conde, 30 April 1936, FO371/19940/C3137.
175. PRO, minute, Vansittart, 15 Nov. 1935, FO371/18863/C7600; Jones, *Sport, politics and the working class*, pp.182–5.
176. PRO, minute, Richard Bloore, 8 April 1935, FO370/484/L1833, agreed by Gaselee, head of Library, 8 April 1935; minute, Gaselee, 6 June 1935, FO371/18864/C4324; minute, Capewell, 5 July 1935, FO370/484/L4322.
177. PRO, minutes, Perowne, 13, 18 Nov. 1935, FO371/18863/C7600; *The Times*, 13, 16 Nov. 1935.
178. PRO, minute, Creswell, 27 Aug. 1935, FO371/18866/C6172; minute, Wigram, 11 Nov. 1935, FO371/18884/C7552; Phipps to Eden, 13 Feb. 1936, FO371/19940/C930; Phipps to Foreign Office, 11 Nov. 1935, FO371/18863/C7600.
179. PRO, minutes by Cranborne, Eden, Wigram, Sargent, 7–18 May 1936, FO371/19940/C1639; minute, Lawford, 5 June 1936, FO371/19940/C4049.
180. PRO, minute, Capewell, 25 April 1936, FO371/19940/C3137; C. Torr to Chancery, Berlin, 24 June 1936, FO371/19940/C4149. See also, FO370/484/L4757; FO370/484/L6447, July–Oct. 1935.
181. PRO, minutes, Perowne, 13 Nov. 1935, Wigram, 14 Nov. 1935, Vansittart, 15 Nov. 1935, FO371/18863/C7600.

182. Lord Aberdare, letter to *The Times*, 13 Nov. 1935. Note Lord Aberdare's attendance at the inaugural Anglo-Fellowship meeting mentioned below.
183. CAC, Montefiore to Noel-Baker, 26 Nov. 1935, NBKR 6/54.
184. *The Times*, 17 March 1936; Hart-Davis, p.106.
185. PRO, minute, Orme Sargent, 19 Nov. 1935, FO371/18884/C7566.
186. Stoddart, p.395.
187. USA, Dodd, Berlin, to State Dept., 5 Dec. 1935, RG59, Box 4248, 741.62/106.
188. *Daily Herald*, 2 Dec. 1935.
189. PRO, minutes, Wigram, Perowne, 22 Nov. 1935, FO371/18884/C7737. On the Anglo-German Fellowship, see minute, Wigram, 11 March 1935, FO371/18878/C1901; Richard Griffiths, *Fellow Travellers of the Right: British enthusiasts for Nazi Germany, 1933–39* (Constable, London, 1980), p.185.
190. PRO, E. Tennant to D. Morton, Industrial Intelligence Centre, 15 Nov. 1935 (forwarded to Wigram), FO371/18878/C8299; Ernest W.D. Tennant, *True Account* (Parrish, London, 1957), pp.193–5. See p.206 for an amusing account of Tennant's game of golf played against Ribbentrop, the German Foreign Minister, in 1938.
191. *The Times*, 6 Dec. 1935; Hart-Davis, p.89.
192. PRO, minute, Wigram, 22 Nov. 1935, FO371/18884/C7737. Dodd felt that the German authorities were equally sceptical: USA, Dodd, Berlin, to State Dept., 5 Dec. 1935, RG59, Box 4248, 741.62/106.
193. PRO, minute, Perowne, 22 Nov. 1935, FO371/18878/C8299; minutes, Leeper and Wigram, 22 Nov. 1935, agreed by Orme Sargent and Vansittart, 23, 25 Nov. 1935, FO371/18884/C7737.
194. Viscount Templewood, *Nine Troubled Years* (Collins, London, 1954), pp.183–4; J.A. Cross, *Sir Samuel Hoare: a political biography* (Jonathan Cape, London, 1977), pp.234–50, p.266.
195. Templewood, pp.185–8, p.199.
196. Fred Perry, *An Autobiography* (Hutchinson, London, 1984), p.50.
197. Ibid., p.96, pp.108–11.

8

Footballing Examples of British Propaganda
as it Should, and Should Not, Be:
The Middle to Late 1930s

During the mid-1930s, the Italian invasion of Ethiopia (1935–36), the German remilitarisation of the Rhineland (1936), and the resumption of Japan's advance in China (1937) reflected a growing state of international instability. At the same time, the Spanish Civil War (1936–39) offered a graphic illustration of the European Civil War's impact upon all spheres of life, not excluding sport; indeed, Ricardo Zamora, who kept goal against England in Spain's famous victory in 1929 as well as in the return match at London (1931), was an early casualty of the conflict.[1] Moreover, the fact that the Civil War broke out a few weeks prior to the opening of the Berlin Games heightened the significance of Spain's abortive bid for the 1936 Olympics.

In many ways, international sport suffered from the fact that the countries responsible for both causing and managing the most serious international problems proved leading sporting powers frequently given responsibility for staging major events, like the Olympics (1936: Germany; 1940: Japan) or the World Cup (1934: Italy; 1938: France). Naturally, football, an Olympic sport, was not unaffected. Generally speaking, international football continued with a relatively full programme of fixtures. The 1938 World Cup, played in France, proceeded as usual, and, of course, 'as usual' also meant the absence of British teams. However, other football tournaments suffered, most notably the fourth edition of the International Cup, which closed prematurely following Germany's annexation of Austria (March 1938). Inevitably, international political developments meant that games played between teams representing leading powers, whether defined in the footballing and/or political senses, acquired an even stronger extra-sporting significance. For the British government, it became even more difficult to avoid acknowledging that fixtures with, say, Germany or Italy were far more than mere football matches.

OLYMPIC POLITICS

The Olympic Games, described by the Foreign Office as 'exceptional events', became a prime target for regimes anxious to exploit the perceived correlation between sporting prowess and politics, as highlighted in 1936 when Hitler's attempt to magnify the German race through sport confronted Olympic universalism.[2] As Lord Aberdare, the BOA's chairman, recalled 'above this display of one nation's military might, flew the standard of world solidarity – the flag of the IOC with its rings of blue, yellow, black, green and red – the five colours to be found in the flags of the different nations of the five continents'.[3] De Coubertin, the Olympic movement's father figure, recorded a message for transmission at the opening ceremony in Berlin: 'The important thing at the Olympic Games is not to win, but to take part, just as the important thing about life is not to conquer, but to struggle well'.[4] Hitler's reaction remains a matter for speculation, but Phipps' comment, to the effect that 'with dictators, nothing succeeds like success', suggests a German preference to win rather than merely to take part: 'the German Government attach enormous importance to the Olympic Games from the point of view of propaganda, and hope to be able to take the opportunity of impressing foreign countries with the capacity and solidity of the Nazi regime'.[5]

Henry Channon, a Unionist MP, was one of numerous British visitors to Berlin. He recorded that 'German wins were frequent' and duly celebrated for propaganda purposes: 'Berlin had not known anything like this since the war, and one was conscious of the effort the Germans were making to show the world the grandeur, the permanence and the respectability of the new regime'.[6] Channon, who was dismissed by a fellow MP as a 'well known Nazi', might be deemed an unreliable witness, especially as he enjoyed the frequent parties more than the sport: 'Everyone goes to the Olympic Games all day. We pretended to, and don't, as they are very boring, except when Hitler arrives.'[7] Nevertheless, his general impressions were seconded by the Berlin embassy.

> It is difficult for anyone in England to understand the importance attached to these games in Germany. No trouble or expense was spared to make them an advertisement of the National Socialist regime, both as regards the organisation of the games themselves, and the performance of the German athletes … Taken all in all, however, the games were an extraordinary success for Germany and for national socialism. Dr. Goebbels, with shining eyes, told a member of my staff that the national spirit created by this regime was responsible for the German victories and this view is widely held.[8]

An impressive medals tally (33 gold, 26 silver, 30 bronze), giving Germany top place in the unofficial league table (Table 8.1), was exploited to emphasise the much vaunted link between national power and sport. Olympic achievements were presented to both domestic and external audiences as a function of National Socialism, most notably through visual images captured by Leni Riefenstahl's *Olympia* (1938).[9] Notwithstanding the USA's second place, the league table seemed to establish that authoritarian regimes in Germany, Hungary, Italy, and Japan, were more successful than liberal democracies, like Austria, Britain, Czechoslovakia or France, in mobilising the potential, or at least the sporting potential, of their respective countries.[10]

TABLE 8.1
1936 OLYMPIC GAMES' UNOFFICIAL POINTS TABLE

Position	Country	Points	Gold medals
1	Germany	628.75	33
2	USA	451.33	24
3	Italy	164.59	8
4	Hungary	152.68	10
5	Japan	151.59	6
8	France	134.50	7
10	Britain	108.09	4
11	Austria	83.18	4
14	Czechoslovakia	58.09	3
16	Poland	44.09	0

(Based on American points tabulation: 10 points for first place, 5 for second, 4 for third, 3 for fourth, 2 for fifth, and 1 for sixth.).

Source: Richard Mandell, *The Nazi Olympics*, p.206.

The whole episode, offering British policy-makers an overt example of the Olympics' 'immense' value as propaganda and perhaps the most vivid illustration to date of the politicisation of sport, was witnessed at first hand by Vansittart.[11] Moreover, his stay, taking advantage of his wife's role in assisting Olympic hospitality at the British embassy during the indisposition of her sister, Lady Phipps, demonstrated that sporting functions – to quote Ribbentrop – 'presented very favourable opportunities of staying in touch with politicians and important personages from widely scattered locations'.[12] Despite initial fears that his presence would be mis-represented, Vansittart appreciated that his Olympic visit provided useful cover for quasi-official exchanges on non-sporting issues with Hitler as well as Goering, Goebbels, Hess, and Ribbentrop.[13]

THE OLYMPIC TOURNAMENT POSES QUESTIONS FOR BRITISH FOOTBALL

Following its exclusion from the 1932 Olympics, fears about giving the game second-class status, in conjunction with the DFB's anxiety for the inclusion of Germany's major sport, ensured that FIFA found a basis for agreement with the IOC covering the Berlin Olympics.[14] Although the 1936 Olympics do not figure prominently in the history of British football, the mere fact of participation for the first time since 1920, albeit only as a result of the last minute acceptance of a German invitation, was significant because of the British associations' lengthy history of problems with FIFA over amateurism, their alleged desire to make a 'friendly and sporting gesture' to Germany, and their eventual agreement to send a 'Great Britain' team instead of the usual 'England' side.[15] Participation soon revealed the absence of any clear organisational and funding framework for a 'Great Britain' team, and hence, in future, it was decided to create a British Olympic Football Committee, containing two representatives from each of the four football associations. In the meantime, the FA, 'the senior partner', assumed the major role, leaving its British counterparts to contribute players and one official each (at the FA's expense).[16]

Moreover, the 1936 Olympics provided a rare non-European contact for British football through a first round match with China. But, 'Great Britain', having triumphed 2-0, got no further than the quarter-finals, where Poland, having been 5-1 ahead, hung on to win 5-4. Elimination was followed by an extra game against a German XI (lost 1-4), specially arranged by the DFB at Hamburg to help defray the team's Olympic expenses. Football also represented a rare weak-spot in Germany's Olympic performance, for its team, though containing several players from that visiting London the previous year, also departed at the quarter-final stage, even if its unexpected 0-2 defeat by Norway was often rationalised in terms of Hitler's absence! Meanwhile, Italy, overcoming the USA with characteristically over-robust play, defeated Norway 2-1 in the semi-finals.[17] Then, playing before a 90,000 crowd, Italy beat Austria 2-1; thus, the reigning World Cup holders added the Olympic title to strengthen Italian claims to footballing primacy.

The generally high standard of play at Berlin, alongside the early departure of 'Great Britain', led Wreford Brown and Rous, the officials-in-charge, to argue the case for change, even if, say, the proposed introduction of training raised serious questions about the amateur principle, at least insofar as it was defined in Britain. More revealing was the recommendation, influenced by shamateurism and the frequent overlapping composition between Olympic and full international sides (e.g. Germany, Italy), for a reappraisal of tactics at all levels of the British game:

> It was the view of all, or at any rate, the majority of members of the official party that our style of play in some respects does not compare favourably with that adopted by some of the other national teams – Austria, Norway, Poland, etc. The so-called 'W' formation meets with scant favour by the majority of national teams, and generally speaking, the old methods which have for their object attack more than defence proved more effective and certainly much more interesting to watch. There is some reason to believe that our own professional teams will be reverting this season to the type of football which obtained for so long a period and was only changed because it was thought to meet the situation created by the alteration in the offside rule. If this is so, an improvement in the results of our International Games may follow.[18]

England's failure to win a full international since December 1935 (three defeats by Wales, Austria, Belgium; one draw: Scotland) reinforced the case for action. Although 'the trip was not entirely successful from a football playing point of view', Wreford Brown and Rous believed that participation forged invaluable links with the DFB, the 'German football public', and FIFA. In particular, Rous, taking the opportunity to advocate a more realistic attitude towards international football, pressed the merits of continued British cooperation with FIFA: 'In view of the developments which must inevitably take place in Association Football throughout the world it is important that Great Britain should take her part as the country with most experience in the exploitation of a game which can now affect the social life and happiness of many millions'.[19] FA minutes, albeit recording the Council's acceptance of the report, provide no indication of any plan of action. Certainly, the FA saw no reason to rejoin FIFA, even if the episode reinforced ongoing moves in support of a more systematic British approach to coaching and training.

OLYMPIC GAMES AND WAR GAMES

In summer 1936, the British government was drawn into exchanges about the location of the next Olympics, which the IOC awarded for the first time to an Asiatic country, Japan. In general, the British government, though lobbied beforehand at prime ministerial and departmental level by rival bidders (i.e. Finland, Japan), upheld its traditional course, that is, to 'keep clear of official intervention' because it was 'entirely a matter for the British Olympic Games Committee to do whatever they think best'.[20] Nevertheless, the usual interventionist disclaimers and complaints that 'the Olympic Games always bring more dissension in their train than international amity' failed to prevent the Foreign Office viewing the question in political terms, given the obvious desire of bidders 'to make their country be better known' in the wider world.[21] Indeed, foreign policy considerations led the government to incline towards the Japanese bid, particularly in the wake of the supportive framework established by Anthony Eden, the Foreign Secretary: 'for heaven's sake, let us encourage it. I could even run the mile myself!'.[22]

Then, suddenly, during June 1936, the British government became aware of a rival London bid, submitted by the BOA and the City of London. Inevitably, this move, establishing yet again the manner in which sporting bodies operated independently of the British government, sparked off renewed speculation about potential impacts upon Anglo-Japanese relations, since the bid was bound to be interpreted in Japan as a consequence of government policy.[23] Within the Foreign Office, the Library's backing for London for tourism and other reasons confronted the Far Eastern Department's preference for Tokyo in order to avoid potentially 'deplorable' impacts upon an already difficult Anglo-Japanese relationship.[24] The advice offered by Clive, the British ambassador in Tokyo, to the effect that any consequences would prove 'out of all proportion to the importance of the matter', was significant given the long-standing tendency of British governments to discount the policy priority of sport.

Vansittart inclined to the usual 'leave it to the BOA' line, but appreciated that, '*on this occasion*', 'serious' foreign policy questions necessitated a Cabinet reference.[25] On 9 July 1936, the Cabinet, reportedly taking up a sporting question for the first time, accepted Eden's advice that the withdrawal of London's bid would represent a 'useful gesture' for Anglo-Japanese relations: 'the Cabinet have decided for reasons of high policy & contrary to the normal rule of non-intervention in Olympic Games, it would be desirable that the British Olympic Committee should be urged to withdraw their application'.[26] In any case, ministers, recalling the recent controversy surrounding the England-Germany football match, did not relish the prospect of holding the Olympics in London because of the

218

'element of danger' arising from possible demonstrations directed against 'certain' nations. Cabinet minutes mentioned no names, but undoubtedly Germany was prominent in ministerial thinking. One week later, the Cabinet, reviewing progress, advocated that 'pressure ... be put on the British representatives' for withdrawal.[27] Soon afterwards, the BOA, having been apprised by Vansittart of the government's attitude and realising the futility of proceeding without government support, withdrew London's bid. In public, this decision was presented as a spontaneous action.[28] There was *no mention* of any official intervention, although the Foreign Office ensured that the Japanese authorities were made aware of the British government's supportive action in securing this 'very happy outcome'. Naturally, British officials were gratified when Arita, the Japanese Foreign Minister, expressed his government's pleasure at this example of 'splendid cooperation', which helped to prepare the ground for the IOC's choice of Tokyo in preference to Helsingfors.[29]

Initial British hopes that Olympic considerations would moderate Japan's military activities soon proved abortive. Indeed, the Marco Polo bridge incident (July 1937), inaugurating a further phase in the Sino-Japanese conflict, prompted demands within (e.g. Noel-Baker) and outside Britain to transfer the 1940 Olympics elsewhere.[30] At the same time, Sir Robert Craigie, reporting from Tokyo, warned the British government neither to under-rate the Olympics' political dimension nor to assume any responsibility for a switch, as might happen if London was offered as an alternative location: 'the effect on Anglo-Japanese relations would be out of all proportion to the intrinsic importance of the question'.[31] Craigie's advice formed the basis for informal, albeit politically significant, Foreign Office exchanges with Lord Aberdare and other British IOC representatives.[32] Eventually, in July 1938, Japan's apparent preference for 'performing war games in China', and particularly the resulting delays to Olympic preparations, led the government to surrender the right to stage the 1940 Olympics at Sapporo and Tokyo, which were reallocated subsequently by the IOC to Garmisch-Partenkirchen (winter) and Helsinki (summer) respectively.[33]

Once again, the British government had found it difficult to ignore the political relevance of international sport, most notably its impact upon British relations with another great power and potential in terms of propaganda, leverage, and cover for diplomatic exchanges. Moreover, the episode established the varying, albeit often high, priority attached to sport by foreign governments. On the surface, the British government, referring Olympic matters to the BOA, appeared to follow its 'normal rule of non-intervention', as indicated in a disclaimer revealing an interesting juxtaposition of 'our' for the nation and 'we' for the Foreign Office: 'To those who objected to our participation in the Olympic Games, we have said the matter was nothing to do with the Govt'.[34] However, in private, the British government performed a relatively interventionist role, whether opposing a boycott of the 1936 Berlin Olympics, supporting Japan's bid, securing the withdrawal of London's rival offer, and avoiding any association with links to transfer the Games elsewhere. Unsurprisingly, it was not always easy to find the right balance, as demonstrated vividly on 16 July 1936, when the Cabinet, having decided that 'the matter was not one for which the Government had any responsibility', advocated the exertion of 'pressure' on the BOA for the withdrawal of London's bid![35] Nor was the nature and scale of government action fully appreciated by contemporaries, even if E.A. Montague, writing about the success of Japan's bid, hinted that 'Great Britain played an obscure and not particularly creditable part in these negotiations'.[36]

For Polley, 'the depth and intensity of this example of governmental intervention in sport has made it an almost unique case', which contributed also to a fundamental change of official outlook about sport.[37] Perhaps, the key 'unique' feature concerned Cabinet intervention, since most other features followed on from previous developments. At the same time, Japan's failure to alter course in order to save the 1940 Olympics made the British government realise sport's limitations, particularly respecting its 'leverage' potential. In this regard, the German example had already proved discouraging, for the Rhineland crisis (March 1936) showed that Hitler's policy was 'hardly peaceful' during the period leading up to the Berlin Olympics. Nor were British relations with either Germany or Japan noticeably helped by the government's conscious effort to avoid appearing obstructive to their Olympic bids.[38]

HIGH STANDARDS OF NATIONAL FITNESS AS 'ADDITIONAL PROOF OF THE SUPERIORITY OF DEMOCRACY'

The BOA's official report on the 1936 Olympics acknowledged the relatively moderate performance of the British team, whose four gold, seven silver, and three bronze medals rated no more than tenth place in the league table. Despite being edited by Harold Abrahams, a Jewish critic of the Nazi regime, political aspects were overlooked, except in the sense that the 'international situation' was blamed for aggravating the BOA's usual funding difficulties.[39] Nevertheless, Britain's Olympic shortcomings were seen increasingly as reflecting broader weaknesses at a time when national fitness was being taken seriously by many governments and the British football associations were complaining about both footballers' lack of 'staying power' and their 'meagre response' to training sessions.[40]

During the mid-1930s, Neville Chamberlain (Chancellor of the Exchequer: 1931–37; Prime Minister: 1937–40), inspired by a long-standing concern for social reform, assumed an influential role in efforts to improve national fitness, most notably, through chairmanship of a Conservative Party sub-committee studying what was described as the 'lamentable state of affairs in this traditional games-playing nation'.[41] The sub-committee, guided by official material provided by the Conservative Research Department (CRD), soon confirmed that other governments were often doing far more, most notably respecting the provision of sports facilities and physical training. Significantly, government departments admitted that most was known about Germany's 'cult of sport': 'The Ministry [of Health] know "It is well known that the Germans have been taking sport very seriously. They aim at physical culture with much more conscious purpose than we do".'[42]

As a result, *A Call to the Nation*, the National Government's 1935 election manifesto, called for the removal once and for all 'the reproach that we are a C3 nation'.[43] Then, speaking at the 1936 Margate party conference (2 October 1936), Chamberlain, taking up this 'new idea', reminded his audience about the 'primary importance' of raising national fitness, with particular reference to the youth: 'We ought surely to do all we can to raise the quality of those who are in future to carry on the race'.[44] Foreign examples, most notably, Germany, showed that Britain was lagging behind other countries: 'Nothing made a stronger impression upon visitors to the Olympic Games in Germany this year than the splendid condition of the German youth, and though our methods are different from theirs in accordance with our national characters and traditions I see no reason why we should not be equally successful in our results'. Chamberlain, maintaining the momentum through further speeches (e.g. Leeds: November; Birmingham: January 1937), welcomed media support, as exemplified by the *Daily Telegraph*'s 'Fitter Britain' supplement and supportive editorials.[45] For example, in October 1936, *The Times*' leading article on 'Physical Health' asserted that 'the results achieved in some other countries by official encouragement of physical training show that in this country there is a gap to be filled'.[46] Two weeks later, another *Times* editorial, entitled 'Democratic Need', asserted that national fitness was not the sole preserve of any particular political regime engaged in the European civil war.[47] 'Even if this were not so, it would be a poor recommendation of democracy that it cultivated weediness ... If democracy can combine political freedom with an equally high physical standard this will be an additional proof of the superiority of democracy and not the first step towards the imitation of political heresies.'

Strong support was offered also by the recently established *Central Council of Recreative Physical Training* (CCRPT: 1935) – funded by the Board of Education, this represented the first government agency for British sport – as well as the BOA, whose chairman, Lord Aberdare, wrote personally to Chamberlain in order to second the case for emulating Hitler's 'marvellous' example: 'the whole of Germany seems to be "Olympically-minded" '.[48] For Aberdare, urgent government action was required to 'help our country to hold its own with other nations in friendly competition': 'I'm sure many share my dislike of seeing Germans, Italians, Japanese and other youth being superior to the British'.

In 1937, ongoing debates were informed by a Board of Education pamphlet produced following a delegation's visit to Germany to see the situation at first hand.[49] The resulting report, though describing a more dirigiste and collectivist approach than that likely to find favour in Britain, provided a further stimulus for legislative action through the *Physical Training and Recreation Act* – this recognised that 'bodily fitness makes for national efficiency and personal happiness' – which reached the statute book in July 1937, that is, within weeks of Chamberlain's accession as prime minister.[50] The same month also witnessed one of the more visible manifestations of national fitness propaganda, that is, the 'Festival of Youth' held at Wembley under the auspices of King George's Jubilee Trust. Significantly, Stanley Rous, the FA Secretary, acted as Secretary of the British Sports and Games Association, which had been created in 1935 to raise funding for the event.[51] Rous, who was becoming a major figure on the broader British sporting scene, was also involved in the CCRPT.

The 1937 Act led to the creation of the National Fitness Council (NFC), which was presented as 'one of the major contributions by the Government towards the national well-being' in terms of apprising an uninformed public about the nature, range and benefits of physical training and sport as well as of allocating grants for improved facilities and special events (e.g. £1,500 for Pageant of National Fitness, 1938 Lord Mayor's Show in London).[52] At one time, the idea was floated of broadcasting physical exercise programmes on BBC radio.[53] Occasional exchanges between the NFC (its members included Rous and the RFU's W. Wakefield), Foreign Office and British Council updated Vansittart and Lord Lloyd (chairman of the British Council), among others, about continental developments, like the 'World Congress of Work and Joy' held at Rome in 1938. Meanwhile, the British Council's preparedness to assist the NFC's publicity work overseas enhanced sport's contribution to Britain's cultural propaganda activities.[54]

According to Mason, 'the importance of these initiatives lies in what they reveal about influential opinion on the role of sport in society'.[55] During this period, the government, media and opinion articulated strong admiration of foreign examples, an emerging appreciation of sport's politico-military utility, and the hope that improved standards of national fitness would enable Britain, most notably, its football and Olympic teams, to perform better in a more competitive world. In many respects, Chamberlain's political initiative for the 'improvement of the national physique' represented one of the most overt and important cases of government intervention in sport during the decade, even if its impact could only be measured in the long term. However, by June 1939 the CRD, encouraged by press reports about higher standards of physical fitness currently displayed by military recruits, felt able to assert that 'Britain is no longer a C3 nation. The standard of physical fitness is higher than it has ever been.'[56] Even so, achievements should not be exaggerated, given the fiscal constraints imposed on the NFC's work. In particular, the 'puny' British effort (1937–38: £2m), as reflected also by, say, the reliance of the Olympic team and the 1937 'Festival of Youth' on private funding, compared unfavourably with the 'lavish' public expenditure by Germany and Italy.[57] As one letter writer to *The Times* observed in September 1938, 'we have much to learn'.[58] Although national fitness was generally acknowledged as helping preparedness for war, the rearmament programme meant that the Treasury was unmoved by the NFC's requests for more money; indeed, the large proportion of NFC expenditure devoted to the construction of swimming baths prompted the Treasury's preference for 'simple and less expensive projects'.[59]

THE FOREIGN OFFICE SURVEYS OVERSEAS SPORT

One by-product of the NFC's existence was the improved collection of information about sport in both Britain and other countries. Thus, in 1938, one memorandum, reaffirming association football's status as the national game, recorded that, whereas the RFU claimed *circa* 1,000 affiliated clubs, some 43,000 clubs were affiliated to the FA.[60] Also even the Foreign Office, prompted by questions raised by the 1935 England-Germany international, undertook a rare survey of international sport, that is, a study of foreign governmental practice regarding representation at major sports events.[61] Results, based on returns from 23 embassies and missions (Table 8.2), became available for departmental use in October 1936.[62] In brief, the survey, drawing together a wide range of information, did not tell the Foreign Office anything new. Rather it confirmed major variations in practice, ranging at one extreme from the interventionism characteristic of Germany and Italy to the other extreme typified by the minimalist approach allegedly prevalent in Greece. Frequently, governments gave recognition only to football internationals against leading teams; for example, in March 1935, England's 1-0 victory at Amsterdam was even watched by Queen Juliana, who reportedly attended an international match for the first time ever.[63] One other common feature, even for countries where there was neither official hospitality nor attendance at matches and/or banquets, was the fact that government ministers attended games in a private capacity.[64] Moreover, notwithstanding inconsistent coverage in returns, it became clear that British diplomats stationed overseas normally watched matches played by visiting British national and club sides in their respective countries.[65]

TABLE 8.2

FOREIGN OFFICE SURVEY OF OFFICIAL ATTITUDES REGARDING
SPORT IN OTHER EUROPEAN COUNTRIES

Type of Government Action	Responses	
	Affirmative	Negative
Official recognition	6	17
Government hospitality	4	19
Ministerial/official attendance at match/banquet	13	10

Sources: Information yielded by 23 replies, collected during 1935–36, was drawn together in October 1936. Replies covered Austria, Belgium, Bulgaria, Czechoslovakia, Denmark, Estonia, Finland, France, Germany, Greece, Hungary, Italy, Latvia, Netherlands, Norway, Poland, Portugal, Romania, Spain, Sweden, Switzerland, Turkey and Yugoslavia.

Despite a continuing preference to avoid formal recognition, precedent led the Foreign Office to decide upon official representation at 'the more important function', that is, the match: 'This seems as far as it is desirable to go until some especial occasion for setting a new precedent presents itself'.[66] As a result, this study ushered in no major shift in policy, except that in future, the topic was allocated to the Western Department rather than to any specific political section of the Foreign Office. Nor did it prompt any immediate attempt to improve links between government and the football associations, such as for the purposes of exchanging information about forthcoming fixtures and tours. Pragmatism, guided by precedent, remained the rule.

FOOTBALLING EXAMPLES OF BRITISH PROPAGANDA 'AS IT SHOULD NOT BE'

Nor did repeated official and media pressure on the football authorities for remedial action stem the flow of reports reaching the British government about the poor results and/or behaviour of club sides engaged on close season overseas tours. One of the more vivid examples occurred in summer 1936, when Sir Howard Kennard, reporting from Warsaw, presented Chelsea football club's recent matches in Cracow and Warsaw as 'admirable examples of British propaganda as it should not be'.[67] Kennard, complaining about the 'lamentable impression' given of British sportsmanship, forwarded detailed press extracts to establish the harm done to Britain's image in the eyes of the Polish people as well as to draw attention to the unfavourable comparisons made with other countries about both British footballing standards and sportsmanship.

Following a win at Warsaw, Chelsea travelled to Cracow, where Wisla's 1-0 victory was widely praised as a landmark in Polish footballing history.[68] Press acknowledgement of British football's positive qualities regarding, say, dribbling and heading skills, was overridden by more detrimental comments.[69] Even allowing for the usual problems consequent upon varying interpretations of the rules (e.g. charging the goalkeeper), the Chelsea players were described as unsporting, even 'brutal', in their play.[70] Deliberate fouls forced Polish players to leave the field injured in both games; indeed, one newspaper tactfully described how one Polish player fell 'with the evident aid of an English [full] back'.[71] Repeated dissent compounded the problem, particularly as one Chelsea player, having spat at the referee, refused to leave the field for ten minutes. Press reports, articulating a new confidence in the strength of Polish football, suggested a more sceptical attitude towards the 'fairy tales' about the qualities of the British game.[72] *I.K.C.* was not alone in claiming that Chelsea's visit undermined Polish images of Britain as the home of good football, sportsmanship and fair play. Moreover, recent visits by Austrian, German and Hungarian club sides prompted unfavourable comparisons with the rather 'dull', 'boring' impression conveyed about the state of the British game, given Chelsea's high First Division placing (8th) during the 1935–36 season.[73] For the Polish press, the era of British footballing superiority seemed under serious threat, if not over, for the much vaunted and 'unequalled' English players were revealed as mere mortals! Within weeks, Poland's victory over 'Great Britain' in the Berlin Olympics merely reaffirmed such images.

Kennard, who attended one match alongside 'the two biggest men in the country' (i.e. Generals Rydz-Smigly and Sosnkowski), confessed to unease and embarrassment when the 20,000 crowd began to boo and catcall the British team. Displaying a clear recognition of the role of international football as cultural propaganda capable of reaching both political elites and the masses in other countries, Kennard reminded the Foreign Office about the need to give the right sort of image across the whole range of cultural activities, not excluding sport.

> It seems to me that it is quite useless for the British Council and Embassies and Legations to waste time and money on cultural propaganda which appeals only to a few hundred people when the unsportsmanlike behaviour of British footballers does infinite harm amongst the millions which have been accustomed to respect the British standard of play in all games, and I would suggest it is far more important for the Council to take strong measures with the authorities concerned to prevent a repetition of such incidents as occurred here on Saturday, than to send British conductors, professors and so forth abroad, who cannot in years wipe out the opinion which must now be held here on what used to be one of our greatest assets, namely, our sense of sportsmanship.[74]

Kennard, whose annoyance was compounded by the isolationist sentiments voiced on a recent visit to Poland by two MPs belonging to the Imperial Policy Group of the Conservative Party, pointed out that, within a short space of time, 'our best assets', that is, 'parliamentary government and our sense of sportsmanship', have been shown in such an 'extremely unfavourable light' to a large foreign audience.[75]

Within the Foreign Office, Orme Sargent and Sir George Mounsey, Assistant Under-Secretary of State, sympathised with Kennard's complaints about the way in which a football team 'defeated at almost one stroke' long-standing efforts to improve Anglo-Polish relations.[76] But, as Viscount Cranborne, a junior minister at the Foreign Office, minuted, there were limits to what the government could do: 'we can't control the footballers, I'm afraid'. Similarly, Orme Sargent, replying to Kennard, deplored Chelsea's misdemeanours, but observed that it was as difficult to control footballers abroad as MPs.[77] Nor was it, he noted, the embassy's job to keep footballers in order. The fundamental problem remained, as demonstrated by Kennard's further representations on the subject to both the Foreign Office and British Council.

This episode also acquainted the Foreign Office with both the rising quality of continental football and the manner in which the game was viewed in the international political context. Similar messages emanated from Portugal, where Sir Walford Selby, following up discussions held in March 1937 by Anthony Eden and Armindo Monteiro, the Portuguese ambassador in London, pushed sport as one way of alleviating the 'strained' state of the Anglo-Portuguese relationship.[78] An England-Portugal football international, like equestrian and yachting contests, came to be perceived as a 'cheap and effective' form of cultural propaganda helping to promote improved relations as well as to counter increased German penetration of the Iberian peninsula.[79] But Selby, having witnessed a convincing 4-0 Portuguese victory over Hungary (9 January 1938), introduced a note of caution: 'The Portuguese struck me as a remarkably well set up lot of men physically'. Exhibiting an up-to-date interest in the contemporary soccer scene, Selby evaluated the result's broader significance; thus, he pointed out that Czechoslovakia, which was narrowly defeated (4-5) in December 1937 by 'our best English combination', lost 3-8 to Hungary the previous September. The marked improvement in Portuguese football led him to advise the Foreign Office to warn the FA to think twice before arranging an England-Portugal fixture: 'continental football must be taken more seriously in England'. Unless the best possible team was chosen, England 'will be simply "gallopped [*sic*] off the field" '. In fact, hindsight suggests that Selby over-reacted to the Hungarian result, since Portugal's record both prior to and after this fixture was far from impressive. Thus, the team, having failed to win a single game since April 1933 (one draw, five defeats), did little better between the Hungarian game and September 1939 (one draw, three defeats). Nor did Portugal qualify for the 1938 World Cup.

Perhaps Selby was over-impressed by the large number of young people brought to watch the Portugal-Hungary game in cold, wet conditions: 'They had been brought to watch their national team play, and watch it they had to. The new Portugal! It seemed to me certainly a case of the survival of the fittest.' The propagandist element was to the fore: 'I fully realise one must not unduly exaggerate the importance of prowess in the field of sport. At the same time, we cannot ignore it. My own view is that this football result has undoubtedly some significance as a symptom of a new spirit among the Portuguese.'[80] If the country's military strength developed in a similar manner under Salazar's presidency, Portugal's support would prove a 'formidable asset'. In any case, the German threat led Selby to demand positive action 'in one direction or another'.[81] Certainly, the visible German presence caught the eye of Geoffrey Dawson, the editor of *The Times*, who visited Portugal to interview Salazar in May 1938: 'the German embassy dominates the diplomatic quarter of Lisbon in striking contrast to our own inconspicuous office'.[82] Naturally, sport represented a key part of the German propaganda effort, as evidenced by both its links with the *Mocidade* (Portuguese youth movement) and the Germany-Portugal international played at Frankfurt in April 1938. A few months later a desire to loosen German links with the *Mocidade* prompted official efforts to ensure British participation in a forthcoming international yachting rally held on the Tagus, even if eventually it proved impossible to send a team.[83]

The need to safeguard Britain's image in the wider world led Selby to move on to recommend that diplomatic representatives abroad should be instructed not only to liaise more closely with visiting British sports teams but also to report regularly on both their performance and the strengths of other countries for the guidance of relevant British sporting bodies.[84] In effect, British diplomats, having been required traditionally as part of their duties to spy on other countries, were now expected also to spy on both foreign and visiting British sportsmen! In this vein, Selby, referring back to his previous posting in Austria, recalled the damage caused to foreign images of Britain by the often disappointing performances of visiting clubs: 'I saw some of our very best teams defeated in Vienna, and though it is true it was at the end of the "British" season, it was not exactly helpful from our point of view'. Poor performances damaged the national interest: 'Having regard to the prestige which our football even today succeeds in retaining, it would not help from a national point of view'. Significantly, his advice, reaching London at a time when the Foreign Office proved more sensitive than usual about the type of national image projected through football, did not fall on deaf ears. As a result, on 11 February 1938, the Foreign Office, feeling that the footballing authorities should 'know what the position is', 'strongly' urged the FA to send 'the best team they can collect' for any future fixture arranged with Portugal.[85] Significantly, Rous, when acknowledging the communication, mentioned ongoing correspondence about a Portuguese fixture, even if no game was actually arranged. The archives fail to indicate the reasons, but the first meeting between the two countries did not occur until May 1947, when England gained a crushing 10-0 victory in Lisbon.

Although the Spanish Civil War ruled out another England-Spain international, in March 1937 George Elvin, Secretary of the British Workers' Sports Association (BWSA) and formerly a member of the TUC, sought government permission to accept a Catalan invitation to send a football team to Barcelona in order to show solidarity with Spanish workers and the republican cause, make contact with the Catalans, and provide cover for a TUC representative to report on the situation in Barcelona. But the Passport Office, upholding the government's non-intervention policy towards the war, refused to issue visas. Nor was the Foreign Office, which allowed British subjects to visit Spain only for 'urgent and serious reasons', prepared to change course, as asserted by Sir George Mounsey, the Assistant Under-Secretary of State: 'I hardly thought playing football could be covered by these conditions'.[86] This recommendation, seconded by Cadogan, was validated at ministerial level by both Eden and Cranborne, especially as current policy requirements were underpinned by the usual fear of establishing a precedent liable to be exploited by 'frivolous applications'.[87]

BRITAIN AND A FOOTBALLING ENIGMA

Whereas it was relatively well informed about the position in the fascist dictatorships, the Soviet sporting scene remained an enigma for British governments. The same was also true of the British football associations, whose lack of knowledge about Soviet football became apparent during the mid-1930s when several British clubs received invitations to visit the Soviet Union.

Writing in 1937, Samuel Shipman presented sport as one of the most significant phenomena in Soviet life.[88] By this time, the basic organisational framework, based on a unified top-down structure, was in place centred upon the All-Union Physical Culture and Sports Council, whose prime political role in the 1930s was to raise standards through a growing emphasis upon competitive sport.[89] Football, whether measured through the number of players or spectators, established itself as the major national sport, and the introduction of league and cup competitions (1936), reflecting a new competitive approach, merely reinforced its primacy, as explicitly acknowledged in 1937, when ten of 22 recipients of the Master of Sport title were footballers.[90] The All-Union Committee's *Physicultura i Sport* soon built up a large circulation, and even *Pravda* carried match reports. But the premium placed on success prompted frequent complaints, such as in *Pravda*, about the fiscal and other material rewards (e.g. accommodation) used to attract leading players, like the Starostin brothers.[91] Stronger criticism was reserved for increased misconduct on and off the field, such as in July 1937 when fighting broke out between players and spectators at a league match between Leningrad Dynamo and Dynamo

Moskva.[92] Nor did the problem go away, as demonstrated by the 83 players sent off in 1939.

Politico-ideological reasons, pressing sport's role in fortifying 'the international workers' front', continued to rule out affiliation to the IOC, FIFA and other international sporting bodies, and hence participation in the Olympics, the World Cup, and fixtures versus most other countries.[93] Unsurprisingly, there exists a virtual blank in the Soviet Union's international sporting record between the wars, a period when foreign contacts were confined largely to workers' sports associations, like Britain's BWSF.[94] The only full internationals recorded for the inter-war period were two matches played versus Turkey in 1924 and 1925, but further 'internationals' seemed to have taken place during 1931, 1932, 1933, 1934 and 1936.[95] Reportedly, games played at Ankara and Istanbul in 1932 were treated as 'politically significant' by the Turkish government, as evidenced by the prime minister's attendance and the provision of government hospitality.[96] In July 1933, the *New York Times*, impressed by 'how the Russian public has taken to sport', reported that 60,000 Muscovites watched a 7-2 victory over a Turkish team.[97]

Within this context, the virtual absence of Anglo-Soviet footballing contacts seems hardly surprising, particularly given the generally difficult relationship, even occasional non-relationship, existing between the two countries; indeed, in 1930 political reasons led the British government to refuse entry visas to a Soviet team.[98] Despite the resumption of diplomatic links in December 1929, relations seldom became close, as highlighted during the late 1930s when the Chamberlain government not only failed to see any reason for Soviet participation in the 1938 Munich conference but also proved lukewarm towards the Anglo-French-Soviet alliance negotiations conducted the following year. During the 1930s, the British football associations were also outside FIFA's ranks and non-entrants to the World Cup, but, unlike the Soviet Union, remained in regular contact with FIFA, while stipulating that international fixtures were only allowed against teams from countries affiliated to FIFA.

Despite this restriction, the mid-1930s saw occasional reports about Soviet invitations involving, say, Arsenal, Manchester City or West Ham.[99] Perhaps the most substantial episode involved Third Lanark, defeated finalists in the 1935–36 Scottish Cup. In May 1936, Third Lanark, following exchanges with the Soviet embassy in London and FIFA, approached the SFA for permission to undertake a six-match Soviet tour commencing on 30 May. Although permission was refused initially on the grounds of Soviet non-affiliation to FIFA, the SFA agreed to reconsider its decision upon being informed of FIFA's willingness to give special permission as part of a new course adopted in October 1934 in the light of rumours about a Soviet application for membership.[100] FIFA, presenting itself to Moscow as 'a purely sporting organisation, without political purposes', agreed to grant 'exceptional' approval for, say, Czech, French (e.g. Racing Club de Paris) and Turkish teams to play Soviet sides as part of its search for 'un rapprochement du sport de football *soviétique* à la FIFA'.[101] At one time, there was even speculation about Soviet tours involving, say, Australia or the USA.[102] Following exchanges with FIFA, the SFA qualified its initial opposition, so as to make approval conditional on FIFA's receipt of a Soviet application for membership within one month and agreement to play according to the IFAB's laws of the game.[103] No Soviet membership application was received by the FIFA, and hence Third Lanark's tour never took place.[104] Subsequently, in June 1936 the British associations, meeting at Troon for the IFAB, reaffirmed FIFA's line.[105] The British government does not seem to have become involved in this episode, especially as, unlike the early or late 1920s, Anglo-Soviet diplomatic relations were now in place.

Meanwhile, FIFA, fearing that 'exceptional permission' would become a meaningless gesture if granted indefinitely, was impatient with the lack of progress, since Soviet affiliation seemed no nearer than in late 1934. Hitherto, FIFA had proved particularly sympathetic towards the predicament of the Turkish football federation, given its precarious fiscal position and dependence on the support of a government attaching high political importance to sporting links with the Soviet Union.[106] However, the 1936 FIFA Congress, held at Berlin, was used by Rimet for informal conversations with Turkish representatives to prepare the ground for a tougher line, and soon afterwards, the Turkish footballing authorities, having been apprised about 'the gravity of the situation', were informed of the resulting termination of FIFA's practice of granting exceptional permission to play Soviet teams alongside the risk of disaffiliation for unauthorised fixtures.[107] In February 1937, Schricker, responding to further FA enquiries about the Soviet Union, emphasised the change of course, while outlining FIFA's abortive efforts to improve relations with Moscow.[108] Inevitably, occasional problems still occurred, as happened in November 1939, when reports about a Soviet visit led FIFA to remind the Bulgarian footballing authorities about the ban on playing unaffiliated associations.[109]

In general, the relative lack of results as reference points rendered it difficult to evaluate the standard of Soviet football, even during the late 1930s.[110] Despite FIFA's receipt of 'some good reports' and occasional fixtures versus non-Soviet teams, Soviet football remained largely an unknown quantity. FIFA, albeit treated generally as the fount of information on world football, conceded shortcomings regarding the quality and accuracy of its information on the Soviet Union, including weaknesses in the *FIFA Handbook*'s coverage thereof. Frequently, it was forced to use the Turkish football association for relevant details, including contact addresses.

CONCLUSION

During this period, sport, like most other aspects of life, was politicised, ideologised and polarised. Within this context, in January 1937, Dr G. Randolph Manning, chairman of the USFA's Foreign Relations Committee, voiced concern about the 'very clouded' Olympic atmosphere: 'It seems that national Olympic Associations are losing control of the Olympiads to government supervision by military and political party domination for their own purposes. Tokio, 1940, already is going along that line – we are making of the games a great propaganda spectacle instead of adhering to fundamental Olympic ideals and simplicity!'.[111] One year later, E.A. Montague, regretting their growing 'political bias', complained about 'the already excessive tendency to turn the Olympic Games, and to a lesser degree other sporting contests like international football matches, into tests of national prestige, instruments of diplomacy, and, in short, one more element of discord in a world which grows yearly more discordant'.[112]

As a result, it proved increasingly difficult for the British government to avoid acknowledging that international sport, exerting 'important' and 'serious' impacts upon national interests, including the appeasement policy, was too important to be left to sporting bodies.[113] Football, which was affected also by official exchanges about the Olympics, remained a central focus for the British government, whose attention at this time was devoted primarily to the game's impact upon overseas perceptions of Britain. During June 1936, Valentine Lawford articulated a typical official preoccupation with international sport: 'Quite enough harm is done already by sending abroad indifferent athletics teams who are trounced by teams representing countries like Belgium and Austria'.[114] Although it was not 'trounced' in Poland, Chelsea's tour was widely interpreted in diplomatic circles as exerting a harmful impact on the work of the British Council and other agencies; indeed, as Kennard observed, within 90 minutes a football team was capable of undermining, even undoing, years of patient cultural propaganda. Nor were footballers the only culprits, as evidenced by Kennard's complaints about visiting MPs!

Of course, any British sports group abroad could exert similar impacts, as demonstrated in December 1937, when the British vice-consul at Toulon complained about the 'lamentable', drunken behaviour of members of the British Empire Games team *en route* by sea to Australia.[115] The incident, albeit resolved locally by team officials (e.g. compensation for damage), prompted exchanges between the Foreign Office and the British Empire Games Federation about the propaganda implications, thereby validating the observation made by the British embassy in Tokyo about sport's ability to produce consequences 'out of all proportion' to an event's perceived sporting significance. Certainly, the growing emphasis on national projection in a competitive world imparted considerable significance to what was, in reality, a relatively trivial incident at Toulon. At the same time, the episode gave added credence to a somewhat flippant remark made in July 1936 by Geoffrey Fry, Stanley Baldwin's private secretary, about Count Soyeshima's request for a meeting with the prime minister to discuss Japan's Olympic bid: 'The question for the Olympic Games of 1940 is presumably not one in which the Government is concerned, but these athletic affairs are, I suppose, becoming so important as to deserve some consideration, and one day a defeat and a bit of barracking may precipitate a world war'.[116]

NOTES

1. FIFA, Rimet, Minutes of 23rd Congress, Berlin, 13–14 Aug. 1936, p.10.
2. PRO, minutes, Leigh Smith, Aug. 1936, Charles H. Johnston, 30 Oct. 1936, FO371/20449/W8826.
3. Lord Aberdare, 'The Olympiad in Britain', *Everybody's*, 1 June 1946, 5.
4. Mandell, p.150.
5. CAC, Phipps' diary, 11 Nov. 1935, 14 May 1936, PHPP 10/2, p.143, p.215; PRO, Phipps to Eden, 13 Feb. 1936, FO371/19940/C930; Phipps to Foreign Office, 11 Nov. 1935, FO371/18863/C7600; minute, V. Lawford, 18 May 1936, FO371/19940/C3697; Hart-Davis, pp.46–9.
6. Robert Rhodes James (ed.), *Chips: the Diaries of Sir Henry Channon* (Weidenfeld & Nicolson, London, 1967), pp.105–12.
7. Ibid.; Carmarthenshire Archives Service, Carmarthen (hereafter CAS), J.P. Thomas to anon., 12 April 1938, Viscount Cilcennin Collection (Cilc.Coll.), Acc.5605, Cilc.Coll.40.
8. PRO, Phipps to Foreign Office, 1 August 1936, FO371/19940/C5677; B. Newton, Berlin, to Eden, 18 Aug. 1936, FO371/19940/C5983.
9. Mandell, pp.165–6, pp.258–70.
10. Ibid., p.xiii, p.205, p.280.
11. PRO, minute, V. Lawford, 21 Aug. 1936, FO371/19440/C5983.
12. Quoted, Hart-Davis, pp.145–6.
13. Ian Colvin, *Vansittart in Office: an historical survey of the origins of the Second World War* (Gollancz, London: 1965), p.111; Polley, 'Foreign Office and International Sport', p.136; Norman Rose, *Vansittart: Study of a Diplomat* (Heinemann, London, 1978), pp.196–9; CAC, Vansittart to Phipps, 23 June 1936,

PHPP 2/18, folio 20; PRO, Vansittart to R. Hankey, 27 May 1935, Cab21/540, 14/2/23 (Pt.1).

14. FIFA, Minutes of 22nd Congress, Rome, 24–25 May 1934, p.11.

15. FA, German Olympic Committee to FA, 14 April 1936, encl. ISC, 20 April 1936, minute 4, Meeting of the British football associations, 4 July 1936, ISC sub-committee, 13 July 1936, Olympic sub-committee, 13 July 1936, 1935–36.

16. FA, C. Wreford Brown and S. Rous, 'Report on the Olympic Games of Berlin, 1936. Association Football, Sept. 1936' (hereafter 'Olympic Report 1936'), Council, 24 Aug. 1936, minute 6, 1936–37; IFA, Council, 25 Aug. 1936, 1925–44; SFAMT, EFC, 1 July 1936, minute 5, 22 July 1936, minute 18, Acc.9017/33, 1936–37.

17. Mandell, pp.192–3.

18. FA, 'Olympic Report 1936', pp.2–3, Council, 24 Aug. 1936, minute 6, 1936–37; FIFA, Manning, USFA, to Schricker, n.d. (Aug. 1934), USA correspondence, 1932–69; Glanville, *Soccer Nemesis*, p.63, pp.75–6. The 'W' formation, encouraged by offside rule changes in the mid-1920s, meant that forwards lined up as if on the points of the letter.

19. FA, 'Olympic Report 1936', p.3, Council, 24 Aug. 1936, minute 6, 1936–37; author's interview with Rous, 28 March 1980.

20. PRO, Sir Eric Drummond, Rome, to Simon, 20 Dec. 1934, FO370/455/L7469; Drummond to Simon, 12 Feb. 1935, FO370/484/L1054; minute, Capewell, 15 Feb. 1935, FO370/484/L1078; minutes, Capewell, 25 March 1935, and R. Bloore, 8 April 1935, FO370/484/L1833; Drummond to Simon, 23 March 1935, FO370/484/L2032; minute, Vansittart, 8 July 1936, FO370/511/L4772.

21. PRO, A. Grant Watson, Helsingfors, to Eden, 11 June 1936, FO370/510/L4008.

22. PRO, minute, Eden, n.d. (9 Jan. 1936), FO371/20279/F149; minute, Gaselee, 18 June 1936, FO370/510/L4049; Gaselee to N. Butler, Prime Minister's Secretary, 15 July 1935, FO370/484/L4322; minutes, Eden, Vansittart, 15 Jan. 1936, FO371/20279/F149; minute, Vansittart, 8 July 1936, FO370/511/L4772.

23. PRO, Crowe, Dept. of Trade, to C. Norton, 8 July 1936, FO370/510/L4771.

24. PRO, Sir Robert Clive, Tokyo, to Foreign Office, 8 Jan. 1936, minutes, 9 Jan. 1936, FO371/20279/F149; minutes, Boniface, 17 June 1936, Gaselee, 18 June 1936, FO370/510/L4049; Clive to Foreign Office, 10 July 1936, FO370/510/L4715.

25. PRO, minute, Vansittart, 8 July 1936, FO370/511/L4772; Hoyer Millar to C. Gamon, Lord Mayor's Secretary, 15 July 1936, FO370/511/L4822.

26. PRO, Cabinet Minutes, 9 July 1936, Cab23/85, 51 (36) 4; Vansittart to Clive, 16 July 1936, FO370/511/L4775.

27. PRO, Cabinet Minutes, 16 July 1936, Cab23/85, 53 (36) 4.

28. PRO, minute, Norton, 15 July 1936, FO370/511/L4775; Crowe to Norton, 21 July 1936, FO370/511/L4947; *Evening News*, 30 July 1936.

29. PRO, minute, Gaselee, 31 July 1936, FO370/511/L4947; Arita to Clive, 7 Aug. 1936, encl. Clive to Eden, 13 Aug. 1936, FO370/511/L5963; Clive to Foreign Office, 3 Aug. 1936, FO370/511/L5168.

30. CAC, Noel Baker to 'Bevil' (C.B. Rudd), 8 April 1938, NBKR 6/15/2.

31. PRO, Sir R. Craigie to Foreign Office, 15 Feb. 1938, FO371/22189/F1906; Craigie to Foreign Office, 24 Feb. 1938, FO371/22189/F2186.

32. PRO, minute, William Davies, Far Eastern Dept., 26 March 1938, FO371/22189/F3238; Sir Edward Monson, Stockholm, to Halifax, 8 July 1938, FO371/22189/F7384.

33. PRO, minute, Davies, 24 Feb. 1938, FO371/22189/F2186; Craigie to Foreign Office, 15 July 1938, FO371/22189/F7630; Junko Tahara, 'Count Michimasa Soyeshima and the cancellation of the XII Olympiad in Tokyo: a footnote to Olympic history',

Int.J.Hist.Sport, 9 (1992), 470–1.
34. PRO, minute, Wigram, 30 April 1936, FO371/19940/C1639; Martin Polley, 'The British Government and the Olympic Games in the 1930s', *The Sports Historian*, 17 (1997), 35.
35. PRO, Cabinet Minutes, 16 July 1936, Cab23/85, 53 (36) 4.
36. Montague, *The Olympic Games*.
37. Polley, 'Foreign Office and International Sport', pp.150–1.
38. PRO, minute, I. Maxse, 9 Jan. 1936, FO371/20279/F149.
39. H. Abrahams (ed.), *The Official Report of the XIth Olympiad: Berlin 1936* (BOA, London: 1937), p.46, quoted Polley, *Foreign Office and International Sport*, p.136.
40. FAW, *Annual Report 1935–36* (FAW, 1936), p.2; *Annual Report 1936–37* (FAW, 1937), p.1; Council, 25 Aug. 1936, minute 4421, 1935–37.
41. BL, Brooke, CRD, to Director, 7 June 1934, CRD 1/60/2 folio 2, J. Ball to Chamberlain, 3 Dec. 1934, CRD 1/60/2 folio 15; Birmingham University (hereafter BU), memorandum, Ball, 26 Oct. 1936, Neville Chamberlain papers (hereafter NC), NC8/23/10; *The Times*, 3 Dec. 1934; Feiling, pp.238–9, p.287; Jones, 'State intervention in sport', 165–8; Jones, *Sport, Politics and the Working Class*, pp.132–6; Grant, pp.165–93; John Ramsden, *The Making of Conservative Party Policy: the Conservative Research Department since 1929* (Longman, London, 1980), pp.79–89.
42. BL, memorandum, 20 July 1934, CRD 1/60/2, folio 10, pp.9–10.
43. BL, *A Call to the Nation*, November 1935, p.27, encl. CRD 1/60/6.
44. BU, Chamberlain's diary (on conversation with Chief Whip), 7 Oct. 1936, NC2/23A; BL, Chamberlain's Margate speech, 2 Oct. 1936, CRD 1/24/2, p.16.
45. BL, Chamberlain to Ball, 8 Oct. 1936, Ball to Chamberlain, 12 Oct. 1936, CRD 1/24/2; Ball to Chamberlain, 18 Nov. 1936, CRD 1/60/6 folio 34; *Daily Telegraph*, 7 Dec. 1936.
46. *The Times*, 6 Oct. 1936 (Chamberlain probably saw this: BU, file NC8/23).
47. *The Times*, 19 Oct. 1936 (in BU, file NC8/23).
48. BU, Lord Aberdare to Neville Chamberlain, 3 Oct. 1936, NC8/23/1.
49. Hajo Bernett, 'National Socialist Physical Education as reflected in British appeasement policy', *Int.J.Hist.Sport*, 5 (1988), 170–2.
50. Board of Education, p.3; *Physical Training and Recreation*, Cmd 5364 (Jan. 1937); PRO, National Advisory Council, memorandum on the powers of local authorities under the Physical Training and Recreation Act, 9 Aug. 1937, ED10/263. See, McIntosh, pp.107–10; Tony Mason, *Sport in Britain* (Faber & Faber, London, 1988), p.101; Jones, 'State intervention in sport', 166.
51. See SFAMT, Acc.9017/410; H. Justin Evans, *Service to Sport: the story of the CCPR – 1935–1972* (Pelham, London, 1974), p.40.
52. PRO, Earl de la Warr, Board of Education, to Sir John Simon, Treasury, 2 Nov. 1938, ED113/25; National Advisory Council Paper (38) 9, 7 Dec. 1938, p.8, ED10/263; Justin Evans, p.30, pp.35–46.
53. PRO, Stephen Tallents, BBC, to Sir M. Holmes, Board of Education, 18 Nov. 1938, ED113/27.
54. PRO, British Council to Capt. L. Ellis, NFC, 10 Aug. 1938, BW2/85. Noel-Baker, who was now back in parliament, took a particular interest, as evidenced by his use of questions to illuminate, say, shortcomings in the number of qualified physical training instructors: *Hansard (Commons) 5th Ser.* CCCVL, 585–6, 16 March 1939.
55. Mason, *Sport in Britain*, p.101.
56. BL, Points for Propaganda, Jan. –July 1939, CRD 1/78/2 no.1; *News Chronicle*, 15 June 1939.

57. PRO, de la Warr to Simon, 2 Nov. 1938, ED113/25.
58. C. Roemer, letter, *The Times*, 2 Sept. 1938.
59. PRO, Simon to de la Warr, 28 Nov. 1938, ED113/25; F. Tribe, Treasury, to D. Davidson, Board of Education, 28 March 1939, ED113/30.
60. PRO, National Advisory Council Paper (38) 9, 7 Dec. 1938, p.13, ED10/263.
61. PRO, minute, Sargent, 19 Nov. 1935, FO371/18884/C7566; Hoare to H.M. representatives in overseas missions, 28 Nov. 1935, FO371/19647/W10098.
62. PRO, minutes, Leigh Smith, Aug. 1936, Charles H. Johnston, 30 Oct. 1936, FO371/20449/W8826.
63. PRO, Sir Hubert Montgomery, The Hague, to Hoare, 7 Dec. 1935, FO371/19647/W10632.
64. PRO, S. Waterlow, Athens, to Hoare, 20 Dec. 1935, FO371/19647/W10977.
65. PRO, Montgomery to Hoare, 7 Dec. 1935, FO371/19647/W10632.
66. PRO, minutes, Johnston, 30 Oct. 1936, Garran, 31 Oct. 1936, FO371/20449/W8826.
67. PRO, Kennard, British ambassador in Warsaw, to Leeper, 26 May 1936, Kennard to Orme Sargent, 3 June 1936, FO371/20462/W5343.
68. PRO, *Kurjer Poranny*, 25 May 1936. The following section is based on the detailed press coverage forwarded by the British embassy: Kennard to Leeper, 26 May 1936, FO371/20462/W5343.
69. PRO, *Gazeta Polska*, 24 May 1936.
70. See A. Verdyck, 'About the laws of the game: charging the goalkeeper', *Football World*, 3 (January 1939).
71. PRO, *I.K.C.*, 25 May 1936; *Kurjer Poranny*, 25 May 1936.
72. PRO, *I.K.C.*, 25 May 1936.
73. PRO, *I.K.C.*, 26 May 1936; *Kurjer Warszawski*, 24 May 1936. The First Division is now called the Premier League.
74. PRO, Kennard to Leeper, 26 May 1936, FO371/20462/W5343.
75. PRO, Kennard to Orme Sargent, 3 June 1936, FO371/20462/W5343.
76. PRO, minutes, Sir George Mounsey, 15 June 1936, Sargent and Mounsey, 17 June 1936, FO371/20462/W5343.
77. PRO, minute, Viscount Cranborne, 22 June 1936, Sargent to Kennard, 23 June 1936, FO371/20462/W5343.
78. PRO, Eden to Sir C. Wingfield, Lisbon, 16 March 1937, FO371/21269/W6676; Sir Walford Selby, British ambassador in Lisbon, to Mounsey, 9 Jan. 1938, FO395/568/P673; Sir Walford Selby, *Diplomatic Twilight, 1930–1940* (John Murray, London, 1953), p.83.
79. PRO, minutes, 12, 26 April 1937, FO371/21269/W6676; Selby to Mounsey, 9 Jan. 1938, FO371/22591/W800.
80. PRO, Selby to Mounsey, 9 Jan. 1938, FO371/22591/W800.
81. Selby, p.85.
82. BL, memorandum, G. Dawson, n.d. (May 1938), MS Dawson 79, folio 182.
83. PRO, Scott, Lisbon, to G. Corley Smith, 31 Aug. 1938, FO395/596/P2602.
84. PRO, Selby to Mounsey, 9 Jan. 1938, FO371/22591W800.
85. PRO, Rowland Kenney to Rous, FA, 11 Feb. 1938, Rous to Kenney, 12 Feb. 1938, FO395/568/P673.
86. PRO, minute, Mounsey (for Cranborne), 15 March 1937, FO371/21394/W5467; minute, W. Pollock, 4 April 1937, FO371/21394/W7390.
87. PRO, minute, Cadogan, 15 March, Eden (n.d.), Cranborne and Mounsey, 17 March 1937, FO371/21394/W5467.
88. Shipman, 81.
89. Riordan, *Soviet Sport*, pp.116–17; Riordan, 'The USSR', pp.24–5.

90. Riordan, *Soviet Sport*, pp.115–17; Shipman, 84; Robert Edelman, *Serious Fun: a history of spectator sports in the USSR* (Oxford University Press, Oxford, 1993), pp.45–8, pp.59–72.
91. *Pravda*, 5 May 1937; Riordan, *Soviet Sport*, pp.119–20; Jim Riordan, 'The strange story of Nikolai Starostin, football and Lavrentii Beria', *Europe-Asia Studies*, 46 (1994), 684.
92. Riordan, *Soviet Sport*, p.117; Morton, p.141; Edelman, pp.67–9.
93. Riordan, 'The USSR', p.21.
94. Riordan, *Soviet Sport*, p.115, pp.144–5; Jones, *Sport, Politics and the Working Class*, pp.170–86; Peppard and Riordan, p.43.
95. FIFA, Hamdi Emin to Schricker, 31 Oct. , 9 Nov. 1932, Turkey correspondence 1932–70; Edelman, pp.48–51.
96. PRO, minute, C.H. Johnston, 30 Oct. 1936, FO371/20449/W8826; Shipman, 84.
97. *New York Times*, 23 July 1933.
98. See Chap. 6, pp.140–2, for the 1930 episode. Similar bans occurred elsewhere, including Spain: *Mundo Obrero*, 23 March 1933, 28, 30 July, 27, 29 Aug. 1934. *Mundo Obrero* was the Communist Party daily. I am indebted to Professor Christopher Cobb for this information.
99. *Football Pictorial*, 30 Nov. 1935; FIFA, Rous to Schricker, 1 March 1935, England 1932–57; Peskett, pp.161–2.
100. FIFA, Circular 1934/36, 3 Sept. 1934, Circular 1934/38, 19 Oct. 1934. The abortive Soviet tour proposal is not mentioned in the club history: Bell.
101. FIFA, Schricker to Emin, 21 Sept. , 5 Dec. 1933, Turkey correspondence, 1932–70. See Circulars 21/1935, 26 Aug. 1935, 23/1935, 27 Aug. 1935, 29/1935, 18 Dec. 1935, 5/1936, 14 March 1936.
102. FIFA, Schricker to Rous, 1 Nov. 1937, England correspondence 1932–57; Manning to Schricker, 14 Jan. 1937, USA correspondence 1932–69; USA, J. Davies, US ambassador, Moscow, to State Dept., 12 April 1937, RG59, Box 6703, 861.4063/2.
103. FIFA, FIFA to G. Graham, SFA, 5 May 1936, Scotland correspondence 1932–67; SFAMT, Office-Bearers, 14 May 1936, minute 2, EFC, 5 June 1936, minute 1, Accc.9017/33, 1936–37; Circulars, 9/1936, 1 May 1936, 11/1936, 11 May 1936.
104. FIFA, Schricker to Rous, 15 Feb. 1937, England correspondence 1932–57.
105. FIFA, Graham to Schricker, 15 June 1936, Scotland correspondence 1932–67; Circular 13/1936, 19 June 1936.
106. FIFA, Schricker to Emin, 21 Sept., 5 Dec. 1933, 18 June 1936, Turkey correspondence, 1932–70.
107. FIFA, Schricker to Emin, 28 Aug. 1936, Turkey correspondence 1932–70.
108. FIFA, Schricker to Rous, 15 Feb. 1937, England correspondence 1932–57.
109. FIFA, Circular, 15 Nov. 1939.
110. FIFA, Schricker to Rous, 15 Feb. 1937, England correspondence 1932–57.
111. FIFA, Manning, USFA, to Schricker, 14 Jan. 1937, USA correspondence, 1932–69.
112. Montague, 'The Olympic Games'.
113. PRO, Sir Noel Curtis Bennet to Crowe, Dept. of Trade, 2 July 1936, encl. Crowe to Orde, 6 July 1936, FO370/510/L4537; minute, C. Norton, 15 July 1936, FO370/511/L4775; Hoyer Millar to Gamon, 15 July 1936, FO370/511/L4822.
114. PRO, minute, Lawford, 5 June 1936, FO371/19940/C4049.
115. PRO, Leeper to British Empire Games Federation, 11 Jan. 1938, FO395/568/P28; J. Leigh Wood, Commander of British Empire Games Team, Sydney, to Foreign Office, 1 Feb. 1938, FO395/568/P1201.
116. PRO, Geoffrey Fry to Hoyer Millar, 9 July 1936, FO370/511/L4821.

9

Britain's 'Football Ambassadors' Perform
Work of 'National Importance':
The Late 1930s

The period leading up to the outbreak of the Second World War was described by Joseph Avenol, Secretary-General of the League of Nations, as one of *'demi-guerre'*.[1] Repeatedly, international order was threatened by major crises prompted largely by the territorial ambitions of Germany, Italy and Japan, whose restlessness concentrated the mind of a British government led by Neville Chamberlain, a prime minister striving for appeasement.[2]

Inevitably, international conditions ensured that the British government, though still disinclined either to adopt a more coherent policy on the topic or to assign it high priority, became increasingly aware of sport's policy value, most notably, its politico-military potential. As ever, German and Italian models figured prominently in official thinking, as evidenced in September 1937, when Robert Vansittart evaluated sport's contribution to Nazi propaganda preparing the German people, especially the youth, for war.[3] For instance, the Nuremberg party rallies were used to stage the Hitler youth movement's sports finals, in which five consecutive events offered 'a picture of the physical performance required from a troop of soldiers going into action, as far as this can be presented through sport'.[4] A 20 kilometre walk, carrying a ten kilogram military pack, followed by a 200 metre obstacle race involving walls and ditches, simulated the advance to battle. A further three events, including shooting in both lying and standing positions as well as the hurling of a small club resembling a grenade, replicated a conflict scenario.

The way in which sportsmen and women representing Germany were interpreted as embodying the qualities of the whole nation, and particularly those fostered by the Nazi regime, was illustrated vividly in June 1936, when Hitler telegraphed Max Schmeling in New York to congratulate him on his twelfth round knock-out victory in a non-title bout over Joe Louis, the world heavyweight boxing champion: 'I know you fight for Germany; that it was a German victory. *We* are proud of you.'[5] Unsurprisingly, *Der Angriff* attributed Schmeling's success to his meeting with the Führer:

'from that moment his will to victory was boundless'.[6] Schmeling returned on the Zeppelin 'Hindenburg' to be welcomed by Hitler at the Reich Chancellery, while political exploitation of an event adjudged to enhance the superiority of 'our race' – the fact that Louis was black helped this message – was maximised by widespread newsreel, press and radio coverage.[7] Two years later, Schmeling's first round defeat to Louis in another highly visible sporting encounter held in New York, where the German ambassador was joined at the ringside by Clark Gable, Gary Cooper, Douglas Fairbanks and J. Edgar Hoover, among others, forced a change of strategy. Ivone Kirkpatrick, reporting from the British embassy at Berlin, indicated that Goebbels had prepared grandiose victory plans celebrating 'the innate superiority of Nordic over nigger'.[8] Instead, *Völkische Beobachter* took refuge in the rapidly changing fortunes of the ring: 'the defeat of a boxer is no national loss of prestige; it is a lost battle only for the boxer himself'. Even then, Louis' win was ascribed to the seemingly unfair manner in which a succession of blows prevented Schmeling from displaying his allegedly superior ring-craft skills! By implication, brute force triumphed over skill. As Kirkpatrick remarked, 'the German has a genius for not only feeling but saying the wrong thing'. Meanwhile, Schmeling himself soon realised the premium placed on sporting success by the Nazi regime: 'I was dropped by the German high command like a hot potato'.[9]

CULTURAL PROPAGANDA AND THE 'FIERCE WAR OF IDEAS'

For the British government, the Schmeling episode illuminated yet again the manner in which sportsmen and women were projected variously as fighting, playing, running or scoring for their respective imagined communities during a period in which – to quote Richard Butler, Minister of State at the Foreign Office – 'the world is full of propaganda today on a scale as great, if not greater, than at the time of war'.[10] Inevitably, the widespread use of propaganda as a 'weapon of aggression' by Germany and Italy, among other governments, forced British policy-makers to realise the need for counter-measures to uphold national interests and prestige in the wider world.

Following the First World War, as Vansittart observed, propaganda activities 'were allowed to take their course regardless of what other countries were doing in this respect'.[11] Eventually, the creation of the British Council (1934–35) ushered in a more activist and systematic strategy, but the level of activity, especially funding, fell far short of that

239

found in other countries: 'We cannot rely indefinitely on our general political prestige ... In the last resort, like can only be met with like, and propaganda with propaganda.'[12] To some extent, the Chamberlain government (1937–40) showed signs of heeding the message. In December 1937, Chamberlain himself conceded that traditional 'stand-upon-your-dignity methods' were no longer applicable in the face of the 'new methods of propaganda' characteristic of the 'rough and tumble of international relations'.[13] Soon afterwards, the prime minister, supporting the Foreign Office's 'sensible' initiative for extending the British Council's 'excellent' work, informed parliament of his government's desire for a 'better understanding of this country and of the British people abroad'.[14] Then, on 16 February 1938, the House of Commons urged the government 'to give the full weight of its moral and financial support to schemes to further the wider and more effective presentation of British news, views and culture abroad'.[15] As usual, Treasury constraints, justified increasingly by the demands of rearmament, limited the amount of additional funding. Thus, during its first five years of life the British Council's funding rose rapidly, but, as ever, totals (1938–39: £178,466, including the Foreign Office grant of £130,500) fell far short of those allocated for similar purposes in other countries, hence limiting the amount available for sport.[16]

INTRODUCING 'BRITISH SPORTING SPIRIT IN GREECE'

During the late 1930s, the British Council's work in the Middle East and Mediterranean region was influenced largely by the 'urgent need' to respond to the intensification of French, German and Italian cultural propaganda.[17] An emerging focus was Greece, whose propaganda potential had been identified already in 1936, when Humphrey Payne, Director of the British School of Archaeology at Athens, presented cultural diplomacy as an 'effective means' of furthering British interests in a country where such activities were viewed, to quote the Director of the British School at Rome, as 'an index of the importance of the nation which maintains them, as a kind of national propaganda, not in any bad sense of the word, which we tend now to associate with Germany and Italy'.[18] Subsequently, Greece's political priority was reaffirmed when it was one of the countries guaranteed in spring 1939 as part of British efforts to contain the territorial ambitions of the Axis powers.

In Greece, the British Council's work was characterised by the usual concentration on literary, linguistic and artistic activities, even if this elitist focus was gradually complemented by greater attention to football and

240

other sports.[19] Notwithstanding a genuine desire to develop the game in Greece, Sidney Waterlow, the British Minister in Athens, conceded that the prime objective was 'to introduce British sporting spirit in Greece' as part of a broad cultural propaganda programme.[20] Waterlow, hoping that 'propaganda through sport and athletics' would become a regular part of the council's work, felt that images of British fair play and sportsmanship offered a useful 'corrective' to intensive German 'Olympic' propaganda, especially as its ability to reach opinion-formers was ensured by the prominent role played in Greek sport by politicians. For example, one request for British help derived from Kotzias, who was not only President of the Hellenic Football Federation but also the Minister-Governor of Athens.

In November 1937, Waterlow, reviewing the council's plans, observed that the despatch of a British football coach, as requested by Kotzias, would serve as a token of friendship between the two countries and provide the basis for further sporting links.[21] Indeed, he went as far as to suggest that the project should be assigned priority over more traditional forms of cultural propaganda. Both the British Council and Foreign Office, welcoming Waterlow's 'very good proposal' as promising 'considerable' policy benefits at minimal cost, moved quickly to implement the recommendation with the help of the FA.[22] As usual, Rous, who was encouraged by officials to see the FA's contribution within the broader cultural propaganda context, proved responsive to the government's request for assistance. Thus, he drew up a short list of possible coaches, paying due regard to the need for continental experience, good references, and preparedness to accept the specified annual salary of £400. More revealing was the British Council's requirement that any appointee must not be a 'roughneck', which was taken to mean evidence of satisfactory educational and social skills; in fact, one candidate, currently working in Smyrna, was rejected in part because of unfavourable reports about his relationship with a local Turkish woman.[23]

Rous moved quickly, so that in February 1938, W. Baggett, whose playing experience (e.g. Bolton, Reading) was reinforced by attendance at a FA coaching course, was appointed to the post, much to the pleasure of the footballing authorities in Greece, where his coaching work was reinforced by efforts to reorganise the game, such as through the introduction of a British-style domestic cup competition.[24] Baggett also assumed responsibility for the national side's abortive efforts to qualify for the 1938 World Cup finals.[25] Following two victories over Palestine, the team travelled to Budapest, where Hungary's crushing 11-1 victory foiled Greek hopes. This result, though demonstrating the limitations of Baggett's impact to date, should be interpreted in part as a reflection of the strength of Hungary, whose 2-0 victory over Switzerland in the early stages of the 1938 World Cup finals contrasted with England's 1-2 loss in Zurich a few weeks earlier.

Soon afterwards, the British legation at Athens, encouraged by Baggett's initial achievements, proposed a visit by a British team. Subsequent exchanges, involving the Foreign Office, British Council, and FA, touched on a range of questions, including finance, geographical coverage, and timing, but perhaps the most illuminating discussion focused on the respective merits of the despatch of either a professional or amateur team. Despite departmental prejudices about professional sport, the British legation's stipulation, that for prestige reasons it was 'necessary that the team should be able to win, and by a controllable margin', resulted in a strong preference for the former.[26] In the event, the FA failed to find a suitable team, much to the irritation of the British legation.[27]

Early in 1939, Waterlow, reviewing the British Council's work, claimed that British influence through culture was 'very much on the ascendant' in Greece: 'British propaganda aims at keeping alive the tradition of Greek friendship for Britain and admiration of British institutions. Our aim is defensive: to preserve and consolidate what we already have in the face of the aggressive economic thrust of Germany.'[28] His survey, acknowledging the 'excellent work' being undertaken by both Baggett and a British swimming coach at Salonica, referred in glowing terms to the 'resounding popular success' of British sport in Greece.[29] Inevitably, he sought to involve other sports, as highlighted in May 1939, when he urged the entry of a strong British team in the biennial Greek marathon race.[30] Of course, Waterlow was not an unbiased observer, but during the late 1930s it is clear that sport made an 'important contribution' to the British Council's efforts to compete for influence in Greece, particularly among the youth. The perceived need to counter the German challenge by 'keeping sport in our hands' was uppermost, as conceded in March 1939 by a meeting held at the British legation at Athens in the presence of Lord Lloyd, the Council's chairman.[31]

Frances Donaldson's otherwise authoritative and comprehensive history is written as if the British Council had nothing to do with sport during the late 1930s.[32] Admittedly, sport was a relatively minor part of its work, but in certain countries, like Greece, such activities were perceived both in London as well as by the men on the spot to offer – to quote the British consul-general in Salonica – 'a sound investment from the propaganda point of view' yielding meaningful contacts and impacts at all levels of society for minimal outlay.[33] Greece, whose value as a case study is reinforced by the ready availability of archival materials, should not necessarily be seen as typical, since much depended on the personal enthusiasm and support of Waterlow. Even then, sport accounted for less than 10 per cent of the council's budget (1938–39: £7,329) for Greece, where only modest sums – these included £400 for a football coach or £150 for a Greek physical training instructor to visit Britain – were actually allocated to sport.[34]

In general, the British Council's work was interpreted by the Foreign Office as offering effective support for British diplomacy, most notably in terms of preventing the 'gradual but distinct dissolution of old friendships due to the indifference shown by this country'.[35] In turn, the patchy nature of its work by country was paralleled by the uneven role played by sport in cultural propaganda programmes undertaken in any one country. The British Council, albeit arranging occasional visits to Britain for foreign teams (e.g. an Afghan hockey team, 1936) and overseas experts, concentrated largely on the despatch overseas of British coaches and instructors for, say, athletics, boxing, football, physical education, swimming and tennis. However, the British Council, to which any applications were passed on routinely for reply by the Foreign Office, was neither prepared nor able to meet foreign requests for information about British sport, modes of organisation, and number of participants, as evidenced in April 1938, when it received a Greek request for statistical and other information for use at a forthcoming sports exhibition. The British legation at Athens, recording that other countries, like Germany, would be only too willing and able to send 'wagon loads' of material, advised that it was 'most important for us to make as good a showing as possible'.[36] However, the Foreign Office News Department, recalling its inability to meet a previous Turkish request, merely rationalised the situation on the grounds that the British were 'less statistically-minded than some other nations'![37] Subsequently, the NFC's assumption of an international role through the British Council, as outlined in the previous chapter, helped to alleviate the problem.[38]

SPORT AS A COVER FOR DIPLOMATIC EXCHANGES

In 1936 Vansittart's visit to the Berlin Olympics highlighted the manner in which sports events provided cover for diplomatic exchanges. A more notorious example occurred in November 1937, when Lord Halifax, the Lord President of the Council, visited a Berlin hunting exhibition.[39] For Lord Halifax, hunting proved a personal passion; indeed, Lord Butler, looking back to their period at the Foreign Office (1938–40), advised that 'the best insight into Halifax's character is that he is an M.F.H. [Master of Fox Hounds].[40] Chamberlain, vexed by the Foreign Office's apparent failure under Eden to take advantage of opportunities to improve links with Berlin, saw attendance as providing both the occasion and 'cover' for advancing Anglo-German relations, especially as an 'unofficial visit free from politics' benefited from the absence of strong pressure to produce quick results.[41]

As a result, Halifax's five-day German visit, having been undertaken ostensibly to see 'something in the way of German sport', assumed 'quite a different aspect' by providing a meaningful point of contact with Hitler and other leading members of the regime. Reportedly, a shoulder strain ruled out plans to go 'shooting foxes in Pomerania', but Halifax left Berlin impressed by a visit depicted as opening the door between London and Berlin: 'Unless I am wholly deceived, the Germans, speaking generally, from Hitler to the man in the street, do want friendly relations with Great Britain. There are no doubt many who don't: and the leading men may be deliberately throwing dust in our eyes. But I don't think so – and the general attitude of the crowd whom I saw in the Hunting Exhibition and of people in the streets was one of obvious friendliness.'[42] Halifax's positive report reaffirmed Chamberlain's belief in his appeasement policy: 'The German visit was from my point of view a great success because it achieved its object, that of creating an atmosphere in which it was possible to discuss with Germany the practical questions involved in a European settlement'.[43] By contrast, Anthony Eden, the Foreign Secretary, was unhappy about the Prime Minister's 'attempt to run foreign affairs in his own way'.[44] Even worse, Halifax's impressions came to underpin government thinking, as noted by Jim Thomas, Eden's Parliamentary Private Secretary: 'the real danger of the visit was that Halifax, on his return, informed the Cabinet that Hitler had stated definitely to him that he had no aggressive intentions in Central Europe. To this remark, the PM clung through the months that followed in spite of warnings from official quarters that Austria was in danger'.[45]

THE FA'S MORE SYSTEMATIC APPROACH TO INTERNATIONAL FOOTBALL

Despite repeated official pressure urging the FA to take action against British teams guilty of unsporting behaviour and poor results in foreign fixtures, negative reports continued to reach London, where officials viewed them with growing impatience. During July 1938, Kennard, the

British ambassador in Poland, used a visit to London to follow up complaints through an exchange of views with Lt.-Colonel Bridge, Secretary-General of the British Council. Kennard, who was never able to expunge the unpleasant memories of Chelsea's visit to Poland in 1936, referred to the harm caused to national prestige by British footballers playing in Czechoslovakia, Germany and Poland, among other countries; thus, he complained that carefully cultivated foreign images of Britain 'can be rendered nugatory in a few minutes' by events on the football field.[46] Following this exchange, Bridge urged action on the Foreign Office: 'Although football is a private undertaking over which the Government cannot exercise control, I submit that something can and must be done to try and preserve our British reputation for sportsmanship from the stigma to which such incidents must submit it ... Otherwise, as Kennard says, why waste the taxpayers' money on trying to disseminate among foreigners an appreciation of the glories of British culture?' One proposal involved the despatch of a dossier of incidents to the FA as the basis for future discussions with the British Council and Foreign Office. In addition, Bridge, pointing to professional football's profit motive, proposed the non-attendance of diplomats at tour matches unless teams made contact with overseas missions and guaranteed the good behaviour of players. But this proposal, seemingly based on the somewhat naive view that the absence of British diplomats would reduce gate receipts, seemed unlikely to remedy the situation.

During 1938 Vansittart, having been 'kicked upstairs' to become 'Chief Diplomatic Adviser', assumed responsibility for the recently established Committee for the Co-ordination of British Publicity Abroad.[47] In this capacity, he took – to quote Gaselee – 'a special interest' in the 'very important' question of international football.[48] In July 1938, the Foreign Office, having expressed pleasure about the recent Germany-England match discussed in this book's opening chapter, summoned the FA for talks with a view to action prior to next season. The prospects for meaningful collaboration were enhanced by the fact that during 1937–38 the FA was already adopting a more systematic approach towards international football. For example, in December 1937 the FA, accepting the merits of a long-term strategy, instructed Rous to prepare a fixtures programme for the next three to four years.[49] At the same time, closer monitoring of overseas fixtures, particularly those undertaken by clubs, was adjudged desirable in the wake of the close season tours conducted in May 1938. In part, the FA was spurred into action by the unexpectedly strong 'German XI' put into the field against Aston Villa as well as by the heavy losses suffered by Preston (e.g. 1-6 to Slavia, Prague), among other clubs. In June 1938, the

FA, having reviewed results, decided that, when arranging international fixtures, selecting national teams, and approving club proposals for overseas tours, due regard should be paid to 'the strength and standing' of foreign teams alongside 'any other circumstances' adjudged liable to impact upon national prestige. Significantly, 'other' factors were deemed to include political considerations, such as when periods of international tension meant that 'more than the playing of the match is at stake, and when it is particularly necessary for the English prestige in sport to be maintained'.[50]

These moves provided a useful background for the meeting between the Foreign Office and the FA, held on 25 August. Vansittart acknowledged both the government's reliance on the footballing authorities and the limits of the FA's control, but was pleased to secure Rous' acceptance of the value of future collaboration with the government in order to instil 'a sense of responsibility' in players about the need to give 'a good impression' abroad for reasons of national prestige.[51] Subsequently, the FA, having reviewed its procedures, issued a revised set of rules in March 1939; thus, clubs, which were still only allowed to play teams affiliated to national associations belonging to FIFA, were required henceforth to submit reports to the FA within 14 days of their return from abroad.[52] Nor could inter-club matches played overseas be billed as international fixtures. At the same time, the Foreign Office, albeit welcoming its apparent receptiveness to official pressure, continued to believe that the FA possessed only a 'very restricted' ability to control clubs.[53] As ever, the Foreign Office failed to credit, possibly because of lack of knowledge, the extent to which British associations dealt already with breaches of their regulations; for example, in April 1937, the FA, guided by its Disciplinary Committee's report about numerous instances of player misconduct during the past two seasons, rejected an application from Wolverhampton Wanderers to tour central Europe in the close season.[54]

BRITISH TEAMS PLAY ON THE CONTINENT IN 1938, BUT NOT IN THE WORLD CUP

In May 1938, both England and Scotland played on the continent during the weeks immediately preceding the third World Cup finals (Table 2.3, Chapter 2), which were awarded to France in 1936 in the face of rival bids from Argentina and Germany. England even played France at the Colombes Stadium in Paris (26 May 1938) – the stadium had been specially enlarged for the World Cup – a mere nine days before the opening of the tournament.

At one time, Scotland was also scheduled to play France during May, but its projected close season tour was scaled down eventually to one game played against the Netherlands (Scotland won 3-1) at Amsterdam on 21 May. Hitherto, Wales had played only one full international outside Britain, but in December 1937, the FAW gave serious consideration to an invitation to tour Austria and Czechoslovakia in May 1938.[55] In the event, the FAW decided not to go ahead with a tour, that is, before the *Anschluss* removed the possibility of the Austrian fixture.

Despite the inevitable British focus on Scotland's Dutch visit and England's close season tour of Germany, Switzerland and France – this tour was discussed in detail in the opening chapter – the 1938 World Cup finals, played between 4 and 19 June, occupy a more prominent place in the history of football. In fact, despite British non-entry in the World Cup, the juxtaposition of these events meant that results against teams due to play in the World Cup finals a week or so later offered one basis for assessing the strength and quality of British football. From this perspective, the position was not encouraging in the sense that Germany and Holland lost their first-round matches, while neither France nor Switzerland got beyond the quarter-finals.

Although a record entry required a qualifying competition to produce 16 finalists for France, the absence of several major footballing countries established the impossibility of keeping international sport clear of politics. Civil war ruled out Spain, while another notable absentee was Austria, a semi-finalist in the 1934 World Cup and generally regarded as one of Europe's leading teams. Although Austria qualified for the 1938 finals, the *Anschluss* ended the country's existence as an independent political and footballing authority. However, Czechoslovakia, defeated finalists in 1934, was present, even if the May war scare crisis suggested the emerging German threat to Czech territorial integrity and independence. Meanwhile, the escalating Sino-Japanese conflict, prompting Japan's withdrawal, left the Dutch East Indies as the only Asian entrant. Only two other non-European countries, Brazil and Cuba, participated, so that the 1938 tournament seemed less global than its predecessor. The non-participation of Argentina, seemingly annoyed by its abortive bid to host the event, and Uruguay proved more serious from the footballing point of view.

Once again, the British associations refused FIFA's invitations to enter the competition. The key decision was made in March 1937, when the FA, whose minutes prove characteristically uninformative, decided against entry in a competition treated, to quote William Pickford, as 'the recognised battleground of national football abroad'.[56] Subsequently, the IFAB, meeting at Llandudno in June 1937, left decisions to individual associations, but there was little likelihood of the FAW, IFA or SFA adopting a more forthcoming attitude than the FA.[57] FIFA's alternative suggestion for a 'Great Britain' team, though acceptable for the 1936 Olympics, was even less attractive to British associations extremely sensitive about their autonomy respecting full internationals.[58] In the event, Britain's self-imposed 'splendid isolation' was accentuated by the fact that, as mentioned earlier, both England and Scotland, played on the continent against four finalists just prior to the start of the tournament. Nevertheless, the British associations exhibited a more sympathetic attitude towards the event as compared to the preceding World Cup. Whereas they had refused FIFA's request to switch the IFAB from Cannes to Rome to link with the 1934 tournament, in 1938 the IFAB's meeting was transferred from Northern Ireland to Paris to facilitate members' attendance at the World Cup. More importantly, for the first time, both the FA and SFA were represented at the World Cup final itself![59] Even so, it was easy for people in Britain to be almost unaware of the World Cup finals, given the relatively modest level of British press coverage thereof.

Italy, though requiring extra time to overcome Norway in its opening game, progressed to its second successive World Cup success following a 4-2 win over Hungary in the final. World Cup victories in 1934 and 1938, plus the 1936 Olympic gold medal, reinforced Italian pretensions to claim the best team in the world, even if the absence of British and several Latin American teams left room for debate. Brazil, the only serious non-European contender, and Czechoslovakia were involved in a notorious quarter-final, labelled the 'Battle of Bordeaux', which raised yet again question marks about the extent to which international sport's cooperative tendencies were able to overcome extra-sporting pressures for success. Meanwhile, FIFA, meeting at Paris during the tournament, deferred a decision about the location of the 1942 finals until its 1940 Congress – rival bidders included Argentina, Brazil and Germany – by which time the outbreak of the Second World War meant that the next championship was not held until 1950.[60]

THE U-TURN ON GERMAN FIXTURES

The Czech problem reached crisis point in September 1938, when the British government, pursuing Anglo-German détente, performed a leading role in the moves culminating in the conclusion of the Munich Agreement. Significantly, the FA, sharing the general sense of relief at the manner in which events failed to escalate into war, sent Chamberlain a congratulatory letter praising his 'great achievement' in averting war.[61]

Soon afterwards, on 26 October 1938, England played FIFA's 'Rest of Europe' team at Highbury as part of the FA's 75th anniversary celebrations. FIFA, highlighting the ambivalent nature of its relationship with British football, had launched this initiative in order to allow members to 'show their gratitude for the pioneer work which the British countries have done for the development of football on the continent'.[62] But, the FA, stressing its separate identity, rejected initial proposals for a Great Britain-FIFA game, thereby prompting the SFA's abortive efforts to extend the FIFA team's visit for an extra match north of the border.[63] England's decisive 3-0 victory over a team representing the 'Rest of Europe' – in fact, the team was dominated by two Germans and seven Italians – reinforced impressions of traditional footballing superiority, especially as British commentators glossed over the problems facing scratch teams. Once again, the Foreign Office's role was confined to minor practical issues, as evidenced by its positive response to Rous' request for the Passport Office to allow *circa* 300 German spectators attending the match on an excursion organised by *Fussball-Woche* to enter Britain with less expensive tourist visas.[64] This concession, occurring in the wake of the Munich agreement, harmonised with the government's aim on 'political grounds' to encourage Germans, especially the youth, to visit Britain for sporting and leisure activities.[65] Likewise, Lord Lloyd emphasised the British Council's desire to 'do all we possibly can' to reach the man in the German street through sport.[66]

During the early months of 1939, growing doubts about German intentions, most notably the durability of the Munich Agreement respecting Czechoslovakia, failed to prevent the arrangement of close season fixtures between British and German clubs, even if other countries, like Holland (November 1938), had already banned international fixtures against Germany. At this stage, there was no attempt by the British government to ostracise the Axis powers; indeed, the Chamberlain government continued to court both Hitler's Germany and Mussolini's Italy, as highlighted by Chamberlain's visit to Rome in January 1939. Having finalised arrangements for England's 1939 tour to Italy, Romania and Yugoslavia, on 11 March 1939, the FA approved club proposals for close season tours to a range of countries, including Germany.[67] Soon afterwards, the rapid deterioration in the international situation consequent upon Germany's occupation of Prague (15 March), Hitler's emerging threat to Poland, and Italy's advance into Albania (7 April), prompted a re-assessment of British foreign policy, as reflected by guarantee treaties for Greece, Poland and Romania.[68] As a result, the FA, following consultations with the Foreign Office, withdrew approval for close season matches arranged against German clubs by Arsenal, Everton and Stoke 'in consequence of the international situation'.[69] The FA's sudden U-turn, illuminating the transformation in Anglo-German relations, forced clubs to alter their tour schedules; for instance, Arsenal's board, resolving to 'Cancel close-season games in Germany', readjusted its projected tour to concentrate on Belgium, Norway and Sweden.[70] Inevitably, serious question marks were raised about the return England-Germany international fixed provisionally for 1939–40.

In this manner, events confirmed that association football functioned within the broad international political framework, as demonstrated also in France, where both association and rugby football internationals against Germany were cancelled in April 1939.[71] In fact, France's cancellation of the scheduled football international against Germany led Scotland, and then Wales, to be invited to fill the gap at short notice. The SFA, committed to a North American tour, refused, but the FAW, tempted also by the prospect of profit, accepted, thereby resulting in Wales' second full international against a non-British side. The match, played at Paris on 20 May, was lost 1-2.[72] However, German football was not ostracised by all countries; thus, during May and June 1939 internationals were played versus Denmark, Estonia, Norway, and the Republic of Ireland (1-1, Bremen, 23 May). Nor was Germany ignored by all British sports (e.g. athletics, tennis), as mentioned below.

ENGLAND'S 'SPORT AMBASSADORS' CONTEST THE 'REAL BATTLE FOR WORLD HONOURS'

Italy, marked out by the British Council as a possible additional country for action, figured prominently in England's 1939 close season tour, which also included Romania and Yugoslavia.[73] Surprisingly, despite its recent invasion of Albania (7 April 1939), Italy escaped the footballing sanctions imposed on its Axis partner; thus, the FA, having consulted the Foreign Office, decided that the tour should go ahead.[74]

As happened in 1938, one tour game occupied centre-stage, that is, England's game versus Italy, scheduled to be played at Milan on 13 May: 'in view of the political situation, this match had assumed, in the eyes of the Press and the Public, a greater significance than it otherwise would have'.[75] Tactfully, this FA report, albeit specifying 'the press and the public', omitted any mention of the two governments, which took a close interest in a match taking place at a time when Anglo-Italian relations were deteriorating in the wake of the Austrian, Czech, Albanian, Spanish and other problems. For example, at this time, the generally hostile tone of the

Italian media, most notably, the 'objectionable' propaganda transmitted by *Radio Bari* towards Egypt and Palestine, caused considerable irritation on the part of the British government.[76]

Nor were sporting considerations of peripheral importance for a fixture presented as the 'real battle for world honours' testing 'The Masters of football' against 'The World Cup holders'.[77] Already in June 1937, Bologna's victory in the Paris Exhibition tournament – this was secured through a victory over Chelsea – had been employed not only to sing the praises of fascism but also to argue that the myth of British footballing primacy had been 'exploded'; indeed, British football, as represented by Chelsea, the 'WM' style of play and an excessively physical approach, was described as 'outdated', even 'absolutely ineffective'.[78] Memories of previous England-Italy encounters, most notably the 1934 'Battle of Highbury', imparted an added edge to a game viewed in both countries as possessing an obvious propaganda value because of widespread media and public interest within and outside Italy.[79] Over 300,000 applications were received for some 60,000 plus tickets, while the match commentary was scheduled to be broadcast both within and outside the country, such as to Albania and Yugoslavia as well as to Britain. Moreover, the fascist regime, seeking, as in 1933, to bolster its position in Malta through football, brought 400 Maltese people to the game to 'watch a real football team lick the English'![80]

Percy Loraine, who had recently arrived in Rome as British ambassador, reported that 'the Italians regarded the event as a test in which the prowess of the new Italy would be matched against the skills of the country where football has its home'.[81] The embassy, recalling previous England-Italy matches, reported that Italian players were lectured about the need for both a win and good behaviour, even if the 'Battle of Highbury' suggested that, in the event of any conflict, the former objective would take precedence.[82] Moreover, in March 1937, Italy's game versus Austria was abandoned, and FIFA's subsequent report thereupon – 'there was no sport at all' – implied the primacy of political considerations in a game followed by anti-Italian demonstrations in Austria.[83] An appreciation of the Italy-England game's extra-sporting significance led FA officials accompanying the tour party to apprise players about the merits of a good performance, as measured by a successful result achieved in a sporting manner; thus, Matthews, realising the game's propaganda dimension, believed that 'we were fighting for English prestige'.[84] Players were urged strongly to avoid retaliation regardless of provocation, but were warned to expect trouble, given Italy's history of rough play.

More significantly, FA officials, glossing over adverse comment about the Nazi salute given at the 1938 Berlin game, decided that players should give the fascist salute to each corner of the ground during the playing of the Italian national anthem.[85] Subsequently, the FA, claiming that the gesture was 'greatly appreciated' by the large crowd at the San Siro stadium, justified the decision in terms of ensuring the success of the fixture and winning over the Italian spectators. In many respects, this assessment was verified by the American ambassador in Rome: 'A gesture which was warmly applauded by the Italian spectators was provided by the British team which gave the Fascist salute when the Italian national anthem was played and there was little doubt, according to Embassy information, that the appearance of the British side was greeted with considerable enthusiasm'.[86] However, the players' action – reportedly, they gave the salute in a somewhat half-hearted manner – failed to prevent England's opening goal being greeted by virtual silence![87] Nor, unlike May 1938, did the episode prompt much controversy in Britain or feature in players' memoirs.

The game, refereed by Bauwens of Germany, ended as a 2-2 draw. England, helped by an early goal, dominated the first half, but proved less impressive after the break. Only a late equaliser secured a draw. The match itself was generally regarded as having lived up to expectations, even if the British press raised question marks about Italy's second goal – this was generally adjudged 'doubtful' because of handball – and its players' frequent use of elbows. For L.W. Manning, it merited high praise as 'the match of the century ... the greatest international match I have seen'.[88] Nor was the extra-sporting dimension overlooked, since it was impossible for the match to avoid being 'pulled into the quagmire of politics ... It was a political gamble and it came off. Thanks not to the politicians, but to the twenty two players who took part in it – and to the German referee.'[89]

Loraine, who travelled to Milan with his military and naval attachés, among other embassy staff, attended both the game and post-match dinner; in fact, he used his speech at the latter to praise the way in which the match demonstrated and strengthened the friendly state of Anglo-Italian relations.[90] Having been greeted at the stadium by Bufferini-Guidi, the Under-Secretary for the Interior, and Marinelli, the Administrative Secretary of the fascist party, Loraine watched the game seated in the same enclosure as Mussolini's sons and several members of the government. His report, informed by a subsequent exchange of views with King Victor Emmanuel III about the match's broader implications, pointed to the visibility given to British footballing skills and sportsmanship alongside the event's 'valuable contribution to friendship between the two nations'.[91] In particular, the ambassador, impressed by the enthusiastic welcome given to the England team in Milan, felt that the whole episode offered '*an interesting insight into the attitude of the Italian masses to Anglo-Italian relations*'.[92] A high profile football international, providing a meaningful point of contact at all levels of Italian society, gave – to quote Andrew Noble, a former member of the British embassy in Rome – 'the Italians an opportunity for showing that they still like us'.[93] Certainly the match, occurring soon after Loraine's arrival in Rome, offered a useful instrument for reinforcing relations, and particularly for accommodating his hope that no bridges, 'which one day the Italians might wish to re-cross', were burned.[94] In this vein, the fixture, complementing other contacts, might be interpreted as patching up the structures of the increasingly rickety 'bridge' joining London and Rome, even if for the Italian government the Axis link with Germany remained the crucial relationship, as demonstrated soon afterwards, that is, on 22 May 1939, by their conclusion of the Pact of Steel.

Hitherto, the British government, albeit irritated by the generally hostile tone of Italian propaganda, concluded that overt counter-measures would lead merely to 'unrestrained competition'.[95] From this perspective, association football, the national game in both countries, offered an effective method of British projection throughout Italy in terms of providing a rare opportunity to reach all sections of Italian society with the active compliance of both the fascist authorities and media. As the American ambassador commented, the Italian press, though dominated by reports of Mussolini's tour to Piedmont, still gave considerable space to the match.[96] Moreover, England had not only avoided defeat – this was adjudged a possibility given Italy's recent record – but also displayed the appropriate blend of skill and sportsmanship to maintain, even enhance, Italian images of British sporting prowess. Naturally, the Foreign Office, though only too aware of international football's unpredictability and ability to project the wrong sort of national image, welcomed the match's seemingly beneficial consequences, even if this outcome failed to prevent the usual departmental jibe to the effect that this proved 'an all too infrequent result of international contests of this kind'.[97]

The general preoccupation with the Italian game made it easy to forget that it represented merely the opening encounter of a close season tour involving two other countries, Romania and Yugoslavia, which were also relevant to British efforts to contain the Axis powers.[98] Unsurprisingly, the remaining fixtures proved an anti-climax in both the political and footballing senses. From Milan, the tour party travelled to Belgrade, where England, suffering from inconsistent refereeing, a difficult pitch and Matthews' early injury, was defeated 1-2 by Yugoslavia in the first-ever fixture between the two countries.[99] Subsequently, on 24 May, slight amends were made by a 2-0 victory over Romania in the final tour game played at Bucharest.[100]

England's tour, though conducted against the background of an increasingly unstable international situation, was generally adjudged successful from the political point of view. Reportedly, it was characterised throughout by friendly and enthusiastic official and popular receptions of the England team, which attracted a sell-out crowd in Milan and large attendances at Belgrade (25,000) and Bucharest (40,000). Certainly, the tour can be interpreted as supporting the Chamberlain government's ongoing efforts to improve relations with Italy, Romania (guarantee treaty, 13 April 1939), and Yugoslavia.[101] Even the FA found it difficult to overlook the tour's underlying political dimension. Looking back as the FA member-in-charge, B.A. Glanvill recalled initial doubts about the wisdom of undertaking the tour at such a sensitive time, but felt that the effort and risk proved worthwhile: 'the remarkable reception accorded to us from the time we reached Milan until we left Bucarest [*sic*] proved conclusively from a football point of view that the friendship which has existed for many years has not diminished one iota'.[102] Similarly, the FA report concluded that 'the main object of the visit was achieved – to show that International matches can be played between teams of England and continental countries before big crowds in a vigorous yet friendly spirit'.[103]

British newspaper comment, pressing the manner in which football rubbed shoulders with power politics, echoed these sentiments, even to the extent of frequently depicting players as 'sports ambassadors' engaged on a 'great peace-through-football role'.[104] Significantly, the Romanian press, reporting 'the most prominent sporting event of the year', welcomed the England team as 'Ambassadors from the land of the birth of the football game'.[105] The *Daily Dispatch*'s Ivan Sharpe praised football's 'powerful' contribution as cultural propaganda: 'The Football Association showed great courage and wisdom in persevering with this tour into troubled territory at a ticklish time. The reward has been a splendid and opportune fillip for British prestige.'[106] Similarly, L.W. Manning (*Daily Sketch*) claimed that England's 'football ambassadors' performed a task of 'national importance', most notably, by reaffirming British values to the man in the street in the countries visited.[107] Moreover, these political benefits were secured at minimal cost to the government:

> My view is that if ever there arose the danger of the F.A. dropping the European tour Whitehall should step in and make it compulsory. The sixteen players who stepped off the train at Victoria … have done a grand job of work for their country. Sixteen professional footballers,

paid £24 for the job … They have blazed a lasting trail of friendships, and in every legation, every consulate in the countries visited there is, I know, an appreciation of the national importance of their achievement.

As indicated here, players received the princely sum of £8 per match, as approved by the IFAB in June 1937, but the FA, following the 1938 precedent, awarded players a small gift in recognition of their 'splendid sportsmanship'.[108] Reportedly, Italian players, though still nominally amateur, were promised the equivalent of a £50 bonus to beat England.[109]

In many respects, the tour's broader dimension encouraged commentators to overlook England's relatively modest record (one win, one draw, one defeat), including a loss to a 'second class soccer power' beset by ethnic problems and possessing a poor recent record, including defeats by Germany (2-3) and Romania (0-1) as well as failure to qualify for the 1938 World Cup finals.[110] Even so, England's visit to Belgrade still possessed a propaganda value, whose impact was accentuated by the fact that Italy played therein just over a fortnight later. Any kudos attached to Italy's 2-1 win over Yugoslavia was easily outweighed by the manner of its victory. Rough play, fisticuffs, and time-wasting saw Italian players booed off the field at the end of the game. The Italian flag was torn up, the team's motor coach was stoned, and the Italian Minister in Belgrade protested about the derogatory comments made by Yugoslav ministers.[111] The resulting rift, though a mere storm in a tea-cup, benefited Britain, given England's sporting attitude displayed in defeat at Belgrade a fortnight earlier. Reportedly, the British Minister in Belgrade attracted 'demonstrative ovations', while the Yugoslav Minister for Social Policy praised the gentlemanly conduct of England players.[112] From this perspective, a sporting performance in defeat appeared to possess as much, if not more, propaganda value as a victory achieved in an unsporting manner.

One media reservation expressed about the tour concerned the FA's failure to address the adverse impacts exerted on players by lengthy rail/sea journeys: 'Endlessly travelling, changing from train to train, packing and unpacking, the cramped sleeping berths, the crowds'.[113] Admittedly, these problems appeared less problematic, when viewed against those experienced by FA representative teams touring, say, Australasia in 1937 or South Africa in 1939, but the FA's continued reluctance to use air travel paralleled the *ad hoc*, even unprofessional, manner in which the England team was still managed and functioned.[114] Thus, the continued lack of a permanent manager, though reflecting the practice of many clubs, was reinforced by problems in securing the release of players for pre-match training.[115]

THE 'NEW WORLD' CHALLENGES THE OLD WORLD'S FOOTBALL HEGEMONY

Latin America ranked second only to the Middle East in the British Council's priorities, and, like many other areas during the 1930s, was subjected to enhanced levels of propaganda emanating from Germany, Italy and the USA, among other states.[116] Naturally, sport contributed to efforts to express and expand their hemispheric influence, as shown by the USA's 'baseball diplomacy'.[117] However, despite baseball's hold over certain parts of the region, particularly Central America, association football proved the major sport for most countries. Indeed, football's claim to be a world game acquired credibility from its strong hold throughout Latin America, where – to quote the British ambassador in Argentina – 'football bulks, if anything, even larger here than in England'.[118] The game's strength therein was validated by Uruguay's World Cup (1930) and Olympic successes (1924, 1928), Brazil's third place in the 1938 World Cup, the proven standing of Argentina (e.g. runners up in 1928 Olympics and 1930 World Cup), and a well-established regional championship dating back to 1916. Peru made a brief, albeit controversial, mark at the 1936 Olympics, where its team crushed Finland and led Austria in a match abandoned due to crowd trouble.[119]

The first World Cup tournament, staged in 1930 at Montevideo, was won by Uruguay, whose success exerted – to quote Eugen Millington Drake, the British representative therein, in 1937 – a significant 'moral' impact making the whole country 'sport conscious and sport confident'.[120] Already, in 1924, the Uruguayan football team, returning triumphant from the Paris Olympics, had been welcomed home by the president as well as 'demonstrations without precedent'.[121] In this vein, diplomats based overseas repeatedly made the British government aware of the political significance attached to sport in Latin America, and particularly its hold over the national imagination. For example, in September 1938, Evelyn Rawlins, reporting from La Paz, noted the paradoxical way in which the Bolivian team, having finished last in the Bolivarian Games held at Bogota, returned to a hero's welcome from the president, people, and media; indeed, one newspaper, *La Cronica*, devoted five pages to the celebrations.[122] By contrast, Bolivian troops returning from the lengthy Chaco campaign were accorded only a low-key reception. For Rawlins, 'it shows a lamentable lack of any sense of proportion on the part of the government and public who saw fit to welcome, in such a spectacular manner, the return of a few mediocre sportsmen'. But, Bolivia was not alone in lauding sport as a central part of national life. Indeed, the similar welcome accorded the

Peruvian team on its return from Bogota by the head of state, people and press led Ogilvie Forbes to impress upon the Foreign Office 'the wholly disproportionate importance now attached to sport in Peru, and, I think, also in other Republics in Latin America'.[123] He warned that, if sporting rivalries continued with the same intensity, 'they are quite likely to lead in the end to bad international relations': 'The matter is *very important* because these people do not know how to lose, and take defeat as a personal affront'.

In January 1937, Millington Drake reminded the Foreign Office of the way in which sport propagated British values throughout the region, and, in the case of, say, Montevideo Rowing Club, brought 'all the benefits of one of the oldest English sports'.[124] Certainly, Britain's role in the origins and development of most popular games helped British visibility in a region, where football was often the national sport and clubs not only often used English names but also competed for British-sponsored trophies.[125] At the same time, meaningful footballing exchanges between Britain and Latin America were conspicuous by their absence. Any contacts, proving both occasional and limited, occurred below full international level, as highlighted by England's failure to play a Latin American national side until the 1950 World Cup. For the other home countries, the position was even worse; thus, Northern Ireland, Scotland and Wales never took the field with Latin American teams until either 1954 (Scotland) or 1958 (Northern Ireland, Wales). Nor did the Olympic Games match up British and Latin American football sides until 1960. This failure to play any Latin American team prior to the Second World War, albeit encouraged by British non-entry to the pre-1939 World Cup competitions, reflected also the impact of practical problems posed by geography, most notably, the length of the sea passage, travel distances within South America, and the extensive period required for any tour. Traditional isolationist thinking, in conjunction with the ever-present pressures of home internationals and domestic league competition, explained the British football associations' relative lack of enthusiasm for crossing the Channel, let alone the Atlantic, to play matches, as typified in 1930 by the FA's abrupt refusal of the Uruguayan invitation to participate in the inaugural World Cup competition. Subsequently, the adoption of a more outgoing attitude, helped by changes in personnel at both the FA and SFA, was confined to continental Europe, even if representative teams were despatched occasionally to Australasia, Canada, and South Africa. The fact that Canadian tours often included matches in the USA merely accentuated the failure of Britain's national sides to visit Latin America.

As a result, between the wars, footballing contacts were largely confined to intermittent club tours and the appointment of British coaches. Even so, club visits proved no more frequent than during the years prior to the First World War, when the profit motive attracted Everton, Exeter, Nottingham Forest, Southampton, Swindon, and Tottenham Hotspur, among other clubs.[126] Unfortunately, from the British point of view, the rare tour between the wars was often undertaken by relatively weak club sides (e.g. Plymouth Argyle, 1924), which did little to suggest, let alone enhance, Britain's footballing reputation. Poor results, unsportsmanlike behaviour, 'perfunctory' attitudes towards matches, fatigue, and a seeming lack of match fitness induced by 'alcoholic indulgence' on a long sea voyage, were typical causes for complaint. Indeed, these images became a central feature of official thinking about overseas tours. Memories of Third Lanark's allegedly unfortunate 1923 visit to Argentina and Uruguay became a reference point for British diplomats based in the region, even if the key problems arose from crowd trouble rather than results (i.e. fours wins, two draws, two defeats).[127] For instance, during the opening match against an 'Argentine Select' team, crowd problems, prompted in part by the uncompromising tackling of the Scottish team, forced the Third Lanark players to leave the field for a short period.[128] Latin American visits to Britain proved even rarer, but in October 1933 neither the FA nor FIFA raised objections to Newcastle and West Ham playing visiting clubs from Chile and Peru.[129] During the 1930s several Latin American players, capitalising on World Cup and Olympic successes, moved to continental Europe, especially Italy, but not to Britain, given the restrictions on the employment of foreigners.[130]

In many respects, the presence of a few British coaches exerted a more effective, albeit still limited, impact in terms of inculcating British footballing values in Latin America. Significantly, British diplomats and the British Council frequently performed an active role in such appointments. For example, in July 1937 Millington Drake, the British Minister in Montevideo (1934–41), was approached by the president of the *Club Nacional de Football*, which sought a coach to improve Uruguayan football 'by the influence of English technique and training systems'.[131] Millington Drake, assisted by the FA and SFA, even used part of his home-based leave to interview William Raeside, who had played for Stockport and Dumbarton and coached in Norway. More importantly, this 'nice fellow of gentlemanly appearance', having visited South America in 1934 with Spain's *Real Club Celta de Vigo*, even spoke Spanish.[132] A series of good results, including unexpected victories over both *Penarol*, *Club Nacional*'s traditional rivals, and *Independiente* of Buenos Aires, soon followed Raeside's arrival, as reported by Millington Drake: 'there is great glee here, especially on the part of my baker, who is a fervent supporter of Club

258

Nacional'.[133] Moreover, his 'tremendous success' was deemed to possess broader benefits: 'We can consider that we "delivered the goods" and the extra superfine quality'.[134] Raeside's achievements, though hindered by *Club Nacional*'s chronic financial problems, fostered discussion of the club's visit to Britain alongside enquiries from the Peruvian Minister in London made on behalf of his government about the availability of British football coaches.[135] However, any benefits should be viewed in perspective, particularly given alternative influences upon Latin American football, most notably 'the Central European style'. There was also a conscious effort to throw off British influences, as evidenced during the mid-1930s when the word *'fútbol'* came to be favoured instead of 'football'.[136]

The first regular football tournaments outside the British Isles were contested by Argentina and Uruguay for the Lipton (Sir Thomas Lipton, the British tea entrepreneur) and Newton (an early British resident) cups donated in 1905 and 1906 respectively. Although both competitions became less regular in the 1930s – they were contested only in 1937 – they provided a foundation for further examples of sports sponsorship helping British visibility in the region. Once again, much depended on the personal initiative of resident diplomats, like Millington Drake, whose standing in Uruguay was indicated by the fact that he assumed the presidency of the Uruguayan Lawn Tennis Association, and even attended the 1936 Berlin Olympics as honorary president of the Uruguay delegation.[137] Unsurprisingly, Millington Drake, a keen rower and tennis player, proved a prime mover in sporting matters, as evidenced by his donation of a cup for Uruguayan football and a belt for Argentine boxing (1930) in recognition of the sport's British origins.[138] Extensive Argentine press coverage of successive title bouts led the Foreign Office to admit the 'incalculable value' of such sporting initiatives for Anglo-Argentine relations.[139] Similar sentiments were expressed in London about the 'Auld Lang Syne Cup' donated in 1934 for polo in Colombia. Spencer Dickson, the moving force, informed London about the Colombian president's attendance at the cup game as well as widespread local press coverage. Significantly, the Colombian press, perhaps finding it difficult to find the right words, left untranslated Dickson's references to 'playing the game', thereby reaffirming sportsmanship as a central component of Colombian images of Britain.[140]

Information and advice furnished by British diplomatic missions in Latin America formed an influential framework of reference for London-based officials, whose perceptions about, say, football in Latin America were marked by an appreciation of the manner in which popular passions were complicated by the subtle inter-relationship of politics and sport therein. Governments, like public opinion, proved – to quote the British ambassador in Argentina – extremely 'touchy' on footballing matters.[141] Official British visions of Latin American football were dominated by impressions of volatility, since unsporting, even violent, behaviour on the part of both players and spectators proved commonplace in reports reaching London.[142] Reportedly, bottles, knives and pistols were taken away from spectators attending 1930 World Cup games, while the widespread use of barbed wire fences was taken to reflect the risks posed to visiting players.[143] Peru's footballing history was particularly troubled, as highlighted by the 1936 Olympics. Peru withdrew from the tournament upon being required to replay a match disrupted by crowd trouble. Austria was declared the winner by forfeit, but the episode, prompting exchanges between Rimet and the Peruvian ambassador at Paris as well as discussions at the 1936 FIFA Congress, exerted a 'startling' impact in Peru, where crowds stoned the German legation and consulate in Lima.[144] Subsequently, in August 1938 Peru's 4-2 victory over Colombia in the Bolivarian Games was marked by fighting between players.[145]

Naturally, the Second World War further curtailed the already limited prospects of footballing exchanges between Britain and Latin America. Nevertheless, the war's early months saw the British government devote serious attention to an invitation for the participation of British and French teams in an Argentine festival of physical fitness and sport scheduled for March 1940.[146] Dr Adrian Escobar, the President of the Argentine Football Federation and also Director-General of Argentine Posts and Telegraphs, was a prime mover in the proposal, which included matches against neighbouring countries. Inevitably, war ensured the primacy of propaganda factors respecting a country deemed specifically relevant to national political, economic and cultural interests. The prospect of improving, or at least preventing any further deterioration, in Anglo-Argentine relations was accompanied by fears that Argentina, pressurised by the Axis powers, might take advantage of Britain's wartime preoccupations to press long-standing claims to the Falklands Islands, South Georgia, or parts of Antarctica.[147] Sir Esmond Ovey, the British ambassador in Buenos Aires, advised London that, 'in theory – and possibly in practice – the propaganda value of a visit of a first class football team would be enormous, for the football "fans" of Argentina are legion'.[148] A visit offered a potentially valuable means of national projection reaching both the Argentine government – President Ortiz was reportedly interested in the project – and the man in the Buenos Aires street. Furthermore, any Anglo-French tour promised to show the flag, promote images of allied solidarity, create much-needed goodwill for the allied cause within and beyond Argentina, and contain the impact of Axis propaganda in the region.

Countervailing arguments centred upon long-standing anxieties about the potential for trouble. Official memories of the steady stream of complaints received about poor and unsporting performances by British teams abroad were compounded by images of the volatility of Latin American football. Ovey pressed the case for strict instructions about appropriate modes of team behaviour on and off the field, even to the extent of enforcing discipline by claiming that players were engaged on 'war service'! But, he feared that even a well-behaved performance might prompt complications, given differing interpretations of the rules and Latin America's perennial crowd problems. Ovey, pointing to one death and numerous injuries in a recent riot (May 1939), observed that an Argentine football crowd was prone to 'punctuate its vociferations by the hurling of bricks and, if the target is sufficiently close, by the drawing of knives'.[149]

On balance, Ovey inclined to caution, for the risk of complications outweighed the theoretical benefits: 'I believe that international tests of athletic prowess *in the professional field* to be little short of disastrous'.[150] His considered view, to the effect that 'the dangers of disaster are such, that I could not possibly advise that the risk be taken', fell upon receptive ears in London, where Oliver Bonham Carter, a member of the Ministry of Information (MOI)'s Latin American division, endorsed the ambassador's assessment:

> From *personal* experience of the behaviour of Argentine football crowds, I can confirm every word that Ovey says, and it is absolutely essential that the whole idea be shelved at once. It would be fatal if a team went out from here to play football in the Argentine, as nothing arouses the passion of the locals so much as this perfectly sound form of exercise. When one knows that the spectators have to be wired in and that the police are armed with tear-gas bombs, and that shootings have been known to occur, there is little need for me to enlarge upon the inadvisability of sending a team out.[151]

In any case, player availability and travel difficulties, alongside fears of adverse parliamentary and press criticism about wartime football tours, would have posed serious question marks, even if the proposed tour had been interpreted as politically desirable.[152] Nor did the proposal attract much enthusiasm in Paris, but this failed to prevent the British government apprising the French government of its view that the tour would serve 'no useful purpose' in order to ensure allied consensus.[153]

This episode, though ending in a negative manner, illustrated not only the selective, small scale and pragmatic nature of British sporting activities in Latin America between the wars but also the manner in which the government viewed such an 'international test of athletic prowess' primarily as 'a medium of propaganda'. Significantly, Argentine representatives, having been informed about Britain's rejection, tried to save the tour by arguing that no better method of Allied propaganda in Latin America existed than football!

CONCLUSION

Despite being confronted by a series of major international crises during the late 1930s, Chamberlain attempted to continue his personal sporting interests, even if a penchant for 'sticky wicket' type phrases obscured his disinterest in major sports like cricket. According to Thomas Jones of the Cabinet secretariat, 'nor was he attracted by Wimbledon or Lord's. He was a fisherman, and he loved birds, flowers and music'.[154] Chamberlain's private papers, illuminating his shooting and walking interests, include detailed fishing diaries covering the period 1921–39![155] However, events conspired increasingly to interrupt his leisure plans. For instance, the 1938 Czech 'May Crisis' forced the premature curtailment of a fishing excursion: 'those d----d Germans have spoiled another weekend for me'.[156] Subsequently, 'the very great and prolonged' mental strain, consequent upon the German occupation of Prague in March 1939, prompted complaints that Hitler had given him yet another 'completely wrecked holiday' by causing him to fish 'carelessly and badly'.[157]

Nevertheless, despite the Prime Minister's lack of personal interest in major sports, the Chamberlain government launched a significant initiative concerning national fitness, while becoming involved on an occasional basis in a diverse range of international sports, including not only the Olympics but also athletics, boxing, football, ice hockey, motor cycling and swimming. Most interventions, drawing in not only the Foreign Office but also other departments, were of the usual *ad hoc*, functional character concerned principally with travel, visa and related questions but, in the case of international football, occasionally covered more substantive issues like fixtures, the need for a good result, and the conduct of players.[158] The late 1930s saw increases in the frequency and quality of contact, at least at the informal and personal levels, between the British Council, the Foreign Office and the football associations on overseas fixtures and coaching appointments. In particular, the FA, though preferring still to do its own thing, was increasingly forced to recognise that international football did not take place in a political vacuum, as conceded by Rous: 'the FA were always conscious of the political implications of tours by our national team and we kept in close touch with the Foreign Office over arrangements'.[159] Unsurprisingly, the Foreign Office's desire to 'exercise some control' extended to other sports, as evidenced by ongoing efforts to improve liaison between touring sports teams and British missions and embassies abroad.[160] A British basketball team's tour to France, Germany, Italy, and Poland, offered an early manifestation of this new strategy.

International sport, though treated in a pragmatic manner, was interpreted within the broader international political framework, as demonstrated during 1938–39 by the supportive attitude adopted on 'policy grounds' towards the 'friendly contests' arranged by England versus teams from 'antagonistic nations' like Germany (1938) and Italy (1939).[161] The British government's reluctance to interfere with these fixtures contrasted vividly with strong opposition to the BWSA's proposed tour to Spain the previous year. Whereas the former were perceived as likely, on balance, to support the policy of appeasement, the BWSA's proposal conflicted with the government's non-intervention stance respecting the Spanish Civil War. Moreover, during 1938–39, England's well-publicised visits to Berlin and Milan demonstrated football's ability to provide a subtle, albeit effective, instrument of national projection in countries where overt British propaganda was either difficult, if not almost impossible, or deemed undesirable on policy grounds. From this perspective, international football offered an extra dimension for policy-makers by providing a highly visible, often impressive, British presence in two countries omitted from the British Council's current sphere of operation for reasons articulated by Kenneth Johnstone: 'Before the war the Council entered the field, very belatedly, to find it already dominated by militarist and hostile cultural propagandists concerned with glorification of their own and depreciation of other countries. Even so, the Council, rightly or wrongly, did not attempt to meet stridency with stridency or display with display.'[162]

As a result, sporting exchanges, which continued in spite of the fluctuations in British relations with the Axis powers, loomed large in respect of projecting national interests, such as by illustrating a range of qualities, like fair play and sporting skills, or reminding the authorities and people therein about the value of continued links with Britain. In general, a premium was placed upon success as the best form of sports propaganda, but the 1939 Yugoslavia-England match suggested that even defeats, when accepted in a sporting manner, were capable of exerting positive impacts.[163] As ever, the government's prime focus was placed on England (see Table 2.3, Chapter 2). Scotland's international fixtures failed to attract the same level of official interest (Table 2.3, Chapter 2), despite the fact that between 1936 and 1938 it played several politically significant countries (i.e.

Austria, Czechoslovakia, Germany, Holland and Hungary), attracted considerable overseas media and public visibility (e.g. crowds of 63,000 and 28,000 in Vienna and Prague respectively, May 1937), and secured an impressive set of results against non-British teams (i.e. 1936–38: five wins, one draw, no losses).[164]

Despite gathering war clouds, British teams continued to play their part in the world of international football. Thus, summer 1939 witnessed England's tour to Italy, Romania and Yugoslavia, visits by FA and SFA teams to South Africa and Canada/USA respectively, Wales' second trip to France, and the usual wide range of close season fixtures undertaken by British clubs. However, the appearance of normality, conveyed by the appearance of British footballers in, say, Belgrade, Bucharest, Copenhagen, Gothenburg, Milan, or Paris, was undermined after April 1939 by the ostracism of Germany, at least from the point of view of British football. But this occurred on a selective basis by sport, and in June, both Nevile Henderson and Osten watched Germany take a 3-0 winning lead over the Great Britain tennis team in the Davis Cup.[165] Then, in July, German tennis players played at Wimbledon – Menzel won his opening match on the centre court – thereby giving added meaning to *The Times*' preview of the tournament, where 'all the week through, British and foreign players will be banging lawn tennis balls at each other in fierce and friendly contests'.[166] Moreover, what proved the final weeks of peace saw further Anglo-German sporting contests. Indeed, a British army team participated in a six-day international motor cycle meeting commencing at Salzburg on 22 August, even if the worsening international situation led the government to instruct the riders to return home immediately before the close of the tournament.[167] Also, at Cologne a few days earlier, on 20 August, a crowd of 60,000 watched the German athletics team defeat Great Britain (93.5 to 42.5 points). By contrast, the British team's next contest against France, scheduled for early September, proved a casualty of the rapidly deteriorating international situation.[168]

In July 1939, *The Times*, previewing the forthcoming week's events, expounded international sport's qualities in promoting British values through friendly competition: 'At Wimbledon, at St Andrews, and at Henley, this tremendous swell of a week will see visitors from other lands doing their best to beat the natives of the British Empire and walk off with the honours that are world-wide'.[169] Of course, the Foreign Office often articulated a more pessimistic view about international sport's cooperative potential, especially as the late 1930s yielded plenty of evidence justifying this line. For example, during 1938–39, the consolidation of German power over Czechoslovakia involved the use of both cultural exhibitions (June

1939) and 'friendly' football matches to foster Czech-German links.[170] One fixture, played at Prague on 8 June, ended controversially.[171] Czech spectators were manhandled by German troops, while three *Prague XI* players, criticised for 'vigorous tactics' insulting the Reich, were warned by the German authorities that any repetition of such misconduct would warrant arrest.[172] Nor were relations on the football field between Germany and former 'Austrians' more harmonious, as shown on 18 June 1939 by the German League championship final. *FC Schalke 04* defeated *Admira Wien* 9-0 in a bad tempered game marred by the sending off of an *Admira* player for punching Szepan, the *Schalke* captain, who had led Germany against England in 1935.[173] Subsequently, Osten praised the forbearance of *FC Schalke*, while *Admira Wien* was suspended for the rest of the season and threatened with dissolution unless remedial action was taken.

By August 1939, attention was fixed increasingly upon the escalating crisis over Poland, as shown by the Home Office's exchanges with the FA about Air Raid Precautions and the Board of Education's adoption of plans to suspend the NFC's activities upon the outbreak of war.[174] Nevertheless, British sport continued to plan for the future, and on 21 August the FA, preparing for the forthcoming season, discussed arrangements for the 1940 Olympics as well as for an international versus France in May 1940.[175] In the event, the German army, not the England football team, entered France on that date. Meanwhile, on 26 August, the new league season opened in England, where a 45,000 crowd watched Arsenal draw 2-2 at Wolverhampton.[176] Despite the growing sense of crisis, football internationals continued as scheduled elsewhere. Indeed, on 27 August, Poland, representing the country at the storm centre, defeated Hungary 4-2 in Warsaw. But, within days, Poland's sporting success was overtaken by military invasion. Poland's record in five football internationals played against Germany since Hitler's accession in 1933 was poor – one draw was accompanied by four losses – and after September 1939, when Polish-German rivalry moved from the football field to the battlefield, the country fared no better in the face of the military moves escalating into the Second World War.

On 3 September 1939, the British government declared war on Germany. Within Britain, both domestic and international football were seriously affected; thus, England's return match with Romania, scheduled for December, proved an early wartime casualty. In turn, the Second World War, foiling plans also for 1940 England-Germany fixture, explained why the two countries' national sides did not face each other on the football pitch again until December 1954, when Germany, or rather West Germany, took the field at Wembley as recently crowned world champions!

NOTES

1. Quoted, James Barros, *Betrayal from Within: Joseph Avenol, Secretary-General of the League of Nations 1933–1940* (Yale University Press, New Haven, 1969), p.164, p.189, p.192.
2. Young, *Britain and the World*, pp.114–27; Parker.
3. CAC, Vansittart, memorandum, Sept. 1937, Lord Vansittart Papers (VNST), VNST II 2/13; York, N. Henderson to Lord Halifax, 29 Nov. 1937, A4 410. 3. 2. (ii); *The Times*, 2 Sept. 1938 (letter, C. Roemer).
4. CAC, *Völkische Beobachter*, 20 July 1937, quoted Vansittart, memorandum, Sept. 1937, VNST II 2/13.
5. Joe Louis Barrow Jr and Barbara Munder, *Joe Louis: the Brown Bomber* (Arthur Barker, London, 1988), p.9; William J. Baker, *Sports in the Western World* (University of Illinois Press, Urbana, 1982 rev. edn), p.251, pp.258–9.
6. Quoted, *New York Times*, 28 June 1936.
7. Hart-Davis, p.123; *New York Times*, 27, 28 June 1936.
8. PRO, I. Kirkpatrick, British embassy, Berlin, to W. Strang, 27 June 1938, minute, Vansittart, 6 July 1938, FO371/21781/C6586.
9. Quoted, Barrow Jr and Munder, p.18.
10. TC, R. Butler, 23 May 1938, RAB K4/8.
11. PRO, memorandum, K. Johnstone, 10 Oct. 1936, BW2/85; Vansittart to Chamberlain, 28 May 1938, PREM1/272/29–30.
12. PRO, memorandum, Johnstone, 10 Oct. 1936, BW2/85.
13. Chamberlain, *Hansard (Commons) 5th Ser.*, CCCXXX, 1803, 21 Dec. 1937.
14. PRO, Eden to Chamberlain, 18 Jan. 1938, minute, Chamberlain, n.d., PREM1/272/56–8; Chamberlain, *Hansard (Commons) 5th Ser.*, CCCXXXI, 670–1, 7 Feb. 1938.
15. *Hansard (Commons) 5th Ser.*, CCCXXXI, 1909–10, 16 Feb. 1938; Taylor, *Projection of Britain*, pp.222–4.
16. Donaldson, p.382; PRO, Wilson to E. Hale, Treasury, 11 Aug. 1938, T161/907/S35581/03/38/1; Sir Findlater Stewart, Report on the British Council, 8 Feb. 1945, p.5, FO924/262/LC2697.
17. Taylor, *Projection of Britain*, pp.169–74; PRO, Lord Lloyd, British Council, to Vansittart, 25 May 1938, T161/907/S35581/03/38/1.
18. PRO, Humphrey Payne to Lord Lloyd, 21 Jan. 1936, C. Hardie, Director of British School at Rome, 'Some notes on Cultural Relations in Mediterranean', 3 June 1936, BW34/8.
19. PRO, S. Waterlow to Eden, 29 June 1937, BW34/8.
20. PRO, Waterlow to Eden, 26 Nov. 1937, BW34/8; Foreign Office to Waterlow, 15 Nov. 1937, Waterlow to Eden, 29 Nov. 1937, FO395/556/P5091.
21. PRO, Waterlow to Eden, 26 Nov. 1937, BW34/8.
22. PRO, R. Kenney, Foreign Office, to Bridge, British Council, 3 Dec. 1937, J. Jennings to Johnstone, 31 Dec. 1937, Rous to Jennings, 4 Jan. 1938, BW34/8.
23. PRO, Greig, Consul-General at Smyrna, to Foreign Office, 10 Jan. 1938, FO395/565/P183; Johnstone to Waterlow, 22 Jan. 1938, FO395/565/P468.
24. PRO, Henry Hopkinson, Athens, to Johnstone, 11 Feb. 1938, BW34/8.
25. PRO, W. Baggett to Jennings, 2 Aug. 1938, BW34/8.
26. PRO, Chancery, British legation, Athens, to British Council, 12 Dec. 1938, BW34/8.
27. PRO, Bridge to Hopkinson, 21 April 1939, BW34/9.
28. CAC, Waterlow to Halifax, 22 Feb. 1939, GLLD 19/9; PRO, Waterlow to Lord Halifax, 18 July 1938, BW34/8.

29. PRO, Waterlow to News Dept., Foreign Office, 2 May 1939, FO395/656/P1811.
30. Ibid.
31. PRO, record of meeting at British Legation, Athens, 4 March 1939, BW34/9.
32. Donaldson, *The British Council: the first fifty years* (Jonathan Cape, London, 1984).
33. PRO, Edwyn Hole, British consul-general, Salonica, to British Council, 18 May 1938, BW34/8.
34. PRO, British Council to Foreign Office, 24 May 1938, BW34/8.
35. PRO, Eden to Simon, 23 Dec. 1937, T161/907/S35581/03/38/1.
36. PRO, Chancery, Athens, to News Department, 20 April 1938, BW34/8.
37. PRO, Kenney to L. Adie, British Council, 3 Feb. 1938, FO395/609/P512; News Department to Chancery, Athens, 3 May 1938, BW34/8.
38. PRO, British Council to Capt. L. Ellis, NFC, 10 Aug. 1938, BW2/85.
39. York, E. Parker, editor, *The Field*, to Halifax, 13 Oct. 1937, Halifax to Parker, 21 Oct. 1937, A4.410. 3. 2. (i); Andrew Roberts, *The Holy Fox: a life of Lord Halifax* (Macmillan, London, 1992 edn), pp.63–73.
40. TC, memorandum, Butler, n.d. (June/August 1939), RAB G10/28, RAB F80/100. In 1957, Halifax stressed his lifetime's devotion to hunting: York, note, Lord Halifax, Dec. 1957, A4 410 7. 15a.
41. BU, Chamberlain to Hilda Chamberlain, 24 Oct. 1937, NC18/1/1025; Chamberlain to Ida Chamberlain, 14 Nov. 1937, NC18/1/1028; York, Lord Halifax, 'My visit to Berlin, November 1937', 6 May 1946, A4. 410. 3. 3 (vi); CAS, Jim Thomas, 'Account of Eden's resignation', p.7, n.d. (1940), Cilc.Coll.50.
42. York, Henderson to Halifax, 29 Oct. 1937, 29 Nov. 1937, A4.410. 3. 2. (ii); memorandum, Lord Halifax, Nov. 1937–Jan. 1938, A4.410 3. 3. (vi); Parker, pp.97–101.
43. BU, Chamberlain to Ida Chamberlain, 26 Nov. 1937, NC18/1/1030.
44. CAS, Thomas, 'Account of Eden's resignation', p.8, n.d. (1940?), Cilc.Coll.50.
45. Ibid.
46. PRO, Lt.-Col. C. Bridge, Secretary-General, British Council, to R. Leeper, 12 July 1938, FO395/568/P2241.
47. Taylor, *Projection of Britain*, p.222; CAC, Vansittart to Eden, 10 Feb. 1941, VNST II 1/9. Rose's biography discounts the political significance of this job, while typically ignoring its sporting dimension: Rose, pp.210–14.
48. PRO, minute, J. Corley-Smith, 14 July 1938, C. Warner to Rous, 27 July 1938, FO395/568/P2241.
49. FA, ISC, 2 Dec. 1937, minute 3, 1937–38; ISC, 26 Sept. 1938, minute 9, 1938–39.
50. FA, ISC, 24 June 1938, minute 10, 1937–38.
51. PRO, minute, A. Dougherty, 25 Aug. 1938, FO395/568/P2241; minute, Viscount Cranborne, 22 June 1936, FO371/20462/W5343. FA papers make no mention of this session.
52. FA, ISC, 22 Nov. 1938, minute 10, 12 Dec. 1938, 9 Jan. 1939, minute 5, 11 March 1939, minute 3, 1938–39.
53. PRO, minutes, Corley Smith, 14 July 1938, Warner, 15 July 1938, FO395/568/P2241. See Pickford, 'How soccer is controlled', 656–7.
54. FA, Council, 30 April 1937, minute 4, 1936–37; Percy Young, *The Wolves: the first eighty years* (Stanley Paul, London, 1959), p.119. On Wolverhampton's tours in the 1930s, see Christopher Andrew's interview with Rachel Newnham, 'Making History: 2', *BBC Radio Four*, 7 Dec. 1996.
55. FAW, Council, 29 Dec. 1937, minute 4649, 1937–39.
56. FA, ISC, 8 March 1937, minute 8, 1936–37; Pickford, *Recollections*, p.116.
57. SFAMT, EFC, 23 June 1937, minute 3, Acc.9017/34, 1937–38.

58. FA, ISC, 8 March 1937, minute 8, 1935–46; SFAMT, EFC minute 109, Acc.9017/33, 1936–37; FIFA, Rous to Schricker, 1 July 1937, encl. FIFA Circular 1937/39, 5 July 1937.
59. FIFA, Graham to FIFA, 5 May 1938, Scotland correspondence, 1932–67; Schricker to Rous, 4 May 1938, England correspondence, 1932–57.
60. FIFA, Xandry, DFB, to Schricker, 10 Jan. 1939, Germany 1938–68.
61. FA, W. Pickford to N. Chamberlain, 4 Oct. 1938, encl. Consultative Committee, 19 Oct. 1938, minute 18; Chamberlain to FA, 24 Oct. 1938, encl. Council, 27 Oct. 1938, minute 10, 1938–39.
62. FA, ISC, 29 April 1938, minute 5, 1937–38; FIFA, Schricker to Rous, 4 April 1938, Rous to Schricker, 19 April 1938, England correspondence 1932–57.
63. FIFA, Graham, SFA, to FIFA, 2 June 1938, FIFA to Graham, 7 June 1938, Scotland correspondence, 1932–67.
64. PRO, N. Bland, Foreign Office, to Rous, 11 Oct. 1938, FO372/3269/T12626. Already, during July 1938 the government approved visa fee exemptions for German and other teams participating in the forthcoming European Swimming Championships at Wembley.
65. PRO, minutes, Makins, Corley Smith, 11–12 Nov. 1938, FO372/3269/T14257.
66. PRO, minutes, Lord Lloyd, 17 Oct. 1938, Johnstone, 13 Oct. 1938, BW32/1.
67. FA, ISC, 9 Jan. 1939, 11 March 1939, 1938–39.
68. Parker, pp.200–20.
69. *The Times*, 4, 17 April 1939; Allison, *Allison Calling*, pp.148–51.
70. Tom Watt, *The End. 80 Years of Life on Arsenal's North Bank* (Mainstream, Edinburgh, 1993), p.61; *Daily Sketch*, 10 May 1939.
71. *New York Times*, 23 March 1939; *The Times*, 20 April 1939.
72. *Annual Report 1938–39* (FAW, 1939), p.1.
73. PRO, minute, Lord Lloyd, 17 Oct. 1938, BW32/1.
74. Author's interview with Rous, 28 March 1980; *Daily Sketch*, 9 May 1939; Hapgood, pp.41–2; Lawton, pp.77–8; Rous, *Football Worlds*, p.104.
75. FA, Report on Continental Tour 1939, encl. ISC, 5 June 1939, 1938–39.
76. PRO, Foreign Office to Lord Perth, Rome, 18 April 1939, FO371/23785/R2972; Sir Miles Lampson, High Commissioner in Cairo, to Foreign Office, 29 April 1939, FO371/23785/R4207.
77. *Daily Dispatch*, 15, 30 May 1939; *Daily Sketch*, 12, 13 May 1939.
78. Lanfranchi, 336–7.
79. *Daily Sketch*, 11 May 1939.
80. PRO, report, n.d., encl. Major J.H. Dodds, Consul-General in Nice, to P. Nichols, 16 May 1939, FO371/23785/R4205; Matthews, pp.92–3.
81. PRO, Percy Loraine, Rome, to Halifax, 16 May 1939, FO371/23785/R4193.
82. PRO, minute, A. Noble, Southern Dept., 22 May 1939, FO371/23785/R4193.
83. *The Times*, 22 March 1937; FIFA, Circular 1937/16.
84. *Daily Sketch*, 12 May 1939; Matthews, p.92.
85. Author's interview with Rous, 28 March 1980; *Daily Express*, 13 May 1939; *Daily Dispatch*, 15 May 1939; Glanville, *Soccer Nemesis*, p.97.
86. USA, W. Phillips, US ambassador, Rome, to State Dept., 19 May 1939, RG59, Box 6870, 865.00/1821.
87. PRO, Report, n.d., enclosed in Dodds, Nice, to Nichols, 16 May 1939, FO371/23785/R4205; *Daily Express*, 22 May 1939; *Daily Dispatch*, 29 May 1939. Gate receipts were £12,000: *Daily Sketch*, 13, 18 May 1939.
88. *Daily Sketch*, 15 May 1939; *New York Times*, 14 May 1939; *Daily Express*, 15 May, 22 May 1939; *Daily Dispatch*, 15 May 1939; FA, Report on Continental Tour, 1939,

encl. ISC, 5 June 1939, minute 3, 1938–39.

89. *Daily Express*, 22 May 1939.

90. Hapgood, p.46.

91. PRO, Loraine to Halifax, 16 May 1939, FO371/23785/R4193.

92. Ibid.; Matthews, p.92, p.97.

93. PRO, minute, Noble, 22 May 1939, FO371/23785/R4193. Agreed by Sargent, 25 May 1939.

94. Gordon Waterfield, *Professional Diplomat: Sir Percy Loraine of Kirkharle, 1880–1961* (John Murray, London, 1973), p.228.

95. PRO, Foreign Office to Lampson, 23 April 1939, FO371/23785/R3104; Lord Perth to Foreign Office, 15 April 1939, FO371/23785/R2899.

96. USA, W. Phillips, US ambassador, Rome, to State Dept., 19 May 1939, RG59, Box 6870, 865.00/1821.

97. PRO, minutes, Broad, 22 May, Ingram, 23 May, Sargent, 25 May 1939, FO371/23785/R4193.

98. PRO, 'Notes on cultural propaganda' by Eleonor Rathbone, MP, April 1937, BW2/85. Rathbone, having returned from Czechoslovakia, Romania and Yugoslavia, feared that British inactivity would benefit Germany and Italy.

99. *New York Times*, 17, 19 May 1939; *Daily Express*, 19 May 1939; *Daily Sketch*, 19 May 1939.

100. *Daily Express*, 25 May 1939; *Daily Dispatch*, 25 May 1939.

101. Donald Cameron Watt, *How War Came: the immediate origins of the Second World War, 1938–1939* (Heinemann, London, 1989), pp.292–6.

102. Quoted, Ivan Sharpe, 'Tell England', *Daily Dispatch*, 30 May 1939.

103. FA, Report of Continental Tour, 1939, encl. ISC, 5 June 1939, minute 3, 1938–39; FIFA, Rous quoted, Schricker to G. Vaccaro, 6 June 1939, Italy correspondence 1939–58.

104. *Daily Sketch*, 10 May 1939; *Daily Express*, 23 May 1939; Sharpe, p.76.

105. Quoted, Hapgood, p.52.

106. Ivan Sharpe, 'Tell England', *Daily Dispatch*, 30 May 1939.

107. L.W. Manning, 'Sixteen men do a fine job of work', *Daily Sketch*, 29 May 1939; *Daily Dispatch*, 24 May 1939.

108. FA, ISC, 5 June 1939, minute 3, 1938–39.

109. *Daily Sketch*, 11 May 1939; Oliver, p.360.

110. *Daily Sketch*, 18, 19 May 1939; *Daily Dispatch*, 29 May 1939.

111. *New York Times*, 5 June 1939; *The Times*, 7 June 1939.

112. *The Times*, 7 June 1939.

113. *Daily Express*, 23 May 1939; *Daily Sketch*, 29 May 1939. *En route* home to Britain, Lawton and Mercer left to join Everton's tour of the Netherlands: Lawton, pp.82–3.

114. *Daily Dispatch*, 29 May 1939.

115. FA, ISC, 16 Dec. 1935, 1935–36; Tony Mason, 'Football', in T. Mason (ed.), *Sport in Britain: a social history* (Cambridge University Press, Cambridge, 1989), p.165.

116. Donaldson, p.105.

117. PRO, C. Joint, San Salvador, to Eden, 22 Dec. 1943, FO371/37921/AS231; minute, Corley Smith, 3 Nov. 1938, FO395/568/P3155; T.H. Batterbee to G. Campbell, Ottawa, 17 Nov. 1938, FO395/568/P3271.

118. PRO, Sir A. Noble, British ambassador in Buenos Aires, to Perowne, 11 Sept. 1945, FO371/44776/AS5040; Murray, pp.114–24.

119. Furrer, Godoy and Blatter, p.72.

120. CAC, E. Millington Drake, Memorandum on 'Physical culture in Uruguay', 14 Jan. 1937, Millington Drake papers (MLDK) MLDK 5/51.

121. USA, American legation, Montevideo, to US State Dept., 8 Sept. 1924, RG59, 851.4063/22, M560 Roll 47.
122. PRO, Evelyn Rawlins, La Paz, to Foreign Office, 10 Sept. 1938, FO371/21447/A7687; Montague Paske-Smith, Bogota, to Halifax, 23 Aug. 1938, FO371/21447/A7245.
123. PRO, Ogilvie Forbes, Lima, to American Dept., 6 Sept. 1938, FO371/21447/A7777.
124. CAC, Drake, memorandum, 14 Jan. 1937, MLDK 5/51.
125. Mason, *Passion of the People*, pp.1–14.
126. Ibid., pp.15–26; Capel-Kirby and Carter, pp.152–60.
127. PRO, Chancery, Santiago, to Foreign Office, 12 Sept. 1945, FO371/45052/AS5071; Chancery, Quito, to Foreign Office, 21 Sept. 1945, FO371/45052/AS5173. In 1938, Rous reported discussions about a possible West Ham tour to Peru: PRO, minute, C.H. Johnston, 31 Jan. 1938, FO395/568/P673.
128. Mason described the tour as being undertaken by a 'Combined Scottish' team, whereas Bell presented it as a strengthened club side: Mason, *Passion of the People*, p.105; Bell, pp.138–41.
129. FIFA, Wall to Schricker, 8 Aug. 1933, Schricker to Wall, 14 Aug. 1933, England correspondence, 1932–57.
130. Archetti, 206.
131. CAC, A. Falco, Montevideo, to Drake, 22 July 1937, MLDK 5/52.
132. CAC, Drake to Rev. D. Bruce, Buenos Aires, 14 March 1938, MLDK 5/52.
133. CAC, Drake to I. Anderson, Glasgow, 8 Dec. 1937, Drake to Raeside, 24 Jan. 1938, MLDK 5/52.
134. CAC, Drake to Anderson, 25 Jan. 1938, Drake to Bruce, Buenos Aires, 14 March 1938, MLDK 5/52.
135. CAC, Drake to Anderson, 6 April 1938, 4 Aug. 1938, MLDK 5/52.
136. Archetti, 203–5.
137. CAC, Drake, memorandum, 14 Jan. 1937, MLDK 5/51; Donaldson, p.105.
138. *The Times*, 12 Sept. 1938 (on Willingdon Cup for Uruguayan football).
139. *La Prensa*, 1 Nov. 1933; PRO, Drake, Buenos Aires, to Simon, 10 Nov. 1933, Duff, 8 Dec. 1933, FO395/503/P2824.
140. PRO, Spencer Dickson, British legation, Bogota, to Simon, 20 Sept. 1934, FO371/17514/A8257.
141. PRO, Sir A. Noble, British ambassador in Buenos Aires, to Perowne, 11 Sept. 1945, FO371/44776/AS5040; Murray, pp.134–5.
142. PRO, minute, P. McQuillen, 12 Jan. 1944, FO371/37921/AS231.
143. Cottrell, pp.58–9.
144. PRO, Ogilvie Forbes, Lima, to American Dept., 6 Sept. 1937, FO371/21447/A7777; Hart-Davis, p.220; Mandell, pp.193–5; FIFA, minutes of 23rd Congress, Berlin, 13–14 Aug. 1936, pp.4–5, pp.7–8.
145. PRO, M. Paske Smith, Bogota, to American Dept., 21 Oct. 1938, FO371/21447/A8613..
146. Peter J. Beck, ' "To play, or not to play?", That is the Anglo-Argentine Question', *Contemporary Review*, 245 (1984), 70–4.
147. Peter J. Beck, *The International Politics of Antarctica* (Croom Helm, London, 1986), pp.30–6.
148. PRO, Sir E. Ovey to Halifax, 9 Nov. 1939, FO371/22715/A8182.
149. *New York Times*, 15 May 1939. See Bell, pp.139–41.
150. PRO, Ovey to Halifax, 9 Nov. 1939, FO371/22715/A8182.
151. PRO, O. Bonham Carter, Ministry of Information, to Hugh Montgomery, 8 Dec. 1939, FO371/22715/A8633.

152. PRO, minutes, Montgomery, Perowne, Balfour, 24 Nov. 1939, Balfour to Ovey, 1 Dec. 1939, FO371/22715/A8182.
153. PRO, E. Daladier to R. Campbell, 20 Dec. 1939, FO371/22715/A9150.
154. Thomas Jones, 'Neville Chamberlain' (book review), *The Times*, 10 Dec. 1946.
155. BU, Chamberlain to Lord Weir, 1 Aug. 1937, NC7/11/30/139; Chamberlain to Hilda Chamberlain, 25 June 1938, NC18/1/1057; Chamberlain to Ida Chamberlain, 17 Dec. 1938, NC18/1/1080; Chamberlain's fishing diaries, 1921–1939, NC6/3/2–4; Winston Churchill, 'Neville Chamberlain', *Sunday Dispatch*, 17 Nov. 1940.
156. BU, Chamberlain to Hilda Chamberlain, 22 May 1938, NC18/1/1053.
157. BU, Chamberlain to Ida Chamberlain, 9 April 1939, NC18/1/1093.
158. See PRO, FO372/3269/T9612.
159. Rous, *Football Worlds*, 104; author's interview with Rous, 28 March 1980.
160. PRO, minute, Corley Smith, 20 Oct. 1938, FO395/568/P2968.
161. PRO, minutes, Makin, Corley Smith, 11 Nov. 1938, FO372/3269/T14257; Polley, 'Foreign Office and International Sport', p.174.
162. PRO, Kenneth Johnstone, memorandum, The British Council, 8 Jan. 1946, encl. British Council to Montagu Pollock, Foreign Office, FO924/266/LC421.
163. PRO, News Dept. to Chancery, British embassy, Brussels, 5 Feb. 1938, FO395/568/P532.
164. Gallagher, p.109.
165. *Daily Dispatch*, 5 June 1939; *The Times*, 5 June 1939. On the German effort to use sport to maintain an air of normality, see Krüger, 'The role of sport in German international politics, 1918–1945', in Arnaud and Riordan (eds), *Sport and International Politics*, p.90.
166. 'Peak of the Season' (editorial), *The Times*, 3 July 1939.
167. *The Times*, 7 August 1939; PRO, Henderson, Berlin, to Foreign Office, 25 Aug. 1939, FO371/23059/C11988.
168. Maria Hartman, *BBC Radio Four*, 'Today programme', 19 June 1991; Hartman, quoted in *The Independent*, 23 June 1991; *The Times*, 21, 29 Aug. 1939.
169. *The Times*, 16, 27 June 1939, 3 July 1939.
170. *The Times*, 13 June 1939.
171. *The Times*, 19 May 1939.
172. *The Times*, 10, 13 June 1939; *New York Times*, 13 June 1939.
173. *The Times*, 20 June 1939.
174. PRO, minute, Sir Maurice Holmes, 29 Aug. 1939, ED113/25; Green, p.497.
175. FA, ISC, 23 June 1939, minute 8, 21 Aug. 1939, minutes 7–8, 1939–43.
176. *The Times*, 26, 28 Aug. 1939.

10

Conclusion:
'Good Kicking is Good Politics'

Between 1900 and 1939, international sport, though often presented in Britain as an autonomous activity, operated in a highly competitive world of nation states and conflicting ideologies. The international political environment, in conjunction with sport's inherently competitive and divisive nature, ensured that major sporting events impinged on politics, even prompting governments, the press and public opinion in several countries to perceive meaningful links between the performance of, say, national football or Olympic teams and abstract considerations of national prowess. Although this practice was associated mainly with Hitler's Germany and Mussolini's Italy, the *Daily Express*, commenting in January 1929 *à la* Macaulay on recent exchanges between the Foreign Office and the FA, provided one British manifestation of this trend:

> The Consul's brow was sad, and the Consul's speech was low,
> And darkly looked he at the goal and darkly at the foe.
> 'They surely score again', he cried, 'before the game doth cease',
> 'And if they once defeat our team what hope for Europe's peace?'.[1]

Of course, this was far from being universally accepted, and Brian Glanville, among others, questioned 'what correlation was there between kicking an inflated bladder between three wooden posts more times than one's opponents, and acquiring national prestige?'.[2]

BRITISH FOOTBALL 'STILL STANDS AT THE TOP OF THE LIST'

Speaking soon after the 1938 Munich Crisis about Britain's role in upholding the 'standard of democracy' against the dictators, Lord de la Warr, the Lord Privy Seal (1937–38), articulated the Chamberlain government's appreciation of the perceived need for Britain to prove itself in *all spheres of activity*: 'Great Britain is as great and as peaceful as ever ... But we must face the fact that we live in a new world, one that is virile, assertive and questioning. Nothing is taken for granted, not even what seems so obvious to us – the inherent superiority of the British race over all others. In the modern world, men and nations must prove themselves.'[3]

In the world of football also, it was no longer enough to be the game's pioneers. British football had to prove itself continually on the field as the masters of the game against an ever-wider range of former pupils, given what the FAW described as the continued growth in the popularity of 'our great world's game' by 'leaps and bounds season after season'.[4] Nevertheless, the British football associations still assumed national primacy, since images of ascendancy fostered by results (Table 2.3, Chapter 2), at least by national sides, were reinforced by their seemingly independent global role outside of FIFA, most notably by continued control over the laws of *their* game through the IFAB.[5] Nor were the football associations alone in their thinking. Similar views were held uncritically throughout much of British society, as typified in 1939 by Ivan Sharpe, a leading football correspondent: 'England's football reputation abroad, despite a number of defeats during the past six years, still stands at the top of the list'.[6]

Eduardo Archetti, reviewing the period from an Argentinian viewpoint, identified British football's cultural imperial role:

> The spread of football was caused by Britain's world power status and active presence in commerce, industrial production, territorial control and international finance ... Not only was the game a British export but so too were the standards and quality of play. In the first decade of the twentieth century Argentinian football grew under the influence of the great British teams that came to play in Buenos Aires and Rosario ... The myth of British invincibility in football was then created, and was intelligently manipulated by the British themselves, and not only in relation to the Argentinians.[7]

As Willy Meisl observed, foreign teams tended to suffer from an inferiority complex, at least when playing British national sides.[8] In many ways, Britain's high footballing reputation rested on mythologies as well as the inertia characteristic of foreign impressions of the British game, but it proved also in part a function of the fact that, notwithstanding their complete absence from lists of Olympic and World Cup footballing honours between the wars, England and Scotland had good, even outstanding, results in high profile games against foreign sides (see Table 2.3, Chapter 2). Impressive performances against Italy (one win, two draws, no defeats), the 1934 and 1938 world champions and 1936 Olympic football gold medallists, reinforced England's image as 'masters of the game' during a decade when Scotland, though displaying less overall consistency, finished with a strong run of results (1936–38: five wins, one draw, no losses) against leading continental sides, including Austria and Germany. Moreover, in 1938, England beat FIFA's 'Rest of Europe' team 3-0 in a match played to mark the FA's 75th anniversary.

Against this background, one Hungarian writer, looking back to the inter-war years following a period when his own country's national team proved pre-eminent, observed that 'in those days, and for a long time to come, no team was ashamed to being beaten by the England eleven; it was the rule'.[9] Of course, neither England nor Scotland, though unbeaten at home by non-British teams, went undefeated by foreign sides, even if England's first such loss did not occur until 1929. In any case, defeats often seemed capable of rationalisation in terms of, say, poor foreign referees, varying interpretations of the laws of the game, uneven pitches, adverse climatic conditions, excessive travelling, and tiredness after a long league season, that is, factors preventing British players from displaying their assumed innate superiority. In turn, it proved easy for the British footballing authorities, media and people to interpret Britain as having nothing to prove in the World Cup. For British football, the real test remained the home international tournament, or rather, for England and Scotland, the prime goal was to win their annual contest.

Nevertheless, over time, the complacent, even arrogant, nature of British thinking was qualified gradually by a grudging acknowledgement of an ever-changing footballing balance of power (Figure 10.1), given what Jimmy Hogan – his current managerial post at Aston Villa followed experience of coaching abroad – described in October 1938 as 'the growth of continental football from a mere weakling to a strong, sturdy man'.[10] Soon afterwards, Ivan Sharpe, albeit unshaken in his acceptance of British superiority, admitted reappraising his views following England's recent visits to Belgrade and Bucharest: 'these Balkan countries are stronger than we bargain for'.[11] L.W. Manning echoed his thoughts: 'I would have liked to be able to say that we gave the Rumanians [sic] a soccer lesson, but this would not be correct. They pulled out just as much good football as we did.'[12] Significantly, even the FA's 1939 tour report conceded that 'once more the advance of continental football is to be noted. In the Balkans, which we visited for the first time, the standard of play pleasantly surprised us'.[13] Undoubtedly, continental standards, frequently benefiting from the work of Hogan and other British coaches, were improving rapidly, particularly respecting individual skills and tactics rather than heading or shooting.[14] The same was equally true of Latin America, but hitherto British football, like the media and people in Britain, was only vaguely aware of developments therein. Easy victories could no longer be taken for granted, except in, say, Scandinavia, Australasia, North America, or South Africa.

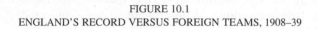
FIGURE 10.1
ENGLAND'S RECORD VERSUS FOREIGN TEAMS, 1908–39

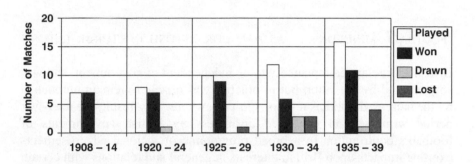

During the late nineteenth century, British football, responding to the growing problem of shamateurism, led the way towards professionalism, even if it proved easy to forget, particularly in official circles, that the vast majority of British footballers were amateurs. Other countries followed more slowly in spite of growing evidence that 'amateurs' elsewhere were often well rewarded. Moreover, the amateur status of players in, say, Germany and Italy belied the more professional approach adopted towards the game therein, such as in terms of coaching, tactical awareness, training, the appointment of permanent managers/coaches, and the use of air travel for lengthy journeys. Indeed, 'amateur' teams representing Belgium, Switzerland and Yugoslavia defeated England in the 1930s! By contrast, the British associations, though fielding national sides composed either wholly or largely of professionals, operated in a more traditional manner, as highlighted by the FA's continued reliance on placing England in the charge of individual committee members for each game rather than of a permanent manager, the enduring primacy of club over country, the low priority accorded to coaching, and use of rail-sea travel for foreign travel. Walter Winterbottom, who became England's first manager in 1946, complained that prior to the Second World War 'we were so insular that we wouldn't believe that other methods could be used for doing things, other ways of playing the game could be better than ours'.[15] Nevertheless, British football, albeit falling well short of continental practice, did show signs of becoming more 'coaching-minded' during the 1930s, when the FA offered coaching services to grammar schools (1934), held its first instructional course (July 1935) and commenced publication of a coaching journal entitled *The Bulletin* (May 1939).[16] Significantly, the latter's first issue included an article by a Briton coaching on the continent apprising readers about the superior ball control, positional play and attacking play of foreign players![17]

'FOOTBALL MINDEDNESS' AS A MAJOR BRITISH CULTURAL EXPORT

British sport claimed repeatedly to be independent of government, and was so presented by the latter, but in practice was unable to remain untouched by the increased politicisation of sport elsewhere. As a result, the inter-war period witnessed an enhanced awareness by British governments of football's contribution to a broad programme of national advertisements exerting impacts upon British interests in general and relations with certain countries in particular. Of course, it is impossible to assess precisely the role, if any, of, say, the England-Germany internationals of 1935 and 1938 as instruments of British foreign policy, but association football, more than any other sport, offered British governments a relatively cheap, even no-cost, form of national projection, which helped to ensure that the country was seen on the 'world's screen' – to quote Tallents' *The Projection of England* – 'for what it is – a great nation' espousing worthy values.[18] In particular, football's ability to reach the man in the street as well as opinion-makers in other countries complemented the elitist focus of other forms of cultural propaganda, especially as 'sport can be a focus of collective emotion which has no equal in art, religion or politics'.[19]

At the same time, an international match's character as a highly visible, head-on confrontation between British and foreign teams might be seen as compromising the British government's desire to 'avoid the idea that it [propaganda] is directed against any other country, or indeed that it is competitive', but generally speaking sport was treated as avoiding the political risks associated with overt forms of propaganda.[20] Also, Britain's early lead in football, as validated by results against foreign teams during the early decades of the twentieth century and Olympic successes in 1908 and 1912, meant that football internationals were equally capable of giving rise to negative impacts, most notably, regarding impressions of decline. Even worse, the likely loss of national prestige in the eyes of foreign audiences through defeats was compounded by the risk of fostering international friction through incidents on and off the field, thereby explaining why official intervention often took the form of damage-limitation exercises designed either to prevent or to contain such unwelcome impacts.

In many respects, the game's propaganda value was accentuated by the apolitical character of the British football associations, whose jealously guarded independence and freedom of action in arranging international fixtures and approving club tours, offered at first sight an 'uncompromising context for government intervention'.[21] British football, though willing to cooperate with the government, wished to keep the game as far away as possible from any rival authority, whether this be the British government or FIFA. During 1937, William Pickford, having outlined the FA's *modus operandi*, asked 'Who controls the controllers?'.[22] According to colleagues, he did, given his status as FA President. By implication, his account, notable for its omission of any reference to government, emphasised the FA's autonomous character. Paradoxically, this feature became a key attraction for British governments seeking to conduct propaganda at arm's length through seemingly non-governmental organisations. Of course, in reality, no British sporting body was completely autonomous, for all operated within the overall domestic (e.g. law and order, taxation) and international framework defined by government. Thus, it was difficult, if not impossible, for a fixture to be arranged with any country either lacking diplomatic relations with Britain (e.g. Soviet Union, 1917–24, 1927–29) or subjected to an official non-intervention policy (e.g. Spain, 1937).

Nor were the footballing authorities entirely unaware of the game's extra-sporting significance, most notably, regarding the value of upholding a national reputation for footballing skill and fair play, as implied in 1939, when Ted Robbins, the FAW's Secretary, claimed that 'Great Britain always plays the Game – so much so that our sides are welcomed and asked for everywhere'.[23] Subsequently, in 1948, the Earl of Athlone employed his presidential address to the FA's AGM to articulate the game's propaganda potential, and his views, though made outside this book's period of coverage, are relevant to any study of British thinking:

> At a time when exports were of paramount importance, football (or what one might perhaps call 'football mindedness') was far from being insignificant; a successful English referee in the Argentine, or our International team in Italy carried a message to other Nations in a language ordinary people could well understand; the football fan in Buenos Aires or Turin had much in common with the football fan in Manchester or Colchester – and *that* was a thing worth remembering.[24]

For the Earl of Athlone, who became president in 1939, 'football mindedness' provided an invaluable common language for the world,

277

whether divided by either the 1930s European Civil War or the post-1945 Cold War.

At times, the four home associations even appeared to act in a political manner independent of government, as demonstrated by the intransigent position adopted towards fixtures with ex-enemy states during the immediate post-1919 period. To some extent, their position proved in part a function of the inevitable anti-German sentiments fostered by a long war and the second-class status (e.g. initial exclusion from the League of Nations) accorded to defeated states, but the FA, which took the lead role, did seem to be acting in pursuit of its own politico-sporting agenda. Subsequently, British footballing associations, seeking to maximise their freedom from state influence, repeatedly emphasised their autonomy, as reiterated in November 1945 by Rous upon his return from the meeting at Zurich used to discuss British re-entry to FIFA: 'We have made it clear that in international football we do not allow politics, race or religion to interfere in any way with the game'.[25] However, this assertion was not in complete accord with developments during the past decade or so, when Rous himself had adopted a cooperative, even receptive, line towards government interference in footballing questions. Significantly, Arnaud, pointing to British football's post-1919 ban respecting the Central powers, argues 'that the initial boycott operations, often attributed to authoritarian regimes from the 1930s, were actually implemented from 1919 by democratic states, on the initiative of England, and then relayed effectively by Belgium and France'.[26]

At the same time, the British football associations operated within the broader footballing framework defined by the IFAB and FIFA, especially as the ban on fixtures against foreign teams from associations unaffiliated to FIFA (e.g. Soviet Union) was maintained even following British withdrawal in 1928. In general, membership of FIFA, a transnational actor pursuing an universalist agenda, did not result in the British associations adopting positions towards international questions out of line with British foreign policy.[27] Indeed, withdrawal in 1920 and again in 1928 highlighted their efforts to contain FIFA's supranational tendencies and reluctance to follow a line (e.g. definitions of amateurism) of which they disapproved. As Wall asserted, 'we want to govern ourselves both on and off the field'.[28] Against this background, the period 1900–39 also offered interesting insights into the operations and inter-relationships of national and international sports bodies.[29]

AN INTERVENTIONIST INTERPRETATION OF NON-INTERVENTION

During the 1930s, Orme Sargent, among others, advised that 'it is undesirable that the Foreign Office should be too closely associated with international football'.[30] The Foreign Office, remaining relatively unenthusiastic about international sport *per se*, inclined to the view that the promotion of friendly relations with other countries was 'an all too infrequent result of international contacts of this kind'.[31] In any case, officials, imbued through education and upbringing with the amateur ethic, failed to credit the football associations' tough stance on amateurism and the game's predominantly amateur character. As a result, they adopted a rather unsympathetic opinion about British football, as evidenced by assumptions that professional footballers played for themselves, or rather their wallets, not their country. Nor did British policy-makers display much sympathy towards the Olympic movement, which still enshrined the amateur principle in spite of occasional infringements (e.g. broken-time payments).

During 1938, Charles Fone even claimed that 'it has been our policy to discourage the staging of football matches with foreigners'.[32] In fact, the government seldom acted in this manner. Bans on the entry of foreign teams (e.g. a Soviet side, 1930) or overseas visits (e.g. a BWSA visit to Spain, 1937) were exceptional, and generally speaking, the Foreign Office, acknowledging its inability to contain the rapid growth of international football, adopted a more realistic stance seeking to ensure that fixtures exerted positive rather than harmful impacts. Despite an understandable unwillingness to challenge traditional images regarding the separation of politics and sport, British governments, apprised by diplomatic representatives stationed abroad about the extent of political intervention elsewhere, were forced to an equally reluctant acceptance of the fact that international football was too important to be left entirely to sporting bodies. Even worse, other governments, like those headed by Hitler and Mussolini, valued victories over British teams for reasons designed to establish simultaneously the dynamic impact of their respective dictatorships and the alleged decadence of Britain and other liberal democracies. Thus, matches involving British teams were interpreted elsewhere as politically significant regardless of the position taken by the British government.

Intervention in footballing questions, albeit assuming a more subtle and occasional form than the more totalitarian variants found elsewhere, proved both more substantial and frequent than implied by Fone. In fact, even he conceded that 'on more than one occasion, we have drawn attention to the embarrassing situation' created by the unsatisfactory performance of British club sides abroad.[33] Policy-makers, appreciating gradually that 'sport creates politically usable resources', found it impossible to stand aside from events, as British governments became increasingly involved in international football fixtures versus Germany (e.g. 1928–29, 1935 and 1938), Italy (e.g. 1928, 1933–34, 1939), the Soviet Union (e.g. 1930) and Spain (e.g. 1937).[34] Contrary to appearances, even a decision against intervention to stop a match (e.g. 1935 England-Germany game), though presented publicly in terms of keeping politics out of football, was often made for reasons related to an appreciation of the political benefits arising from allowing the match to go ahead. After all, even decisions not to do something normally reflected political contingencies. Moreover, as the late Stephen Jones remarked, the government's 'intervention was characterised by gross discrimination' determined by policy priorities, so that sporting contacts with Germany, Italy and Japan were treated far more sympathetically than those with the Soviet Union or republican Spain.[35] Unsurprisingly, George Sinfield, a communist, complained about the manner in which 'the Government allocates to itself the right to determine what is "right" and what is "safe" and what is "political" '.[36]

For policy-makers, England, alongside English club sides, constituted the prime focus. Scotland's international fixtures failed to attract the same level of official interest, while neither Wales, which only played two full internationals against non-British teams prior to 1939, nor Northern Ireland – its foreign fixture list was blank during this period – attracted the attention of British foreign policy-makers (Table 10.1, Figure 10.2).

International sport proved a rare Cabinet agenda topic. For this reason, the Cabinet's role during 1936 in securing the withdrawal of London's bid for the 1940 Olympics for the sake of good Anglo-Japanese relations remains of historical interest, particularly given the policy preference accorded to Japan over Finland and the resulting exertion of clandestine official pressure on the BOA, another supposedly apolitical sporting body. Nor did individual ministers become involved on a regular basis; thus, the Hoare-Simon exchanges about the 1935 England-Germany match proved the exception rather than the rule. Normally, international sport, like most other topics, was dealt with largely at the official level, principally through the Foreign Office, with other departments, most notably the Home Office (e.g. for law and order, visas), the Board of Education (e.g. for national fitness, sport at schools), the Treasury (e.g. taxation, visa fees) and the defence ministries (e.g. military participation in Olympic teams, wartime football), being drawn in, as appropriate. International sport came to be viewed also as a useful, albeit minor, function of the British Council

TABLE 10.1
BRITISH FOOTBALL BECOMES LESS ISOLATIONIST, 1900–39*

		Total games played	No, against non-British teams	Per cent against non-British teams
England	1900–19	54	7	13
	1920–29	49	18	37
	1930–39	56	28	50
Northern Ireland	1900–19	46	0	0
	1920–29	30	0	0
	1930–39	29	0	0
Scotland	1900–19	45	0	0
	1920–29	34	3	9
	1930–39	41	12	29
Wales	1900–19	45	0	0
	1920–29	32	0	0
	1930–39	30	2	7

* Amateur football gives a rather different picture. Excepting six games played versus Belgium, France and South Africa (1920–24), disputes concerning the definition of amateurism meant that between 1925 and 1939 England's amateur internationals were confined to the home countries.

FIGURE 10.2
PERCENTAGE OF INTERNATIONALS VERSUS BRITISH TEAMS

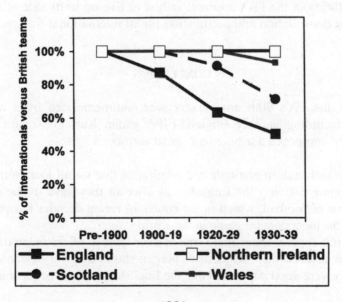

(created 1934–35), even if its overseas representatives frequently complained also about the damage inflicted upon their work by the misconduct of club footballers engaged on close season tours.

Although it is tempting to identify the gradual emergence of a long-term strategy linked to the growing role of the state, in reality official intervention took the form of pragmatic one-off responses to events, even if reference to precedent helped to provide a unifying theme. What occurred was the exertion of varying degrees of pressure upon the footballing authorities to secure specific objectives. Generally speaking, cultural propaganda, as pursued through international football, placed a premium on results. Winning, rather than merely taking part, was treated as the most effective form of propaganda, although a sporting display was increasingly valued. In turn, the inter-departmental squabbles characterising the official exchanges surrounding the 1935 England-Germany match highlighted the fragmented and incoherent nature of government approaches towards international sport, most notably the unclear lines of departmental responsibility. Nor was the appointment of a minister of sport a matter of practical politics, even during the mid-1930s when the creation of the CCRPT, the first official sporting agency, paved the way for the 1937 Physical Training and Recreation Act and the NFC's national fitness campaign.[37] As regards football, the outbreak of the Second World War interrupted ongoing efforts to harmonise political and sporting priorities through the adoption of more formal procedures for international fixtures, although it is worth recording repeated government complaints during the late 1940s about the FA's apparent failure to live up to its side of the deal (i.e. prior consultation and notification for all international fixtures).

CONCLUSION

In 1953, the FA's 90th anniversary was commemorated by a range of events, including another England-FIFA game. Kurt Gassmann, FIFA's Secretary, composed a tribute to a 'great member':

> It is with a deep gratitude and admiration that we all look to this great sporting nation – the English – as after all they gave us the glorious game of football, which in the course of recent decades has proved to be the most popular game in the world.
>
> If it appears today that some of their 'pupils' of the olden days have now reached their standard of play, it shows in a very clear way that they were good pupils and that the English were even better teachers ...

They not only taught us their methods of play but they made known to us these true English traditions, the famous English sporting attitude, sportsmanship and fair play as well. These characteristics matter much more than the bare result as, after all, football is a game. They also taught us 'How to lose without dry faces and how to win without grimaces'.[38]

In many respects, this extract suggests the enduring success of British football during the period 1900–39 in exporting selected images and values to the wider world, and hence of exerting impacts possessing an extra-sporting significance.

Unsurprisingly, British governments, wishing to avoid challenging traditional images about the autonomy of sport, took pains to appear in public as staying on the sidelines of international sport. Despite occasional controversies, their efforts proved largely successful, given the general belief both within and outside the country that sporting fixtures in Britain neither possessed political implications nor occasioned governmental interference.[39] The seeming independence of the footballing associations, described frequently by ministers and officials as 'a law unto themselves', helped to consolidate such images, particularly as compared to continental Europe where the politicisation of sport was often taken for granted.[40] There, 'sport diplomacy', taking advantage of an activity attracting high visibility, emerged as an increasingly important instrument by which nations conducted their international relations.[41] In turn, it proved increasingly difficult for British club and national sides playing foreign teams to avoid being seen as projecting the values of their imagined national community.[42] Henceforth, supposedly apolitical British footballers, albeit largely motivated by personal motives (e.g. interest in sport, financial), were unable to prevent their footballing exploits being given a broader political meaning by governments, media and people. Following Jarvie and Polley, 'perhaps we should question the axiomatic identification with football as a national symbol', even if a more critical approach, though acknowledging that numerous other symbols contribute to imagined communities, will still find it difficult to deny the game's prime role in fostering a complex blend of frenzied emotion and nationalist fervour.[43]

For Britain, football's cultural export role was reinforced by its apparent capacity to accommodate more specific diplomatic objectives, most notably, the despatch of messages suggesting the tone and temper of relations with other countries.[44] Policy-makers came to view international football as an instrument for meeting diverse goals, whether this involved developing and reinforcing bilateral relations, exerting varying degrees of pressure to secure a change of course by another government, indicating disapproval of another regime, or preventing a sporting contact adjudged prejudicial to the government's overall foreign policy.

According to Tony Mason, 'by 1939 the Foreign Office was much more alert to the place of sport in culture and propaganda than it had been in 1918 but neither the government nor the ruling élite of British sport wanted a state-controlled sport as seemed to be in place in the Fascist West and the Communist East'.[45] The notion that British sport, a free voluntary, private activity, has nothing to do with anything else, and particularly politics, has a long and revered history as well as an energetic present; thus, a `dominant ideology of non-interference' characterised Britain during the period 1900–39.[46] Neither governments nor the media made much effort to acknowledge, let alone codify, international sport's role as a diplomatic resource. Nor is it easy for historians to identify the existence of a clear and coherent government policy towards international sport in general and international football in particular. For Mason, a chapter on politics, though essential to studies of German, Italian, Soviet or Latin American football, 'would probably not exist in a book on British football'.[47] Writing from Mexico City in 1955, one British diplomat warned the Foreign Office that his report about the Pan-American Games possessed 'more political interest than would at first seem apparent from its subject matter'.[48] In this vein, contrary to appearances, 'good kicking' was viewed increasingly as 'good politics' by British governments, thereby suggesting the case for far more than a mere chapter detailing not only instances of official interference regarding international football but also the fact that frequently British governments adopted a rather interventionist interpretation of non-intervention.

NOTES

1. *Daily Express*, 1 Jan. 1929.
2. Brian Glanville, *Soccer: a panorama* (Eyre & Spottiswoode, London, 1969), p.82; Allison, 'Sport and politics', p.5; Polley, *Moving the Goalposts*, pp.35–6.
3. *The Times*, 10 Oct. 1938.
4. FAW, *Annual Report 1935–36* (FAW, 1936), p.1.
5. Graham, p.21.
6. *Daily Dispatch*, 18 May 1939; Matthews, p.106; Walvin (1994 edn), p.143. Exceptions included Brian Glanville, who felt that British football reached its zenith in 1914: Glanville, *Soccer Nemesis*, p.11.
7. Archetti, 203.
8. Willy Meisl, *Soccer Revolution* (Phoenix, London, 1955), p.62.
9. József Vetö, *Sport in Hungary* (Corvina Press, Budapest, 1965), p.52.
10. FAW, Jimmy Hogan, *Wales-England Match Programme, Cardiff, 22 October 1938*, 1937–39.

11. *Daily Dispatch*, 25 May 1939.
12. *Daily Sketch*, 25 May 1939.
13. FA, Report of Continental Tour, 1939, encl. ISC, 5 June 1939, minute 3, 1938–39.
14. Glanville, *Soccer Nemesis,* pp.101–2.
15. Winterbottom, quoted, Taylor and Ward, p.89.
16. *The Blueprint for the Future of Football* (FA, London, 1991), p.63; Walter Winterbottom, *Soccer Coaching* (Naldrett Press, London, 1952), p.5.
17. "T.M", 'Coaching on the continent', *The Bulletin (FA)*, 1 (May 1939), 8; Sharpe, 'Football on the Continent', 1.
18. Tallents, pp.39–40.
19. Allison, 'Sport and politics', p.3.
20. PRO, memorandum, Leeper, 23 April 1934, FO395/504/P1255.
21. Houlihan, *Sport and International Politics*, p.207.
22. Pickford, 'How soccer is controlled', 657.
23. FAW, Ted Robbins, *Wales-England programme, Wrexham, 18 November 1939*, p.23, 1939–40.
24. FA, 45th AGM of FA, 7 June 1948, 1948–49.
25. FIFA, Rous quoted, I. Schricker to G.R. Manning, 14 Dec. 1945, USA correspondence 1932–69.
26. Arnaud, 'Sport – a means of national representation', in Arnaud and Riordan (eds), *Sport and International Politics*, p.12.
27. See Houlihan, *Sport and International Politics*, p.207.
28. Wall, p.220.
29. Taylor, 'Sport and international relations', pp.42–6.
30. PRO, Sargent, 19 Nov. 1935, FO371/18884/C7566; Duff, minute, 18 March 1933, FO395/492/P673.
31. PRO, minutes, Broad, 22 May 1939, Orme Sargent, 25 May 1939, FO371/23785/R4193.
32. PRO, minute, C.H. Fone, Library Dept., 25 Jan. 1938, FO395/568/P673.
33. PRO, minute, Fone, 25 Jan. 1938, FO395/568/P673.
34. Allison, 'Sport and politics', p.12.
35. Jones, *Sport, Politics and the Working Class*, p.187.
36. Ibid.
37. Polley, *Moving the Goalposts*, pp.12–34. No minister of sport was appointed until 1963.
38. Kurt Gassmann, 'Tribute to a great member', *FIFA Official Bulletin*, 3 (Sept. 1953), 1.
39. *The Times*, 2 Jan. 1929, 3 Dec. 1935.
40. PRO, Willert to Don MacEachen, 3 Jan. 1930, FO395/434/P1900.
41. Peppard and Riordan, pp.1–3.
42. The singular has been used here for Britain, given uncertainty regarding the extent to which foreign perceptions distinguished between 'British' as opposed to say 'English' or 'Scottish' national communities.
43. Hobsbawm, p.143; Montagu; Grant Jarvie, 'Giving the game away' (review article), *The Sports Historian*, 17 (1997), 212; Polley, *Moving the Goalposts*, pp.35–41.
44. Houlihan, *Sport and International Politics*, p.12, p.209.
45. Mason, *Sport in Britain*, p.102.
46. Ibid., p.7; Holt, 'Sport and History', 231, 240; Neil Macfarlane with M. Herd, *Sport and Politics: a world divided* (Willow, London, 1986), p.7; Green, pp.503–4; Polley, *Moving the Goalposts*, pp.29–34, p.160, pp.166–71.
47. Mason, *Passion of the People*, p.ix.
48. PRO, M. Chevallier to Eden, 20 April 1955, FO371/114012/A1801.

Bibliography

PRIMARY SOURCES (UNPUBLISHED)

Official documents

Public Record Office, Kew, London (PRO): British government records – Board of Education (ED), British Council (BW), Cabinet (CAB), Foreign Office (FO), Home Office (HO), MEPO (Metropolitan Police); PREM (Prime Minister's Dept.), Treasury (T).

National Archives, College Park, Maryland, USA (Archives II) (USA): General Records of United States State Department.

Private papers

University of Birmingham: Special Collections Department, Library (BU). Neville Chamberlain (NC).

Cambridge University: Churchill Archives Centre, Churchill College (CAC). Lord Noel-Baker (NBKR); Sir Alexander Cadogan (ACAD); Sir Winston Churchill (Chartwell); Eugen Millington Drake (MLDK); Sir Hughe Knatchbull-Hugessen (KNAT); Lord Lloyd (GLLD); Sir Eric Phipps (PHPP).

Cambridge University: Wren Library, Trinity College (TC). Lord Butler of Saffron Walden (RAB).

Cambridge University: Manuscripts Room, University Library (CU). Viscount Templewood; Earl Baldwin.

Carmarthen: Carmarthenshire Archives Service (CAS). Viscount Cilcennin (Cilc.Coll. Acc.5605).

FIFA, Zurich (Note: the FIFA archives are not generally available for public access).

Football Association, London.

Football Association of Wales, Cardiff.

Irish Football Association, Belfast.

Oxford University: Modern Papers Room, Bodleian Library (BL). Conservative Party (CRD); Geoffrey Dawson (MS Dawson); Viscount Simon (MS Simon).

Scottish Football Association. These papers, which were used at the National Library of Scotland, Edinburgh, as Acc.9017, are now located at the Scottish Football Association Museum Trust (SFAMT), Hampden Park, Glasgow.

University of York (York): Borthwick Institute of Historical Research. Lord Halifax.

Yale University: Sterling Memorial Library, New Haven, Connecticut, USA (Yale). Sir Arthur Willert (MG 720).

Oral testimony

Interview with Sir Stanley Rous, 28 March 1980; telephone interviews with Frank Broome, 6, 10 May 1980.

Rogan Taylor and Andrew Ward, *Kicking and Screaming: an oral history of football in England* (Robson Books, London, 1995).

PRIMARY SOURCES (PUBLISHED)

Official documents

Board of Education, *Educational Pamphlet No. 109: Physical Education in Germany* (National Advisory Council for Physical Training and Recreation/HMSO, London, 1937).

Department of Culture, Media and Sport Press Release, DCM 50/97 (department web site). http://www.culture.gov.uk.

Hansard, Parliamentary Debates. Official Reports. 5th Series, House of Commons.

National Fitness: the First Stage (National Advisory Council for Physical Training and Recreation, 1937).

Sport: raising the game (Dept. of National Heritage, London, 1995).

Newspapers

Newspapers, which were consulted mainly at the British Library's Newspaper Library, Colindale, are listed in the endnotes.

Radio

Christopher Andrew interviewing Rachel Newnham, 'Making History', *BBC Radio Four*, 7, 14 Dec. 1996.

Maria Hartman interviewed, 'Today', *BBC Radio Four*, 19 June 1991.

Roy Hattersley, 'Who Goes Home?', *BBC Radio Four*, 9 Jan. 1995.

Memoirs, diaries

George F. Allison, *Allison Calling: a galaxy of football and other memories* (Staples, London, 1948).

Cliff Bastin (with B. Glanville), *Cliff Bastin Remembers. An Autobiography* (Ettrick Press, London, 1950).

John Graves (ed.), *Herbert Chapman on Football* (Garrick, London, 1934).

Robert Graves, *Goodbye to All That* (Penguin Books, Harmondsworth, 1960 edn).

Eddie Hapgood, *Football Ambassador* (Sporting Handbooks, London, 1945).

Ruth Elwin Harris (ed.), *Billie. The Nevill Letters, 1914–1916* (Julia MacRae, London, 1991).

Alan Hudson (with Ian Macleay), *The Working Man's Ballet* (Moon over Miami Productions, Sheffield, 1996).

Robert Rhodes James (ed.), *Chips: the Diaries of Sir Henry Channon* (Weidenfeld & Nicolson, London, 1967).

Tommy Lawton (with Roy Peskett), *Football is my Business* (Sporting Handbooks, London, 1946).

Neil Macfarlane (with M. Herd), *Sport and Politics: a world divided* (Willow, London, 1986).

Stanley Matthews, *Feet First* (Ewen & Dale, London, 1948).

Fred Perry, *An Autobiography* (Hutchinson, London, 1984).

Roy Peskett (ed.), *Tom Whittaker's Arsenal Story* (Sporting Handbooks, London, 1957).

William Pickford, *A Few Recollections of Sport* (private printing, Bournemouth Guardian, Bournemouth, 1938).

Ben Pimlott (ed.), *The Political Diary of Hugh Dalton, 1918–40, 1945–60* (Jonathan Cape/LSE, London, 1986).

Stanley Rous, *Football Worlds: a lifetime in sport* (Faber, London, 1978).

Siegfried Sassoon, *Memoirs of a Fox-Hunting Man* (Faber & Faber, London, 1960 edn).

Sir Walford Selby, *Diplomatic Twilight, 1930–1940* (John Murray, London, 1953).

Ivan Sharpe, *Forty Years in Football* (Hutchinson, London, 1952).

Viscount Templewood, *Nine Troubled Years* (Collins, London, 1954).

Ernest W.D. Tennant, *True Account* (Parrish, London, 1957).

Frederick Wall, *Fifty Years of Football* (Cassell, London, 1935).

SECONDARY SOURCES

Books

Anthony P. Adamthwaite, *The Making of the Second World War* (Allen and Unwin, London, 1977).

Thomas Alexander and Beryl Parker, *The New Education in the German Republic* (Williams & Norgate, London, 1930).

Lincoln Allison (ed.), *The Politics of Sport* (Manchester University Press, Manchester, 1986).

Lincoln Allison (ed.), *The Changing Politics of Sport* (Manchester University Press, Manchester, 1993).

Pierre Arnaud and James Riordan (eds), *Sport and International Politics: the impact of fascism and communism on sport* (E. & F.N. Spon, London, 1998).

William J. Baker, *Sports in the Western World* (University of Illinois Press, Urbana, 1982 rev. edn).

Michael Balfour, *Propaganda in War: organisations, policies and publicity in Britain and Germany* (Routledge Kegan & Paul, London, 1979).

James Barros, *Betrayal from Within: Joseph Avenol, Secretary-General of the League of Nations 1933–1940* (Yale University Press, New Haven, 1969).

Joe Louis Barrow Jr and Barbara Munder, *Joe Louis: the Brown Bomber* (Arthur Barker, London, 1988).

Peter J. Beck, *The International Politics of Antarctica* (Croom Helm, London, 1986).

Bert Bell, *Still Seeing Red: a history of Third Lanark A.C.* (Glasgow City Libraries and Archives, Glasgow, 1996).

J.C. Binfield and J. Stevenson (eds), *Sport, Culture and Politics* (Sheffield Academic Press, Sheffield, 1993).

Derek Birley, *Playing the Game: sport and British society, 1910–45* (Manchester University Press, Manchester, 1995).

Alan Breck's Book of Scottish Football (Scottish Daily Express, Glasgow, 1937).

Asa Briggs, *The History of Broadcasting in the United Kingdom. Vol. II: the golden age of wireless* (Oxford University Press, Oxford, 1965).

Bryon Butler, *The Official History of the Football Association* (Queen Anne Press, London, 1991).

Peter Byrne, *Football Association of Ireland: 75 years* (Sportsworld, Dublin, 1996).

W. Capel-Kirby and Frederick W. Carter, *The Mighty Kick: romance, history and humour of football* (Jarrolds, London, 1933).

Cato, *Guilty Men* (Gollancz, London, 1940).

Peter Clarke, *Hope and Glory: Britain 1900–1990* (Allen Lane, The Penguin Press, London, 1996).

Ian Colvin, *Vansittart in Office: an historical survey of the origins of the Second World War* (Gollancz, London, 1965).

Committee on Fair Play in Sports, *Food for Thought* (Committee on Fair Play in Sports, New York, 1935).

Committee on Fair Play in Sports, *Preserve the Olympic Ideal: a statement of the case against American participation in the Olympic Games* (Committee on Fair Play in Sports, New York, 1936).

289

B.O. Corbett, *Annals of the Corinthian Football Club* (Longmans, Green, London, 1908).

Peter Corrigan, *100 Years of Welsh Soccer: the official history of the Football Association of Wales* (Welsh Brewers Ltd., Cardiff, 1976).

John Cottrell, *A Century of Great Soccer Drama* (Hart-Davis, London, 1970).

F.N.S. Creek, *A History of the Corinthian Football Club* (Longmans, Green, London, 1933).

F.N.S. Creek, *Association Football* (Dent, London, 1937).

J.A. Cross, *Sir Samuel Hoare: a political biography* (Jonathan Cape, London, 1977).

Deutschland Weltmeister im Fussball, 1954 (Wilhelm Limpert, Frankfurt am Main, 1954).

Frances Donaldson, *The British Council: the first fifty years* (Jonathan Cape, London, 1984).

Vic Duke and Liz Crolley, *Football, Nationality and the State* (Longman, Harlow, 1996).

Robert Edelman, *Serious Fun: a history of spectator sports in the USSR* (Oxford University Press, Oxford, 1993).

Niall Edworthy, *England: the official FA history* (Virgin, London, 1997).

Christiane Eisenberg (ed.), *Fussball, Soccer, Calcio: ein englischer Sport auf seinem Weg um die Welt* (DTV, Munich, 1997).

H. Justin Evans, *Service to Sport: the story of the CCPR – 1935–1972* (Pelham, London, 1974).

Keith Feiling, *Neville Chamberlain* (Macmillan, London, 1946).

FIFA 1904–1929 (de Bussy, Amsterdam, 1929).

FIFA Handbook, 1927 edn (J.H. de Bussy, Amsterdam, 1927).

FIFA Handbook 1931, 4th edn (de Bussy, Amsterdam, 1931).

FIFA Handbook, 1935, 7th edn (Rüegg, Zurich, 1935).

FIFA Handbook 1950, 9th edn (FIFA, Zurich, 1950).

Nicholas Fishwick, *English Football and Society, 1910–1950* (Manchester University Press, Manchester, 1988).

Football Association, *The Blueprint for the Future of Football* (FA, London, 1991).

Football Association of Wales: 75th Anniversary 1876–1951 (FAW, Cardiff, 1951).

Günther Furrer, Paulo Godoy and Joseph Blatter, *FIFA 1904–1984* (FIFA, Zurich, 1984).

Brian Glanville, *Soccer Nemesis* (Secker & Warburg, London, 1955).

Brian Glanville, *Soccer: a panorama* (Eyre & Spottiswoode, London, 1969).

Philip Goodhart and Christopher Chataway, *War Without Weapons* (W.H. Allen, London, 1968).

George G. Graham, *Scottish Football Through the Years* (Scottish Daily Record and Evening News, Glasgow, 1947).

Mariel Grant, *Propaganda and the Role of the State in Inter-War Britain* (Clarendon, Oxford, 1994).

Victoria de Grazia, *The Culture of Consent: mass organisation of leisure in fascist Italy* (Cambridge University Press, Cambridge, 1981).

Geoffrey Green, *The History of the Football Association* (Naldrett Press, London, 1953).

Richard Griffiths, *Fellow Travellers of the Right: British enthusiasts for Nazi Germany, 1933–39* (Constable, London, 1980).

Allen Guttmann, *The Games Must Go On: Avery Brundage and the Olympic movement* (Columbia University Press, New York, 1984).

Allen Guttmann, *The Olympics: a history of the modern games* (University of Illinois Press, Urbana, 1992).

John Hargreaves, *Sport, Power and Culture: a social and historical analysis of popular sports in Britain* (Polity Press, Cambridge, 1986).

Duff Hart-Davis, *Hitler's Games: the 1936 Olympics* (Harper & Row, New York, 1986).

Eric Hobsbawm, *Nations and Nationalism since 1780: programme, myth, reality* (Cambridge University Press, Cambridge, 1990).

Richard Holt, *Sport and the British: a modern history* (Clarendon Press, Oxford, 1992 edn).

Nick Hornby, *Fever Pitch* (Gollancz, London, 1992).

Barrie Houlihan, *The Government and Politics of Sport* (Routledge, London, 1991).

Barrie Houlihan, *Sport and International Politics* (Harvester Wheatsheaf, Hemel Hempstead, 1994).

Barrie Houlihan, *Sport, Policy and Politics: a comparative analysis* (Routledge, London, 1997).

Stephen G. Jones, *Sport, Politics and the Working Class: organised labour and sport in interwar Britain* (Manchester University Press, Manchester, 1988).

D.B. Kanin, *A Political History of the Olympic Games* (Westview, Boulder, CO, 1981).

A. Krüger and J. Riordan (eds), *The Story of Worker Sport* (Human Kinetics, Leeds, 1996).

Clive Leatherdale (ed.), *Scotland's Quest for the World Cup: a complete record, 1950–1986* (John Donald, Edinburgh, 1986).

R.B. Lockhart, *Giants Cast Long Shadows* (Methuen, London, 1964).

B. Lowe, D.B. Kanin and A. Strenk (eds), *Sport and International Relations* (Stipes, Champaign, IL, 1978).

Rod Macleod, *100 Years of the Scottish Football Association, 1873–1973* (Scottish Television, Glasgow, 1973).

Bruno Malitz, *Die Leibesübungen in der Nationalsozialistischen Idee* (Verlag Fritz Eher, Munich, 1933).

Richard D. Mandell, *The Nazi Olympics* (Macmillan, New York, 1971).

Laurence Martin and John Garnett, *British Foreign Policy: challenges and choices for the 21st century* (RIIA/Pinter, London, 1997).

Arthur Marwick, *The Deluge: British society and the First World War*, 2nd edn (Macmillan, London, 1991).

Tony Mason, *Association Football and English Society, 1863–1915* (Harvester Press, Brighton, 1980).

Tony Mason, *Sport in Britain* (Faber & Faber, London, 1988).

Tony Mason (ed.), *Sport in Britain: a social history* (Cambridge University Press, Cambridge, 1989).

Tony Mason, *Passion of the People?: football in South America* (Verso, London, 1995).

Peter McIntosh, *Sport in Society* (C.A. Watts, London, 1983 edn).

Walter M. McLennan (Sir Walter Citrine), *Under the Heel of Hitler: the dictatorship over sport in Nazi Germany* (General Council, TUC, London, 1936).

Willy Meisl, *Soccer Revolution* (Phoenix, London, 1955).

David Miller, *Stanley Matthews: the authorised biography* (Pavilion, London, 1989).

Henry W. Morton, *Soviet Sport* (Collier, New York, 1963).

Kurt Münch, *Deutschkunde über Volk, Staat, Leibesübungen: Hilfsbuch für die politische Erziehung in den Vereinen des deutschen Reichsbund für Leibesübungen* (Limpert, Berlin, 1935).

Bill Murray, *Football: a history of the world game* (Scolar, Aldershot, 1994).

Fred Ollier, *Arsenal: a complete record, 1886–1992* (Breedon, Derby, 1992).

R.A.C. Parker, *Chamberlain and Appeasement: British policy and the coming of the Second World War* (Macmillan, London, 1993).

Victor Peppard and James Riordan, *Playing Politics: Soviet Sport Diplomacy to 1992* (Jai Press, Greenwood, CT, 1993).

Martin Polley, *Moving the Goalposts: a history of sport and society since 1945* (Routledge, London, 1998).

John Ramsden, *The Making of Conservative Party Policy: the Conservative Research Department since 1929* (Longman, London, 1980).

David Reynolds, *Britannia Overruled: British policy and world power in the 20th century* (Longman, Harlow, 1991).

James Riordan (ed.), *Sport under Communism: the USSR, Czechoslovakia, the GDR, Cuba* (Hurst, London, 1978).

James Riordan, *Soviet Sport: background to the Olympics* (Blackwell, Oxford, 1980).

Andrew Roberts, *The Holy Fox: a life of Lord Halifax* (Macmillan, London, 1992 edn).

Norman Rose, *Vansittart: study of a diplomat* (Heinemann, London, 1978).

Alan Rowlands, *Trautmann: the biography* (Breedon, Derby, 1991).

Dave Russell, *Football and the English: a social history of association football in England, 1863–1995* (Carnegie, Preston, 1997).

Norman Schneidmann, *Soviet Road to the Olympics* (Routledge, London, 1979).

Sir Stephen Tallents, *The Projection of England* (Faber, London, 1932).

Hugh Taylor, *'Go Fame': the story of Kilmarnock Football Club, 1869–1969* (n.d. [1969]).

Philip Taylor, *The Projection of Britain: British overseas publicity and propaganda* (Cambridge University Press, Cambridge, 1981).

Philip M. Taylor, *Munitions of the Mind: war propaganda from the ancient world to the nuclear age* (Patrick Stephens, Wellingborough, 1990).

Neil Tranter, *Sport, Economy and Society in Britain, 1750–1914* (Cambridge University Press, Cambridge, 1998).

Barbara Tuchman, *Practicing History: selected essays* (Ballantine, New York, 1982).

Wray Vamplew, *Pay Up and Play the Game: professional sport in Britain, 1875–1914* (Cambridge University Press, Cambridge, 1988).

József Vetö, *Sports in Hungary* (Corvina Press, Budapest, 1965).

James Walvin, *The People's Game: a social history of British football* (Allen Lane, London, 1975). Revised edn 1994.

Gordon Waterfield, *Professional Diplomat: Sir Percy Loraine of Kirkharle, 1880–1961* (John Murray, London, 1973).

D.C. Watt (ed.), *Hitler's Mein Kampf* (Hutchinson, London, 1969).

Donald Cameron Watt, *How War Came: the immediate origins of the Second World War, 1938–1939* (Heinemann, London, 1989).

Tom Watt, *The End. 80 Years of Life on Arsenal's North Bank* (Mainstream, Edinburgh, 1993).

David J. Whittaker, *Fighter for Peace: Philip Noel-Baker 1889–1982* (William Sessions, York, 1989).

Gareth Williams, *1905 and All That* (Gomer, Llandysul, 1991).

Trevor Wilson, *The Myriad Faces of War* (Polity Press, Cambridge, 1986).

Walter Winterbottom, *Soccer Coaching* (Naldrett Press, London, 1952).

Thomas Woody, *New Minds. New Men?: the emergence of the Soviet citizen* (Macmillan, New York, 1932).

John W. Young, *Britain and the World in the Twentieth Century* (Arnold, London, 1997).

Percy Young, *The Wolves: the first eighty years* (Stanley Paul, London, 1959).

Percy M. Young, *A History of British Football* (Stanley Paul, London, 1968).

Articles (articles in newspapers, though cited in full in endnotes, are listed only selectively here)

'Half a century of history: the FIFA is 50 years old', *FIFA Official Bulletin*, No. 7 (Sept. 1954).

'Not "a German Football Wonder" ', *The Bulletin* (Bonn), 25 November 1954.

'The Burning Question', *The B.E.F. Times*, 1 Nov. 1917.

'The Italian Football Federation: 75th anniversary', *Italy: Documents and Notes*, 23 (1), (1974).

Lord Aberdare, 'The Olympiad in Britain', *Everybody's*, 1 June 1946.

Nathan D. Abrams, 'Inhibited but not "crowded out": the strange fate of soccer in the United States', *International Journal of the History of Sport*, 12 (1995).

Christopher Andrew, 'Secrets of our national game', *The Guardian*, 26 Nov. 1996.

Eduardo P. Archetti, 'In search of national identity: Argentinian football and Europe', *Int.J.Hist.Sport*, 12 (1995).

P.J. Baker, 'Olympiads and the noble English press', *The Granta*, xxvi (578), 23 Nov. 1912.

Philip J. Baker, 'Olympiad and Liars', *The Outlook*, 19 Oct. 1912.

Philip Baker, 'The Olympic Games', *The Empire Review*, May 1924.

Philip J. Baker, 'The Olympic Games – a retrospect', *The Independent*, 113, No. 3876, 30 Aug. 1924.

Philip Baker, 'Britain and the Olympic Games', *Daily News*, 19 July 1924.

P.J. Baker, 'The NUS and International Sport', *NUS Scene*, 3 April 1928.

P.J. Bauwens, 'England-Italien', *World's Football. Official Bulletin of FIFA*, No. 44, 15 Jan. 1935.

Peter J. Beck, 'Politics and the Olympics: the lesson of 1924', *History Today*, 30, 7 (1980).

Peter J. Beck, 'England v Germany, 1938', *History Today*, 32, 6 (1982).

Peter J. Beck, ' "To play, or not to play?", That is the Anglo-Argentine Question', *Contemporary Review*, 245 (1984).

Peter J. Beck, 'Was the League of Nations really a failure?: the "new diplomacy" in a period of appeasement', *History Teaching Review Yearbook of the Scottish Association of Teachers of History*, 9 (1995).

Walter Bensemann, 'Missionaries of sport', *World's Football*, 37 (1933).

Walter Bensemann, 'Tutti Frutti', *World's Football*, 40 (1933).

Hajo Bernett, 'National Socialist Physical Education as reflected in British appeasement policy', *Int.J.Hist.Sport*, 5 (1988).

Tony Blair, 'Stan's my man', *New Statesman and Society* (20 Jan. 1995).

Gerald Carr, 'Sport and party ideology in Third Reich', *Canadian Journal of History of Sport and Physical Education*, 5 (1974).

Gerald Carr, 'The synchronization of sport and physical education under National Socialism', *Canadian Journal of History of Sport and Physical Education*, 10 (1979).

Winston Churchill, 'England, My England!', *Answers* (12 Aug. 1933).

Winston Churchill, 'Sport is a stimulant in our workaday world', *News of the World* (4 Sept. 1938).

Lord Decies, 'Sport can kill war', *World's Football*, 37 (1933).

Kurt Gassmann, 'Tribute to a great member', *FIFA Official Bulletin*, 3 (Sept. 1953).

Heiner Gillmeister, 'The first European soccer match: Walter Bensemann, a twenty-six year old German student, set the ball rolling', *The Sports Historian*, 17 (1997).

John Hargreaves, 'The political economy of mass sport', *Bulletin of the Society for the Study of Labour History*, 32 (1976).

Simon Hoggart, 'When the Nazis came to Tottenham', *The Observer* (14 March 1982).

Per Olof Holmäng, 'International sports organizations 1919–25: Sweden and the German question', *Int.J.Hist.Sport*, 9 (1992).

Richard Holt, 'Contrasting nationalisms: sport, militarism and the unitary state in Britain and France before 1914', *Int.J.Hist.Sport*, 12 (1995).

Richard Holt, 'Sport and History: the state of the subject in Britain', *Twentieth Century British History*, 7 (1996).

Richard Holt and J.A. Mangan, 'Prologue: heroes of a European past', *Int.J.Hist.Sport,* 13 (1996).

Grant Jarvie, 'Giving the game away' (review article), *The Sports Historian*, 17 (1997).

Stephen G. Jones, 'State intervention in sport and leisure in Britain between the wars', *Journal of Contemporary History*, 22 (1987).

Thomas Jones, 'Neville Chamberlain' (book review), *The Times* (10 Dec. 1946).

J.T. Kelly, 'Football in the Free State', *Football World*, 4 (Feb. 1939).

Arnd Krüger, '*Sieg Heil* to the most glorious era of German sport: continuity and change in the modern German sports movement', *Int.J.Hist.Sport*, 4 (1987).

Arnd Krüger, 'On the origins of the notion that sport serves as a means of national representation', *History of European Ideas*, 16 (1993).

Pierre Lanfranchi, 'Bologna: the team that shook the world', *Int.J.Hist.Sport*, 8 (1991).

René Lehmann, 'Allemagne-France', *World's Football*, 37 (April–May 1933).

"T.M", 'Coaching on the continent', *The Bulletin (FA)*, 1 (May 1939).

J.A. Mangan, ' "Muscular, militaristic and manly": the British middle-class hero as moral messenger', *Int.J.Hist.Sport*, 13 (1995).

Tony Mason, 'Land of Sport and Glory' (review article), *History*, 82 (1997).

E.A. Montague, 'The Olympic Games', *Manchester Guardian* (11 March 1938).

H.F. Moorhouse, 'One state, several countries: soccer and nationality in a "United Kingdom" ', *Int.J.Hist.Sport*, 12 (1995).

Charles Nevin, 'Adolf's lads: my part in their downfall', *Daily Telegraph* (14 May 1988).

P.J. Noel-Baker, 'International sport and international good understanding: Great Britain, Germany and the USA', *British Olympic Journal* (Autumn 1926).

P. Noel-Baker, 'Olympic Games Memories', *Midland Daily Telegraph*, 18 August 1928.

R.W. Pickford, 'The psychology of the history and organization of association football, Part 2', *British Journal of Psychology*, XXXI (1940).

William Pickford, 'How soccer is controlled', *The Listener* (29 Sept. 1937).

Martin Polley, 'The British Government and the Olympic Games in the 1930s', *The Sports Historian*, 17 (1997).

Martin Polley, ' "No business of ours"?: the Foreign Office and the Olympic Games, 1896–1914', *Int.J.Hist.Sport*, 13 (1997).

David Ransom, '1929 South American Tour', *Chelsea Historian*, 5 (Sept. 1996).

Jim Riordan, 'The strange story of Nikolai Starostin, football and Lavrentii Beria', *Europe-Asia Studies*, 46 (1994).

Sir Stanley Rous, 'Football as an international sport', *FIFA Official Bulletin*, 3 (1953).

Sir Stanley Rous, 'Reflections on the 100th anniversary of the Football Association', *FIFA Official Bulletin*, 39/40 (Nov. 1963).

W. Schmid-Parker, 'Continental menace to our football supremacy', *Football Pictorial* (12 Oct. 1935).

W. Schmid-Parker, 'German invasion, Dec. 4', *Football Pictorial* (19 Oct. 1935).

W. Schmid-Parker, 'A splendid game without a single foul', *Football Pictorial* (14 Dec. 1935).

Ivan Sharpe, 'Football on the Continent', *Football World*, 10–11 (Aug.–Sept. 1939).

Samuel S. Shipman, 'Sports in the Soviet Union', *Current History*, XLVII (1937).

George Sinfield, 'When our British players gave the Russians a shock', *Daily Worker* (13 Nov. 1954).

Michael Stenton, 'British propaganda and raison d'état, 1935–1940', *European Studies Review*, 10 (1980).

Junko Tahara, 'Count Michimasa Soyeshima and the cancellation of the XII Olympiad in Tokyo: a footnote to Olympic history', *Int.J.Hist.Sport*, 9 (1992).

Trevor Taylor, 'Sport and world politics: functionalism and the state system', *International Journal*, XLIII (1988).

Colin Veitch, 'Play up! Play Up! And Win the War', *Journal of Contemporary History*, 20 (1985).

A. Verdyck, 'About the laws of the game: charging the goalkeeper', *Football World*, 3 (Jan. 1939).

John N. Washburn, 'Sport as a Soviet tool', *Foreign Affairs*, 34 (1956).

Sir Arthur Willert, 'National Advertisement', *The Fortnightly* (Jan. 1939).

Richard A. Woeltz, 'Sport, culture, and society in late Imperial and Weimar Germany: some suggestions for future research', *Journal of Sport History*, 4 (1977).

Yamone, 'Football Game in Japan', *Football World*, 2 (Dec. 1938).

Chapters

Teresa Gonzalez Aja, 'Spanish sports policy in republican and fascist Spain', Pierre Arnaud and James Riordan (eds), *Sport and International Politics: the impact of fascism and communism on sport* (E. & F.N. Spon, London, 1998).

Lincoln Allison, 'Sport and politics', Lincoln Allison (ed.), *The Politics of Sport* (Manchester University Press, Manchester, 1986).

Pierre Arnaud, 'Sport – a means of national representation' and 'French sport and the emergence of authoritarian regimes, 1919–1939', Pierre Arnaud and James Riordan (eds), *Sport and International Politics: the impact of fascism and communism on sport* (E. & F.N. Spon, London, 1998).

Lord Noel-Baker, 'Stockholm, 1912', Lord Killanin and John Rodda (eds), *Olympic Games* (Macdonald & Jane's, London, 1979).

Alan Bairner, 'Football and the idea of Scotland', Grant Jarvie and Graham Walker (eds), *Scottish Sport in the Making of the Nation: ninety minute patriots?* (Leicester University Press, London, 1994).

David Bull, 'Politicians as Football Fans – incredible!', David Bull and Alastair Campbell (eds), *Football and the Commons People* (Juma, Sheffield, 1994).

David Cannadine, 'The context, performance and meaning of ritual: the British monarchy and the "invention of tradition", *c.*1820–1977', Eric Hobsbawm and Terence Ranger (eds), *The Invention of Tradition* (Cambridge University Press, Cambridge, 1983).

David Childs, 'The German Democratic Republic', J. Riordan (ed.), *Sport under Communism: the USSR, Czechoslovakia, the GDR, Cuba* (Hurst, London, 1978).

Kenneth Clarke, 'Forest first and foremost', David Bull and Alastair Campbell (eds), *Football and the Commons People* (Juma, Sheffield, 1994).

Theodore Cook, 'Public World and Public Duty', *The Field*, 15 August 1914, T. Cook (ed.), *Kaiser, Krupp and Kultur* (John Murray, London, 1915).

Bernard Crick, 'The English and the British', B. Crick (ed.), *National Identities: the constitution of the United Kingdom* (Blackwell, Oxford, 1991).

Gordon Daniels, 'Japanese sport: from Heian Kyó to Tokyo Olympiad', J.C. Binfield and J. Stevenson (eds), *Sport, Culture and Politics* (Sheffield Academic Press, Sheffield, 1993).

J.G. Dixon, 'Physical education as moral education in Germany', P. McIntosh (ed.), *Fair Play: ethics in sport and education* (Heinemann, London, 1979).

Christiane Eisenberg, 'Deutschland', C. Eisenberg (ed.), *Fussball, Soccer, Calcio: ein englischer Sport auf seinem Weg um die Welt* (DTV, Munich, 1997).

W.G. Gallagher, 'Scotland Abroad', A.H. Fabian and G. Green (eds), *Association Football, vol. 4* (Caxton, London, 1960).

Alexander Grant and Keith Stringer, 'Introduction: the enigma of British history', Alexander Grant and Keith Stringer (eds), *Uniting the Kingdom?: the making of British History* (Routledge, London, 1995).

C.A.W. Hirschman, 'Notes sur la Fondatin de la F.I.F.A.', *FIFA 1904–1929* (de Bussy, Amsterdam, 1929).

Richard Holt, 'The Foreign Office and the Football Association: British sport and appeasement, 1935–1938', 'Interwar sport and interwar relations: some conclusions', Pierre Arnaud and James Riordan (eds), *Sport and International Politics: the impact of fascism and communism on sport* (E. & F.N. Spon, London, 1998).

Steve Ickringill, 'Amateur and professional: sport in Britain and America at the turn of the twentieth century', J.C. Binfield and J. Stevenson (eds), *Sport, Culture and Politics* (Sheffield Academic Press, Sheffield, 1993).

Michael John, 'Österreich', C. Eisenberg (ed.), *Fussball, Soccer, Calcio: ein englischer Sport auf seinem Weg um die Welt* (DTV, Munich, 1997).

Stephen Jones, 'The British Workers' Sports Federation: 1923–1935', A. Krüger and J. Riordan (eds), *The Story of Worker Sport* (Human Kinetics, Leeds, 1996).

W. Unite Jones, 'International football', Alfred Gibson and William Pickford (eds), *Association Football and the Men who Made it: vol. 4* (Caxton, London, 1906).

Arnd Krüger, 'The German way of Worker Sport', A. Krüger and J. Riordan (eds), *The Story of Worker Sport* (Human Kinetics, Leeds, 1996).

Arnd Krüger, 'The role of sport in German international politics, 1918–1945', Pierre Arnaud and James Riordan (eds), *Sport and International Politics: the impact of fascism and communism on sport* (E. & F.N. Spon, London, 1998).

John Major, 'A blue on the blues', David Bull (ed.), *We'll Support you Evermore* (Duckworth, London, 1992).

J.A. Mangan, 'Prologue. Britain's chief spiritual export: imperial sport as moral metaphor, political symbol and cultural bond', J.A. Mangan (ed.), *The Cultural Bond: sport, empire, society* (Frank Cass, London, 1992).

Tony Mason, 'Football', T. Mason (ed.), *Sport in Britain: a social history* (Cambridge University Press, Cambridge, 1989).

Alex Natan, 'Sport and politics', J.W. Loy Jr and G.S. Kenyon (eds), *Sport, Culture and Society: a reader on the sociology of sport* (Collier-Macmillan, New York, 1969).

George Orwell, 'The Sporting Spirit', Sonia Orwell and Ian Angus (eds), *The Collected Essays, Journalism and Letters of George Orwell, vol. 4: In Front of Your Nose, 1945–1950* (Secker & Warburg, London, 1968).

Hans von Tschammer und Osten, 'German sport', *Germany Speaks by 21 Leading Members of Party and State* (Thornton Butterworth, London, 1938).

Hans von Tschammer und Osten, 'Sport und Leibesübungen im Nationalsozialistischen Staat', H.H. Lammers and H. Pfundtner (eds), *Grundlagen Aufbau und Wirtschaftsordnung des Nationalsozialistischen Staates* Band 1, Gruppe 1 Beitrag 10a (Spaeth & Linde, Berlin, 1936).

Harold Perkin, 'Epilogue. Teaching the nations how to play: sport and society in the British Empire and Commonwealth', J.A. Mangan (ed.), *The Cultural Bond: sport, empire, society* (Frank Cass, London, 1992).

James Riordan, 'The USSR', J. Riordan (ed.), *Sport under Communism: the USSR, Czechoslovakia, the GDR, Cuba* (Hurst, London, 1978).

James Riordan, 'Worker sport within a worker state: the Soviet Union', A. Krüger and J. Riordan (eds), *The Story of Worker Sport* (Human Kinetics, Leeds, 1996).

Brian Stoddart, 'Sport, cultural politics and international relations: England versus Germany, 1935', N. Müller and J. Rühl (eds), *1984 Olympic Scientific Congress Official Report: Sport History* (Schors-Verlag, Niedernhausen, Germany, 1985).

Andrew Steed, 'British propaganda and the First World War', in I. Stewart and S.L. Carruthers (eds), *War, Culture and the Media: representations of the military in 20th Century Britain* (Flicks Books, Trowbridge, 1996).

John Sugden and Alan Bairner, 'Northern Ireland: sport in a divided society', L. Allison (ed.), *The Politics of Sport* (Manchester University Press, Manchester, 1986).

Colin Tatz, 'The corruption of sport', Geoffrey Lawrence and David Rowe (eds), *Power Play: essays in the sociology of Australian sport* (Hale & Iremonger, Sydney, 1986).

Trevor Taylor, 'Sport and international relations: a case of mutual neglect', Lincoln Allison (ed.), *The Changing Politics of Sport* (Manchester University Press, Manchester, 1993).

Angela Teja, 'Italian sport and international relations under fascism', Pierre Arnaud and James Riordan (eds), *Sport and International Politics: the impact of fascism and communism on sport* (E. & F.N. Spon, London, 1998).

Alan Tomlinson, 'Going Global: the FIFA story', A. Tomlinson and G. Whannel (eds), *Off the Ball: the football world cup* (Pluto Press, London, 1986).

Donald C. Watt, 'The European Civil War', in Wolfgang J. Mommsen and Lothar Kettenacker (eds), *The Fascist Challenge and the Policy of Appeasement* (George Allen & Unwin, London, 1983).

Paula Welch, 'Paris 1924', J.E. Findling and K.D. Pelle (eds.), *Historical Dictionary of the Modern Olympic Movement* (Greenwood Press, Westport, 1996).

Jean Moorcroft Wilson, *Siegfried Sassoon, the Making of a War Poet: a biography (1886–1918)* (Duckworth, London, 1998).

Unpublished theses

David B. Kanin, 'The Role of Sport in International Relations', PhD dissertation, Fletcher School of Law and Diplomacy, Tufts University (1976).

Martin Polley, 'The Foreign Office and International Sport, 1918–1948', unpublished PhD thesis, St David's University College, University of Wales (1991).

Reference works

British Society of Sports History website bibliographical and other databases: http://www.umist.ac.uk/UMISTSport/bssh.html.

Richard W. Cox (ed.), *Sport in Britain: a bibliography of historical publications, 1800–1987* (Manchester University Press, Manchester, 1991; Second edition, Sports History Publishing, Frodsham, 1997)

FIFA Museum Collection: 100 years of Football (Edition q, Berlin, 1996).

Ron Hockings and Keir Radnedge, *Nations of Europe: a statistical history of European international football, 1872–1993, vol. 1* (Articulate, Emsworth, 1993).

Guy Oliver, *The Guinness Book of World Soccer: the history of the game in over 150 countries* (Guinness Publishing, Enfield, 1992).

Peter J. Seddon (ed.), *A Football Compendium: a comprehensive guide to the literature of Association Football* (British Library, Boston Spa, 1995).

Index

Aberdare, Lord, 202, 204, 211 (note 182), 214, 219, 222
Aberdeen FC, 82, 83, 104
Abrahams, Harold, 100 (note 87), 201, 220
Admiralty, the, 85, 281
air travel to internationals, 6, 28, 193, 255, 275
Albania, 147, 249–51
Alexander, Thomas, 88
Allison, George, 38
Allison, Lincoln, 43
Amateur Athletic Association (AAA), 24, 40, 93, 95, 264
amateurism and professionalism, 42, 52, 53, 58, 61, 64, 65–6, 69, 74 (note 15), 101, 108–10, 113, 115–16, 118, 122, 123, 136–7, 146–7, 151, 156, 166, 167 (note 39), 171 (note 144), 189-90, 205, 209 (note 102), 216, 217, 242, 255, 261, 275, 278–9
Anglo-German Fellowship, the, 203-04
appeasement, 1, 3, 7, 99 (note 69), 232, 238, 244
Archetti, Eduardo, 273
Argentina, 26, 51, 58, 68, 104, 143–4, 155, 156, 246, 248, 256–62, 273
Arsenal FC, 35, 36, 93, 141, 146, 154, 171 (note 165), 190, 191, 230, 249–50, 265
Astley Cooper, J., 12
Aston Villa FC, 2, 4, 7, 15 (note 51), 73, 245, 274
Athlone, Earl of, 29, 277–8
Attlee, Clement, 13, 41, 185
Australia, 26, 28, 58, 87, 106, 107, 165–6, 231, 233, 255, 275
Austria, 1, 14 (note 16), 31, 54, 57, 60, 65, 70, 71, 80–3, 103-5, 118, 120, 125, 130–1, 132, 133, 142, 145, 154, 156, 158–61, 162, 163, 216, 225, 228, 244, 247, 250, 251, 256, 264–5, 274; 1938 *Anschluss*, 1, 4, 213, 215, 247
Avenol, Joseph, 238

Baggett, W., 241–2
Baker, Philip *see* Noel-Baker, Lord

Baldwin, Stanley, 36, 40, 141, 194, 204, 233
baseball, 58, 136, 256
Bastin, Cliff, 1, 7, 36, 158
Bauwens, Peco, 146, 252
BBC, 158–61
Belgium, 54–5, 56, 81–2, 84, 87, 88, 89–91, 93, 96, 117, 131, 132, 133, 144, 146, 148, 164, 197, 275
Bensemann, Walter, 53, 70, 151, 155, 163
Beresford, Jack, 91-2
Blair, Tony, 13, 17, 39
Board of Education, 65, 222–3, 265, 280
Board of Trade, 70
Bolivia, 256
Bologna, 148, 251
Bosanquet, R.C., 61
boxing, 41, 94, 130, 159, 238–9, 243, 259, 262
Brasher, Christopher, 36
Brazil, 26, 65, 143, 145, 156, 247, 248, 256
Bridge, Lt.-Colonel, 245
Briggs, Asa, 158
Brighton police (German tour), 4
British Council, 9, 17, 18, 20–2, 27, 33, 134, 174, 222–3, 226–7, 232, 239–43, 245, 249, 250, 256, 258, 262–3, 280
British Empire, 23, 26, 28, 43, 62, 79, 87, 103, 104, 105, 106–7, 118, 131, 149, 165, 233, 255, 265
British home international tournament, 26–7, 32, 50, 52, 57, 59, 66–7, 69, 70, 71, 79, 102–4, 107, 108, 111, 130, 132, 142, 274
British Olympic Association (BOA), 36, 38, 55, 61, 62, 64, 81, 84–7, 95–6, 101, 109, 136, 201-3, 214, 218–20, 222, 280
British Workers' Sports Association (BWSA), 228-9, 263, 279
British Workers' Sports Federation (BWSF), 88, 139–42, 230
Britishness, 22-3, 29, 31, 42, 50, 102, 162, 195, 285 (note 42)
broadcasting, 19, 35, 158–61, 162, 188, 239, 251
Broome, Frank, 1, 6, 7

301

Bulgaria, 131, 231
Burnley FC, 114
Butler, Richard, 17, 41, 239, 243–4

Cabinet, 9, 174, 218–20, 262, 280
Cadogan, Sir Alexander, 41, 229
Canada, 28, 55, 65, 87, 104–6, 107, 131, 132–3, 250, 257, 264, 275
Capel-Kirby, W., 162–4
Carter, F.W., 162–4
Cato, 1
Celtic FC, 56, 68, 104, 133
Central Council of Recreative Physical Training (CCRPT), 222, 282
Chamberlain, Sir Austen, 120
Chamberlain, Neville, 1, 3, 12, 21, 36, 41, 48 (note 137), 204, 221–3, 230, 238, 240, 244, 248, 249, 254, 262, 272
Channon, Henry, 214
Chelsea FC, 34, 39, 103, 143–4, 225–7, 232, 245, 251
Chile, 51, 58, 258
China, xi, 27, 136, 213, 216
Churchill, Sir Winston, 13, 36, 38
Citrine, Sir Walter, 185, 187, 189, 190–2, 198–9
Clarke, Kenneth, 41
Clarke, Peter, 12
Clegg, J.C., 66, 172 (note 179), 194
Clive, Robert, 218
Clynes, Samuel, 138, 140
Colombia, 259, 260
Colonial Office, 149–50
Cook, Theodore, 61, 64–5, 72
Corinthian FC, 65, 74 (note 22)
Corrigan, Peter, 133
Craigie, Sir Robert, 219
Cranborne, Viscount, 226, 229
cricket (including test matches), 23, 25, 28, 33, 35, 39, 40, 41, 45 (note 39), 48 (note 137), 50, 58, 106, 124, 136, 157, 165–6, 190, 262
Crossman, Richard, 39
Crowe, Eyre, 64–5, 80, 86
Crozier, W.P., 201
Cuba, 247
Czechoslovakia, 1, 3, 25, 103, 120, 125, 131, 132, 142, 154, 156, 215, 227, 231, 245, 247, 248, 250, 262, 264–5; May 1938 war scare, 2, 8, 247, 262; Munich Conference, 1, 230, 248, 249–50, 272; Occupation of Prague, 1939, 249–50

Daily Express, 2, 5, 7, 11, 26, 119–24, 173, 174, 272
Daily Herald, 178, 192
Daily Mail, 8, 72, 192
Daily Telegraph, 150, 221

Daily Worker, 174, 192, 193
Dawson, Geoffrey, 36, 228
De Coubertin, Pierre, 37, 38, 64, 214
Decies, Lord, 36, 38, 165
Denmark, 24, 55–6, 60, 68, 82-3, 104, 114, 131, 250
Desborough, Lord, 61, 64
Deutscher Fussball Bund (DFB), 2, 4, 53, 58, 59, 69, 71, 117–18, 121, 134, 144, 179–80, 188, 194, 197, 216–17
Diem, Carl, 38, 193
Dodd, William, 35, 198, 203
Dollfuss, Engelbert, 159–60
Donaldson, Frances, 242
Douglas, James, 29
Duff, Charles, 150, 153

Eden, Anthony (Lord Avon), 9,13, 21, 41, 202, 218, 227, 229, 244
Egypt, 27, 87, 156, 255
England, internationals, 13, 14 (note 16), 32, 42, 53–4, 102–3, 123, 129 (note 115), 130–2, 145-7, 216-17, 246-7, 250, 264, 265, 273-5; Austria, 4, 13, 54–5, 60, 103, 112, 157, 159–61, 163, 165, 180, 186, 197; Czechoslovakia, 3, 154, 163; FIFA XI, 24, 112, 249, 274, 282; France, 4, 9, 10, 35, 123, 145–7, 161, 162–3, 164–5, 183, 246, 247; Germany (1930), 23, 54, 93, 103, 118, 142, 164, 180, 189, 279; Germany (1935), 28, 35, 53, 54, 112, 141, 161, 166, 173-205, 218, 223, 265, 276, 281–2; Germany (1938), 1–10, 42, 54, 245, 247, 263, 276, 279; Germany (1954), 10, 54, 265; Hungary, 54, 60, 123, 154, 163; Italy (1933), 23, 147–51, 163, 251, 279; Italy (1934), 16 (note 58), 132, 148, 154–8, 161, 163, 183, 186, 195, 251, 279; Italy (1939), 11, 249–55, 263, 264, 279; Latin America, 27, 103, 256-62; pre-1914, 53–60, 69, 71; Spain, 23, 118, 123–4, 132, 161, 162–3, 213, 228–9, 279; Switzerland, 4, 10, 11, 16 (note 58), 151–2, 242, 247
Ethiopian crisis, 147, 158, 184, 204, 213
European 'civil war', 2, 9, 20, 21, 23, 31, 147, 153, 198, 221–3, 239, 272–3, 278, 279, 283–4
Evening Standard, 189, 190
Everton FC, 162, 249–50, 258, 269 (note 113)

fair play, 5, 10, 22, 28–9, 34, 38, 39, 42, 70, 72, 79, 80, 91–2, 113–17, 119–21, 122–3, 143–4, 146–7, 150, 152, 158, 163, 194, 196–7, 198, 225–7, 241, 244–6, 251, 252, 255, 259, 261–3, 277–8, 282
FIFA, 4, 24, 25, 26, 27, 38, 43, 50, 53, 54, 55, 56–60, 65, 67–70, 72, 80–3, 101–2, 108–13,

131, 136–7, 138–40, 142–5, 151, 154–5, 164, 165, 166 (note 2), 179, 216, 217, 230–2, 246, 247–8, 249, 251, 258, 260, 273, 278, 282
Finland, 26, 56, 62, 82, 87, 88, 91, 93, 131, 138–9, 218, 219, 256, 280
First World War, 19, 25, 52, 63, 65–7, 71–3, 79, 92, 105, 114, 146, 164, 180, 239; Battle of the Somme (1916), 72
Fishwick, Nicholas, 40
Fone, Charles, 279
Football Association (FA), 1, 3–6, 10, 24, 25, 29, 32, 51, 52–60, 65–8, 69, 70–1, 73, 80–3, 84, 85–6, 101, 102–13, 114, 116, 119, 124–5, 131–2, 140, 143–4, 148, 149, 150, 155, 156, 163–5, 180–1, 182, 185–90, 192, 193–4, 195, 197, 199, 216–17, 221, 222, 225, 228, 241–2, 244–52, 254–5, 257–8, 262, 265, 272, 275, 277–8, 280, 282
Football Association of Ireland (FAI), 25, 45 (note 52), 102, 103, 130, 133–4, 197, 250
Football Association of Wales (FAW), 25, 32, 42, 51, 52, 57, 65–8, 71, 73, 79, 82–3, 101, 103–13, 116, 127 (note 49), 133, 140, 164, 221, 247, 248, 250, 273, 277, 278, 280
football propaganda, 10, 23–6, 29–31, 33–6, 38, 40, 42, 70–1, 114–17, 118–21, 122–3, 133, 140, 148–51, 153, 155, 157, 162, 175–6, 179, 182, 187, 192, 193, 195, 197, 198, 203, 225–8, 232, 240–3, 245–6, 251–5, 261–2, 263, 273, 276–8, 282
Foreign Office, 5, 9, 10, 17, 19, 20, 25, 33, 38, 60–5, 70, 80, 84–7, 90, 92, 95–7, 113–25, 135, 139–42, 144, 145, 147, 149–53, 157, 160–1, 174, 180, 181–9, 194, 198–200, 202–3, 214, 218, 219, 222, 223–5, 227–9, 233, 240, 241–3, 245–6, 249, 253, 254, 262–4, 272, 279, 280, 283–4
France, 26, 53, 56, 57, 61, 70, 71, 82, 88, 89–91, 93, 96, 98 (note 33), 103–5, 117, 118, 131, 132, 133, 140, 144, 145–7, 148, 162–3, 164–5, 166, 184, 213, 215, 231, 247, 250, 260–2

Gaselee, Sir Stephen, 5, 119, 245
Gassmann, Kurt, 282
Germany, 1–11, 28, 31, 53, 54, 57, 59, 64–5, 70, 71–2, 73, 80–3, 86, 88–91, 93, 94–5, 96, 97 (note 11), 98 (note 33), 103–4, 105, 113–21, 131, 134, 139, 141, 142, 145, 147–8, 156, 164–5, 173–205, 213–16, 221–4, 225, 238, 243–4, 245, 246, 248–50, 253, 255, 260, 263–5, 274, 275, 278, 279–80, 284
Glanville, Brian, 38, 272, 284 (note 6)
Gloucester, Duke of, 24
Goebbels, Joseph, 8, 195, 214, 239

golf, 23, 40–1, 42, 58, 212 (note 190)
Graham, George, 30, 103
Graham, Sir Ronald, 33, 151
Grandi, Count, 157, 158
Graves, Robert, 41
Greece, 33, 131, 179, 185, 224, 240–3, 249
Grimm, Hans, 89
Guérin, Robert, 56
Gurney, Wentworth, 135
Guttmann, Allen, 37

Halifax, Lord, 41, 243–4
Hapgood, Eddie, 7, 151, 158
Hardie, C.G., 18, 240
Hart-Davis, Duff, 200
Headlam Morley, James, 80
Henderson, Nevile, 2, 6, 8, 9, 14 (note 7), 264
Henley Regatta, 91, 264
Hess, Rudolf, 8, 216
Heuss, President, 10
Hirschman, Carl, 51, 56, 110, 111, 131, 139
Hitler, Adolf, 2, 6, 8, 38, 135, 173–4, 176–7, 180–2, 187, 189, 192, 200, 202, 204–5, 214–16, 220, 238–9, 244, 262, 265, 272, 279
Hoare, Samuel, 21, 40, 184, 186–7, 189, 190, 202, 204–5, 280
Hobsbawm, Eric, 12–13
Hogan, Jimmy, 14 (note 24), 38, 71, 163–4, 274
Hoggart, Simon, 174
Holt, Richard, 41, 50, 70
Home Office, 4, 139–42, 174, 181–95, 198–200, 265, 280
Hornby, Nick, 39
Hotblack, Colonel, 176
Houlihan, Barrie, 43
Hungary, 54, 60, 80–3, 103, 105, 112, 118, 123–4, 125, 130–1, 132–4, 135, 142, 148, 154, 163–4, 179, 215, 225, 227, 241–2, 248, 264, 265, 274
hunting, 41, 243–4

IARHC, 89–91, 114–17
Illustrated London News, 72
International Football Association Board (IFAB), 24, 52, 56, 58–9, 68, 69, 101–2, 110–12, 151, 155, 156–7, 231, 247–8, 255, 273, 278
International Olympic Committee (IOC), 60, 64, 70, 80–1, 83, 101, 109, 136–7, 138, 142, 201, 214, 216, 219, 230
Ireland *see* Football Association of Ireland; Irish Football Association
Irish Football Association (IFA), 25, 27–8, 32, 43, 50, 51, 52, 57, 59, 65–8, 73, 82–3, 101, 103–13, 116, 133–4, 146, 164, 221, 248,

257, 278, 280, 284
Italy, 8, 11, 26, 82, 88, 103, 105, 118–19, 123,
    130–1, 132, 142, 145, 147–58, 162, 169
    (note 100), 174, 180, 213, 215, 216, 224,
    238, 248, 249–55, 258, 263, 273, 275, 280,
    284
Janner, Barnett, 135, 181
Japan, 27, 135–6, 147, 167 (note 34), 174, 213,
    215, 217–20, 233, 238, 247, 280
Jarvie, Grant, 283
Jewish Chronicle, 182, 199
Johnstone, Kenneth, 18, 19, 27, 263
Jones, Stephen, 140, 166, 280

Karnebeek, H.A. van, 33
Kennard, Sir Howard, 152, 225–7, 232, 244–5
Kilmarnock FC, 104
Kilmarnock, Lord, 114–17
Kirkpatrick, Ivone, 239
Knighton, A.L., 188

Labour movement, 179, 181, 185, 187, 190–6,
    200
Laffan, R.S. de Courcey, 64, 86
Latin American football, 24, 26–7, 36, 51, 55,
    68, 103, 104, 108, 130, 142, 145, 156,
    256–62, 274–5, 284
Laval, Pierre, 204
Lawford, Valentine, 192, 232
League of Nations, 80, 93, 113, 121, 135, 164,
    165, 204, 238, 278
Lebuman, Ernest, 84
Leeper, Rex, 19, 20, 21, 134, 153, 204
Lehmann, R.C., 62–3
Lewald, T., 193, 204
Lillelien, Bjorge, 13
Lindley, Sir Francis, 135-6
Lloyd, Lord, 9, 21, 222, 242, 249
Locarno Treaties, 93, 95, 117
Lockhart, R. Bruce, 137
Loraine, Percy, 251–3
Louis, Joe, 238–9

MacDonald, Ramsay, 40, 137, 141
Macleod, Rod, 113
Major, John, 13, 39
Malitz, Bruno, 177
Malta, 149–50, 251
Manchester Guardian, 35, 195, 201
Mangan, J.A., 43
Manning, G.R., 136, 232
Manning, L.W., 252, 254–5, 274
Mao Zedong, xi
Mason, Tony, 50, 223, 283–4
Matthews, Sir Stanley, 1, 6, 7, 13, 39, 158, 194,
    251, 253
McIntosh, Peter, 34

M'Dowall, John K., 103
Meisl, Hugo, 142, 163
Meisl, Willy, 273
Millington Drake, Eugen, 256–9
Ministry of Health, 221
Ministry of Information, 19, 261
Ministry of Labour, 103
Ministry of Transport, 85
Montague, E., 220, 232
Montefiore, L., 201, 202
Motherwell FC, 45 (note 39), 104, 133
Mounsey, Sir George, 226, 229
Mount Temple, Lord, 204
Münch, Kurt, 177, 196
Murray, Bill, 42, 70
Mussolini, Benito, 34, 147–8, 151, 154, 156,
    158, 249, 252, 253, 272, 279

national fitness (and the NFC), 43, 220–3, 243,
    262, 282
National Union of Railwaymen (NUR), 181–2,
    191
Nazi salute incident (1938), 1, 6–7, 251–2
Nerz, Otto, 121, 190, 194
Netherlands, 11, 33, 53, 56, 82, 88, 91–2, 93,
    103–4, 130, 131, 142, 184, 189, 224, 247,
    249, 264
New York Times, 8, 121, 122, 151, 230
New Zealand, 58, 87, 106, 107, 255
Newbolt, Henry, 72
Newcastle Utd. FC, 39, 125, 162, 258
News Chronicle, 192
Newsam, F., 182, 190, 191
Noble, Andrew, 253
Noel-Baker, Lord, 22, 36, 37, 38, 40, 63, 72,
    85, 92, 94–5, 100 (note 87), 142, 165,
    177–8, 200–1, 219, 235 (note 54)
Northern Ireland *see* Irish Football Association
Norway, 13, 82, 83, 86, 103–4, 111, 117, 118,
    125–6 (note 14), 131, 133, 139, 216, 250

Observer, The, 196
Oesterreichischer Fussball-Bund (OFB), 4
Olympic Games, 69, 101, 108–9, 138, 230,
    232, 257, 265, 279–80; London (1908), 26,
    55, 61, 70, 86, 276; Stockholm (1912), 37,
    55, 62, 63, 86, 276; Berlin (1916), 63-5, 70,
    72; Antwerp (1920), 26, 80–1, 84–7, 91, 92,
    94; Paris (1924), 80, 83, 86, 91, 94, 96, 100
    (note 87), 108, 113, 256; Amsterdam
    (1928), 37, 86, 91, 93, 95, 96, 109, 113,
    118, 136, 145, 165; Los Angeles (1932), 27,
    135–7, 161–2; Berlin/Garmisch (1936), 6,
    38, 136, 173–5, 178, 179, 183, 185, 193,
    199–203, 204, 213–17, 221–2, 241, 243,
    248, 259, 260; Tokyo/Sapporo (1940), 27,
    136, 213, 217–20, 232–3, 265, 280; London

(1948), 24, 121
O'Malley, Owen, 157
Orwell, George, 38
Osten, Hans von Tschammer und, 2, 8, 178–9, 185, 191, 193–4, 201, 204, 264–5
Ovey, Sir Esmond, 260–61

Parker, Beryl, 88
Payne, Humphrey, 240
peace treaties (1919), 80–2, 89–91, 98 (note 50), 114, 135, 175, 181, 183, 184
Percy, Sir Eustace, 21
Perowne, John, 150, 186, 204
Perry, Fred, 204–5
Peru, 256–60, 270 (note 127)
Pesti Naplo, rankings, 130–1, 145, 154, 159, 163
Phipps, Sir Eric, 175–7, 179, 193, 196, 200, 214
Pickford, William, 82, 110, 111, 247, 277
Plymouth Argyle FC, 103, 258
Poland, 34, 55, 104, 182, 216, 225–7, 232, 245, 249, 265
Polley, Martin, 43, 151, 220, 283
Portugal, 25, 31, 55, 56, 104, 131, 144, 227–8
Pozzo, Vittorio, 155, 163
Preston North End FC, 245
Preston, Thomas, 30, 118–19, 121
professionalism *see* amateurism
propaganda/cultural propaganda: British, 1, 6, 9, 10, 17–23, 80, 91–2, 95, 114, 134, 159, 174–5, 193, 239–43, 260–1, 269 (note 98), 272–3, 276; French, 18–19, 61, 70, 91; German, 2, 18, 31, 70, 88–91, 175–9, 182, 187, 196, 198, 202, 204, 214, 223, 227–8, 238, 239, 240, 242–3, 256; Italian, 18, 150, 153, 155, 157, 239, 240, 251, 253, 256, 260–1
Punch, 71

Raeside, William, 258–9
Raising the Game, policy initiative, 13
Rangers FC (Glasgow), 56, 83, 104, 132–3, 172 (note 172)
Reitervereine, 89–91
Rhineland reoccupation (1936), 175, 213, 220
Ribbentrop, Joachim von, 8, 215–16
Riefenstahl, Leni, 215
Rimet, Jules, 108–10, 112, 131, 136, 142, 145, 152, 231, 260
Riordan, James, 137, 138
Robbins, Ted, 277
Robertson, Sir Malcolm, 19
Romania, 131, 144, 249, 250, 253–5, 264, 265, 274
Rous, Sir Stanley, 5, 6, 7, 10, 11, 38, 53, 112, 113, 164, 193, 217, 222, 228, 241, 245–6,

249, 262, 278
rugby football, 25, 26, 35, 40, 48 (note 137), 52, 94, 113–15, 146–7, 152–3, 166, 183, 223, 250
Russia *see* Soviet Union

Salazar, Antonio de O., 227–8
Sargent, Sir Malcolm , 203
Sargent, Orme G., 116, 149, 184–5, 186, 203, 226, 279
Sassoon, Siegfried, 73
Schmeling, Max, 238–9
Schmid-Parker, W., 180, 196
Schricker, Ivo, 53, 155, 156, 164, 231
Scotland, internationals, 11, 14 (note 10), 27, 32, 43, 103–4, 107, 124, 130–1, 132–3, 145, 147, 149, 154, 171 (note 140), 197, 246–7, 257, 263–4, 274, 280; Germany (1929), 93, 104, 117, 124, 142, 164; Austria (1933), 112, 132, 154, 158–61, 162
Scotsman, The, 25, 34, 121
Scott, Sir Russell, 185, 191
Scottish Football Association (SFA), 25, 27, 30, 32, 50, 51, 52, 56, 57, 58, 65–8, 73, 79, 82–3, 93, 101, 102–13, 116, 117, 124, 125–6 (note 14), 132, 140, 143, 155, 158–61, 164, 221, 230–1, 248, 249, 250, 257, 258, 264, 278
Scottish Office, 160–1
Second World War, 10, 248, 260–2, 265, 282
Seeldrayers, R., 111, 112
Selby, Sir Walford, 227–8
Shankly, Bill, 12
Sharpe, Ivan, 7, 163, 254, 273, 274
Shipman, Samuel, 229
Simon, Sir John, 28–9, 40, 157–8, 160, 173–5, 179, 184, 186–95, 198–9, 280
Sinfield, George, 139, 142, 280
Smith, Chris, 17
Snow, Edgar, xi
South Africa, 28, 45 (note 39), 51, 53, 55, 65, 75 (note 31), 87, 104–6, 107, 118, 133, 255, 264, 275
Soviet Union (and Russia), 38, 55, 62, 69, 88, 92, 137–42, 152, 182, 184, 229–32, 277, 278, 279–80, 284
Spain, 23, 26, 56, 82, 92–3, 103, 104, 105, 118, 130, 131, 132, 134, 142, 144, 147, 162–3, 213, 228–9, 237 (note 98), 247, 250, 263, 277, 280
spectators *see* sports tourism
Sport and: history, 11–12, 13, 22, 39, 43, 118–19, 151, 157–8, 196, 284; nationalism, 12–13, 30–1, 36–7, 43, 50, 90, 220, 283; politics, 2–5, 11, 13, 22, 24, 30–1, 34, 36–41, 41–3, 59, 60–5, 69–71, 80–3, 84–7, 88–97, 107–8, 114, 115–25, 134–5, 137,

139–42, 147, 149–50, 152–3, 158, 161–2, 164–6, 173–9, 180–4, 188, 190–4, 196–200, 202–3, 213, 215, 217–20, 223–4, 227, 232–3, 238, 252, 254–5, 256–7, 259–60, 263–4, 272, 276–84; propaganda, 21, 22–3, 33, 70–1, 87, 88, 91, 95, 114–17, 149, 153, 174–5, 200, 213–14, 218, 222-3, 238–9, 249, 254–5, 257, 262 (*see also* football propaganda)
sporting values *see* fair play
sports tourism, 161, 162, 165, 166, 173, 181–4, 186–7, 191–3, 196
Star, The, 181, 193
Steel-Maitland, Sir Arthur, 40
Stoddart, Brian, 197
Stresemann, Gustav, 120
Sunday Referee, 198–9
Sunderland FC, 68
Sweden, 33, 56, 57, 60, 62, 63, 82, 83, 105, 131, 136, 138–9, 142
Swindon FC, 68, 258
Switzerland, 34, 56, 59, 82, 103, 105, 108, 131, 132, 134, 148, 204, 242, 247, 275

Tallents, Sir Stephen, 20, 22, 23, 42, 134, 276
Tatz, Colin, 43
Taylor, Philip, 19, 159
Taylor, Trevor, 43
Temperley, Lt.-Colonel, 92, 93, 95
Templewood, Lord *see* Hoare, Samuel
Tennant, Ernest, 203
Tennant, H.J., 66–7
tennis, 23, 41, 264
Thatcher, Margaret, 13, 17, 39
Third Lanark FC, 56, 104, 230–1, 237 (note 100), 258, 270 (note 128)
Thomas, J.P., 214, 244
Times, The, 4, 7, 8, 24, 25, 30, 31, 66, 79, 94, 120, 146, 192, 195–6, 202, 221–2, 223, 228, 264
Tomlinson, Alan, 29, 36–7
Trades Union Congress (TUC), 181, 185, 187, 189–93, 194–6, 201, 202, 203–4, 228–9
Treasury, 70, 85, 135, 223, 240, 280
Trenchard, Lord, 185
Tschammer und Osten, Hans von *see* Osten, Hans
Tuchman, Barbara, 12
Turkey, 131, 139, 164, 230–2, 243
Turner, Richard, 38

United Nations (UN), 51, 165

Uruguay, 26, 27, 31, 68, 108, 118, 130, 142–5, 156, 247, 256–9
USA, 26, 27, 28, 36, 51, 55, 58, 63, 65, 89, 95, 104, 107, 132–3, 135–7, 144, 156, 215, 216, 231, 232, 256, 257, 264, 275
Usill, Harley, 3

Vansittart, Sir Robert, 5, 6, 20, 41, 64–5, 177, 182–4, 186, 202, 204, 215–16, 219, 222, 238, 239, 243, 245–6
Villiers, Gerald, 85, 86, 92, 95
von Hoesch, Leopold, 182, 188–9, 193, 204

Wakefield, W., 222
Wales, internationals, 27, 32, 42, 52, 106, 130, 132, 133, 247, 250, 257, 280; France (1933), 133, 146, 250
Wall, Sir Frederick, 24, 29, 30–1, 53, 57, 108, 110, 112, 119–21, 123, 143–4, 151, 156, 164, 172 (note 179), 193, 278
Walvin, James, 12
War Office, 63–7, 71, 73, 85, 90, 113–17, 280
Warr, Earl de la, 272–3
Waterlow, Sidney, 241–3
Weldon, J.E.C., 31
West Ham FC., 103, 114, 117, 230, 258, 270 (note 127)
Whittaker, David, 37, 40
Wigram, Ralph, 182–3, 186, 189–90
Willert, Sir Arthur, 20, 88, 146
Wilson, Harold, 39
Wimbledon tennis, 23, 41, 264
Winterbottom, Walter, 275
Woeltz, Richard, 175
Wolverhampton Wanderers FC, 246, 265
Woolfall, Daniel, 50, 58, 59, 65, 68
World Cup, 59–60, 69, 101, 112, 181, 230, 274; (1930), 26, 27, 130, 142–5, 146, 155, 165, 256, 257; (1934), 8, 26, 27, 130, 147, 151, 154–7, 164, 189, 213, 248; (1938), 4, 10, 11, 26, 27, 35, 147, 213, 227, 241–2, 246–8, 255; (1950s), 10, 26, 248, 257; (1966), 39
Wreford Brown, C., 6, 53, 217

Xandry, Georg, 121, 194

Yencken, Arthur, 34, 115
York, Archbishop of, 29, 200
Yugoslavia, 36, 131, 144–5, 249, 250, 251, 253–5, 263, 274, 275

Zhou Enlai, xi